Households, Sects, and the Origins of Rabbinic Judaism

by

Alexei M. Sivertsev

BRILL
LEIDEN • BOSTON
2005

This book is printed on acid-free paper.

Library of Congress Cataloging-in-Publication Data

Sivertsev, Alexei, 1973–
    Households, sects, and the origins of rabbinic Judaism / by Alexei M. Sivertsev.
        p. cm. — (Supplements to the Journal for the study of Judaism, ISSN 1384-2161 ; v. 102)
    Includes bibliographical references and index.
    ISBN 90-04-14447-1 (alk. paper)
    1. Households—Religious aspects—Judaism. 2. Judaism—History—Post-exilic period, 586 B.C.–210 A.D. 3. Jewish sects—History—To 1500. 4. Judaism—Social aspects. 5. Rabbinical literature—History and criticism. I. Title. II. Series.

BM176.S52 2005
296'.09'014—dc22

2005047142

ISSN 1384-2161
ISBN 90 04 14447 1

PRINTED IN THE NETHERLANDS

CONTENTS

PART ONE

HOUSEHOLDS AND THE ORIGINS OF JEWISH SECTARIANISM

PART TWO

RABBIS AND HOUSEHOLDS: NEGOTIATING HOLINESS

PREFACE

This book serves as a direct continuation of my earlier work published by Mohr Siebeck in 2002 under the title *Private Households and Public Politics in 3rd–5th century Jewish Palestine*. It examines the Second Temple and early Rabbinic periods to elaborate my previous thesis about the crucial role of Jewish households and their traditions in shaping what we call today "Rabbinic Judaism." This project was both started and completed during the first three years of my service at the Department of Religious Studies, DePaul University. I would like to express profound gratitude to members of our department for their constant support and collegiality that allowed me to succeed in the daunting task of completing a book project. I would like to particularly thank our New Testament scholar, Dr. Christopher Mount, for his advice on matters relevant to my research, as well as his gracious offer to help proofread this work and his valuable remarks on matters of both content and style. Fr. James Halsted, O.S.A., Dr. Frida Kerner Furman, and Dr. Naomi Steinberg offered constant inspiration and support in the course of these years.

I am especially grateful to Prof. John J. Collins of Yale University and the second anonymous reader of my book for recommending it for publication. Their suggestions allowed me to enormously improve its final version. I am also thankful to Mattie Kuiper and Willy de Gijzel of Brill Academic Publishers for speedy and efficient handling of the manuscript. My former academic advisor, Prof. Lawrence H. Schiffman of New York University, and other members of the Skirball Department of Hebrew and Judaic studies have maintained a presence in my academic life throughout these years by offering helpful suggestions and moral encouragement.

Anne Elizabeth Parsons of New York University and Tom Blanton of the University of Chicago did a great job with the initial proofreading of the manuscript. I deeply appreciate their help and take full responsibility for any mistakes or omissions found in the text.

The completion of my work would have been impossible without continuous and generous financial support from both internal and external grants. The University Research Council of DePaul University awarded me two 18-month research grants as well as a full quarter research leave in autumn 2004 allowing timely completion and editing of the manuscript. Two summer grants from the College of Liberal Arts and Sciences allowed me to spend summer months by focusing entirely on research. Last but not least, the 2004 summer grant from the National Endowment for the Humanities came at the crucial time of research and allowed me to successfully complete its final stages.

Parts of chapters one and three have been published as an article "Sects and Households: Social Structure of the Proto-Sectarian Movement of Nehemiah 10 and the Dead Sea Sect" by *The Catholic Biblical Quarterly*, vol. 67, No. 1 (January 2005), 59–78. I am grateful to *CBQ* for permission to include substantial portions of this article in my book.

Finally, my special thanks go to my parents, Tamara and Michael Sivertsev, whose constant presence in my life allows me to undertake and fulfill ambitious projects.

INTRODUCTION

This book analyzes the social dynamic that underlay the evolution of Judaism during the Second Temple and early Rabbinic period. It seeks to understand both continuity and discontinuity of social structures behind the movements of the first and second centuries CE. It further seeks to answer the question, what social structures of the time served to embody and transmit Jewish religious practices and beliefs. What were the basic social units within which religious traditions were formed, learned, and disseminated? The period we are about to explore is arguably one of the most extensively studied periods in Jewish history. Still, the question of the social basis of both Second Temple sectarian movements and early Rabbinic Judaism remains largely unanswered. Methodological changes in scholarship that occurred over the past several decades have effectively undermined many of the earlier assumptions about this period. On the other hand, new interpretations have been slow in coming, although scholars have made a number of useful suggestions that need to be developed. Before I formulate the goals of the present work, it would be worthwhile to map out trends in recent scholarship and put my own research in context.[1]

Traditional Paradigm: Disciple Circles as the Matrix of Second Temple Religious Learning and Piety

The idea of a school as the basic social unit within which Judaism takes its shape goes all the way back to the medieval portrayal of Jewish history as leading up to and culminating in the reign of Rabbinic Judaism. Starting with *Wissenschaft des Judentums*, modern

---

[1] My definition of a "sect" is similar to that proposed by S.J.D. Cohen, *From the Maccabees to the Mishnah* (Philadelphia: The Westminster Press, 1987), 125: "A sect is a small, organized group that separates itself from a larger religious body and asserts that it alone embodies the ideals of the larger group because it alone understands God's will." A. Baumgarten, *The Flourishing of the Jewish Sects in the Maccabean Era: An Interpretation* (Leiden: Brill, 1997), 5–15, provides a more "sociological" (but equally helpful) description of what constitutes a "sect." He also reviews other definitions of a "sect" in modern scholarship and their application to the Second Temple Jewish movements.

Jewish and Christian scholarship has embraced this vision and further perpetuated it.[2] The school consisting of disciples gathered around
their master and receiving religious knowledge from him became a
paradigmatic social unit embodying and transmitting teachings of
Judaism. The emergence of such schools in the early Hellenistic
period, according to many scholars, started the process of formation
of the tradition that would eventually result in mature Rabbinic
Judaism around 200 CE. This process coincided with (and in fact
was part of) another process that was described as "democratization
of access" to Judaism. Whereas prior to the Hellenistic period religious knowledge about Judaism and its laws and practices had been
essentially confined to priests, from the Hellenistic period on lay intellectuals were increasingly gaining prominence as tradents and interpreters of the Law. Sometimes, these intellectuals were identified as
"lay scribes," who replaced an increasingly corrupt and ossified priesthood in handling the Torah.[3]

Starting with Elias Bickerman, scholars began to make consistent
attempts to establish a connection between this rise of Jewish schools
formed around lay intellectuals and Hellenistic influences on Judaism.
Bickerman suggested that the Pharisees had embraced the Hellenistic
emphasis on education as the single most important social task.[4] The
Pharisees sought to transform Jews into a holy nation through education, just as Hellenism believed that "education could so transform
the individual and the entire people that the nation would be capable of fulfilling the divine task set it [sic]." According to the Pharisees,

[2] See for example Z. Frankel, *Darkhe ha-Mishnah, ha-Tosefta, Mekhilta, Sifra, we-Sifre* (Warsaw: Cailingold, 1923), 1–21, H. Graetz, *History of the Jews* (Philadelphia: Jewish Publication Society, 1891), vol. 1, 396–97 and vol. 2, 17–20, I. Halevy, *Dorot Ha-Rishonim: Sefer Divre ha-Yamim Li-Vene Yisrael* (Berlin: Harz, 1923), vol. 1, 607–09, and Z. Jawitz, *Sefer Toldot Yisrael* (Jerusalem: Ahiever, 1926), vol. 6, 211. Cf. E. Schürer, *History of the Jewish People in the Age of Jesus Christ (175 BC–AD 135)*, revised and edited by G. Vermes and F. Millar (Edinburgh: Clark, 1973–1975), vol. 2, 322–30. Albeck's historiographic review of major theories about origins of the Mishnah unintentionally shows essential continuity between medieval rabbinic and 19th century "modern" theories about Second Temple origins of Rabbinic Judaism. See H. Albeck, *Mavo La-Mishnah* (Jerusalem: Byalik, 1966), 63–87.
[3] See Schürer-Vermes, *History of the Jewish People*, vol. 2, 322–23, and Moore, *Judaism in the First Century* (London: Sheldon Press, 1989), vol. 1, 308–09. Cf. S. Safrai, *Literature of the Sages* (Assen: Van Gorcum, 1987), 3–4, and Cohen, *From the Maccabees to the Mishnah*, 160–61 and 172–73.
[4] E. Bickerman, *From Ezra to the Last of the Maccabees: Foundations of Post-Biblical Judaism* (New York: Schocken Books, 1962), 160–65.

"piety was teachable" and could be "attained only through teaching."[5] Bickerman further observes that the Pharisees did not limit their education to the Torah of Moses. Instead, "they added many principles wanting in the Torah," something that eventually would evolve into the "Oral Law" of Rabbinic Judaism. According to Bickerman, "the Pharisaic idea of education promoted the tendency to develop the Torah as time and circumstance demanded." In other words, it was the centrality and religious value of education that resulted in the formation of the "Oral Law" and determined its importance for Rabbinic Judaism.[6] Bickerman's observation that the ideal of formalized (Greek-style) study and the idea of the "Oral Law" are interrelated will prove crucial for a proper understanding of Rabbinic Judaism, although his attempt to place this combination back into the Hasmonean period was probably anachronistic. This attempt is better explained by the power of historiographic tradition on this subject than by anything else.

Martin Hengel's thorough discussion of cultural and educational changes brought about by Hellenism in Jewish Palestine puts meat on the bones of a somewhat schematic outline of these changes provided by Bickerman. Hengel specifically focuses on Jason's attempt to introduce Greek education in Jerusalem in the time immediately preceding the Maccabean revolt, as well as on subsequent Greek-style educational institutions in Second Temple Jewish Palestine.[7] He then proceeds to discuss "the development of the Jewish school," which emerges as a result of these changes in educational and cultural patterns.[8] Hengel observes that the description of disciple circles and their studying techniques in rabbinic literature closely parallels that of the Greek rhetorical schools. Like Bickerman, Hengel correctly notices the centrality of Hellenistic cultural and educational patterns for understanding Rabbinic Judaism. Like Bickerman, he tries to locate this development sometime during the Hellenistic and Hasmonean periods and then see it unfold into the mature rabbinic form by 200 CE.[9]

---

[5] Bickerman, *From Ezra*, 162.
[6] Bickerman, *From Ezra*, 163–64.
[7] M. Hengel, *Judaism and Hellenism: Studies in Their Encounter in Palestine During the Early Hellenistic Period* (Philadelphia: Fortress Press, 1974), vol. 1, 70–78.
[8] Hengel, *Judaism and Hellenism*, vol. 1, 78–83.
[9] Cf. also a more recent discussion of the increased accessibility of literacy during the Second Temple period and its implications for Jewish sectarianism in Baumgarten, *Flourishing of Jewish Sects in the Maccabean Era*, 114–36.

Birger Gerhardsson's important study on methods of transmission of oral traditions in Judaism follows similar methodological assumptions. Like the two previous scholars, Gerhardsson recognizes the centrality of Greek-style study circles and their learning techniques in the formation of some of the basic notions of Rabbinic Judaism (including the centrality of oral traditions in early Rabbinic Judaism). Gerhardsson also tries to trace these developments back to the Hellenistic period, emphasizing the importance of formalized teaching and teaching techniques for the preservation and transmission of the Torah.[10] He further discusses the importance of "schools for the study of Oral Torah" for preservation and transmission of the Oral Law.[11] In both cases, Gerhardsson freely uses predominantly rabbinic evidence to account for what was going on in Second Temple Judaism. He also interprets Second Temple Judaism *in light of* this later evidence, thus unintentionally imposing the perspective of later rabbinic sources on Second Temple Jewish texts. The latter practice is in fact characteristic of all three authors and illustrates just how powerful the traditional reading of these texts is. Still, like Bickerman and Hengel, Gerhardsson correctly recognizes the centrality of formalized Hellenistic studying practices and their institutional settings for the development of Rabbinic Judaism. He further stresses their importance for the development of oral tradition and its predominant status in Rabbinic Judaism.[12]

As we shall see below, more recent studies have basically affirmed the importance of Hellenistic social patterns (exemplified first and foremost by study circles centered around particular masters and emphasizing formalized oral study as the main mode of learning) for a proper understanding of Rabbinic Judaism. On the other hand, the centrality of such patterns in Second Temple Judaism has been increasingly called into question. David Goodblatt's article on Jewish education during the Second Temple period provides a useful correction to earlier views.[13] Goodblatt first rejects a number of later

---

[10] B. Gerhardsson, *Memory and Manuscript: Oral Tradition and Written Transmission in Rabbinic Judaism and Early Christianity* (Grand Rapids: Eerdmans, 1998), 56–66.

[11] Gerhardsson, *Memory and Manuscript*, 85–92.

[12] Gerhardsson, *Memory and Manuscript*, 93–170.

[13] D. Goodblatt, "Talmudic Sources on the Origins of Organized Jewish Education," in B. Oded, ed., *Studies in the History of the Jewish People and the Land of Israel* (Haifa: University of Haifa, 1980), vol. 5, 83–103 (in Hebrew). Cf. F. Golka, *The Leopard's Spots: Biblical and African Wisdom in Proverbs* (Edinburg: T&T Clark, 1993), 4–15, and R. Whybray, *The Intellectual Tradition in the Old Testament* (Berlin: Walter de Gruyter),

talmudic sources as anachronistic and then provides a thorough review of Second Temple Jewish texts to see if they provide evidence to substantiate the thesis about organized religious education in that time. His conclusions question the existence of formal education in Second Temple Jewish society. Rather, he asserts the importance of home-based and family-based education, a point to which we shall return below.[14] Goodblatt's observation fits well into an overall reluctance of scholars to assert the importance of organized public education in the biblical and early Second Temple periods. Instead, they increasingly look for alternative forms of education and training, including family-based forms of learning. In all probability, there were two basic formats of knowledge transmission in Ancient Israel and the early Second Temple period. On the one hand, there were official (state-sponsored?) scribal schools that trained professional bureaucrats for royal service (just as existed in other Near Eastern monarchies of the time). On the other hand, they probably operated on a limited scale, and a good deal of education took place within informal and often family-based circles, including those of scribes and priests. In fact, the two modes of learning might have overlapped. As we shall see, the transmission of professional skills within particular families is repeatedly attested during the Second Temple period and was probably considered "normal" by everyone involved. The family was perceived as a locus of knowledge transmission far beyond elementary education.[15]

31–48, for similar observations. See also C. Hezser, *The Social Structure of the Rabbinic Movement in Roman Palestine* (Tübingen: Mohr Siebeck, 1997), 94–95.

[14] Baumgarten, *Flourishing of Jewish Sects in the Maccabean Era*, 114–36, argues that the spread of literacy, democratization of education, and its detachment from the earlier family setting constituted one of the prime reasons for the birth of sectarianism during the Hellenistic period. I think that one has to distinguish between two processes here: the spread of literacy in non-priestly circles does not necessarily mean the emergence of public education outside of one's own family. In fact, a good deal of evidence cited by Baumgarten reflects the continuous importance of family-based transmission of knowledge. So, as Baumgarten convincingly demonstrates, there was a spread of literacy in Hellenistic Judah, but it probably took place within a traditional household setting.

[15] See P. Davies, *Scribes and Schools: The Canonization of the Hebrew Scriptures* (Louisville: John Knox Press, 1998), 74–88, and L. Grabbe, *Priests, Prophets, Diviners, Sages: A Socio-Historical of Religious Specialists in Ancient Israel* (Valley Forge: Trinity Press, 1995), 171–74, for summary of the debate. Cf. J. Crenshaw, *Education in Ancient Israel: Across the Deadening Silence* (New York: Doubleday, 1998), 85–113, and L. Perdue, "The Israelite and Early Jewish Family: Summary and Conclusions," in L. Perdue et al., *Families in Ancient Israel* (Louisville: John Knox Press, 1997), 172–73.

Another related aspect of describing Second Temple sectarian movements in modern historiography sees them as a product of changes in social and economic life in Greco-Roman Judaea. Specifically, the emergence of sects as identifiable and influential groups within Judaism is related to the urbanization of Judaea in Hellenistic and Roman times, as well as the emergence of urbanized civil society in Jewish Palestine of that period. Louis Finkelstein's attempt to see competition among the sects (especially between the Pharisees and the Sadducees) in terms of "class struggle" between urban population represented by scribes/Pharisees and rural population represented by priests/Sadducees has received mixed reaction in subsequent historiography.[16] Although other scholars were very cautious in embracing his extremely reductionistic approach in its entirety, his idea about Pharisees as an ideological mouthpiece of a new urban middle class gained popularity and acceptance. Thus, for example, Victor Tcherikover talks about "the class of scribes, the flesh and bone of the broad city populace, which took upon itself the task of interpreting the Torah neglected by the priests."[17] It was these "intellectual leaders of the urban population" that were ultimately responsible for creating the Oral Law "as a continuation, interpretation and supplementation of the Written Law." Ellis Rivkin relates the rise of the Pharisees to power to the public assembly that elected Simon the Hasmonean to the high priesthood.[18] He correctly emphasizes the revolutionary nature of this act and its relationship with Hellenistic civil practices. The Pharisees as a leading political and cultural force were born out of the confluence between Jewish society and Hellenism, and specifically out of transformation of social and political structures of Jewish society into those of the larger Hellenistic world. He draws interesting parallels between social and political institutions established by the Pharisees (or, rather, ascribed to them later in rabbinic sources) and Greco-Roman institutions.[19] Overall, according to Rivkin, it was the emergence of a new Jewish society that catapulted the Pharisees (= scribes) into a position of

---

[16] L. Finkelstein, *Pharisees: The Sociological Background of Their Faith* (Philadelphia: Jewish Publication Society, 1962), vol. 1, 82–100.

[17] See V. Tcherikover, *Hellenistic Civilization and the Jews* (Philadelphia: Jewish Publication Society, 1959), 124–25.

[18] E. Rivkin, *A Hidden Revolution* (Nashville: Abingdon, 1978), 211–51.

[19] See E. Rivkin, "*Beth Din, Boule, Sanhedrin*: A Tragedy of Errors," *HUCA* 46 (1975), 181–99.

power. Most recently, Albert Baumgarten has referred to urbanization as a crucial factor that contributed to the development of classical Jewish sectarianism in the Hasmonean times.[20] His well-informed
study, however, once again tends to rely too heavily on later rabbinic
sources (and on the reference to the two Yose's in M 'Abot 1, in
particular) to describe the social reality of Hasmonean Judaea. As
was the case with cultural Hellenization, the discussion of urbanization makes a valid observation about the social background of religious developments within Judaism but chronologically misplaces it.

Starting with Arnold H. Jones, scholars have convincingly argued
that the true urbanization of Jewish Palestine does not begin until
the reign of Herod and especially until that of his sons.[21] The latter launched a major building program and were credited with founding (or rebuilding) the first "Jewish" *poleis*, such as Sepphoris and
Tiberias. These were the cities organized along Greek constitutional
lines but predominantly populated with Jews and governed by Jewish
city councils. Prior to that time, Jewish Palestine was a predominantly rural entity dominated by the temple-city of Jerusalem. The
latter was a typical representative of an earlier Near Eastern type of
temple-dominated city, just as Judaea of that time continued to be
a more or less typical Near Eastern temple-state. Neither during the
Hellenistic nor during the Hasmonean age was there any consistent
attempt to change this situation. There is no indication that any
other Jewish settlement besides Jerusalem sought to be promoted to
city status. Nor is there any sign that a city-based civil society played
any role in Judaea during this period of time. Even the abortive
attempt to convert Jerusalem into a Greek-style *polis* took place within
a fairly traditional social framework (which probably contributed to
its ultimate failure). It is also highly unlikely that any Greek-style
civil institutions emerged during this period of time. As David
Goodblatt has convincingly demonstrated, all references to the public
assembly in our sources have to be taken with the grain of salt.[22]
As a whole, it was precisely during the reign of Herod and his sons

---

[20] See Baumgarten, *Flourishing of Jewish Sects*, 137–51. Cf. Safrai, *Literature of the Sages*, 5–7.
[21] See A. Jones, "Urbanization of Palestine," *JRS* 21 (1931), 78–85. Cf. R. Horsley, *Archaeology, History, and Society in Galilee: The Social Context of Jesus and the Rabbis* (Valley Forge: Trinity Press, 1996), 43–65.
[22] D. Goodblatt, *The Monarchic Principle: Studies in Jewish Self-Government in Antiquity* (Tübingen: J.C.B. Mohr, 1994), 77–130.

(and the time of Roman domination) when Jewish Palestine began
to transform from a rural temple-dominated society into an urbanized province of the Mediterranean urban empire built by Rome. It
was during this period that city-based public institutions came to
dominate Jewish social life. The true internalization of Hellenism by
Jewish society began only then. Prior to that time, Jewish Palestine
had continued to follow basic social patterns and conventions going
all the way back to Achaemenid times.[23]

In light of all this, it seems that the urban stage in the development of Jewish sectarianism starts only in the first century BCE, perhaps even not earlier than the first century CE. All previous observations
about urbanization as a crucial factor in the religious development
of Judaism remain valid and accurate, but the chronology should be
pushed into the Herodian (or even post-Herodian) period. It was
during this time that Judaism had to adapt to a changing social environment by reformulating itself as a religion for an increasingly
urbanized population. And it did, in many important ways. The
emergence of the first synagogues in Palestine precisely during this
period of time provides clear evidence for the changing nature of
Jewish piety.[24] The earliest unambiguous examples of disciple circles
formed around religious "sophists" come from the same period.[25]
Judaism increasingly follows Greco-Roman cultural patterns in constructing itself in this new social environment. It internalizes Hellenism
and gets reborn in the process, just as Jewish society at large internalizes new cultural and social order by becoming part of the
Mediterranean Roman Empire. And just as the Jewish society of
Galilee in the second and third centuries CE would become a culmination of this process of social and cultural integration, the Rabbinic

---

[23] For a convenient summary of cultural transformation during the reign of Herod
and his sons see M. Hengel, *The "Hellenization" of Judaea in the First Century after Christ*
(London: SCM Press, 1989), 32–40. See also his observations on stylistic differences
between the "Jewish-Greek" of pre-Herodian literature and that of Josephus and
Justus of Tiberias (p. 24). See also D. Fiensy, *The Social History of Palestine in the
Herodian Period: The Land is Mine* (Lewiston: Edwin Mellen Press, 1991), 133–45. He
discusses the impact of social and economic changes during the Herodian period
on the position and structure of peasant households.
[24] L. Levine, *The Ancient Synagogue: The First Thousand Years* (New Haven: Yale
University Press, 2000), 42–73 and 124–59. Cf. L. Grabbe, "Synagogues in Pre-70
Palestine: A Re-assessment," *JTS* 39 (1988), 401–10, and S. Schwartz, *Imperialism
and Jewish Society, 200 BCE to 640 CE* (Princeton: Princeton University Press,
2001), 222–25.
[25] See Schwartz, *Imperialism and Jewish Society*, 88.

Judaism of the second and third centuries would ironically become a culmination of Judaism's internalization of Hellenistic cultural values. To put it bluntly, the Hellenization of Jewish beliefs and traditions of Second Temple times produced Rabbinic Judaism.

Let us now revisit earlier historiography about the centrality of Hellenistic cultural norms for Second Temple Jewish sectarianism. All these studies suffer from an attempt to project social and cultural norms of the later rabbinic society (which were profoundly Hellenized as we shall see below) back into the Hellenistic and Hasmonean times. They try to find continuity where indeed there was a good deal of rupture. One of the things that precisely *distinguishes* Rabbinic Judaism from Second Temple sectarian movements is the profound Hellenization of its social structure and cultural norms. Rabbinic Judaism emerged as part of the transformation of Palestinian Jewish society into an urbanized provincial society of the Roman Empire. Prior to that moment, Judaism remained essentially a family-dominated religion of the Near Eastern temple-centered state.

Disciple circles constitute one of the prime settings (although not the only one) in which classical Rabbinic Judaism took shape. Such circles formed around particular masters ("rabbis"), known for their halakhic expertise and/or piety. The transmission and creation of rabbinic traditions took place within this educational setting, primarily as a result of dialogical give-and-take between the rabbi and his disciples.[26] Scholars have long since noticed remarkable similarities between the educational setting of rabbinic traditions and that of Greco-Roman philosophical and rhetorical schools. To begin with, the very notion of disciple circles, in which oral transmission of the text serves as a prime medium of learning, is profoundly Greek. Near Eastern scribal schools tended to emphasize the study of the written word and written text as a prime medium of wisdom.[27] In

---

[26] S. Lieberman, *Hellenism in Jewish Palestine: Studies in the Literary Transmission, Beliefs and Manners of Palestine in the I century BCE–IV century CE* (New York: JTSA, 1950), 83–99, convincingly demonstrates that systematization and "publication" of the Mishnah took place within educational setting of disciple circles. Cf. Gerhardsson, *Memory and Manuscript*, 93–170. For more recent discussion see M. Jaffee, *Torah in the Mouth: Writing and Oral Tradition in Palestinian Judaism, 200 BCE–400 CE* (Oxford: Oxford University Press, 2001), 65–83 and 126–52, and A. Tropper, *Wisdom, Politics, and Historiography: Tractate Avot in the Context of the Graeco-Roman Near East* (Oxford: Oxford University Press, 2004), 157–88.

[27] See M. Fishbane, *Biblical Interpretation in Ancient Israel* (Oxford: Clarendon Press, 1985), 24–43.

contrast, the notion of oral dialogue between the sage and his disciples as a way of achieving wisdom was part of Greco-Roman educational technique. Judah Goldin has convincingly demonstrated how the portrayal of Yohanan b. Zakkai and his disciples in M 'Abot 2:8–14 reflected the social structure and functioning of Greek philosophical circles.[28] Shaye Cohen took his observations one step further by comparing the depiction of R. Judah the Prince in talmudic sources and those of heads of Hellenistic academies in Greco-Roman texts.[29] Indeed, both rabbinic schools and Hellenistic academies resorted to the same types of "founding myths" about their origins. As Henry Fischel has shown, both rabbis and their Greek counterparts used the literary genre of *chreia* (short didactic stories, designed to capture and transmit essential points about human nature and behavior) to tell stories about founding fathers of their groups.[30] In the rabbinic case, it was the stories about Hillel the Elder that constituted the "foundational myth" of the movement. Finally, the very notion of the rabbinic teaching being handed down over generations through a chain of masters and their disciples finds numerous parallels in both Greek and early Christian writings. The etiological construct of the "chain of tradition" was a common tool used to legitimize one's school and its claims for authority in the Hellenistic world.[31] Overall, rabbinic study circles emerge as Jewish counterparts of educational institutions in the second and third century Greco-Roman milieu.

---

[28] See J. Goldin, *Studies in Midrash and Related Literature* (Philadelphia: Jewish Publication Society, 1988), 57–76. For further helpful observations on the philosopher-like portrayals of some of R. Yohanan's disciples see H. Fischel, *Rabbinic Literature and Greco-Roman Philosophy: A Study of Epicurea and Rhetorica in Early Midrashic Writings* (Leiden: Brill, 1973), 1–97.

[29] S. Cohen, "Patriarchs and Scholarchs," *PAAJR* 48 (1981), 57–85.

[30] See H. Fischel, "Story and History: Observations on Greco-Roman Rhetoric and Pharisaism," in idem, ed., *Essays in Greco-Roman and Related Talmudic Literature* (New York: KTAV, 1977), 443–72, and "Studies in Cynicism and the Ancient Near East: The Transformation of a Chria," in J. Neusner, ed., *Religions in Antiquity: Essays in Memory of Erwin Ramsdell Goodenough* (Leiden: Brill, 1968), 372–411.

[31] E. Bickerman, "La Chaîne de la Tradition Pharisienne," *Revue Biblique* 59 (1951), 153–65, and Tropper, *Wisdom, Politics, and Historiography*, 158–72. Cf. M. Herr, "Continuum in the Chain of Torah Transmission," *Zion* 44 (1980), 43–56, who contrasts this approach with the revelation-based doctrine of the Dead Sea Sect. D. Boyarin, *Border Lines: The Partition of Judaeo-Christianity* (Philadelphia: University of Pennsylvania Press, 2004), 74–86, traces "the transformation of the chain of tradition of a Hellenistic philosophical school into the institution for the protection of the faith" and sees this development as central for the formation of both Rabbinic Judaism and early Christianity.

In fact, the very idea of the Oral Law as it emerged in classical Rabbinic Judaism might have been part of this "foundational myth" (or perhaps "institutional myth") of the disciple circles. As Martin Jaffee has observed, "of particular importance for the study of oral and written foundations of rabbinic tradition is the educational setting in which its texts were mediated."[32] Both Jacob Neusner and Peter Schäfer have convincingly argued for a post-70 setting of this concept.[33] In particular, they both associate it with early rabbinic study circles at Yavneh. It was the new institutional format of oral study and transmission of Jewish law that eventually became conceptualized in the idea of the "Oral Law" transmitted from Moses to rabbis through multiple generations of masters and their disciples. The Oral Law emerged as an essential part of the foundational myth of the schoolhouse, developed by tannaitic rabbis.[34] Martin Jaffee has recently argued that early Palestinian Amoraim made further steps in perfecting this myth and giving it its final form.[35] The myth became ideology stressing the primacy of the oral word and mode of learning over the written one. It is not surprising that Jewish and Greek study circles shared similar techniques of textual interpretation as well. In addition to generally acknowledging the centrality of the oral dialogical form of study, Greek Sophists and Jewish rabbis applied specific exegetical methods to mine sacred (and written) texts of their traditions for new meanings. Although scholars disagree about the precise extent of similarities, substantial overlaps between technical approaches to textual exegesis used on both sides are quite clear.[36]

---

[32] Jaffee, *Torah in the Mouth*, 128.

[33] J. Neusner, *The Rabbinic Traditions about the Pharisees Before 70* (Leiden: Brill, 1975–1978), vol. 3, 143–79, and P. Schäfer, "Das Dogma von der mündlichen Torah," in idem, *Studien zur Geschichte und Theologie des Rabbinischen Judentums* (Leiden: Brill, 1978), 153–97. Cf. Jaffee, *Torah in the Mouth*, 65–83.

[34] See S. Fraade, *From Tradition to Commentary: Torah and Its Interpretation in Midrash Sifre to Deuteronomy* (Albany: State University of New York Press, 1991), 69–121 and Jaffee, *Torah in the Mouth*, 84–99.

[35] See Jaffee, *Torah in the Mouth*, 126–52.

[36] D. Daube, "Rabbinic Methods of Interpretation and Hellenistic Rhetoric," *HUCA* 22 (1949), 239–64, and "Alexandrian Methods of Interpretation and the Rabbis," in H. Fischel, *Essays*, 165–82, interprets rabbinic exegetical rules as essentially a Jewish version of interpretive techniques current in contemporaneous Greco-Roman schools of rhetoric. Lieberman, *Hellenism in Jewish Palestine*, 47–82, offers a much more cautious (but not necessarily more correct) assessment. See further P. Alexander, "*Quid Athenis et Hierosolymis?* Rabbinic Midrash and Hermeneutics in the Graeco-Roman World," in P. Davies and R. White, eds., *A Tribute to Geza Vermes: Essays on Jewish and Christian Literature and History* (Sheffield: JSOT Press, 1990),

Among other things, they served to translate authoritative written texts of either Hellenic or Jewish tradition into the new oral modality of learning and comprehension. Through these exegetical methods the Torah passed from its original cultural and social setting in Second Temple Judaism to a new setting in Rabbinic Judaism, just as Homer and other classical Greek texts were appropriated and transformed within the Second Sophistic. The new social setting of religious learning transformed the learning itself.

Overall, the paradigm of disciple circles adequately describes mature forms of Rabbinic Judaism. It further demonstrates profound similarities with contemporaneous Greco-Roman modes of education. Disciple circles of Rabbinic Judaism demonstrate cultural naturalization and internalization of Hellenistic intellectual values within Jewish society. In many ways, what makes Rabbinic Judaism distinct from its Second Temple predecessor is precisely this process of profound Hellenization. On the other hand, Jewish sectarian movements of the Second Temple period were deeply steeped in cultural and social conventions of traditional Near Eastern society. The Herodian and post-Herodian periods witnessed the gradual transformation of these conventions into new forms. But prior to that time, we have to search for another paradigm to explain the social structure of Jewish religious movements. Disciple circles do not adequately account for the realities of Second Temple Judaism.

Looking for Alternative Paradigms: The Household as the Matrix of Second Temple Religious Learning and Piety

Over the past several decades an increasing number of scholars have focused their attention on extended families and households as the main social and economic units within ancient Jewish society. Most of their work deals with early stages of Israelite history (prior to the Babylonian exile), with relatively little work done in the area of post-exilic Jewish history.[37] In addition to emphasizing the social and

---

101–24. See also Jaffee, *Torah in the Mouth*, 128–40, who demonstrates how the rhetorical technique of producing a multiform *chreia* worked in both Hellenistic and rabbinic settings.

[37] On Jewish families in Second Temple and early Rabbinic periods see J. Collins, "Marriage, Divorce, and Family in Second Temple Judaism," in L. Perdue et al., *Families in Ancient Israel* (Louisville: Westminster John Knox Press, 1997), 104–62,

economic importance of extended families for Jewish society of the pre-exilic period, several scholars have also addressed the centrality of Jewish households in shaping Judaism of that time. Thus Rainer Albertz has argued that early forms of Israelite religion evolved within a household setting and came into existence within the family environment of Israelite tribal society.[38] This situation changed with the emergence of monarchy, with its attempt to centralize and bureaucratize Israelite religion along with other aspects of Israelite society.[39] With the Babylonian exile, the state-controlled structures collapsed and the traditional family once again became central to the preservation and development of Judaism.[40] Unfortunately, Albertz focused most of his research on pre-exilic times, virtually dismissing post-exilic Judah from consideration by stating that in the aftermath of the restoration in 539 BCE the nature of Judaism changed from an ethnic clan-based tradition to a more inclusive and universalistic religion, which surpassed ethnic boundaries.[41] Later scholars have duly criticized this view,[42] but in spite of several isolated cases to be discussed presently, no attempt has been made to create a comprehensive picture of the possible role of Jewish households in shaping Second Temple and (later) Rabbinic Judaism. Still, despite some shortcomings, Albertz's work maintains its significance in emphasizing the extended Israelite family as the main locus in which the formation of Israelite religion took place. It correctly stresses the nature of pre-monarchic and exilic Judaism as essentially household religions, preserved, refined, and transmitted within individual families and/or clans.[43]

---

and M. Satlow, *Jewish Marriage in Antiquity* (Princeton: Princeton University Press, 2001). See also S. Safrai, "Home and Family," in idem and M. Stern, eds., *The Jewish People in the First Century: Historical Geography, Political History, Social, Cultural & Religious Life & Institutions* (Assen: Van Gorcum, 1976), vol. 2, 728–833.

[38] See R. Albertz, *History of Israelite Religion in the Old Testament Period* (Louisville: John Knox Press, 1994), vol. 1, 25–39 and 94–103.

[39] Albertz, *History of Israelite Religion*, vol. 1, 105–56.

[40] R. Albertz, *Persönliche Frömmigkeit und offizielle Religion* (Stuttgart: Calwer Verlag, 1978), 178–90 and *History of Israelite Religion*, vol. 2, 399–411.

[41] Albertz, *Persönliche Frömmigkeit*, 190–92.

[42] See C. Camp, *Wisdom and the Feminine in the Book of Proverbs* (Decatur: Almond Press, 1985), 249–50.

[43] J. Blenkinsopp, "The Family in First Temple Israel," in Perdue, ed., *Families in Ancient Israel*, 78–84, further emphasizes the centrality of family religion and family values for pre-exilic and (judging from his discussion of Proverbs) post-exilic Judaism. Cf. also Perdue, "Israelite and Early Jewish Family," 172–73 and 203–07 (with special emphasis on the family setting of "oral tradition" on pp. 206–07).

To assert the religious importance of Jewish households in the post-exilic period would be a natural conclusion from Albertz's work and especially from his extensive discussion of the revival of the family's religious role during the Exile. Claudia Camp's analysis of the feminine imagery of Wisdom in the Book of Proverbs follows Albertz's methodology but relates to the post-exilic period and its literature.[44] She maintains that the importance of female imagery in the portrayal of Wisdom in the Book of Proverbs reflects the centrality of family and household structures for Jewish society and Judaism of that time. She further sees the Jewish extended family as one of the prime loci of religious creativity in the early post-exilic period, of which the Book of Proverbs is only one example. Camp notices the importance of extended families and their heads in the social, economic, and political organization in post-exilic Judah, and maintains that it was within such families that contemporaneous religious values were also shaped. In addition to Camp's research, Carole Fontaine has further emphasized the importance of traditional Israelite families and family-based social structures for the development of biblical wisdom texts. In fact, she maintains that families and clans provided one of the main social settings in which these texts emerged and developed. Once again, Fontaine does not draw any explicit distinction between pre-exilic and post-exilic Israelite society. As far as wisdom traditions were concerned, the latter served as a direct continuation of the former.[45]

In her subsequent research Camp takes this discussion of feminine wisdom imagery one step further to include Ben Sira and the Wisdom of Solomon.[46] She observes that the Hellenization and urbanization of Jewish society led to the transformation of the family's role, which became reflected in changing images of feminine wisdom. The association of Wisdom with Torah in Ben Sira leads to its abstraction and gradual loss of feminine (and familial) characteristics. Furthermore, "the study and teaching of the Torah have been removed from the domestic domain, where the wife and mother shares the responsibility with her mate, and placed in the institution

---

[44] Camp, *Wisdom and the Feminine in the Book of Proverbs*, 233–82.

[45] C. Fontaine, "The Sage in Family and Tribe," in J. Gammie and L. Perdue, eds., *The Sage in Israel and the Ancient Near East* (Winona Lake: Eisenbrauns, 1990), 155–64.

[46] C. Camp, "The Female Sage in Ancient Israel and in the Biblical Wisdom Literature," in Gammie and Perdue, *Sage in Israel*, 185–203.

of the school."[47] Overall, Hellenistic influence and Hellenistic social values result in "constricting" the role of a female sage just as they result in challenging the authority of the traditional family. I shall argue below that Camp probably overstresses the degree of Hellenization and subsequent erosion of the traditional family in the time of Ben Sira. Much of our evidence stemming from that time shows that the traditional family continued to shape Judaism for centuries after Ben Sira. Indeed Ben Sira's discourse itself does not necessarily presuppose the transition of wisdom learning from households to schools. Still, Camp's basic line of argument is surely correct. Judaea's integration into the Hellenized urban society of the Mediterranean basin resulted in a profound transformation in the sociology of Judaism. The family-dominated and family-enshrined religious traditions of the Second Temple period became transformed into abstract religious doctrine analytically studied, perfected, and transmitted within disciple circles and not within natural kinship groups. It was precisely this development that ushered in the era of classical Rabbinic Judaism.

Adiel Schremer has more recently suggested a somewhat similar thesis in connection with the development of Torah study in the Dead Sea sect and in Second Temple Judaism in general.[48] She argues (on analogy with modern orthodox Judaism) that one has to distinguish between a "tradition-based observance" (identified as "the *living tradition* of fathers and forefathers") and a "text-based observance" appealing to "written—therefore authoritative—texts, as the primary source from which one should draw halakhic guidance."[49] Schremer emphasizes the revolutionary nature of one's appeal to the written text as the main source of halakhic knowledge during the

---

[47] Camp, "Female Sage," 199. Cf. similar observations in J. Berquist, *Controlling Corporeality: The Body and the Household in Ancient Israel* (New Brunswick: Rutgers University Press, 2002), 181–96, and J. Gammie, "From Prudentialism to Apocalypticism: The Houses of the Sages Amid the Varying Forms of Wisdom," in Gammie and Perdue, *Sage in Israel*, 484–85. According to the latter, the existential religious value of traditional families began to disappear with the emergence of belief in individual salvation after death.

[48] See A. Schremer, "[T]he[y] did not Read in the Sealed Book': Qumran Halakhic Revolution and the Emergence of Torah Study in Second Temple Judaism," in D. Goodblatt et al., eds., *Historical Perspectives: From the Hasmoneans to Bar Kokhba in Light of the Dead Sea Scrolls* (Leiden: Brill, 2001), 105–26. Cf. M. Goodman, "A Note on Josephus, the Pharisees and Ancestral Tradition," *JJS* 50 (1999), 17–20.

[49] Schremer, "[T]he[y] did not Read," 105–06.

Second Temple period. Prior to that moment, halakhic observances had been informed by one's "tradition of the fathers." The new text-based mode of religious authority resulted in the transformation of basic religious structures, including the development of institutional-ized education intended to transmit text-based knowledge to subse-quent generations and the increased role of scholars versed in the sacred texts.[50] At the same time the accuracy and authority of non-textual traditions became increasingly questionable. Schremer does not associate this shift in halakhic authority with the arrival of Hellenism but rather with the internal development of text-based authority in Second Temple Judaism.

Several other scholars have addressed the question of how tradi-tional Jewish families contributed to the formation of the ideas and values of Second Temple Judaism.[51] Christine Hayes has made a major contribution to this topic by discussing the concept of "sacred seed" in Second Temple Jewish literature.[52] In such texts as the Book of Ezra, *Jubilees*, and 4QMMT, all Israel was portrayed as the "holy seed," which is naturally distinct from any other nation. The preser-vation and transmission of its purity was regarded as one of the prime obligations of any Israelite family, both priestly and lay. This goal determined many aspects of Jewish family laws in this period and made the family into a key unit of Jewish religious identity. Only in the Rabbinic period, Hayes maintains, did this perception of marital relationships begin to change by shifting to "a moral-reli-gious rationale for the prohibition of intermarriage" rather than the "holy seed" concept.[53] Such a change may be associated with a larger shift in the ideals of piety taking place around the same time.

To conclude our discussion of the familial setting of Second Temple Jewish religiosity one has to make an important methodological obser-vation. Religious learning and transmission of knowledge during this

[50] Schremer, "[T]he[y] did not Read," 107 and 113–15.
[51] For methodologically helpful observations on how the household setting might have influenced religious language and ideas of ancient Judaism (both pre- and post-exilic) see Perdue, "The Household, Old Testament Theology, and Contemporary Hermeneutics," in Perdue, *Families in Ancient Israel*, 225–43, and J. Berquist, *Controlling Corporeality: The Body and the Household in Ancient Israel* (New Brunswick: Rutgers University Press, 2002).
[52] C. Hayes, *Gentile Impurities and Jewish Identities: Intermarriage and Conversion from the Bible to the Talmud* (Oxford: Oxford University Press, 2002), 68–91. Cf. D. Schwartz, *Studies in the Jewish Background of Christianity* (Tübingen: J.C.B. Mohr, 1992), 8–9.
[53] Hayes, *Gentile Impurities*, 145–92.

period should be considered in the broader context of dominant perceptions of piety and holiness in the contemporaneous Jewish society. Religious learning constituted an essential part of the much larger "holiness project" pursued by various Jewish groups of the time. I shall argue below that many of these groups perceived family life and routine household functions as religiously meaningful loci of sanctity. By meticulously observing halakhic regulations pertaining to everyday household activities these groups tried to achieve religious ideals of purity, piety, and ultimately, holiness and salvation. Religious instruction and its possible familial settings should be treated as part of this much larger endeavor. Hence, the rise of disciple circles in the concluding centuries of the Second Temple period was part of a great paradigmatic shift in the discourse of holiness. This shift occurred when new associations of like-minded adult individuals began to sideline more traditional kinship groups in their capacity as "sacred communities." As a result, new "holiness projects" had to be worked out, which would either accommodate both social types or deny religious validity to one of them. The development of different modes of piety during the later part of the Second Temple period and first post-Destruction centuries was intimately connected with the variety of responses to this particular problem.

Several lines of argument in modern historiography converge on the key role of households for rabbinic discourse. Over the past several decades a number of studies have emphasized the centrality of the "body" and body-centered discourse for rabbinic halakhic anthropology. Howard Eilberg-Schwartz calls attention to the importance of body-related religious rites (such as circumcision), which heighten an individual's awareness of one's corporeality and its religious significance.[54] Daniel Boyarin contrasts such an approach with Hellenistic philosophical anthropology, which perceives the soul and disembodied spirituality as the true path toward illumination and ultimately salvation but degrades the human body as something inferior and secondary, an unfortunate by-product of our physical existence.[55] The religious value of the human body and body-related

---

[54] H. Eilberg-Schwartz, *The Savage in Judaism: An Anthropology of Israelite Religion and Ancient Judaism* (Bloomington: Indiana University Press, 1990), 141–94, and "The Problem of the Body for the People of the Book," in idem, ed., *People of the Body: Jews and Judaism from the Embodied Perspective* (Albany: State University of New York Press, 1992), 17–46.

[55] D. Boyarin, *Carnal Israel: Reading Sex in Talmudic Culture* (Berkeley: University of

practices serves as a distinct characteristic of Rabbinic Judaism in its Greco-Roman environment. As subsequent studies have shown, the rabbinic discourse treats an individual body inseparably from the larger "body" of a household.[56] These two "bodies" are of vital interest to the early rabbinic thought, worldview, and legal system. The sages wanted to design means by which a traditional Jewish family could sanctify its everyday life and economic activities. By using archaeological evidence, a recent work by Cynthia Baker demonstrates that rabbinic interest in families and their functions reflects the central role of the household in the social and economic life of Galilee in the second and third centuries CE.[57]

In his discussion of pharisaic and early Rabbinic Judaism, Jacob Neusner repeatedly mentions the household as the prime setting of pharisaic and early rabbinic religious values. In his early works Neusner seeks to develop a sociological paradigm suggested by Morton Smith. The latter tried to identify the Pharisees (as well as the Dead Sea Sect and possibly other sectarian groups of that time) with "table fellowships."[58] In this scenario individual households did not play any significant role. Instead, the emphasis was placed on communal table gatherings and participation in common meals, which had religious significance. Neusner, however, quickly revised Smith's theory in at least one important way. For him, pharisaic meals were conducted in regular household settings among family and (sometimes) friends and did not possess any characteristics of a sacred meal. The goal rather was to eat one's regular food in a state of ritual purity. It was one's household that had to be rendered pure by observing food purity laws and tithing one's agricultural produce.[59] In his later works, Neusner specifically articulates the centrality of Jewish households and their everyday concerns for shaping mishnaic laws, including

California Press, 1993), 1–10 and 231–35. Cf. E. Stiegman, "Rabbinic Anthropology," in *ANRW* 19 (1977), 508–23.

[56] See C. Fonrobert, *Menstrual Purity: Rabbinic and Christian Reconstructions of Biblical Gender* (Stanford: Stanford University Press, 2000), 40–67, and C. Baker, *Rebuilding the House of Israel: Architectures of Gender in Jewish Antiquity* (Stanford: Stanford University Press, 2002), 34–76.

[57] Baker, *Rebuilding the House of Israel*, 34–47, 77–94, and 114–22.

[58] See M. Smith, "The Dead Sea Sect in Relation to Ancient Judaism," *NTS* 7 (1960), 347–60. Cf. J. Neusner, "The Fellowship (הבורה) in the Second Jewish Commonwealth," *HTR* 53 (1960), 125–42, and "Two Pictures of the Pharisees: Philosophical Circle or Eating Club," *ATR* 64 (1982), 525–28.

[59] See Neusner, *From Politics to Piety: The Emergence of Pharisaic Judaism* (New York: KTAV, 1979), 82–90.

their earliest stratum.[60] Hayim Lapin takes a similar approach in his work on legal traditions of M Baba Metsia and their social setting.[61] He emphasizes the centrality of Jewish households of means and their everyday economic activities for the formation of this tractate. Indeed, just as households constituted the main unit of production in Jewish society of the time, they also formed the prime setting in which civil law of the Mishnah took shape.

Shaye Cohen's vision of the sociology of Jewish sectarianism seems to have undergone a development similar to that of Neusner. In his earlier works he repeatedly stresses that one of the main social characteristics of Jewish sects was to overcome natural family boundaries and to create a viable alternative to natural kinship ties.[62] On the other hand, in his later article on the origins of the rabbinic movement, Cohen asserts the centrality of the traditional family and its values for the formation of Rabbinic Judaism.[63] He moreover questions a traditional assumption that disciple circles constituted the single most important line of transmission of rabbinic traditions. Instead, he points to rabbinic families as another possible line of transmission and stresses their importance at the original stages of the rabbinic movement. Moving along similar lines, Catherine Hezser has recently proposed a social network theory to explain the nature and functioning of rabbinic circles in Roman Palestine. In addition to stressing the importance of teacher-disciple relationships, she has also emphasized the significance of social networks involving rabbinic households and everyday relationships among them. Along with networks of study circles and rabbinic schools, there also existed networks of rabbinic families interacting with one another on an everyday informal basis.[64] Overall, there has been a trend to abandon (or significantly revise) the earlier paradigm of "table fellowships" (and/or "philosophical circles") in favor of traditional patriarchal households

---

[60] J. Neusner, *Judaism, the Evidence of the Mishnah* (Chicago: University of Chicago Press, 1981), 250–56, and *The Economics of the Mishnah* (Chicago: University of Chicago Press, 1990), 50–71.

[61] H. Lapin, *Early Rabbinic Civil Law and the Social History of Roman Galilee: A Study of Mishnah Tractate Baba Mesia* (Atlanta: Scholars Press, 1995), 119–241. Cf. Satlow, *Jewish Marriage*, 12–21, for a broader Greco-Roman perspective.

[62] See Cohen, *From the Maccabees to the Mishnah*, 115–19, 160–64, and 172–73.

[63] S. Cohen, "The Rabbi in Second-Century Jewish Society," in W. Horbury et al., eds., *The Cambridge History of Judaism* (Cambridge: Cambridge University Press, 1999), vol. 3, 926–27, 930–36, and 948–50.

[64] Hezser, *Social Structure of the Rabbinic Movement*, 93–110, 228–39 and 307–27.

as an important setting of pharisaic and early rabbinic movements. On the other hand, as we have observed above, there exists a basic consensus among scholars that in its mature forms (as expressed by the Mishnah, Tosefta, and Tannaitic midrashim) early Rabbinic Judaism is essentially a product of disciple circles and their unique worldview. It remains to be seen how this transition from one social matrix to another exactly took place and what it implied about the rabbinic religious project.[65]

Plan and Goals of This Work

In light of this research, I can now formulate the goals of the present work. I will argue that as far as the chronology of the Second Temple and early Rabbinic periods is concerned, there were two stages in the development of Jewish religious groups. The first period embraces the time of Achaemenid rule and the Hellenistic and Hasmonean periods, stretching roughly from 539 BCE to 63 BCE. During this period Judaism remained a patriarchal religion, and its family-based nature shaped most of its religious identity as well as religious movements within it.[66] One should not underestimate the ability of traditional Jewish institutions to absorb new Hellenistic influences without undergoing much of a change in the process. The Second Temple Jewish sects that emerged during this time were essentially alliances of individual families bound together by their common understanding of Torah.[67] Jewish law took its form within the family setting and was often indistinguishable from the ancestral

---

[65] See chapter on Rabbinic Judaism for further discussion of relevant historiography.

[66] For the centrality of families or family-based groups in post-exilic Judea see in particular J. Weinberg, *The Citizen-Temple Community* (Sheffield: JSOT Press, 1992), 49–61, and J. Blenkinsopp, "Temple and Society in Achaemenid Judah," in P. Davies, ed., *Second Temple Studies* (Sheffield: JSOT Press, 1991), vol. 1, 22–53. The articles contain summaries of earlier scholarship. See also S. Japhet, "Sheshbazzar and Zerubbabel," *ZAW* 94 (1982), 66–98, esp. 87–89, and S. McEvenue, "Political Structure in Judah from Cyrus to Nehemiah," *CBQ* 43 (1981), 353–64.

[67] On the importance of Jewish Law and its interpretation for early sectarian movements see Blenkinsopp, "Interpretation and the Tendency to Sectarianism: An Aspect of Second Temple History," 1–26. Albertz, *Persönliche Frömmigkeit*, 178–90, and *History of Israelite Religion*, vol. 2, 399–411, convincingly demonstrates that Jewish extended families constituted the main social setting, within which Judaism developed during the exilic period. Camp, *Wisdom and the Feminine*, 243–54, emphasizes the centrality of familial structures for wisdom texts of post-exilic Judaism.

practices of individual households. In this respect, priestly families and their legal traditions were not unique. Rather, they represented a common trend that dominated Jewish society of the time. This period witnessed the emergence of a particular "discourse of holiness" that perceived a traditional patriarchal household and its religious practices as the prime settings and true embodiments of sanctity. Early sectarian movements (the community of Ezra and Nehemiah being the first clearly attested example of such sort) structured themselves around this notion both institutionally and doctrinally.

The situation began to change sometime during the first century BCE. Jewish Palestine was increasingly becoming part of the larger Mediterranean society comprised and represented by the Roman Empire. Urbanization and Hellenization became two main social trends. This process only accelerated in the wake of unsuccessful Jewish revolts against Rome in the late first and early second centuries CE. The traditional family setting of Judaism did not disappear completely. As we shall see, its elements were preserved well into the third and fourth centuries CE. But alongside it there emerged new types of religious learning. During this time family traditions were increasingly abandoned and transformed in favor of more universal, eternal, and abstract modes of presentation. The traditions were no longer transmitted as part of ancestral family lore but as anonymous collections of texts organized either by subject or as running commentaries on biblical books. On a social level this development corresponded to the increased prominence of study circles, in which traditions were transmitted from teachers to their disciples, not from fathers to their sons. The traditions came to lose their family-based setting. They became more universal and abstract. They were no longer "embodied" or "owned" by specific households. This transition from a household to a disciple study circle as the basic social unit of religious learning and piety within Judaism was what, I would argue, marked the transition from Second Temple to Rabbinic Judaism (as well as Christianity). Household religion was transformed into a universal teaching that existed independent of families. This process in many ways reflected the transformation of religious and cultural values of the traditional clan-based society into the religious and cultural values of a provincial civic society within the Roman Empire.

This work consists of two parts. In part one I shall argue that starting with the Return in 538 BCE and through the Hasmonean

period religious movements within Judaism had pretty much the
same social structure. They should be seen as networks of patriarchal families united by a common interpretation of Torah, shared
halakhic practices, and a shared "discourse of holiness." I shall further argue that the patriarchal family (either priestly or lay) constituted the main social unit, within which religious teachings and
practices were formed, learned, and transmitted. These practices were
truly "traditions of the fathers" in the most immediate sense of this
term. In order to substantiate my argument, I shall use three basic
groups of texts: the books of Ezra and Nehemiah, pseudepigraphic
texts from the early Second Temple period (*1 Enoch*, *Jubilees* and
related texts), and texts produced by the Dead Sea sect. All these
documents will be critically evaluated separately from one another
and on their own merits. Then, we shall put the results of the analysis together to see if they amount to a consistent picture of the historical situation of that period.

At the same time, I shall argue that the Second Temple period
witnessed the gradual emergence of new forms of Jewish sectarianism. This new type of movement encompassed adult male individuals rather than families. It produced a new type of community that
tried to surpass and very often replaced natural kinship ties with a
new sense of common identity based on the common quest for salvation and commonly recognized unique interpretation of sacred
texts. The first clear example of such a group within Judaism comes
from the Dead Sea sect. In fact, the Dead Sea sect may serve as a
litmus test for my entire theory since it reflects both stages in the
development of Jewish sectarianism. I shall argue that while the
group had started as a traditional family-based religious movement,
by the first century CE it evolved into an association of like-minded
individuals built around shared views of salvation, religious observances, and interpretation of sacred texts. Although there is no convincing evidence that even at this stage they abandoned family life,
the latter was clearly no longer part of their religiously meaningful
discourse. The traditional family and its everyday routine no longer
served as the prime locus of sanctity; instead, a new community of
adult devotees came to embody holiness through meticulously regulated practices and rituals. Eventually, some of this new community's
offshoots evolved into eschatological "utopian" groups driven by the
ideals of "scholastic asceticism." The latter physically secluded them-

selves from the rest of society by departing into the Judean Desert and abandoning traditional kinship ties altogether.

The second part of this work will address the history of family-based traditions within pharisaic and early rabbinic groups. It will not treat the development of disciple circles and associated new forms of Judaism, since this topic, I believe, has been adequately covered in previous studies. Instead, this work will focus on the religious role of families at the early stages of the Rabbinic period. It will show how family-centered modes of Judaism continued to exist well into the rabbinic times, now sharing the stage with disciple circles and being gradually transformed into the universal teachings of classical Rabbinic Judaism. Unlike the Dead Sea sectarians, however, rabbis did not discard the religious value of family life. Instead, they tried to integrate families into their grand project of holiness by legislating for them and eventually "rabbinizing" their everyday existence. In Rabbinic Judaism family life continued to remain religiously meaningful, but it had to be determined from outside by the halakhic discourse of newly emerging rabbinic schools. As a result, early Rabbinic Judaism became entangled in a complex web of relationships with the earlier family-based traditions, ranging from outright acceptance to respectful disregard and open hostility.

The transition from "ancestral traditions" to "scholastic piety" also resulted in new types of totalizing discourse intended to create new identities for rabbinic "philosophical schools" and the surrounding world, as well as to justify their existence in this world. In his recently published book Daniel Boyarin makes the following crucial observation about the nature and origins of the early rabbinic movement:

> The appropriation of the *paradosis* and the *diadoche* and their promotion to an apostolic succession list of officeholders, culminating in the patriarchal dynasty, at the time of the redaction of the Mishna—in short, the invention of rabbinic orthodoxy—is the Jewish parallel to the invention of Justin, Irenaeus, and their successors at the same time. The transformation of both nascent Christianity and nascent Judaism from groups of sects—collections of philosophical schools, as Josephus had described Judaism and Brent, third-century Christianity—into orthodox churches with their heretical others would be seen on this reading as part of the same sociocultural process and practice.[68]

---

[68] Boyarin, *Border Lines*, 85. Cf. the discussion in D. Boyarin, "The *Diadoche* of

I hope to demonstrate that the root cause of the tendency noticed by Boyarin lies in a much earlier development of the association-type communities with their tendency to create new identities and their claims of access to the universal (cosmic) truth. Such universalizing agendas of these groups often resulted in a totalizing discourse and produced a particular type of "heresiological mindset" as its by-product. This whole development came as a result of profound Hellenization of the Jewish society and its gradual restructuring along Hellenistic lines, when the household-based social framework was gradually abandoned, and conviction-based alliances of adult individuals with claims for the universal truth were embraced as the prime means of religious self-expression. Both the Dead Sea sect and the Pharisaic-rabbinic movement(s) serve as excellent examples of such a transition.

the Rabbis; or, Judah the Patriarch at Yavneh," in R. Kalmin and S. Schwartz, eds., *Jewish Culture and Society under the Christian Roman Empire* (Leuven: Peeters, 2003), 309–18.

PART ONE

HOUSEHOLDS AND THE ORIGINS OF JEWISH SECTARIANISM

CHAPTER ONE

SECTS AND HOUSEHOLDS DURING THE FORMATIVE CENTURIES OF SECOND TEMPLE JUDAISM

In his article "The Dead Sea Scrolls in Relation to Ancient Judaism," Morton Smith made an important observation about the group described in Nehemiah 10. He characterized this group as one of the earliest sectarian movements of the Second Temple period and in many ways as a precursor of the later sectarian groups such as the Pharisees and the Dead Sea Sect.[1] According to Smith, "the point at which we can first see the formation of a distinct, formally constituted sect, is, I think, the covenant in Nehemiah X."[2] He describes the content of Nehemiah 10 as "the basic covenant of a sect, a group of special observants, in the tradition of Nehemiah, but now particularly concerned with the observance of their obligations towards the Temple."[3] Smith makes a convincing argument that indeed the group described in Nehemiah 10, as well as several other groups from the times of Ezra and Nehemiah, can be accurately described as the earliest Jewish sects of the Second Temple period. This hypothesis has since been accepted and further elaborated by a number of scholars.[4] It will also serve as a starting point for the following discussion.

---

[1] Smith's article further elaborates a more general observation of M. Weber, *Ancient Judaism* (Glencoe: Free Press, 1952), 336–55, that the roots of Second Temple Jewish sectarianism should be sought in the transition from nation-state to a confessional community that happened as a result of the Babylonian exile. Weber's point was further elaborated by S. Talmon, "The Emergence of Jewish Sectarianism" in *King, Cult and Calendar* (Jerusalem: Magnes Press, 1986), 165–201. Talmon observes that the Jewish returnees from Babylonia brought with them Babylonian social structures and attempted to transplant them into the Land of Israel. Unfortunately, neither of these scholars elaborated on specific details of this social structure.

[2] Smith, "The Dead Sea Sect in Relation to Ancient Judaism," 355.

[3] Smith, "Dead Sea Sect," 357.

[4] See, for example, J. Blenkinsopp, "Interpretation and the Tendency to Sectarianism: An Aspect of Second Temple History" in E. Sanders, ed., *Jewish and Christian Self-Definition* (Philadelphia: Fortress Press, 1981), vol. 2, 1–26, and "A Jewish Sect of the Persian Period," *CBQ* 52 (1990), 5–20. Cf. Cohen, *From the Maccabees to the Mishnah*, 137–143.

Social Structure of the Ezra-Nehemiah Movement

Scholars have identified the text of Nehemiah 10 as a covenant.[5] It begins with naming the parties and providing an elaborate list of participants, who "take an oath with sanctions to follow the teaching of God, given through Moses the servant of God, and to observe carefully all the commandments of the Lord our God, his rules and laws."[6] The text that follows specifies these rules and laws. On the one hand, they include laws regulating various economic and social activities of the people signing this document.[7] On the other hand, there are laws specifically addressing the maintenance of the temple.[8] The first category includes the prohibition on marrying "peoples of the land," the prohibition on trading with "peoples of the land on the Sabbath," and the promise to observe the Sabbatical years by suspension of agriculture and cancellation of debts. The second category includes obligations to pay an annual tax of one-third of a shekel for the upkeep of the Temple, to bring wood to the Temple, and to bring the first fruits and the first born of one's herd. It also specifies tithes that have to be paid to the Levites.

This document also contains important hints as to the social structure of the group that agreed to follow it. Nehemiah 10:29 describes this group as "the rest of the people, the priests, the Levites, the gatekeepers, the singers, the temple servants, and all who separated themselves from the peoples of the lands to follow the teaching of God, their wives, sons and daughters, all who know enough to understand." This description is preceded by the reference to three groups of named officials: priests, Levites and "the heads of the people" signing the document.[9] The list of participants seems to indicate that

  [5] See J. Blenkinsopp, *Ezra-Nehemiah: A Commentary* (Philadelphia: Westminster Press, 1988), 308–319. Cf. H. Williamson, *Ezra and Nehemiah* (Sheffield: JSOT Press, 1987), 27, and Y. Kaufmann, *History of the Religion of Israel* (New York: Ktav, 1977), vol. 4, 382–89.
  [6] Neh 10:29–30.
  [7] Neh 10:31–32.
  [8] Neh 10:33–40.
  [9] The list of named participants seems to be an editorial construct drawn from various sources including the books of Chronicles and other lists in Ezra-Nehemiah. Still, as Joseph Blenkinsopp rightly observes, many of these names "represent patronyms rather than individuals." See Blenkinsopp, *Ezra-Nehemiah*, 312–14. This may be indicative of editor's understanding of the nature of the covenant and of the nature of the group that makes it. He envisions the group of Nehemiah 10 as being composed of families and clans rather than individuals.

the family and not the individual constituted the main unit within
the covenant-making community. People take an oath accompanied
by their wives and children, and indeed at least some of the regulations of the covenant envision the family as their prime subject.
The restrictions on marriage would be a prime example of such a
regulation, but not the only one. According to Nehemiah 10:35: "we
have cast lots among the priests, the Levites, and the people, to
bring the wood offering to the House of our God by clans annu-
ally." The main social unit within the covenant is thus identified as
the clan. It is no surprise then that one's wives and children were
mentioned as participants of the covenant ceremony. The focus in
connection with observance of the law was on one's household and
not so much on the individual.[10]

It would be worthwhile to look for other indications of the family-based nature of the covenant as it is envisioned in the book of
Nehemiah. Nehemiah 8–10 is usually seen as a single literary unit,
although its parts might have been composed in different times.[11]
The focus of the entire unit is on the covenant renewal by a particular Jewish group following the reading from the book of the law
by Ezra and mass repentance on the part of the group's leaders.
Family-based language is used to describe this group throughout the
narrative. Following the public reading from the law by Ezra, "the
heads of all the families (ראשי האבות), along with the priests and
the Levites, gathered around Ezra the scribe to give attention to the
words of law."[12] This observation clarifies otherwise fairly unspecific
references to "all the people" and "the whole community that returned
from the exile" assembling to listen to Ezra's reading and interpretation of the law.[13] In social terms the gathering seems to be iden-

---

[10] Cf. L. Perdue, "The Household, Old Testament Theology, and Contemporary
Hermeneutics," in idem, *Families in Ancient Israel*, 239–43. He argues that the "location for shaping the formal character and conceptual understanding of the covenant
and its binding obligations is the household in Ancient Israel and early Judaism."
Perdue mostly uses pre-exilic biblical materials to substantiate his point. Moreover,
our modern distinction between family and individual may be anachronistic when
applied to this period. As Berquist, *Controlling Corporeality*, 44, observes: 'for Israel,
especially in its earlier times and in its rural locations, family and body were almost
coextensive."

[11] Blenkinsopp, *Ezra-Nehemiah*, 278–319. But cf. Williamson, *Ezra and Nehemiah*,
20–25, for an opinion that Nehemiah 8 originally belonged between Ezra 8 and 9.

[12] Neh 8:13.

[13] Neh 8:1–12 and 17.

tical with that of Nehemiah 10. "All the people" appears to refer to
a sum total of clans and families that felt obliged to follow Ezra's
vision of the law. Nehemiah 8:3 describes "the congregation" attending the ceremony for reading of the law as "men, women and those
who could understand." This description parallels almost verbatim
the one in Nehemiah 10:29. In both cases the text describes Israelite
families led by their heads and gathered for the ceremony of the
covenant's renewal. The family is thus envisioned as a core group
within the entire process.[14]

Indeed, according to Nehemiah 8:13, it was the heads of the families who attended the second (and less public) session with Ezra
where the law was interpreted. During this second session, when
"the heads of all the families, along with the priests and the Levites,
gathered around Ezra the scribe to give attention to the words of
law," the discussion specifically focused on the construction of booths
to celebrate the holiday of Sukkot. The subsequent celebration had
a double setting in the temple precincts and in households, thus
marking out the two most crucial religious spaces for the new
movement:

> So the people . . . made themselves booths on their roofs, in their court-
> yards, in the courtyards of the House of God, in the square of the
> Water Gate and in the square of the Ephraim Gate.[15]

For our purposes it is important to observe that the celebration had
a clearly identified family setting along with that in the temple. Once
again, an individual family and its observance of the law as interpreted by Ezra and "the heads of all the families" became a crucial part of the covenant envisioned by Nehemiah 8–10. The family

---

[14] The role of patriarchal families in the community of Ezra and Nehemiah
resembles that in the roughly contemporaneous phratry and deme of Greek cities.
There too natural families played a central role in the formation of pseudo-kinship
groups within the polis. In both cases women were peripheral in this new "imagined" kinship group, although their presence constantly remained in the background
because of their role in natural households. On complex relationships between natural family ties and fictitious ancestral bonds within the phratry see S. Pomeroy,
Families in Classical and Hellenistic Greece: Representations and Realities (Oxford: Clarendon
Press, 1997), 75–82. Cf. Weinberg, *Citizen-Temple Community*, 58–61, who similarly
characterizes *bet 'avot* in the time of Ezra and Nehemiah as "an agnatic band which
came into existence in the peculiar situation of the exile and repatriation, and which
unified a number of families that were related (either genuinely or fictionally)."

[15] Neh 8:16.

courtyard setting was as important for the fulfillment of the covenant as that of the temple courtyard.[16]

Reading and interpretation of the law by Ezra led to another public gathering and public confession of "their sins and the wickedness of their fathers."[17] Prior to the ceremony, "those of the Israelite descent had separated themselves from all foreigners," including probably foreign wives and other members of their households.[18] The initial purification ceremony targeted specifically one's household, the purity of which had to be ensured prior to the repentance and covenant renewal ceremonies. The public confession of sins and transgressions in Nehemiah 9 repeatedly refers to "sins of the forefathers" being confessed by the community.[19] It is not immediately clear whether this phrase implies former generations of the people of Israel in general or rather familial ancestors of particular clans participating in the ceremony. In fact, the phrase may refer to both.[20] Still, the reference of Nehemiah 9:32 and 34 to "our kings, our officers, our priests, our fathers, and all your people" represents a list of Israelite leaders and thus may be specific enough to imply forefathers of particular households, rather than forefathers of Israel in general. If so, the confession of Nehemiah 9 suggests Israelite clans and families as its primary setting. It was the sins of their ancestors (along with those of Israel's political and religious leaders) for which the people repented during the ceremony.

Most of the subsequent religious reforms undertaken by Ezra clearly envisioned families as prime religious units within the community of Israel. Recent studies of Ezra's and Nehemiah's attempts to ban marriages between Jews and non-Jews have focused attention on preservation of the "holy seed" of Israel as a key underlying reason for these actions.[21] The notion of a pure seed of Israel as intrinsically

---

[16] For the liturgical importance of the household as a prime setting of religious celebrations in Ancient Israel cf. Perdue, "Israelite and Early Jewish Family," 205–06.

[17] Neh 9:2.

[18] Cf. Ezra 9–10. But see Blenkinsopp, *Ezra-Nehemiah*, 295–296, for more general interpretation of this phrase.

[19] Neh 9:2, 9, 16, 23, 32, 34, and 36.

[20] The meaning of אבותינו in Neh 9:9, 16, 23 and 34 seems to imply more distant generations of the people of Israel, whereas Neh 9:32 and 34 refers to immediate (familial?) ancestors.

[21] See Hayes, *Gentile Impurities and Jewish Identities*, 27–32, and Satlow, *Jewish Marriage in Antiquity*, 135–40. Cf. Schwartz, *Studies in the Jewish Background of Christianity*, 8–9. He briefly discusses other contemporaneous biblical texts reflecting the cen-

distinct from the profane seed of gentiles apparently evolved during
the Babylonian exile, when a family gradually assumed the role of
the main social, economic, and religious unit within the Jewish community.[22] It was originally applied to the priests, but Ezra's reform
broadened its application to lay Israelites as well.[23] As Michael Satlow
has observed, Ezra attempted to build a new community using the
notion of the genealogical purity of its members.[24] Individual families played the crucial role in this edifice. It was through them that
the "holy seed" of Israel had to be preserved unalloyed and transmitted from one generation to another. Proper preservation and
transmission of the "holy seed" became one of the dominant religious ideals, positioning the family as the key building block within
the religious community. The concept of the "holy seed" preserved
and transmitted through lay families transformed earlier Israelite
tribal practices. Shaye Cohen has convincingly argued that it was
precisely by means of joining her husband's household that a non-
Israelite woman would become a convert under the assumption that
the husband's family determined the religious identity of his wife.[25]
In biblical times a patriarchal Israelite clan constituted the main
source of one's identity, including one's religious identity. Ezra's
reforms preserved the centrality of an Israelite patriarchal clan but
gave it an entirely new religious purpose.

Overall, the text of Nehemiah 8–10 demonstrates remarkable consistency in portraying the social makeup of Nehemiah's movement.
The group described in Nehemiah 8–10 is composed of families and
clans rather than individuals. Families and clans sign the covenant
and agree to follow it, namely, to interpret Jewish law in a particular way and to follow this interpretation in their everyday lives.

---

trality of "seed" ideology for Jewish identity of the time. See esp. Mal 2:15, but
also 1 Chr 16:13 and 2 Chr 20:7. Cf. Esth 6:13, 9:28 and 31, and 10:3.

[22] On this development see Albertz, *Persönliche Frömmigkeit*, 178–90, and *History of
Israelite Religion*, vol. 2, 399–411.

[23] See Hayes, *Gentile Impurities and Jewish Identities*, 28. Hayes argues that Ezek
44:22 reflects the beginning of this trend, when Ezekiel requires that all officiating
priests must marry virgins from the seed of Israel. This was not a universally practiced requirement and its biblical roots were not immediately evident.

[24] Satlow, *Jewish Marriage in Antiquity*, 138–40.

[25] S. Cohen, *The Beginnings of Jewishness: Boundaries, Varieties, Uncertainties* (Berkeley:
University of California Press, 1999), 264–67. Cf. a somewhat similar situation in
the Classical Greek family as discussed by Pomeroy, *Families in Classical and Hellenistic
Greece*, 67–99. In both cases the family and its cult constituted the basis of personal
religious identity.

They also separate themselves from the rest of the Judaean population, constructing a micro-society of their own. The heavy presence of priestly and Levitical families within this group explains its concern with the temple as well as the fact that their covenant was centered on the temple. Throughout the books of Ezra and Nehemiah we also find a relatively new type of religious discourse that identifies families and family life as depositories of sanctity. This discourse became a dominant one at the early stages of Second Temple Jewish sectarianism.

Leadership Structures of Ezra-Nehemiah's Group

The leadership of the movement and especially Nehemiah's inner circle reflected the same family-based structure as the movement in general. Morton Smith has already observed that "Nehemiah's party" included a number of his relatives.[26] An entire saga of Nehemiah's appointment as a governor starts when his brother Hanani, "together with some men of Judah," arrives in Shushan and tells Nehemiah of the miserable state of Jerusalem and of the "remnant who had survived the captivity."[27] During the first days since Nehemiah's arrival in Jerusalem he is surrounded by a close-knit group of people, whose identity is not always revealed but who include his staunchest supporters.[28] Further in the narrative, Nehemiah refers to his inner circle as "my brothers, my servants, or the guards following me," thus providing the first glimpse into the core-group behind his activities, raising the possibility that this group may have been based on the household.[29] In fact, the phrase "my brothers and my servants" is repeatedly used throughout the narrative to characterize Nehemiah's "staff."[30] The further indication of a central role that Nehemiah's household played in shaping social, political and religious life of the province comes from the description of the admin-

---

[26] M. Smith, *Palestinian Parties and Politics that Shaped the Old Testament* (New York: Columbia University Press, 1971), 128–29.

[27] Neh 1:1–3.

[28] Neh 2:12 (original inspection of the state of Jerusalem by Nehemiah). Neh 2:16 explicitly distinguishes the group accompanying Nehemiah during the inspection from official authorities of Jerusalem.

[29] Neh 4:23.

[30] Neh 5:10 and 14. On Nehemiah's "staff" including his relations cf. observations by Smith, *Palestinian Parties*, 151.

istration of Jerusalem established by Nehemiah once the city had been rebuilt. According to Neh 7:1–2, Nehemiah put his brother Hanani in charge of Jerusalem. He further assigned "the inhabitants of Jerusalem to watches, each man to his watch, and each in front of his own house."[31] Neh 13:19 provides a further glimpse into the administration of Jerusalem, when it describes special measures taken by Nehemiah in order to prevent violation of the Sabbath:

> When shadows filled the gateways of Jerusalem at the approach of the Sabbath, I gave orders that the doors be closed, and ordered them not to be opened until after the Sabbath. I stationed some of my servants at the gates, so that no goods should enter on the Sabbath.

The household of Nehemiah apparently constituted the ideological, administrative and perhaps military backbone of the reforms. Nehemiah not only put his brother Hanani in charge of the administration of Jerusalem but also used his servants to enforce the law when necessary. The distinction between private and public domains becomes virtually non-existent once we consider the household of Nehemiah. The latter used his servants as enforcement agents and his relatives as administrators to man key positions of power. In many ways Nehemiah's household reminds us of later high priestly clans described by Josephus and referred to by Rostovtzeff as prime examples of "oriental feudalism" of the Greco-Roman period.[32] Public politics of Second Temple Judah thus find their prime setting and realization within households and clans.

In fact the passage from Neh 7:2 quoted above indicates that the entire political landscape of Jerusalem at that time was shaped and dominated by families fulfilling public functions. Nehemiah's decision to assign "the inhabitants of Jerusalem to watches, each man to his watch, and each in front of his own house" reflects the close connection between the area of one's public responsibility and the private space of his household. The public functions became compartmentalized in accordance with private domains. Each family head was responsible for guarding the part of the wall adjacent to his house. This dispensation resembled the one established during the rebuilding of the walls, when in order to guard builders against a

---

[31] Neh 7:3.
[32] See M. Rostovtzeff, *The Social and Economic History of the Roman Empire* (Oxford: Clarendon Press, 1966), vol. 1, 269.

surprise attack, Nehemiah "stationed the people by families with their swords, their lances, and their bows."[33] The family once again appears to have been a basic unit within the political and social structure of the restored community.[34] The fact that certain professional functions and duties became concentrated in the hands of particular families and eventually identified with those families provides another indication of the lack of boundaries between public and private realms in early Second Temple Judaism. Genealogical lists in 1 Chronicles contain occasional allusions to occupation-specific family groups, such as משפחות ספרים ("families of the scribes") and משפחות בית־עבדת הבץ לבית אשבע ("families of the linen-factory at Beth-Ashbea").[35] The same is true for at least some families mentioned in Ezra-Nehemiah in connection with various temple functions and handling of temple funds.[36] The family-based nature of certain occupations was especially obvious in the case of priests and Levites, although it seems that Nehemiah's attempts to utilize the resources of his family for the purpose of governing Jerusalem may belong to the same category.[37]

As becomes apparent from census lists in Ezra 2 and Nehemiah 7, an extended family and clan were essential units within the restored community in general.[38] "The Congregation of the Exile," repeat-

---

[33] Neh 4:13.

[34] The list of people responsible for rebuilding different sections of the wall in Nehemiah 3 at least partially consisted of families. The latter were usually responsible for sections of the wall adjacent to their houses. See Neh 3:17–18, 23, and 28–30.

[35] 1 Chr 2:55 and 4:21. Pomeroy, *Families in Classical and Hellenistic Greece*, 141–60, convincingly demonstrates that this was also the case in Classical Greece: "the family that enjoys economic success reproduces itself in each generation: the same names and the same professional activities occur."

[36] Neh 3:8 and 31–32 mention one of "the goldsmiths" and one of "the perfumers" repairing parts of wall. Since they appear as part of the list that deals with families repairing parts of the wall, we can assume that the guilds of goldsmiths and perfumers were also family-based establishments. In fact, based on the context, they could be related to the Levitical families.

[37] The list of families that settled in Jerusalem in Nehemiah 11 provides several examples of priestly and Levitical families that apparently "owned" certain temple-related occupations. See Neh 11:10–12, 16–17, 19, and 21–23. Cf. Neh 12:8–9 and 24–26.

[38] The lists identify lay expatriates by either their families (Ezra 2:3–20 and Neh 7:8–25) or their towns of residence (Ezra 2:21–35 and Neh 7:26–38). Priests and Levites are identified by their families (Ezra 2:36–42 and Neh 7:39–45). In the case of Levites, the list also indicates occupations "owned" by particular families. Those include singers and door-keepers (Ezra 2:40–42 and Neh 7:44–45). The list further

edly referred to throughout the Ezra-Nehemiah narrative, was arranged by extended families (בית־אבותם). Ancestral records detailing one's belonging to a particular clan were deemed of prime importance for one's standing within society, this being true for both lay and priestly families.[39] Heads of the clans (ראשי האבות) constituted a backbone of the political and religious leadership of the restored community. They were responsible for making crucial political and religious decisions along with the governor Zerubbabel and are portrayed as a kind of aristocratic council at his side.[40] The rebuilding of the temple, as well as handling of temple's treasury, was entrusted specifically to them.[41] In other words, during this period the family constituted a recognizable public body and a main social unit within the restored community.[42] When Ezra arrived at the scene, he also came accompanied by heads of clans, both lay and priestly.[43] Some of these clans would later provide staunch support for the religious reforms of Ezra and Nehemiah, and eventually for the covenant arrangement of Nehemiah 8–10. What we see throughout the book of Ezra is a number of Jewish families forming alliances and groupings around particular leaders. It was through these families that such leaders as Zerubbabel or Ezra received political, religious and often military support for their programs. The political alignment of Judaean families shaped the structure of the contemporaneous Jewish society as well as its internal fights.[44]

---

includes families of temple servants (Ezra 2:43–54 and Neh 7:46–56) and "Solomon's servants" (Ezra 2:55–58 and Neh 7:57–60).

[39] Ezra 2:61–63 (= Neh 7:63–65) contains list of priestly families that could not prove their genealogical descent and as a result were barred from officiating in the temple. Ezra 2:59–60 (= Neh 7:61–62) provides a similar type of list for lay Israelite families.

[40] Ezra 4:1–3.

[41] See Ezra 1:5 and 2:68–69. The latter text specifies donations made by particular heads of clans, whereas the former states that heads of clans were entrusted with handling of special funds given to them by Cyrus and "their neighbors." The role of private donations by heads of clans seems to be confirmed by Zech 6:9–14 describing donations of silver and gold by three individuals who returned from Babylonia. All three of them were Jewish magnates involved in internal politics of the restored Judaean community, although their precise identities remain unclear. See further Smith, *Palestinian Parties*, 109–10.

[42] On the crucial public role of families in the time of Zerubbabel see further Japhet, "Sheshbazzar and Zerubbabel," 66–98, esp. 87–89, and McEvenue, "Political Structure in Judah from Cyrus to Nehemiah," 353–64. Cf. Weinberg, *Citizen-Temple Community*, 49–61.

[43] Ezra 8:1–14.

[44] The opposition to Ezra and Nehemiah was also based on family alliances. Neh

We get a glimpse into the structure and workings of one of the pro-Ezra clans from the description in Ezra 8:15–20. When Ezra reviewed lay and priestly clans that came to support him, he did not find any Levites among them. To remedy the situation, Ezra sent messengers to one Iddo, "the leader at the place [called] Casiphia:"

> I gave them a message to convey to Iddo and his brother, temple-servants at the place [called] Casiphia, that they should bring us attendants for the House of our God. Thanks to the benevolent care of our God for us, they brought us a capable man of the family of Mahli son of Levi son of Israel, and Sherebiah and his sons and brothers, 18 in all, and Hashabiah, and with him Jeshaiah of the family of Merari, his brothers and their sons, 20 in all.

The group dispatched by Iddo to Ezra was clearly a tightly knit family-based unit. It was also an occupation-specific professional group. All members of this group, being Levites, served as temple-servants. Ezra immediately entrusted it with the safekeeping of the contributions made to the temple by Persian authorities and Jews.[45] This family thus acquired a clearly identifiable public function. Moreover, it appears to have monopolized this function, becoming socially significant because of it. As a result, this particular familial group came to be identified with a particular set of public religious responsibilities because of its support of Ezra. From our perspective, it is important to observe that specific public religious responsibilities became virtually identified with members of a particular family. In exchange the family provided support for Ezra and his religious reforms. It is also important to notice that the clansmen of Iddo probably reflect a larger picture of how alliances were made between particular families and the religious leadership of the community. It appears that the social structure of the covenant movements cobbled together by Ezra and Nehemiah was defined by the same kind of arrangement.

Against this background the family-based nature of the covenant renewal becomes more understandable. Throughout the period under discussion, a household was perceived as the main unit not only of

---

6:17–19 explicitly accuses "the nobles in Judah" of allying themselves with Tobiah "because he was a son-in-law of Shecaniah son of Arah, and his son Jehohanan had married a daughter of Meshullam son of Berechiah." See also Neh 13:4–5 and 28 (the family of the high priest Eliashib was related by marriage to families of Tobiah and Sanballat).

[45] Ezra 8:24–30.

an individual's private life, but also of the public life of the society. In many ways, the society itself was shaped and driven by the alliances and interests of the families constituting it. Both political and religious public functions were distributed among family-based groups. In such a situation it was only natural that the temple and law-centered covenant of Nehemiah 8–10 had individual families as its main participants and that its requirements were set in Jewish households of economic means. The covenant in many ways cemented an alliance of a number of such households that agreed to live their lives in accordance with religious requirements of the covenant. Far from sidelining the traditional familial structures, the covenant of Nehemiah 8–10 used these structures as the social framework of the law- and temple-focused community it built.

Family, Society, and the Arrival of Hellenism

There is an increasing consensus among scholars that the Hellenistic kingdoms, which emerged as a result of conquests of Alexander the Great, in many ways have to be seen as immediate successors of the Achaemenid Persian Empire and its political legacy. As Pierre Briant has observed: "From the geo-political point of view, the period opened by Alexander was merely the final phase of Achaemenid history, with Alexander consolidating globally the territory of the Achaemenids and adopting a number of Persian institutions."[46] The break between the two periods postulated by an earlier historiography is increasingly called into question. The continuity is especially evident in the case of the Seleucid Empire, which in many respects took over and further developed the political and administrative structure of the Achaemenid kingdom.[47] The organization of the imperial provinces provides one of the prime examples of such continuity. As far as Judah is concerned, the decree issued by Antiochus III confirming Jewish privileges was remarkably similar to that issued by Cyrus the

---

[46] P. Briant, "The Seleucid Kingdom, the Achaemenid Empire and the History of the Near East," in P. Bilde et al., eds., *Religion and Religious Practice in the Seleucid Kingdom* (Aarhus: Aarhus University Press, 1990), 44.

[47] See Briant, "Seleucid Kingdom," 40–65, and S. Sherwin-White and A. Kuhrt, *From Samarkhand to Sardis: A New Approach to the Seleucid Empire* (Berkeley: University of California Press, 1993), 7–39 and 40–71.

Great according to the Bible.[48] The formal status of Judah as a temple-centered state was recognized in both documents and both of them contain similar provisions deemed to ensure the economic and political well being of the temple and its servants.[49] In this respect Jerusalem fit into a general pattern of neighboring Near Eastern cities, which demonstrated remarkable continuity with pre-Hellenistic times, even while adopting some Hellenistic institutions and cultural conventions.[50] There is no wonder, then, that basic social structures observed for the Persian period would continue to exist in the early Hellenistic period as well.[51] An extended family fulfilling important public functions would constitute one such structure. And similar to the Persian period, it would provide a basis for the religious movements of the time.[52]

A number of leading families that constituted the local Jewish and Samaritan elite continued to play a dominant role in the society well into the Hellenistic period. These included the family of high priests

---

[48] See the detailed discussion in Briant, "Seleucid Kingdom," 58–60. Cf. E. Bickerman, "La charte séleucide de Jérusalem," in idem, *Studies in Jewish and Christian History* (Leiden: Brill, 1980), vol. 2, 44–85, and "Edict of Cyrus in Ezra 1," in idem, *Studies in Jewish and Christian History*, vol. 1, 72–108.

[49] Judaean coinage of this period also reflects basic social and political continuity between Achaemenid and early Hellenistic times. See L. Mildenberg, "Yehud: A Preliminary Study of the Provincial Coinage of Judaea," in O. Mørkholm and N. Waggoner, eds., *Greek Numismatics and Archaeology: Essays in Honor of Margaret Thompson* (Wetteren: Cultura, 1979), 183–96, and Y. Meshorer, *Ancient Jewish Coinage* (Dix Hills: Amphora, 1982), vol. 1, 14–20. Cf. also D. Barag, "A Silver Coin of Yohanan the High Priest and the Coinage of Judaea in the Fourth Century BCE.," *INJ* 9 (1986–1987), 4–21 (on a coin mentioning the high priest rather than a secular governor during the late Achaemenid period). S. Schwartz, "On the Autonomy of Judaea in the Fourth and Third Centuries BCE," *JJS* 45 (1994), 162, observes some subtle changes in coins that may reflect changing political and administrative reality.

[50] On the Phoenician cities of this period see F. Millar, "The Phoenician Cities: A Case Study in Hellenisation," *Proceedings of the Cambridge Philological Society* 209 (1983), 55–71. Cf. S. Schwartz, "The Hellenization of Jerusalem and Shechem," in M. Goodman, ed., *Jews in a Graeco-Roman World* (Oxford: Clarendon Press, 1998), 37–45.

[51] On the other hand, many aspects of social and economic life in Judah and adjacent territories had been substantially Hellenized long before Alexander's arrival. In this respect, too, there would be no sudden break between the two periods. See Bickerman, *From Ezra*, 14–16, and Smith, *Palestinian Parties*, 57–81. For specific examples see E. Stern, *Material Culture of the Land of the Bible in the Persian Period, 538–332 BC* (Warminster: Aris & Phillips, 1982), 229–37.

[52] On the structure and functions of contemporaneous families in Ptolemaic Egypt see Pomeroy, *Families in Classical and Hellenistic Greece*, 193–229. The traditional patriarchal family continued to play a central role in the Hellenistic society of the time.

in Jerusalem that continued to function uninterrupted under the
Greek government. The legend in *A.J.* 11.325–39 about the meeting between Alexander the Great and the High Priest goes to great
lengths in order to emphasize recognition of the High Priest by the
new Hellenistic rulers of the Near East. It thus stresses the continuity between the leadership of Achaemenid Yehud and that of
Hellenistic Judah, just as it does the continuity between the Persian
leadership and Alexander.[53] Such an approach may constitute the
greatest historical value of this otherwise legendary account.[54] Indeed,
with the disappearance of Persian governors, the public role of the
high priest reached new heights, as he became the only de facto
administrator of Judah. Elias Bickerman has correctly observed that
it is only during the early Hellenistic period that we can speak of
high priests as true leaders of the Jews in both the religious and
administrative realms.[55]

Similar to the Judaean high priests, the family of Sanballat in
Samaria preserved its status during the early Hellenistic period.
Antiquitates' story about Sanballat and his son-in-law Manasseh, who
acquired permission from Alexander to build the temple on Mount
Gerizim, is another legend that reflects unbroken continuity of regional
leadership.[56] Sanballat changed his allegiance from Darius to Alexander
and might have even supplied auxiliary troops for Alexander's conquest of Egypt. The story of the temple on Mount Gerizim is important not only because it reflects ongoing local control on the part

---

[53] See S. Cohen, "Alexander the Great and Jaddus the High Priest according to
Josephus," *AJS Review* 7–8 (1982–1983), 60–64, for the insightful observation that
our story portrays Alexander as a legitimate successor to the "righteous" Achaemenid
rulers of old. He replaces their "wicked and failing" descendants, who no longer
behave benevolently toward the Jews.

[54] On the legendary nature of the story see Tcherikover, *Hellenistic Civilization*,
41–50, and Cohen, "Alexander the Great and Jaddus the High Priest," 41–68.

[55] E. Bickerman, *The Jews in the Greek Age* (Cambridge: Harvard University Press,
1988), 140–47.

[56] *A.J.* 11.321–325 and 340–345. Many scholars have doubts about the story's
reliability. See R. Coggins, *Samaritans and Jews: The Origins of Samaritanism Reconsidered*
(Atlanta: John Knox Press, 1975), 94–97, and L. Grabbe, "Josephus and the
Reconstruction of the Judean Restoration," *JBL* 106 (1987), 236–42. On the other
hand, Cross has presented convincing evidence that its portrayal of Sanballat's
dynasty as continuing into the period of Alexander's reign may very well be correct (see below). Cf. also Purvis, *The Samaritan Pentateuch and the Origin of the Samaritan
Sect* (Cambridge: Harvard University Press, 1968), 102–05. The story itself, even if
it is a legend, certainly asserts continuity between the two periods and its major
players.

of provincial magnates of Achaemenid times, but also because it demonstrates uninterrupted continuity of their inter-family relationships and marriage alliances. During his tenure as a governor, Nehemiah attacked the political and marriage alliance between one of the sons of the high priest Jodaiah and a daughter of Sanballat. *Antiquitates*' story starts with the description of a similar marriage between Manasseh, the brother of high priest Jaddua, and a daughter of another Sanballat, apparently the direct descendant of Nehemiah's adversary.[57] This marriage, according to Josephus, would eventually result in the building of the temple on Mount Gerizim with Alexander's connivance. In other words, not only individual families that defined Judaean and Samaritan politics remained the same, the patterns of their family relationships also remained unchanged from the Achaemenid to the early Hellenistic period. The local provincial structure passed on in its entirety and complexity from one epoch to another. Change took decades (if not centuries) to materialize.[58]

Nehemiah's opponents included not only Sanballat but also one Tobiah "the Ammonite slave." Mazar has convincingly argued that Tobiah of Nehemiah's times was a direct ancestor of the powerful Tobiad clan, known to us from the "Tobiad romance" in *A.J.* 12.160–236 and the Zenon papyri.[59] In both cases we are dealing with a powerful feudal family residing in Trans-Jordan but actively involved in Jerusalem affairs. It is possible, indeed, that the family originally returned from the exile along with other clans in the time

---

[57] *A.J.* 11.302–312. The repeated pattern of several generations of Sanballat's family marrying members of the high priest's family in Jerusalem seems to be confirmed by findings in the Wadi Daliyeh. See F. Cross, "Papyri of the Fourth Century BC from Dâliyeh," in D. Freedman and J. Greenfield, eds., *New Directions in Biblical Archaeology* (Garden City: Doubleday, 1969), 53–61 and "Papyri and their Historical Implications," in P. Lapp and N. Lapp, eds., *Discoveries in the Wadi ed-Dâliyeh* (Cambridge: ASOR, 1974), 18–24.

[58] Samaritan bullae from the Wadi Daliyeh clearly show that cultural Hellenization of the local elite had started long before Alexander's arrival. See M. Leith, *Wadi Daliyeh* (Oxford: Clarendon Press, 1997), vol. 1, 20–33. For Greek inscriptions on several Achaemenid Samaritan coins see Y. Meshorer and S. Qedar, *The Coinage of Samaria in the Fourth Century BCE.* (Jerusalem: Numismatic Fine Arts International, 1991), 13–18.

[59] See B. Mazar, "The Tobiads," *IEJ* 7 (1957), 137–45. D. Gera, *Judaea and Mediterranean Politics, 219 to 161 BCE.* (Leiden: Brill, 1998), 36–58, correctly sees the story in *A.J.* 12 as a romance full with inconsistencies and factual mistakes. The story appears to be a romantic portrayal of an influential Jewish family.

of Sheshbazzar and Zerubbabel.[60] In addition to the name "Tobiah," passed on from one generation to the next within the family, and the family's headquarters in Trans-Jordan, the Tobiads both in Achaemenid and Hellenistic times maintained close relationships with Jewish elite in general and with the high priestly family in particular. In Nehemiah's times, priest Eliashib "was connected by marriage" with Tobiah.[61] The support for Tobiah among Judaean aristocracy overall was very strong. As Nehemiah observes in his memoir:

> In those days the nobles in Judah kept sending letters to Tobiah, and receiving replies from him, for many in Judah were in league with him, because he was a son-in-law of Shecaniah son of Arah, and his son Jehohanan had married a daughter of Meshullam son of Berechiah.[62]

Tobias' influence was based on his family connections with leading aristocratic clans of Judah. The same situation persisted into the Hellenistic period. Joseph in the "Tobiad romance" is the son of Tobias and the sister of Onias, the high priest, and receives support from "his friends in Samaria" for his journey to the Ptolemaic court.[63] On the other hand, both Achaemenid and Hellenistic Tobiads had vassal-like relationships with central authorities and apparently were allowed to have their own military contingents to maintain order in the region.[64] Indeed, the pejorative "Ammonite slave" of Nehemiah may reflect exactly this kind of relationship,[65] whereas the Zenon papyri and the "Tobiad romance" attest the same type and level of relationship for the Ptolemaic period.[66]

The Tobiad castle at 'Araq el-'Amir in Jordan physically embodies and displays both change and continuity between the governing structures of Achaemenid and Hellenistic Judah. According to Josephus, Hyrcanus, the son of Joseph the Tobiad and one of the main characters of the "Tobiad Romance," built this castle sometime in the

---

[60] See Mazar, "Tobiads," 229–38.

[61] Neh 13:4.

[62] Neh 6:17–18. The family of Arah is mentioned among clans that returned from the exile in Ezra 2:5 and Neh 7:10. Shecaniah was probably one of its heads. Meshullam son of Berechiah son of Meshezabel is repeatedly mentioned as a head of powerful clan and local official in the time of Nehemiah. See Neh 3:4, 10:21, and 11:24. See further Mazar, "Tobiads," 144, n. 38–39.

[63] *A.J.* 12.160 and 168.

[64] See *CPJ*, vol. 1, 118–21.

[65] Neh 2:10 and 19. Cf. Mazar, "Tobiads," 144.

[66] See V. Tcherikover, "Palestine under the Prolemies," *Mizraim* 4–5 (1937), 9–90.

late third century BCE.[67] Physical remains of the manorial complex, which exist today, seem to confirm this picture. Lapp has argued that it was built around 200 BCE and thus should be identified with the castle of Hyrcanus described by Josephus.[68] On the other hand, the site of the castle demonstrates clear signs of continuity with earlier periods. Two Aramaic inscriptions carved on the facades of two large halls hewn in nearby cliffs mention "Tobiah" and have been dated to a chronological range from the fifth to third centuries BCE by most epigraphers, although others date them around the time of Hyrcanus.[69] The Zenon papyri also mention the fortress of a local grandee Tobias around the year 259 BCE.[70] Even though the building excavated by Lapp may be relatively recent, it was most probably built on the site that belonged to the Tobiad family. Many scholars believe that the earlier Tobiad residence (the "birta" of the Zenon papyri) was located nearby, whereas present day remains at Qasr el Abd constitute a Hellenistic architectural elaboration of the traditional power seat of the Tobiad family.[71] At any rate, the area where the castle was built has clear signs of continuous association with the Tobiad clan, going all the way back to the early post-exilic period. Moreover, despite its relatively late construction, the architecture of the castle itself is by no means exclusively Hellenistic. Rather it reflects a peculiar blend of Greek and Near Eastern artistic motifs, thus reflecting the dual cultural identity of its inhabitants.[72]

---

[67] *A.J.* 12.230–233.

[68] See N. Lapp, ed., *The Excavations at Araq el-Emir* (Winona Lake: Eisenbrauns, 1983), vol. 1, 133–48 and "'Iraq el-Emir," *NEAEHL*, vol. 2, 646–49. But cf. the critical observations of Gera, *Judaea and Mediterranean Politics*, 42.

[69] See Mazar, "Tobiads," 141–42, for a fifth century dating. For a more cautious fourth century dating see F. Cross, "The Development of the Jewish Scripts," in G. Wright, ed., *The Bible and the Ancient Near East: Essays in Honor of William Foxwell Albright* (Garden City: Doubleday, 1961), 191, n. 13, and 195, n. 75. Cf. also W. Albright, *The Archaeology of Palestine and the Bible* (New York: Fleming H. Revell, 1932), 222, n. 111. Lapp, "'Iraq el-Emir," 647, maintains that the inscriptions could be contemporaneous with the castle and thus come from the time of Hyrcanus.

[70] *CPJ*, vol. 1, 118–21: "Birta of the Ammanitis." Mazar, "Tobiads," 140–41, traces this name back to the Persian period and sees it as another sign of chronological continuity with earlier times. Cf. J. Hoftijzer and K. Jongeling, *Dictionary of the North-West Semitic Inscriptions* (Leiden: Brill, 1995), vol. 1, 155–56.

[71] See Gera, *Judaea and Mediterranean Politics*, 40–44.

[72] See M. Avi-Yonah, *Art in Ancient Palestine: Selected Studies* (Jerusalem: Magnes Press, 1981), 132. For interaction between Greek and native art forms in the Hellenistic Near East see M. Colledge, "Greek and non-Greek Interaction in Art and Architecture of the Hellenistic East," in Bilde, *Religion and Religious Practice*, 134–62.

Those who lived there were by no means a "new elite" of the land and they did not present themselves as such. Rather they were members of the old aristocracy, willing to embrace the changes in civilization and play by the new rules.[73] Overall, similar to the families of Sanballat and the high priests in Jerusalem, the Tobiad clan emerged during the Achaemenid reign as a major power broker in the region and retained this status (both locally and with the central government) in early Hellenistic times. The basic power structures of Judah and Samaria survived the transition from the Achaemenid to the Hellenistic period without any noticeable change.

Underlying problems also remained the same. Throughout the Achaemenid period, boundaries and responsibilities within the political life in Judah remained remarkably ill-defined. Non-priestly families repeatedly tried to assert their influence over temple affairs, whereas the high priest's authority was steadily expanding into the areas of provincial administration. The ongoing intermarriage between high priestly and lay families only contributed to general confusion and enabled various family members to seek extended powers. Thus, priest Eliashib, "who was appointed over the storerooms of the house of our God," allowed his relative Tobiah to make use of a large room within the temple complex. In this room, "they formerly had kept the grain-offering, the frankincense, the temple vessels, the tithes of grain, new vine, and oil prescribed for the Levites, singers, and door-keepers, and the contributions for the priests."[74] In a similar way, Hyrcanus son of Tobias ("a man of very high standing," according to 2 Macc 3:11) had his money deposited for safekeeping in the temple during the Seleucid rule. The family-based nature of public institutions in the restored Jewish community rendered such formal distinctions as "priestly" and "lay" irrelevant.

The events of the Achaemenid period proved time and again just how blurred were the borders between "priestly" and "lay" aristocracy. Nehemiah's policy of administrative and religious reforms had

---

[73] As becomes obvious from letters dispatched by Tobias to Apollonios, composed in Greek and following Greek cultural conventions (such as the "many thanks to the gods" formula). There is no doubt that his ancestors dispatched similar letters (but following different cultural conventions) to Achaemenid kings. See *CPJ*, vol. 2, 125–29. J. Collins, *Jewish Wisdom in the Hellenistic Age* (Louisville: Westminster John Knox Press, 1997), 24–35, attempts to reconstruct the cultural and religious ethos of early Hellenistic Jewish magnates based on contemporaneous literary evidence.

[74] Neh 13:4–5.

direct consequences for the temple (as can be seen from the covenant in Nehemiah 10, discussed above). He eventually set out to regulate marriage laws for the priesthood, although his success in this respect must have been limited.[75] In general, the interference of lay leaders with temple affairs becomes something of a pattern during the Achaemenid period. On the other hand, the alleged struggle between the high priest Joshua and Zerubbabel at the onset of the Restoration,[76] as well as fourth century Achaemenid coins mentioning "Yohanan ha-Kohen," may indicate that the high priestly family also tried to establish its control over the political and social affairs of the province.[77] In other words, the lack of a clear distinction between priestly and lay aristocracy is something that defines Jewish history of the Second Temple period from its inception. Individual aristocratic clans that constituted the backbone of the restored Jewish community tended to cross boundaries between priestly and lay families in both directions. This led to profound uncertainty about their respective responsibilities. The priesthood's monopoly over temple affairs was repeatedly called into question by non-priestly aristocratic clans.

The same situation characterized the Hellenistic period as well. Joseph the Tobiad acquired the right to collect taxes for Ptolemy at the expense of his priestly uncle Onias. Later, one Simon (who was an administrative official in the Temple) and his brother Menelaus (who was entrusted with bringing tax-money to Antiochus and thus probably occupied a similar administrative post) launched a concerted attack to deprive the Oniads of the high priesthood.[78] The internal politics, defined by the ongoing struggle among leading Judaean and Samaritan clans, thus persisted well into the Hellenistic period. The political culture of fluidity within the administrative

---

[75] See Nehemiah 13. Smith, *Palestinian Parties*, 136–44, compares Nehemiah to tyrants of contemporaneous Greek city states. Given certain similarities between the social structure of Nehemiah's movement and a phratry mentioned above this may be not as far fetched as it seems.

[76] On this struggle see Smith, *Palestinian Parties and Politics*, 99–119.

[77] On Yohanan's coins see Barag, "Silver Coin of Yohanan the High Priest," 4–21. Other coins of the same type refer to *Yehizkiyah ha-Pehah* ("the governor"). The two people were presumably different and their relationship is hard to ascertain. On coins bearing the name of Yehizkiyah see further Mildenberg, "Yehud," 183–96. Cf. also Schwartz, "On the Autonomy of Judaea," 159. Chronologically, Yohanan's coins were struck shortly before Alexander's conquest.

[78] 2 Macc 3:4–6 and 4:23–25. Some scholars have suggested that the two brothers were indeed Tobiads, but this is unlikely. See Tcherikover, *Hellenistic Civilization*, 152–57 for discussion and previous scholarship.

system, which derived from the social importance of individual families and family-based institutions (such as the priesthood), continued to determine Judaean politics during most of this time. In this respect, too, Ptolemaic and Seleucid Judah was a direct heir to Achaemenid Yehud.

It only seems logical then that religious movements in Hellenistic Judaea shared a number of common characteristics with religious movements of the Achaemenid era. When Menelaus attempted his reforms, he was acting in a way that was similar to Nehemiah's policy several centuries earlier.[79] Both Nehemiah and Menelaus were leaders of aristocratic factions who challenged high priestly claims to wield exclusive power in Temple affairs. In both cases these factions were backed by the power of a foreign king who exercised his right of patronage over the Temple. Finally, in both cases the leaders who challenged the existing status quo proposed drastic religious reforms that polarized the people and led to civil disturbances. Phenomenologically, the sweeping Hellenization initiated by Menelaus was not all that different from Nehemiah's reforms. There are abundant reasons to believe that the latter owed a great deal to cultural and administrative tastes of the Achaemenid court, as well as cultural and religious convictions of aristocratic Jewish refugees who allied themselves with this court.[80] In the same way, Menelaus' attempt to transform Judaism owed a great deal to cultural tastes and religious convictions of Jewish aristocracy that allied itself with Hellenistic rulers. In both cases religious ideologies of the reformers were contested by staunch opposition of the more "traditionalist" local Judaean population whose practices these reformers sought to transform (and, perhaps, "civilize").

---

[79] On Menelaus' reforms see E. Bickerman, *The God of the Maccabees: Studies on the Meaning and Origin of the Maccabean Revolt* (Leiden: Brill, 1979), 38–90, and M. Hengel, *Judaism and Hellenism*, vol. 1, 255–309. Cf., however, the critique of this approach by F. Millar, "The Background to the Maccabean Revolution: Reflections on Martin Hengel's Judaism and Hellenism," *JJS* 29 (1978), 1–21.

[80] For various aspects of the imperial involvement in the missions of Ezra and Nehemiah see articles collected in J. Watts, ed., *Persia and Torah: The Theory of Imperial Authorization of the Pentateuch* (Atlanta: Society of Biblical Literature, 2001). For similar practices of the Achaemenid government elsewhere in the empire see J. Blenkinsopp, "The Mission of Udjahorresnet and Those of Ezra and Nehemiah," *JBL* 106 (1987), 409–21. Fishbane, *Biblical Interpretation*, 108, observes regarding Ezra's ceremony of public Torah reading, "Such a lexical expansion was arguably influenced by Persian courtier customs of declaiming records and by Iranian terminology."

Even the administrative means of enforcing the reforms remained the same. As we have observed above, an alliance of aristocratic clans centered around the family of Nehemiah was a main driving force behind Nehemiah's reforms. The "community of the exile" (cemented by ideological bonds as well as family ties) established itself as a kind of military colony in Jerusalem.[81] The same was probably true of Menelaus' movement. We know that Menelaus' family formed its backbone, and there are indications that the movement itself can be described as a lose alliance of aristocratic clans united around a particular understanding of Judaism.[82] The foundation of the Akra might have played the same role of establishing an ideologically motivated military colony as the "community of the exile" did.[83] Phenomenologically, religious movements of Achaemenid and Hellenistic Judaea shared the same main characteristics. In both cases alliances of aristocratic clans driven by similar concerns and ambitions dominated the religious scene, just as they dominated political and social life of both Achaemenid and Hellenistic Judaea.

The continuity between the two periods was not limited to leading aristocratic clans. It appears that social and administrative structures on the village level also remained the same as those in Achaemenid times. We have mentioned above that families constituted the main building blocks within the restored community of Judah, whereas "heads of the families" provided local leadership and day-to-day administration of local affairs. It seems that this deeply patriarchal nature of the local Jewish society persisted well into the Hellenistic period. One of Zenon's letters reports how his agent together with the agent of a local official unsuccessfully attempted to collect money which one Ieddous owed Zenon. When they confronted Ieddous and produced a letter authorizing the collection, he "laid hands on them and threw them out of the village."[84] We do not know anything else about Ieddous, but there has been a schol-

---

[81] See K. Hoglund, *Achaemenid Imperial Administration in Syria-Palestine and the Missions of Ezra and Nehemiah* (Atlanta: Scholars Press, 1992), 207–40.

[82] On Menelaus' family and its involvement in the events see 2 Macc 4:23 and 29 (cf. 2 Macc 3:4–6 and 4:1–2). See also Tcherikover, *Hellenistic Civilization and the Jews*, 152–74. On families that supported the reforms see 1 Macc 2:45–46.

[83] See Bickerman, *God of the Maccabees*, 42–53, and J. Sievers, "Jerusalem, the Akra, and Josephus," in F. Parente and J. Sievers, eds., *Josephus and the History of the Greco-Roman Period* (Leiden: Brill, 1994), 195–209.

[84] *CPJ*, vol. 1, 129–30.

arly consensus that he, most probably, was one of the local "sheikhs" or "village strongmen" who controlled everyday affairs in the Judaean countryside.[85] Most of these people were local landowning magnates of means, who demonstrated relative independence from central authorities in Jerusalem, or even, as Ieddous' affair proves, from the imperial authorities. In the Achaemenid period these people would probably be known as "heads of the families" who effectively controlled the countryside and were occasionally convened by the leaders of the province to make decisions about public affairs.

Although we know precious little about Ieddous and the nature of his authority in his home village, the book of Judith provides additional important information about the organization and functioning of village administration during the Hellenistic and early Hasmonean period.[86] This administration looks remarkably similar to what we have observed for the Achaemenid period. Despite the book's emphasis on the figure of Judith and her individual heroic and religious qualities, it also reflects what would be typical local leadership under normal circumstances. At the moment of Holophernes' attack the town of Bethulia was governed by the "town magistrates then in office, Uzziah son of Mica, of the tribe of Simeon, and Chabris son of Gothoniel, and Charmis son of Melchiel."[87] Under exceptional circumstances that went beyond daily administrative routine these three would summon "elders of the town" for public assembly. The latter would often come accompanied by "all the young men and women," apparently their family members.[88] In fact, the three magistrates are sometimes also called "elders."[89] It seems that local paterfamilias held administrative posts in turn, thus guaranteeing equal distribution of public obligations among local households. The distinction between household and village administration was virtually non-existent: after the public assembly one of the magistrates Uzziah

---

[85] See Tcherikover, "Palestine under the Ptolemies," 48–51, and S. Schwartz, "A Note on the Social Type and Political Ideology of the Hasmonean Family," *JBL* 112 (1993), 306.

[86] Smith, *Palestinian Parties and Politics*, 162–63, argues that Judith was written within the milieu of the Judaean gentry and reflects its cultural and religious feelings. This hypothesis must remain an open question due to the lack of persuasive evidence. Still, the book seems to reflect accurately certain aspects of life in the Hellenistic Judaean countryside.

[87] Jdt 6:15.

[88] Jdt 6:16.

[89] Jdt 8:10 and 10:6.

gave a feast for the elders at his home and offered his house to the Assyrian defector Achior for residence and protection.[90] The heads of families continued to control life in the Judaean countryside as they had during the Achaemenid period. The patriarchal family remained the main social unit within Judaean society.

The household serves to provide identity for Judith herself, in spite of the story's focus on her individuality and personal heroism. Jdt 8:1 introduces her by recalling Judith's genealogy. Jdt 8:2–8 tells about her deceased husband Manasses, "who belonged to the same tribe and clan as she did." Jdt 8:7 specifically mentions that "Manasses had left her gold and silver, slaves and slave-girls, livestock and land, and she lived on her property." Judith's status in the local society is determined by her family's prosperity. She is a widow of one of the local "elders," "sheikhs," or "village strongmen," inheriting his status and wealth after his death. Her faithfulness to her deceased husband makes her rightful heir of his property.[91] Prior to her own death, she divides her property "among all those who were most closely related to her husband, and among her own nearest relations."[92] The traditional household is always present behind Judith and marks her status in the society. The author both introduces her and concludes her story by referring to her family and that of her husband. The book of Judith seems to reflect the changing cultural tastes of some of the "heads of families" that dominated political and social landscape of rural Judah during the Achaemenid and Hellenistic periods. The novelistic portrayal of an aristocratic Jewish woman displaying both traditional family piety and personal heroism reflected increased cultural sophistication (and Hellenization?) within these circles.[93]

---

[90] Jdt 6:21. Cf. Jdt 14:6 and 10. Achior eventually converts to Judaism. Was his residence in Uzziah's house part of this conversion process? He joins Israel by becoming member of a respected household.

[91] Jdt 8:4–6 and 16:22: she refuses to marry anyone after her husband's death and is "gathered to his people" when she dies. Judith's faithfulness to her deceased husband makes her the legitimate heir of his wealth and status. She alone continues to embody their household until her death.

[92] Jdt 16:24.

[93] Baumgarten, *Flourishing of Jewish Sects*, 114–36, correctly emphasizes the spread of literacy beyond priestly circles as a major cultural development during this period. It seems that non-priestly households of means became main beneficiaries of this process. Ben Sira may provide a good example of private lay education emerging during this time as well as new religious and cultural ethos shared by prosperous lay householders of Hellenistic Judah. See Collins, *Jewish Wisdom in the Hellenistic*

It was precisely this group of people that was most affected by
the spread of Hellenistic reform initiated by Menelaus and his friends
in 164 BCE. Seth Schwartz has correctly grouped the Hasmonean
family into one category of "village strongmen" with Ieddous and,
possibly, the Tobiads (although the latter seem to have occupied a
more elevated social and political status than the first two).[94] The
Seleucid official who came to Modein addressed Mattathias, the patriarch of the Hasmonean clan, as a "leader, honored and great in
this town, and supported by sons and brothers."[95] Mattathias is
depicted here surrounded by his family as would be appropriate for
any "head of the family" of either the Achaemenid or the Hellenistic
period. It was indeed Mattathias' immediate family that constituted
the core of the original revolt when he and his sons took to the hills
after killing a local renegade Jew along with the Seleucid official.[96]
But the Hasmonean reaction to persecution was not the only way
out. Both 1 and 2 Maccabees contain a series of legendary accounts
of Jews who chose martyrdom over submission to the "evil decrees"
of Antiochus. In most cases, these stories emphasize the heroism and
self-sacrifice of families rather than individuals. Indeed, 1 Macc
1:54–61 describes the persecution itself as a house to house search
intended to root out Judaism and targeting specific families rather
than the people of Israel as a whole. After the "abomination of des-
olation" was set up on the altar of the temple, reformers began to
build pagan altars "in the towns throughout Judaea." More specifically,
"the incense was offered at the doors of the houses and in the
streets."[97] The second stage of the reforms is described as involving
family-based Jewish observances. The story continues that persecutors "put to death women who had had their children circumcised.
Their babies, their families, and those who had performed the cir-
cumcisions were hanged by the neck."[98] 2 Macc 6:10–11 provides
a more detailed version of the same story. It describes how two
women who had had their children circumcised were brought to

Age, 35–41. Ben Sira's ethics is that of a patriarchal householder and represents
remarkable blend of Jewish and Greek ideals. See Collins, *Jewish Wisdom*, 62–79.
   [94] Schwartz, "Note on the Social Type," 305–09.
   [95] 1 Macc 2:12.
   [96] 1 Macc 2:28.
   [97] 1 Macc 1:55.
   [98] 1 Macc 1:60–61.

trial. Then, "with their babies hanging at their breasts, they were paraded through the city and hurled headlong from the ramparts."

The culmination of the persecution account in 2 Maccabees comes with the story of a mother and her seven sons, tortured and executed by Antiochus himself for their refusal to transgress ancestral laws.[99] It emphasizes the heroism of the righteous family and its readiness to die rather than commit sacrilege. The story expects the vindication of the righteous after their death by means of resurrection as well as the punishment of the wicked. Indeed, it is a series of righteous martyrdoms that sets the stage for the Maccabean revolt and victory over the persecutors.[100] From our perspective it is important to observe that martyrdom accounts in 2 Maccabees tend to focus on families rather than individuals. Eleazar, whose story precedes that of the seven brothers and their mother, is exceptional in this respect. However, if we accept Nickelsburg's theory that in the original version of the account Eleazar was father of the seven brothers, even this exception disappears.[101] In addition to the Hasmonean militancy, both 1 and 2 Maccabees reflect an ideology of martyrdom and passive resistance to religious persecution. Just as the Hasmonean family embodies the ideal of armed resistance, other families embody the ideal of righteous martyrdom leading to the eventual vindication of the pious and destruction of the wicked. Whereas the pro-Hasmonean 1 Maccabees dismisses this trend as an idealistic curiosity, 2 Maccabees takes a much more sympathetic look at it. Both works, however, recognize that families provided major resistance to Hellenizers' attempts to spread their version of Judaism throughout the Judaean countryside. Armed resistance and peaceful martyrdom were the two alternative ideologies used at this initial stage.[102]

---

[99] 2 Macc 7:1–42.

[100] See W. Van Henten, *The Maccabean Martyrs as Saviours of the Jewish People: A Study of 2 and 4 Maccabees* (Leiden: Brill, 1997), 125–269, for ideological underpinnings of martyrdom stories in 2 Maccabees. The ethos of martyrdom emerges from his description as a unique blend of Jewish and Greek religious and political ideals.

[101] G. Nickelsburg, *Resurrection, Immortality, and Eternal Life in Intertestamental Judaism* (Cambridge: Harvard University Press, 1972), 98–99.

[102] Nickelsburg, *Resurrection*, 93–109, finds numerous literary parallels and connections between a series of stories about heroic families in 1 Macc 2:29–38 (martyrdom in the cave), 1 Macc 2:15–28 and 49–68 (the story of Mattathias), and 2 Macc 7 and Assumption of Moses 9 (the story of Taxo and his seven sons). He

If 2 Maccabees' account of Jewish martyrs culminates with the story of the seven brothers, 1 Maccabees' (much less sympathetic) treatment ends with the story of "many" who escaped to the desert and mountains "taking their children and their wives and their livestock with them."[103] When royal troops surrounded them on the Sabbath, these families refused to fight in order not to profane the Holy Day and were all slaughtered: "men, women, and children, up to a thousand in all, along with their livestock."[104] As finds in the Wadi Daliyeh show, the Desert of Samaria, where these families most probably tried to escape, served as a classic site of refuge for the local population from at least the times of Alexander the Great.[105] The evidence of a mass slaughter of refugee families found in that area, dating to the time of the unsuccessful Samaritan rebellion against Alexander, along with documents discovered there, proves that the practice of seeking refuge in the hills was widespread among the local population. Those who fled to the Wadi Daliyeh in the time of Alexander were relatively prosperous landowners.[106] Their status was apparently the same as that of the families in Ezra-Nehemiah and Judith discussed above. The martyrs described in 1 Maccabees apparently belonged to the same social class, as parallelism and contrast between their behavior and the Hasmonean success story may indicate. The upshot of this parallelism would be to demonstrate how families coming from the same social background chose different ways to manifest their piety and that history eventually validated the more militant choice of the Hasmoneans. The political biases of 1 Maccabees aside, the story of "Sabbath martyrdom" proves the centrality of prosperous landowning families to the resistance against Hellenistic reforms. The militant response of the Hasmoneans was not a commonly shared ideal within this group. Another ideal had to do with passive resistance, escape into the wilderness and, if necessary, martyrdom. We shall see later on that

interprets all these accounts as belonging to the same literary tradition or group of traditions.

[103] 1 Macc 2:30.

[104] 1 Macc 2:38.

[105] For discussion of this region and its importance in local Jewish history see J. Schwartz and J. Spainer, "On Mattathias and the Desert of Samaria," *RB* 98 (1991), 252–71.

[106] See Cross, "Papyri of the Fourth Century BC from Dâliyeh," 51–52, and "Papyri and their Historical Implications," 17–18.

at early stages in its history the Dead Sea Sect followed the same pattern.

Finally, there were those who fully embraced the reforms or, at least, did not oppose them. It seems that multiple cultural and religious identities were the norm of the day for many (if not most) Jewish households. Earlier in the period Hecateus of Abdera noted that contemporaneous Jewish families followed both native (legislated by Moses) and foreign practices on such key occasions as marriage and the burial of the dead.[107] Some Jewish families, no doubt, actively embraced the change initiated by the Hellenizers. During its initial stages the Hasmonean rebellion seems to have targeted precisely such people. Mattathias and his friends are said to have swept across the Judaean countryside "demolishing the pagan altars and forcibly circumcising all the uncircumcised boys found within the frontiers of Israel."[108] They "hunted down their arrogant enemies," identified elsewhere as "sinners and renegades."[109] To the house-to-house imposition of the Hellenistic lifestyle, manifested through building pagan altars at house doorsteps, the Hasmoneans responded with their own house-to-house uprooting, displayed by tearing down these altars. The households that supported the reforms suffered most. Unfortunately we know next to nothing about these households. Still, the penetration of Greek culture and civilization into the Judaean countryside was probably substantial enough to ensure that quite a few families abandoned the "ways of their fathers" and joined the reform. We simply have no way to tell what the percentage was.

As a whole, our sources repeatedly demonstrate that landowning households residing in the Judaean and Samaritan countryside continued to shape social, political and economic life of these areas during the Hellenistic period. In terms of their organization and powers they were the direct successors of "families" that had returned to Judah in the Achaemenid period. The patriarchal nature of the restored Jewish settlement in Yehud remained virtually unchanged throughout the Hellenistic period. On the other hand, at least some of these households proved to be remarkably receptive to new cul-

---

[107] See Hecateus in Diodorus Siculus, *Bibliotheca Historica* 40.3.8. On the survival of syncretistic cults in the Second Temple Period see Smith, *Palestinian Parties*, 82–98. See also n. 73 above.

[108] 1 Macc 2:45–46.

[109] 1 Macc 2:44 and 47.

tural trends. The spread of new literary genres, such as the Hellenistic
novel and romance, proves the cultural openness of this social group.[110]
The commercialization of the Judaean countryside and its increased
involvement in regional trade undoubtedly contributed to its cultural
and social mobility.[111] Hellenistic artistic styles were now present in
most of the spheres of everyday life: from pottery, seals, and coins
to the architecturally elaborate mansions of local magnates.[112] Epig-
raphical and archaeological evidence suggests that the use of the
Greek language was on the increase in the countryside as well as in
cities.[113] The patriarchal *bet 'av* of Achaemenid Judah demonstrated
its vitality precisely because it was able to accommodate new cultural trends in the society. It also began to play a considerable role
in shaping the society's religious ideals. The ideals of martyrdom
and armed resistance as two responses to religious oppression apparently emerged within these circles. Both of them would shape Judaism
for centuries to come.

---

[110] Smith, *Palestinian Parties and Politics*, 157–63, attributes a whole body of literature to this group. In addition to Judith, discussed above, these texts included Job,
Ecclesiastes, Ruth, Esther, Tobit, Jonah, and the Song of Songs. He observes that
most of this material "is essentially belletristic and as such is sharply distinguished
from the national legend and history, laws and prophecies, preserved by the earlier Yahweh-alone tradition. This belletristic material testifies to the continued existence from the sixth to the second century of a lay circle enjoying wealth, leisure,
and considerable culture" (159). Schwartz, "On the Autonomy of Judaea," 167, follows a similar line of thinking when he suggests that the "new" class of "country
landlords and well-to-do traders" was responsible for shaping new genres in literature. His list, however, omits most of Smith's suggestions and includes Ecclesiastes,
Ben Sira, and *1 Enoch* 1–36.
[111] Schwartz, "On the Autonomy of Judaea," 161–67, correctly emphasizes the
importance of trade in shaping new type of culture in Hellenistic Palestine. I, however, cannot agree with his claims that this culture constituted a significant break
with that of the previous period. See Bickerman, *From Ezra*, 14–16, and Smith,
Palestinian Parties, 57–81. If anything, the involvement of the local elites in regional
and international trade during the Hellenistic period stood in direct continuation
with their commercial activities in Achaemenid times.
[112] For summary and review of archaeological finds from this period see H.-P.
Kuhnen, *Palästina in Griechisch-Römischer Zeit* (Munich: Beck, 1990), 33–87. On architectural remains cf. Schwartz, "On the Autonomy of Judaea," 165.
[113] For everyday business transactions conducted in Greek see F. Cross, "An
Aramaic Ostracon of the Third Century BCE from Excavations in Jerusalem," *Eretz
Israel* 15 (1981), 67–69, and L. Geraty, "The Khirbet el-Kôm Bilingual Ostracon,"
BASOR 220 (1975), 55–61. See Hengel, *"Hellenization" of Judaea*, 64, n. 23, and
Schwartz, "On the Autonomy of Judaea," 166, n. 34, for convenient summaries of
other available data.

Outside of Judah: Families and Judaism in the Early Jewish Diaspora

Patriarchal clans played the same central role in the contemporaneous Jewish Diaspora. In order to quell a revolt in Lydia and Phrygia in Asia Minor, Antiochus III proposed to settle there two thousand Jewish families from Babylonia as a stabilizing factor. His letter to the governor of Babylonia runs as follows:

> Learning that the people in Lydia and Phrygia are revolting, I have come to consider this as requiring very serious attention on my part, and, on taking counsel with my friends as to what should be done, I determined to transport two thousand Jewish families with their property (*Ioudaiōn oikous dischilious syn episkeuē*) from Mesopotamia and Babylonia to the fortresses and most important places ... It is my will, therefore—though it may be a troublesome matter—that they should be transported and, since I have promised it, use their own laws (*nomois autous chrēsthai tois idiois*). And when you have brought them to the places mentioned, you shall give each of them a place to build a house and land to cultivate and plant with vines, and shall exempt them from payment of taxes on the produce of the soil for ten years. And also, until they get produce from the soil, let them have grain measured out to them for feeding their servants.[114]

In many ways the arrangements proposed by Antiochus resemble those associated with the Congregation of the Exile of Ezra and Nehemiah.[115] More important from our perspective is the fact that the social structure of the Jewish colony established by this decree is virtually identical with the social structure of the Congregation of the Exile. In both cases, individual families seem to constitute the main building block within a community. In both cases, they receive land allotments ("fiefs") and are expected to fulfill important public functions as a stabilizing force within the local society. It also seems that, similar to the groups described in Ezra-Nehemiah, the house-

---

[114] *A.J.* 12.149–152. The translations are from the Loeb edition of Josephus and have been amended when necessary.

[115] Sherwin-White and Kuhrt, *From Samarkhand to Sardis*, 53–59, convincingly demonstrate that this and other Seleucid military arrangements were in direct continuation of the military structure of the Achaemenid Empire. On the mission of Ezra and Nehemiah as an attempt to establish a military colony to stabilize the region in face of revolts see K. Hoglund, *Achaemenid Imperial Administration in Syria-Palestine and the Missions of Ezra and Nehemiah* (Atlanta: Scholars Press, 1992), 207–40. Cf. Blenkinsopp, "Temple and Society," 50–53. He argues that the group of Ezra and Nehemiah was organized along social lines imported from Babylonia by Jewish immigrants.

holds of the Babylonian Jews summoned by Antiochus played an
important military role. The document mentions household servants
who, like those of Nehemiah, could apparently be used for military
and policing purposes. An individual household in both cases was
perceived as a public institution carrying out important functions.

In both cases the households were also given the right "to use
their own laws." Unfortunately Josephus does not specify what those
were. But the very right to live in accordance with one's religious
law made these families not only politically and militarily but also
religiously significant. They constituted a separate religious community planted within a non-Jewish environment. Similar to the Congregation of the Exile they had their own religious laws and were
expected to live according to them. An individual household would
as a result become a centerpiece and a focal point of the religious
life of the community. By maintaining their religious identity and dis-
tinctiveness, the individual families that constituted the colony shaped
its public religious identity and uniqueness. The family-centered
religion remained as important a dimension in the public life of the
Jewish colony in Seleucid Asia Minor as it had been in the Congregation of the Exile in early Second Temple Judaea.

On the cultural level, this development corresponded to the centrality of the patriarchal family in the exilic Jewish community in
Mesopotamia during approximately the same period of time. The
Book of Tobit, a wisdom tale apparently produced in the eastern
Jewish Diaspora during the early Hellenistic period, reflects the importance of families, family ties and family purity in shaping the everyday social and economic activities of Mesopotamian Jews.[116] It also
unambiguously states that endogamous marriage within one's own
kin is to be preferred to any other type of marriage.[117] In fact, this
type of marriage is perceived as an important part of one's righteousness and piety. The book provides its most elaborate discussion
of the virtuousness of endogamous marriage as part of the paternal

---

[116] Tob 1:14 and 21–22. The exact date of the Book of Tobit remains unclear.
Since the discovery of the Aramaic original of Tobit at Qumran, the majority of
scholars tend to assign it to the early Hellenistic or late Persian period. It most
probably comes from the Mesopotamian Jewish Diaspora. See G. Nickelsburg, *Jewish
Literature between the Bible and the Mishnah: A Historical and Literary Introduction* (Philadelphia:
Fortress Press, 1981), 35.
[117] Tob 1:9 and 4:12–13.

instruction of Tobit to his son Tobias.[118] The instruction as a whole focuses on the religious dimension of one's life as the head of the household. It lists specific acts of piety (respect to parents, almsgiving, timely payment of workers' wages, etc.) that should be performed while managing one's household. As part of proper management, Tobit instructs his son to take a wife from the "seed of your ancestors" and "from your father's tribe; for we are descendants of the prophets."[119] The marriage within one's kin vouchsafes the prosperity of one's children and their possession of the land. Tobit further brings examples of Noah, Abraham, Isaac, and Jacob, as his family ancestors who "chose wives from their kindred."

Tobit's instruction to his son articulates the centrality of the household for everyday halakhic observances in two respects. First, routine family life constitutes the main setting of all regulations and rules given by Tobit. They imply that the person who follows them is a householder of certain means. He maintains his family, conducts his own business and has sufficient income. Indeed, the pious practices of Tobit himself, described in earlier chapters, take place within his everyday family life and economic activities.[120] The halakhah of Tobit is that of a wealthy Diaspora householder. Second, the instruction itself is transmitted as an oral testimony from a father to his son. Earlier in the book, Tobit describes his own observance of the Jewish law as follows:

> Every third year when I brought it [the second tithe] and gave it to them, we held a feast in accordance with the command prescribed in the law of Moses and the instructions enjoined by Deborah the mother of Hananiel our grandfather. For on the death of my father I had been left an orphan.[121]

Tobit follows the Law of Moses in accordance with instructions of his great grandmother Deborah.[122] In other words, Tobit lives in accordance with halakhic norms that have been preserved within his family. These norms parallel and perhaps supplement the Law of Moses. The law is kept and transmitted through successive genera-

---

[118] Tob 4:1–20.
[119] Tob 4:12–13.
[120] See Tob 1:6–20 and 2:1–7. Notice the household setting of Tobit's celebration of the Shavuot in Tob 2:1–2.
[121] Tob 1:8.
[122] For Tobit's genealogy see Tob 1:1.

tions of individual households. It becomes "traditions of the fathers" in the most immediate sense of this term: it becomes ancestral family halakhah. An individual family and its everyday life thus acquire a religious status as transmitter of this law. The Law of Moses does not exist as an abstract category. It exists as a pious lifestyle of individual families, transmitted from parents to children in the form of individual examples, oral testimonies and moral exhortations. The family becomes a carrier of sanctity and righteousness. In its turn, the practice of endogamy is increasingly perceived as ensuring this sanctity through generations. Unlike Ezra, Tobit does not use the "holy seed" language, but he comes very close to it.[123]

Families also formed a social basis and provided a religious identity for other Jewish splinter groups during Hellenistic period. The most important of them was a group led by the high priestly scion Onias after the deposition of his family from the high priesthood in Jerusalem by Antiochus IV Epiphanes. After Onias had given up any hope of gaining back his position as a legitimate high priest of the temple, he fled to Egypt, effectively requesting asylum there. He also asked for permission to build a temple there, which would create a rallying point for those disaffected first with Seleucid and later with Hasmonean rule.[124] The phenomenon of the temple of Onias has intrigued scholars for quite a while, mostly because of its blatant disagreement with the Deuteronomic notion of a single sacrificial center in Jerusalem. From the perspective of our discussion, it is important to notice that by building his temple, Onias made a very articulate claim that the sacrificial cult was his family affair. From his perspective it was not the location that defined the proper nature of the cult but rather the legitimacy of the family carrying it out. The most central aspect of Judaism was perceived as the legitimate domain of a particular household, that of Onias. A space-centered doctrine of sacredness was countered by a family-centered doctrine of sacredness. No matter where Onias and his family were, it was

---

[123] Cf. Hayes, *Gentile Impurities*, 73, for similar observations.

[124] For a helpful summary and discussion of relevant sources see Schürer-Vermes, *History*, vol. 3.1, 47–79, and F. Parente, "Onias III' Death and the Founding of the Temple of Leontopolis," in F. Parente and J. Sievers, eds., *Josephus and the History of the Greco-Roman Period: Essays in Memory of Morton Smith* (Leiden: Brill, 1994), 69–98. D. Noy, "Jewish Communities of Leontopolis and Venosa," in J.W. van Henten and P.W. van der Horst, eds., *Studies in Early Jewish Epigraphy* (Leiden: Brill, 1994), 162–72, provides detailed discussion of epigraphic evidence.

only there that the legitimate sacrificial cult could be fulfilled. Familial control of public religious space was deemed to be the most essential characteristic of this space.

Josephus describes the temple of Onias and the story of its building both in *Bellum* and in *Antiquitates*.[125] In *B.J.* 1.31–33 he mentions Onias the high priest, who "sought the protection of Ptolemy and having obtained from him land in the *nomos* of Heliopolis, did there construct a small town, modeled on Jerusalem, and a similar temple." Josephus provides a more detailed description of the temple itself, as well as of circumstances that led to its building in *B.J.* 7.420–436, when he talks about its closure as a result of Jewish disturbances in Egypt in the wake of the Great Revolt of 66–73 CE. After news about the Jewish uprising in Egypt reached the Roman emperor, he ordered one Lupus to "demolish the Jewish temple in the district called 'of Onias'." This order provides a context for the historical digression about the temple. Josephus identifies the "district called 'of Onias'" as:

> This is a region in Egypt which was colonized and given this name under the following circumstances. Onias, son of Simon, and one of the chief priests at Jerusalem, fleeing from Antiochus, king of Syria, then at war with the Jews, came to Alexandria, and being graciously received by Ptolemy, owing to that monarch's hatred of Antiochus, told him that he would make the Jewish nation his ally if he would accede to his proposal. The king having promised to do what was in his power, he asked permission to build a temple somewhere in Egypt and to worship God after the manner of his fathers (*kai tois patriois ethesi therapeuein ton theon*).[126]

Ptolemy granted Onias land in the *nomos* of Heliopolis, where Onias "built a fortress and constructed a temple which is not like that in Jerusalem, but is like a tower." Josephus further observes that the altar of the temple imitated that in Jerusalem, as did cult objects with the exception of the lampstand, made in a different way. The entire temple was encompassed with a brick wall, which had stone gates in it. Ptolemy also gave Onias a territory for collecting revenues to sustain the temple and its priests. According to Josephus, Onias envisioned the temple as a rallying point for Jews opposed to

---

[125] For critical analysis of both accounts and their contradictions see Tcherikover, *Hellenistic Civilization*, 276–83, and A. Kasher, *The Jews in Hellenistic and Roman Egypt: The Struggle for Equal Rights* (Tübingen: J.C.B. Mohr, 1985), 132–35.

[126] *B.J.* 7.422–424.

the pro-Seleucid high priest in Jerusalem. He also somewhat idio-
syncratically interpreted the prophecy of Isa 19:18–19, which announced
that a temple would be built in Egypt by a Jew, as a theological
justification for his actions.

A.J. 12.387–388 essentially repeats the succinct statement of *B.J.*
1.31–33 about Onias fleeing from Jerusalem to Egypt and obtain-
ing the permission to build a temple "like that in Jerusalem." However,
it adds that the main reason for Onias' flight was that he saw
Antiochus' attempt "to transfer that dignity [high priesthood] from
his family to another house." Josephus picks up this story again in
A.J. 13.62–73. The main portion of this account consists of a spurious letter allegedly written by Onias to Ptolemy and requesting the
right to build a temple that would unite Jews living in Egypt. This
letter is followed by an equally spurious response from Ptolemy, citing reservations about the entire project based on Jewish law. Still,
the story contains some interesting details, which look authentic.
According to *A.J.* 13.63 Onias approaches king Ptolemy and his wife
Cleopatra with a request "to build a temple in Egypt like the one
in Jerusalem and to ordain Levites and priests of his own stock."
This request is explained through the prophecy of Isa 19:18–19 interpreted as a reference to Onias. After citing the two letters, Josephus
says that Onias "built a temple and an altar to God, similar indeed
to the one in Jerusalem but smaller and less elaborate." He further
observes that "Onias found other Jews like himself, together with
priests and Levites, who performed divine service there." It is unclear
whether these Jews, priests and Levites are identical with priests and
Levites from Onias' own stock mentioned before. Still, the repeated
references to the family of Onias in the version of the story in
Antiquitates make the entire affair look very much like an undertak-
ing of the disenfranchised high priestly family and its head Onias.
It was because of the king Antiochus' move to oust this family from
the high priesthood that Onias fled to Egypt. Later Onias specifically
asks Ptolemy for permission to build a temple where his relations
would officiate, and it is granted. Unlike the narrative in *Bellum*, that
in *Antiquitates* is much more inclined to portray the whole story as a
family affair.[127]

---

[127] Cf. Tcherikover, *Hellenistic Civilization*, 279–81, who also observes that Onias'
relatives and "various dependants of that great family" constituted the core of his
settlement.

In a way, such a portrayal is close to how early rabbis under-stood Onias' project. rabbinic texts refer to the temple of Onias as *bet honyo* (בית חוניו).[128] Priests who officiated there are prohibited from officiating in the temple in Jerusalem. But the overall rabbinic atti-tude to the temple of Onias is ambiguous. The offerings made there are not prohibited. They are simply invalid. Still, there was a debate among rabbis about a person's offering of his hair to become a *nazir*. According to some rabbis, if the person specifically intends to offer his hair in the temple of Onias, he meets his obligations. The term used to designate the temple of Onias, *bet honyo*, may indicate that rabbis' view of this place was similar to that expressed in *Antiquitates*. The temple was an enterprise of Onias' family, "the house of Onias." Family-related connotations of the rabbinic term *bayit* ("house") even when it designates a seemingly public institution, such as a school-house, have been discussed elsewhere.[129] In fact, the very ambiguity of this term as it appears in rabbinic texts indicates blurred bound-aries between private and public domains during that time. This becomes especially evident when the term "the house of X" is used to designate a specific public institution. The same seems to be the case with *bet honyo*. The temple of Onias is called "the house of Onias" simply because it was just that. As such it lacked the pub-lic significance of the temple of Jerusalem but commanded a certain respect due to its association with priestly families.[130] Similar to Josephus in *Antiquitates*, the Mishnah recognizes the temple of Onias as a family-owned public institution. Its religious significance is lim-ited but, according to some rabbis, still exists. Rabbinic texts that deal with the "House of Onias" try to figure out the degree to which priestly families maintain their public role even without the temple in Jerusalem.[131]

---

[128] M Menah. 13:10. See Parente, "Onias III," 77 and 81, for discussion of this mishnah.

[129] See Hezser, *Social Structure of the Rabbinic Movement*, 202–03, and A. Sivertsev, *Private Households and Public Politics in 3rd–5th Century Jewish Palestine* (Tübingen: Mohr Siebeck, 2002), 161–83.

[130] Cf. Tcherikover, *Hellenistic Civilization*, 280.

[131] P. Richardson and V. Heuchan, "Jewish Voluntary Associations in Egypt and the Roles of Women," in J. Kloppenborg and S. Wilson, eds., *Voluntary Associations in the Graeco-Roman World* (London: Routledge, 1996), 226–51, interpret the story in T Menahot 13:1 as a possible reference to women priests in Leontopolis. They also follow B. Brooten, *Women Leaders in the Ancient Synagogue* (Chico: Scholars Press, 1982), 73–90, by interpreting an inscription mentioning one Marin *hierisa* (*CPJ*

Against this background we can better appreciate the statement
of *B.J.* 7.424 that Onias "requested permission to build a temple
somewhere in Egypt and to worship God after the manner of his
fathers." Could Onias refer here to the customs of his family? We
already know that from his perspective only the worship carried out
by members of his family is legitimate. But did he also imply specific
halakhic norms followed by his family and thus considered obligatory by him? Later in *Bellum*, Josephus describes the architecture of
the temple of Onias. He states that unlike the temple in Jerusalem,
that of Onias resembled a tower of huge stones, sixty cubits in alti-
tude.[132] The altar and sacred vessels there were similar to those in
Jerusalem with the exception of the lampstand. Instead of a lampstand, a single golden lamp was hanging on a golden chain.[133] Does
this deviation from the architectural pattern of the Jerusalem temple indicate a particular temple halakhah of the priestly family of
Onias? Onias is also known in connection with his interpretation of
the prophecy of Isaiah, which he applied to himself and saw as a
scriptural warrant to build a new temple in Egypt.[134] Such an idiosyncratic interpretation of a biblical text represents one of the main
characteristics of the Second Temple sectarian mentality. In the case
of Onias, it also justified serious halakhic decisions, such as the building of an alternative temple in Egypt.[135] Overall, there are certain
indications that Onias and his family operated within a halakhic
framework peculiar to themselves. Some of their decisions could be
ad hoc but even so would become part of the family's halakhic lore
and understanding of Judaism. In this respect, Onias is somewhat
close to Ezra and Nehemiah, who also tried to shape the community in accordance with their peculiar vision of Jewish law. In both

---

vol. 2, 1514) as a possible reference to a female priest. Due to the lack of conclusive
evidence this entire issue must remain open. Still, it is possible that women played
an important role in the community of Leontopolis precisely because it was predominantly a family-based religious entity.

[132] *B.J.* 7.427, but cf. *B.J.* 1.33 (= *A.J.* 12.388, 13.63, and 20.236) where he says
exactly the opposite.

[133] *B.J.* 7.428–429.

[134] See *B.J.* 7.432 and *A.J.* 13.64, and 68.

[135] R. Hayward, "The Jewish Temple at Leontopolis: A Reconsideration," *JJS*
33 (1982), 432–41, emphasizes the connection between various architectural characteristics of the temple of Onias and possible (although not necessarily commonly
accepted) interpretations of the Isaiah's text. Thus, discrepancies between the temple of Onias and that in Jerusalem can be explained through the interpretive tradition unique to Onias (and his family?).

cases we deal with family-centered religious groups following a particular interpretation of Jewish law.

Conclusions

During the Achaemenid and Hellenistic periods, public life in Jewish society in the Land of Israel was shaped and dominated by powerful clans of local Jewish magnates both priestly and lay. In many ways the society itself formed and grew around such clans. In fact, the Second Temple Jewish community had been built in this way almost from the first days of its existence. In this situation our modern distinction between public and private spheres of life is utterly meaningless. Family structures were used to establish, solidify and staff public institutions from the temple to the defense of city walls. Individual families formed alliances in order to gain control of particular spheres of the public domain. On the professional level, family-specific professions were well attested throughout the period under discussion. On the political level, the country was controlled by local clans, which often did not have much respect for central authorities either in Jerusalem or in Hellenistic capitals of Egypt and Syria.

Finally, Judaism itself was determined by individual clans and alliances between families. In the temple of Jerusalem the familial lore of the high priests determined sacrificial procedures. And at least from the perspective of some priests (such as Onias), the ultimate sacredness of the temple dwelt with the family, not with the place where the temple was built. Outside of the temple (but with the temple in mind), the Congregation of the Exile led by Ezra and Nehemiah consisted of a number of clans that agreed to follow a particular interpretation of the Jewish law and to structure their lives in accordance with it. The interpretation of the law became a familial affair and part of the family lore. When the Second Temple sectarian movements emerged, they followed largely the same social pattern.

CHAPTER TWO

RELIGIOUS FUNCTIONS OF HOUSEHOLDS IN *JUBILEES* AND RELATED TEXTS

Recent scholarship has repeatedly emphasized the significance of family and proper pedigree for the development of Jewish sectarianism in the Second Temple period. Special attention has been paid to the idea of the "holy seed" of Israel, biologically different from that of gentiles, and to the ways in which this notion shaped the identity of Jewish religious movements of that period. With Ezra we find the first instance of a clear articulation of this notion, but it reaches its full fruition in the Hellenistic period, especially in *Jubilees* and early Qumran writings. As Christine Hayes has put it:

> The author of Jubilees stands in a line of tradition that stretches back to the Holiness Code and Deuteronomy through Ezra. For both Ezra and Jubilees, Israel is a holy seed, by nature distinct and separate from the seed of Gentiles, and intermingling the holy seed with another seed has serious consequences. Whereas Ezra emphasizes the profanation and sacrilege that result from intermarriage, Jubilees places emphasis on intermarriage as an act of *zenut* (sexual immorality) that not only profanes but also defiles the holy seed of Israel, in addition to profaning God's holy name, defiling the sanctuary, and threatening the entire community.[1]

The progeny of Israel constitutes the "holy seed," which has inherent biological characteristics distinguishing it from the progeny of gentiles. This is part of the natural order of the universe and cannot be changed. That is why conversion is really out of the question.[2] Israel constitutes a self-contained group closed to outsiders. It

---

[1] Hayes, *Gentile Impurities and Jewish Identities*, 80.

[2] See further D. Schwartz, "On Two Aspects of a Priestly View of Descent at Qumran," in L. Schiffman, ed., *Archaeology and History in the Dead Sea Scrolls: The New York University Conference in Memory of Yigael Yadin* (Sheffield: JSOT Press, 1990), 165–66, and *Agrippa I: The Last King of Judaea* (Tübingen: J.C.B. Mohr, 1990), 124–30. Schwartz convincingly argues that according to the priestly view, conversion could not make a Gentile into an Israelite because the two were "objectively" different, and no intention, no matter how laudable it was, could change this fact of nature. See D. Schwartz, "Law and Truth: On Qumran-Sadducean and Rabbinic Views

is a holy vessel that contains and transmits the holy seed unadulterated by any contact with gentiles. Jewish texts from this period often interpret the prohibition of intermarriage as an extension of the law prohibiting the mixture of different kinds of plants or animals. In both cases, the mixture of biologically different kinds is perceived as an aberration of the natural order of things. In both cases biologically different species have to be kept strictly apart.[3]

Given the importance of such ideas to the self-identity of Jewish sectarian movements, it is little wonder that the family would play a crucial role in forming the social basis of these movements. Naturally, the family would constitute the major vehicle through which the preservation and transmission of the "holy seed" was possible. The texts that emphasize the idea of the "holy seed" also contain a number of shared perspectives on what makes a proper Jewish household. We have already mentioned that intermarriage was out of question. A convert would be equally unacceptable because the conversion was unable to change inherent characteristics making the seed of Israel different from that of gentiles. It remains unclear whether there were further distinctions drawn among different types of Israelites. For example, it is not clear if priests were always allowed to marry lay Israelites or not. The *Aramaic Levi* Document and 4QMMT contain statements that can be interpreted as either prohibiting intermarriage between Israelites and gentiles or between priests and non-priests.[4] In either case, the prohibition against "mixed species" was the key argument behind the prohibition of intermarriages.

The avoidance of "mixed" marriages quite naturally led to the endorsement of endogamous marriages. As Michael Satlow observes in connection with *Jubilees*, "It is first noteworthy that although *Jubilees* never explicitly polemicizes for endogamous marriage, it does

---

of Law," in D. Dimant and U. Rappaport, eds., *The Dead Sea Scrolls: Forty Years of Research* (Leiden: Brill, 1992), 235–36, n. 20. I would only add that the "realistic" approach that Schwartz attributes to the priests was widely shared by lay Jews during the Second Temple period as well.

[3] See Hayes, *Gentile Impurities*, 68–91, and Satlow, *Jewish Marriage*, 135–43, and cf. discussion below.

[4] 4QMMT 75–82 and 1Q21 34 16 and 18–21. Qimron and Strugnell interpreted 4QMMT to prohibit marriages specifically between lay and priestly families within Israel (see *DJD* vol. 10, 171–72). For a similar view cf. M. Himmelfarb, "Levi, Phinehas, and the Problem of Intermarriage at the Time of the Maccabean Revolt," *JSQ* 6 (1999), 1–24, and Satlow, *Jewish Marriage*, 142. For an opposite view, namely that the prohibition deals with marrying non-Jews, see Hayes, *Gentile Impurities*, 82–89.

consistently emphasize the purity of its personages, established through endogamous marriage."[5] In fact, such a positive attitude toward endogamous marriages reflects wider cultural conventions within Second Temple Jewish society. Michael Satlow has convincingly demonstrated that kin marriage was a culturally acceptable and often encouraged norm of the Jewish society throughout the Second Temple period. Indeed, it corresponded to Greek family practices as well.[6] Overall, the sectarian emphasis on "pure" marriage practices deemed to preserve and transmit the "holy seed" fit well into the surrounding culture. It produced a religious justification for prevalent cultural practices or, alternatively, it used acceptable cultural language to express a specific religious ideology. In either case, the family as a social institute remained the prime building block within the Jewish sectarian movements. The family and its cultural conventions acquired a new meaning in light of the emphasis on the preservation and transmission of the "holy seed" of Israel. They now could play a crucial role in the cosmic drama of Israel's existence, since it was through them that the "holy seed" of Israel was regenerated and reproduced.

We have preciously little information about the social structure of groups that functioned during the early Hellenistic period and produced such texts as *Jubilees* or *1 Enoch*. Given the overall continuity that existed between late Achaemenid and early Hellenistic periods, one can imagine that religious movements within Judaism preserved their basic structures as well. Indeed, as we have argued in the previous chapter, there are remarkable similarities between the Ezra-Nehemiah movement and religious groups that emerged in the first centuries of Hellenistic rule. In both cases we encounter alliances of families wedded to a particular interpretation of Jewish law. They usually united around a family, group of families or, sometimes, individual leaders who were recognized as having special expertise in matters pertaining to the Law. The authority of such leaders was by definition localized and did not extend much beyond their respective groups of followers. At the same time most of these groups tried to expand their understanding of the Law, eventually making it the "law of the land" binding for the entire people of Israel. Some of them were successful (like the Maccabees), while many were not. I

---

[5] Satlow, *Jewish Marriage*, 141.
[6] Satlow, *Jewish Marriage*, 143–47.

shall argue in this chapter that a number of early Hellenistic Jewish texts (such as *Jubilees* and parts of *1 Enoch*) were produced within such groups. For one reason or another, their appeal reached wider circles of the Israelite population thus allowing their preservation and dissemination. But their original setting was within particular Torah-centered alliances of Israelite families with their particular interpretations of what Torah means.

During the Hellenistic period, as in the times of Ezra and Nehemiah, the household apparently remained the matrix of Jewish sectarian movements and many of their ideas. The Sapiential Work from Qumran describes the family and basic relationships within it as a source of cosmic wisdom:[7]

> Honor your father in your poverty and your mother in your steps. For his father is like God to man and his mother like a ruler to a human being. For they are the crucible from which you were born and as He placed them over you as rulers and a frame for the spirit, so serve them, and as He has revealed to you the mystery to come, honor them for your honor's sake (ובאשר גלה אוזנבה ברז נהיה בבדם למען בבודבה) and in . . . the splendor of their face for your life's sake and for the length of your days.[8]

The text describes man's obligation to honor his parents as a path to ultimate wisdom ("the mystery to come").[9] He obtains it not by severing or neglecting family ties but by cherishing them. The parents acquire a semi-divine status in this passage. It remains unclear if this description is related to the sacred purpose of the family to produce and transmit the holy seed of Israel along with its wisdom. Another fragment from the same sapiential work contains a prohibition against mixed species, but the context of this prohibition is

---

[7] For a proposed reconstruction of this text see T. Elgvin, "The Reconstruction of Sapiential Work A," *RevQ* 16 (1995), 559–80. According to him, "the work either belongs to the close predecessors of the Essene community or it derives from the first formative phase of the sectarian movement" (p. 561). Cf. D. Harrington, *Wisdom Texts from Qumran* (London: Routledge, 1996), 40–59, and Collins, *Jewish Wisdom*, 117–27.

[8] 4Q416 2 III, 15–19. Cf. an alternative translation of v. 18 by Strugnell and Harrington: "And as they have uncovered thy ear to the mystery that is to come." See most recently D. Parry and E. Tov, eds., *The Dead Sea Scrolls Reader, Part 4: Calendarical and Sapiential Texts* (Leiden: Brill, 2004), 99. If this translation is more accurate (and I am not sure that it is) it may indicate a family-based transmission of eschatological lore envisioned by our text.

[9] On *raz nihyeh* and its possible meanings see D. Harrington, "The *Rāz Nihyeh* in a Qumran Wisdom Text (1Q26, 4Q415–418, 423)," *RevQ* 17 (1996), 549–53.

not clear.[10] Still, there is good reason to believe that the religious value ascribed to the family in our text may be related to the idea of the holy seed preserved and regenerated through the family. In our case, the family is also the ultimate source of heavenly wisdom acquired by a man.[11]

After exhorting a reader to respect his parents our text shifts its attention to marriage:

> You have taken a wife in your poverty, take the offspring . . . from the mystery to come when you are joined together. Walk with the helpmate of your flesh . . .[12]

The incomplete nature of this passage makes it very difficult to analyze it. The text clearly advocates a marital life and apparently perceives it as part of the "mystery to come." Another excerpt from the same sapiential works provides a more detailed exhortation to marry and establish a family. It also envisions a fairly traditional type of household with a husband exercising patriarchal authority over his wife:

> His father and his mother . . . (He) did not make him (her father) rule over her and He separated her from her mother and toward you [will be her longing] . . . [and she will be] one flesh for you. He will separate your daughter for one and your sons . . .
>
> And you will become one with the wife of your bosom, for she is a flesh of your na[kedness] and whoever rules over her apart from you has changed the boundary of his life. He has made you to rule over her spirit so that she may walk according to your pleasure. Let her not increase vows and free-will offerings . . . Bring back (her) spirit to your good pleasure, and annul by a word of your mouth every binding oath of hers by which to vow a vow. And by your will, stop her . . . of your lips . . .[13]

This passage asserts authority of the head of the household over his wife. It first discusses the transition of authority over one's wife from her parents to her husband, who becomes a new head of the house-

---

[10] 4Q418 103 II. Harrington, *Wisdom Texts from Qumran*, 59, recognizes this uncertainty: the passage may refer either to agricultural laws or to marriage regulations.

[11] Cf. Harrington, *Wisdom Texts*, 45–49, for similar observations. Camp, *Wisdom and the Feminine*, 255–82, and "Female Sage in Ancient Israel," 185–203, demonstrates the importance of familial setting for the development of Second Temple wisdom texts in general. Cf. Fontaine, "Sage in Family and Tribe," 155–64.

[12] 4Q416 2 III, 20–21.

[13] 4Q416 IV, 1–10.

hold. The text then illustrates this authority by quoting the husband's right to annul his wife's vows, the right emphasized elsewhere in the sectarian documents from Qumran.[14] Overall, the text provides an idealized description of a typical patriarchal household and its cultural norms. Within such a household, man's position is defined by his relationships with his parents on the one hand and his wife on the other. If conducted properly, family life leads one to comprehension of the "mystery to come." In fact, family life itself is perceived as part of this mystery.[15]

Families and Their Religious Function in Jubilees

In a footnote to her article "*Jubilees* 30: Building a Paradigm for the Ban on Intermarriage," Cana Werman observes that "according to Jubilees, laws resulting from events find a place in the 'heavenly tablets.'" She further concludes that

> The heavenly tablets allow this book to emphasize the eternal reality of a law, a righteous deed, or a transgression. This is particularly true in cases where interpretation of the law is in dispute.[16]

I would like to use this observation as a starting point for my own discussion of the law in *Jubilees*. Most of the events from which laws in *Jubilees* result take place within a family setting. In other words, the law in *Jubilees* exists in two dimensions: it is written down in the heavenly tablets, and it is practiced by a righteous Jewish household. References to the heavenly tablets provide cosmic perspective on particular household practices, making them an eternal law of the creation. But on the human level, the legislation emerges from authoritative precedents and practices ascribed to the righteous forefathers of Israel

---

[14] CD XVI, 10–12.

[15] It is possible that parts of our text (4Q415 2 II) addresses a female member of the household urging her to keep the covenant. This may indicate that (similar to Ezra-Nehemiah's group and the Dead Sea Sect) women were expected to be active performers of covenantal laws, not just their passive recipients. See Collins, *Jewish Wisdom*, 121.

[16] C. Werman, "*Jubilees* 30: Building a Paradigm for the Ban on Intermarriage," *HTR* 90 (1997), 13, n. 58. Cf. Müller, "Hebräische Sprache der Halacha als Textur der Schöpfung: Beobachtungen zum Verhältnis von Tora und Halacha im Buch der Jubiläen," in H. Merklein et al., eds., *Bibel in jüdischer und christlicher Tradition: Festschrift für Johann Maier zum 60. Geburtstag* (Frankfurt am Main: Hain, 1993), 157–76, for similar observations.

and their families.[17] It is part of their paradigmatic holiness, embodied through their life and pious practices of their families. According to *Jubilees*, Abraham initiated the celebration of Sukkoth by building booths "for himself and for his servants" and by offering sacrifices. After a fairly detailed description of sacrificial offerings the text continues:

> And he observed this feast seven days, rejoicing with all his heart and with all his soul, he and all of those who were in his house. And there was no alien with him or any who were not circumcised. And he blessed his Creator who created him in his generation because by his will he created him for he knew and he perceived that from him there would be a righteous planting for eternal generations and a holy seed from him so that he might be like the one who made everything.[18]

Abraham and his house are the first to celebrate Sukkoth by building booths and offering sacrifices. This vouchsafes for them the divine benevolence and the promise of becoming "a righteous planting for eternal generations and a holy seed."[19] By celebrating the festival, Abraham and his family sanctify themselves. The first celebration of Sukkoth is initiated within a family context of a righteous household. This practice, however, immediately gains divine approval and becomes a permanent law by virtue of having been inscribed in the heavenly tablets:

> And we eternally blessed him and his seed who are after him in every generation of the earth because he observed this feast in its (appointed) time according to the testimony of the heavenly tablets. Therefore it is ordained in the heavenly tablets concerning Israel that they will be observers of the feast of booths seven days with joy in the seventh month which is acceptable before the Lord (as) an eternal law in their generations throughout all (time), year by year.[20]

---

[17] On the central role of the heavenly tablets in Jubilees see F. García Martínez, "The Heavenly Tablets in the Book of Jubilees," in M. Albani et al., eds., *Studies in the Book of Jubilees* (Tübingen: Mohr Siebeck, 1997), 243–60, and H. Najman, "Interpretation as Primordial Writing: Jubilees and Its Authority-Conferring Strategies," *JSJ* 30 (1999), 379–410. Werman's note provides a promising alternative to the predominant view of the heavenly tablets as the single most important source of law in Jubilees. It does not, however, diminish the importance of the heavenly tablets in Jubilees' narrative but only puts it into a due perspective.

[18] *Jub.* 16:25. Quotations from the *Book of Jubilees* are from Wintermute's translation as it appears in James E. Charlesworth, ed., *Old Testament Pseudepigrapha* (Garden City: Doubleday, 1985), vol. 2, 52–142.

[19] *Jub.* 16:26.

[20] *Jub.* 16:29.

The text ends by referring to Abraham's practice of waving branches as a sign for Israelites to do the same thing.[21] The reference to the heavenly tablets serves here to make what appears to be the private piety of Abraham and his house into an authoritative legal precedent. Abraham and his seed in every generation are blessed because they perform this celebration. Abraham's behavior is no longer a pious practice of a righteous individual, which is praiseworthy but not legally binding on everyone else. Rather it becomes part of the cosmic law of Israel, written in the heavenly tablets and governing the behavior of all future generations of Abraham's posterity. The family practice thus acquires the status of a religious law of cosmic dimensions.

In a similar fashion, the law of tithing is established by the practice of Jacob. He gave a tenth of his possessions to his son Levi, who "served as priest in Bethel before Jacob, his father."[22] The first transaction thus takes place within a family. Indeed our text describes this as a family matter arranged between a father and his son. This description, however, is immediately followed by a reference to the heavenly tablets that establish this practice as an eternal law for Israel.[23] Overall, the ceremonial law is repeatedly described as originating in the family practice of the patriarchs and acquiring the status of eternal cosmic law after having been inscribed in the heavenly tablets. Such a description reflects the twofold nature of the Jewish law in *Jubilees*. On the one hand the law emerges from the practices of pious individuals and their families. They embody the law in this world. On the other hand, the law has its cosmic dimension. It is not simply a private practice of righteous individuals but a binding cosmic legislation that determines the very existence and the well-being of the creation.[24] Despite the apparently public nature of

---

[21] *Jub.* 16:31.

[22] *Jub.* 32:8–9.

[23] *Jub.* 32:10–15. *Jub.* 13:25–27 seems to be making a similar claim for Abraham. The text appears after a lacuna that makes it impossible to say whether or not the eternal law of tithing the firstfruits has been preceded by the description of Abraham's action to this effect. Content and style-wise it probably was, most probably in connection with the Melchizedek episode.

[24] On the cosmic and halakhic importance of the heavenly tablets see García Martínez, "Heavenly Tablets in the Book of Jubilees," 243–60, and Najman, "Interpretation as Primordial Writing," 379–410. García Martínez, 255–59, correctly emphasizes the role of the heavenly tablets in promoting and justifying new laws unattested in the Scripture. He further connects this image with the "Oral Law" of later Rabbinic Judaism.

the ceremonial laws, *Jubilees* persistently portrays them as originating in the family practices of pious households. This emphasis on household practices as a major source for public Jewish law is very remarkable and may indicate the role which individual families and their practices played in forming Jewish halakhah in the time when the *Book of Jubilees* was written.

Jubilees takes a similar approach to circumcision and family law. It describes circumcision as another practice of Abraham and his household that acquires the status of cosmic law:

> And Abraham did as the Lord said to him and he took Ishmael, his son, and all of the male servants of his house and also whomever he bought with money, every male who was in his house, and he circumcised the flesh of their foreskins. And that very same day Abraham was circumcised and every man of his house and the servant of his house. And all of those who were purchased for money from the sons of aliens were also circumcised with him.[25]

The circumcision follows a direct divine order to circumcise every male of Abraham's family.[26] The original practice of circumcision is a pious act of the patriarch and his household performed in response to God's explicit command. But this practice is immediately given the eternal status of cosmic law:

> This law is for all the eternal generations and there is no circumcising of days and there is no passing a single day beyond eight days because it is an eternal ordinance ordained and written in the heavenly tablets.[27]

The practice originally performed within a household as part of private piety and family lore acquires the status of binding cosmic legislation. Failure to observe it will result in ultimate destruction. The law of circumcision originates as the response of a righteous man and his household to the divine call. It originally constitutes part of the family halakhah of Abraham. Our text emphasizes the family setting of the original covenant by stating that a male who is not circumcised will be "uprooted from his family because he has broken my covenant."[28] The reference here is to one's family, not one's people. It is an individual family and its members who are portrayed

---

[25] *Jub.* 15:23–24.
[26] *Jub.* 15:11–16.
[27] *Jub.* 15:25.
[28] *Jub.* 15:14.

as prime participants in the covenant. The God of Israel is in fact the God of a particular family. By referring to the heavenly tablets, *Jubilees* elevates this family's law to a cosmic level.[29]

The prohibition of sexual relations with the father's wife or concubine as well as with one's daughter-in-law comes from the stories of Reuben's affair with Bilhah and Judah's affair with Tamar.[30] In both cases, Jacob's sons violate the integrity of their families by performing illicit sexual acts. In both cases they repent of their deeds and obtain forgiveness from God. Neither they nor their families are destroyed. Their actions lead to the announcement of heavenly laws prohibiting these types of family relationships. The text specifically indicates that the behavior of Jacob's sons represents negative examples that should not be followed and that the punishment for doing the same thing in subsequent generations will be much more severe. The family law derived from one's practice thus acquires a heavenly status and becomes normative for generations to come. In a similar way Laban explains to Jacob why he had to take Leah first:

> And Laban said to Jacob, "It does not happen thus in our land, to give the younger woman before the elder. And it is not right to do this because thus it is ordained and written in the heavenly tablets that no one should give his younger daughter before the elder because he should first give the elder and after her the younger. And they will write it down as sin in heaven concerning the man who acts thus."[31]

A family custom is explained here as the cosmic law binding for all generations.[32] Similar to the ceremonial law discussed above, family law is also described in *Jubilees* as existing on two levels. It exists as the customary law of pious households, and it is also inscribed in the heavenly tablets, thus acquiring cosmic and eternal status. According

---

[29] God's command to Abraham to perform circumcision begins with the words, "And you also keep my covenant, you and your seed after you" (*Jub.* 15:11). The seed of Abraham is consecrated by means of the covenant in general and circumcision in particular. Moreover, the covenant itself is embodied through successive generations of Abraham's family. On the concept of the "holy seed" in *Jubilees* and its importance see Hayes, *Gentile Impurities and Jewish Identities*, 73–81.

[30] *Jub.* 33:1–17 and 41:1–28.

[31] *Jub.* 28:6.

[32] In this case, contrary to the previous examples, the heavenly law seems to have preexisted the family custom of Laban and is used to justify it. See Najman, "Interpretation as Primordial Writing," 395–98, for discussion of this and other related passages. She further proposes that *Jubilees* treats this and other narrative passages from Genesis as "crypto-legal texts," which, if read correctly, convey rules of halakhah. Cf. García Martínez, "Heavenly Tablets," 256.

to *Jubilees* the family and the ceremonial law constitute two types of Jewish halakhah that follow the same pattern of development. This is not surprising if we consider that, according to *Jubilees*, the ceremonial law and the very institution of priesthood emerge as part of the pious practices of a righteous household. The two types of law are thus profoundly intertwined with each other. In fact, the ceremonial law represents a form of family halakhah of the patriarchs and their households.

Deathbed testimonies of the patriarchs play a prominent role in *Jubilees*. They serve to summarize and present in the form of exhortation the most essential points of law and moral guidance. They also function as oral exhortations to one's children to observe both the moral and ceremonial aspects of halakhah. In other words, deathbed testimonies serve as a literary tool to transmit the ancestral traditions of the patriarchs from one generation to another. In *Jubilees* they often appear side by side with references to written records of ancestral halakhah transmitted by a patriarch to his children. In other words, the written and the oral modes of transmission are seen as mutually supplemental. In fact, sometimes they are indistinguishable from one another, since patriarchs occasionally *read* to their children from books received from their ancestors. The ancestral traditions are thus passed within the generations of the family in both the written form of sacred books and the oral form of deathbed addresses. In both cases, however, one's immediate family constitutes the social matrix for both types of transmission, which thus truly become "traditions of the fathers."[33]

Some testimonies tend to focus on moral instructions, while others contain substantial and fairly technical halakhic sections. Noah's testimony to his sons contains both general moral exhortation and specific halakhic rules.[34] It takes place within the family circle and addresses Noah's children and grandchildren:

---

[33] Cf. J. Baumgarten, "The Unwritten Law in the Pre-Rabbinic Period," *JSJ* 3 (1972), 12, who observes that the Qumran literature "lacks any trace of the distinction between Written Law and Oral Law which is characteristic of rabbinic sources and which serves as the basis of the contrasting forms of transmission." *Jubilees* fully conforms to this description. See also Jaffee, *Torah in the Mouth*, 20–27, for in-depth discussion of ambiguities of written and oral transmission of the text in the Second Temple period.

[34] *Jub.* 7:20–39. In *Jub.* 7:34–38 Noah transmits specific laws of reserving first fruits and observing the Seventh Year.

> And in the twenty-eighth jubilee Noah began to command his grand-sons with ordinances and commandments and all of the judgements which he knew.[35]

The observance of these rules will result in the prosperity of Noah's descendants and their families,[36] while the failure to observe them will lead to the ultimate destruction of one's "seed."[37] The law which Noah transmits to his children is the ancestral law of their physical fathers, passed on from generation to generation within their family. It is embodied and lived through successive generations of his family as family lore and practice:

> And you will be righteous and your plants will be upright, because, thus, Enoch, the father of your father, commanded Methuselah, his son, and Methuselah (commanded) Lamech, his son. And Lamech commanded me everything which his fathers commanded him. And I am commanding you, my sons, just as Enoch commanded his sons in the first jubilees. While he was alive in his seventh generation, he commanded and bore witness to his son and his grandsons until the day of his death.[38]

Remarkably, in this passage Noah seems to emphasize precisely the oral transmission of the ancestral tradition received as a result of someone "commanding" or "bearing witness" to his sons. When he received the law directly from his ancestors, this law was "commanded," not read from the "books of the forefathers."[39] Apparently, a deathbed testimony summarizes and symbolizes exactly such a "commanding" of the law to one's children. It amounts to an oral transmission of moral instructions and legal rulings to the next generation of one's family.

At the same time, Noah's own traditions were transmitted in written form. As we have observed above, Abraham received his knowledge from the "books of his forefathers," including the "words of Noah." But even in its written form, the transmission takes place strictly within his family:

---

[35] *Jub.* 7:20.
[36] *Jub.* 7:34.
[37] *Jub.* 7:29.
[38] *Jub.* 7:37–39.
[39] On the other hand, Enoch's "testimonies" were most probably perceived as written texts. See *Jub.* 4:16–24. See further Najman, "Interpretation," 384–85, for discussion.

> And he called his children, and they came to him, they and their children. And he divided by lot the land which his three sons would possess. And they stretched out their hands and took the document from the bosom of Noah, their father.[40]

The text describes the division of the earth among Noah's sons. It is not immediately clear if the written text received from Noah specifically deals with this division or embraces other areas of his testimony as well. Another passage states that Noah composed a book containing secrets of healing (and exorcism?) taught to him by one of the angels. This book was specifically designed to protect Noah's offspring from demons and was perceived as part of Noah's family lore:

> And the evil spirits were restrained from following the sons of Noah. And he gave everything which he wrote to Shem, his oldest son, because he loved him much more than all of his sons.[41]

Once again, the reference to a book here may indicate a fairly specific and technical manual of medicine and magical lore rather than a tradition in its entirety. Still, in conformity with other Noah's traditions, this technical knowledge is transmitted within his family, although even his children appear to have a restricted access to it.[42]

The farewell testimony of Abraham also contains both moral and halakhic types of instruction. Abraham begins by a lengthy moral sermon containing exhortations to his children to act righteously and to follow the basic moral principles of biblical Judaism.[43] Soon enough the focus of his address shifts to the issues of family purity and family law as prime manifestations of the more general moral principles stated above.[44] The failure to observe family purity results in destruction (historical examples of the giants and Sodom follow).[45] The observance of these rules, on the other hand, will result in economic

---

[40] *Jub.* 8:11.
[41] *Jub.* 10:13–14.
[42] Cf. *Jub.* 8:1–4, where Cainan, a grandson of Noah, learns the art of writing from his father and then discovers "a writing which his ancestors engraved on stone." The writing contains the forbidden lore of the Watchers, which leads Cainan astray. Becoming privy to the ancestral tradition may have negative as well as positive consequences.
[43] *Jub.* 20:1–3.
[44] *Jub.* 20:3–4.
[45] *Jub.* 20:5–6.

prosperity and fertility. The righteous household is described as an embodiment of the divine blessing:

> So that he might be pleased with you, and grant you his mercy, and bring down rain for you morning and evening, and bless all your works which you have made on earth, and bless your food and your water, and bless the fruit of your womb and the fruit of your land, and the herds of your cattle and the flocks of your sheep. And you will become a blessing upon the earth, and all of the nations of the earth will desire you, and they will bless your sons in my name, so that they might be blessed just as I am.[46]

The righteous household manifests the divine presence through its very existence and observance of the laws. In fact, the law itself is embodied through such a household as becomes clear in the next section of Abraham's testimony. This section is addressed specifically to Isaac and contains a detailed technical discussion of sacrificial laws.[47] The legal material is thus transmitted in the form of a testament from father to son. It is presented here as a family halakhah. Indeed, Abraham concludes his instruction by saying:

> Because thus I have found written in the books of my forefathers and in the words of Enoch and in the words of Noah.[48]

The law which Abraham transmits to Isaac is family halakhah in the most exact sense of this word. Abraham received it from his forefathers, although not as a direct instruction but as a written tradition. This corresponds to an earlier observation made by *Jubilees* that Abraham "took his father's books—and they were written in Hebrew—and he copied them. And he began studying them thereafter."[49] Abraham is thus made privy to the ancestral halakhah of his family. It is the "tradition of his fathers" in the most physical and immediate sense of the term: it is his family halakhah. It was preserved in written form to bridge a gap between the righteous generations of Enoch and Noah and that of Abraham. The written form of transmission also reflects the tradition's relationship with the

---

[46] *Jub.* 20:9–10.

[47] *Jub.* 21:1–10.

[48] *Jub.* 21:10.

[49] *Jub.* 12:27. Cf. *Jub.* 11:16, where Abraham learns writing from his father Terah. *Jubilees* seeks to reconcile the family tradition of Abraham with his father's worship of idols and subsequent departure of Abraham from his family. It persistently portrays Terah in positive light. See for example *Jub.* 12:6–8 and 29–31.

cosmic law of the heavenly tablets, since writing is perceived as sacred action throughout *Jubilees*. However, Abraham's son Isaac receives this tradition (at least partially) in the form of oral instruction from his father's mouth.[50] His own testimony to his sons is phrased as a moral deathbed exhortation.[51] What we are dealing with here is the family halakhah, transmitted and observed within generations of a righteous household in both its oral and written form.[52]

Thus, according to *Jubilees* the written transmission and the oral transmission of the law exist side by side, but both of them take place within the family. They constitute a particular dimension of the familial holiness emphasized by the narrative. The deathbed scene of Jacob demonstrates a profound connection between the transmission of the law of the fathers and the overall veneration of family ancestors:

> And he [Jacob] slept with his fathers. And he was buried in the cave of Machpelah in the land of Canaan near Abraham, his father, in the tomb which he excavated for himself in the cave of Machpelah in the land of Hebron. And he gave all of his books and his father's books to Levi, his son, so that he might preserve them and renew them for his sons until this day.[53]

The unity of the deceased patriarchs of the family corresponds in this description to the unity of their ancestral traditions transmitted in written form to Levi and his children. I am presently not concerned with the clearly pro-priestly agenda of this passage. What seems more important is the powerful family-focused ideology permeating this entire passage. The family law, either in its oral or in its written form, is embodied in generations of the family's ancestors. Just as a family burial cave at Machpelah manifests the physical unity of the kin, so the transmission of family halakhah unites

---

[50] According to *Jub*. 39:5–7, Joseph refuses to commit adultery with Potiphar's wife because "he remembered the Lord and the words which Jacob, his father, used to read, which were from the words of Abraham, that there is no man who may fornicate with a woman who has a husband." By referring to Jacob's reading of the words of his father Abraham, the text ingeniously reconciles potential conflict between oral and written transmission of the family lore.

[51] *Jub*. 36:1–19. The exhortation is followed by a family feast.

[52] On the centrality of the written word and authoritative sacred writing for Jubilees see Najman, "Interpretation," 381–88. This centrality, however, should not negate the significance of oral deathbed testimonies given by the patriarchs to their children. The two appear as complimentary parts of the same process of in-family transmission of the sacred law.

[53] *Jub*. 45:15.

the family of the patriarchs through generations.[54] A family's physical ancestors and their halakhah are carried through the successive generations of their descendants.[55] The prime task of the family is to ensure the preservation of righteousness, which is understood in almost biological terms.[56] Numerous passages in *Jubilees* repeatedly assert that following moral and legal instructions guarantees the survival and prosperity of one's seed, whereas failure to observe them leads to the uprooting of the family.[57] One of the most striking examples of the biological potency of family halakhah comes from the discussion of the longevity of successive generations in *Jubilees*. The text explicitly connects the decreasing life span of each successive generation to its failure to adhere to the law.[58] The eschatological future results from the reversal of this pattern:

> And in those days, children will begin to search the law, and to search the commandments and to return to the way of righteousness. And the days will begin to increase and grow longer among those sons of men, generation by generation, and year by year, until their days approach a thousand years, and to a greater number of years than days.[59]

---

[54] Abraham "was gathered to his fathers" at the end of his farewell testimony and blessings for Isaac and Jacob. At the moment of Abraham's death Jacob "was lying on his bosom" (*Jub.* 23:1–2). Throughout its narrative *Jubilees* repeatedly emphasizes the physical unity of successive generations of a righteous family. Indeed, merits of the deceased parents cause the prosperity of their seed. Cf. *Jub.* 24:11 and 22–23. Another recurrent theme is the blessing of a patriarch's name through his seed. See *Jub.* 20:10 and 25:21–22.

[55] Cf. *Jub.* 36:1–3 (the deathbed testimony of Isaac): "My sons, I am going in the way of my fathers to the eternal home where my fathers are. Bury me near Abraham, my father, in the cave of Machpelah in the field of Efron the Hittite which Abraham acquired for a burial place there." Isaac goes on commanding his sons to "perform righteousness and uprightness upon the earth so that the Lord will bring upon you everything which the Lord said that he would do for Abraham and for his seed." The physical unity of the "holy seed" corresponds here to its unity in righteousness.

[56] The notion of "holy seed" and its connection with righteousness in *Jubilees* and other Second Temple texts has been thoroughly investigated by Hayes, *Gentile Impurities*, 68–91. Cf. Satlow, *Jewish Marriage in Late Antiquity*, 140–47.

[57] See, for example, *Jub.* 35:14, where Rebecca predicts the destruction of Esau and his seed because he "has forsaken the God of Abraham and he has gone after his wives and after their defilement and after their errors, (both) he and his sons."

[58] *Jub.* 23:8–15. J. Kugel, "The Jubilees Apocalypse," *DSD* 1 (1994), 328–29, observes that this drop in longevity is already forewarned in Noah's testimony to his sons and grandsons (*Jub.* 7:20–21). In other words, the family's failure to observe ancestral laws results in such physical consequences as the decreased longevity of its new generations.

[59] *Jub.* 23:26–27. See Kugel, "Jubilees Apocalypse," 333–35, for discussion.

The decision by children to observe the law results in the increased span of their lifetimes. They return to the ways of their righteous forefathers, restoring harmony in the universe and within their families.[60]

According to *Jubilees* a pious family embodies the halakhah, while the halakhah constitutes a central dimension of this family's existence. The law is embodied through the practices of a family's ancestors and is transmitted as ancestral instruction in both oral and written form. The observance of the law vouchsafes the family's prosperity in the world and eventually leads to the eschatological transformation of the future. The family embodying the law constitutes itself as a "holy seed" through the generations, thus perpetuating the existence of its righteous ancestors. The transmission of the ancestral law (identified with the cosmic law of the heavenly tablets) constitutes the crucial part of a household's existence. On the other hand, the law is not detached from the family. It does not possess a quality of abstract legislation imposed from the outside. Rather, it is embodied and ensouled into a generational matrix of households.

Such an approach to halakhah in Second Temple Judaism is by no means limited to *Jubilees*, although this book gives us its most elaborate and extensive example. The *Testament of Levi* apparently originated in the same circles that produced the *Book of Jubilees*.[61] It reflects religious ideology similar to that of *Jubilees* and expresses it in almost the same literary and technical terms. It has been convincingly argued that the two texts indeed might have shared the same literary sources, slightly reworking them to fit their larger agendas.[62] The testimony of Abraham in *Jubilees*, with its technical discussion of the sacrificial system, finds a close parallel in Isaac's testimony to Levi in the *Testament of Levi*. The latter contains a fairly detailed and extensive review of sacrificial procedures communicated by Isaac to his grandson Levi as part of their ancestral family lore:

> When he knew that I was a priest of the Most High God, of the Lord of heaven, he began to command me and to teach me the law of the priesthood. And he said to me, "Levi, keep yourself pure, my son,

---

[60] The return is preceded by children's reproach of their immediate parents for failing to follow the law. See *Jub.* 23:16–17.

[61] On literary similarities between the two and their possible roots in a common "Levi-priestly tradition" see R. Kugler, *From Patriarch to Priest: The Levi Priestly Tradition from "Aramaic Levi" to "Testament of Levi"* (Atlanta: Scholars Press, 1996), 139–69.

[62] See Kugler, *From Patriarch to Priest*, 190–206.

from all uncleanness and from all sin. Your judgement is greater than that of all flesh. And now, my son, the true law I will show you, and I will not hide from you any word, so as to teach you the law of the priesthood."[63]

Isaac's instruction of Levi begins with an introduction promising to reveal to Levi "the law of the priesthood," also referred to as the "true law." This statement of intention introduces a lengthy section detailing various laws pertaining to Levi's priesthood. The first group of regulations has to do with the preservation of genealogical purity:

> First, keep yourself pure of all fornication and uncleanness, and of all harlotry. And you, take for yourself a wife from my family so that you will not defile your seed with harlots. For you are holy seed, and holy is your seed, like the holy place. For you are a holy priest called for all the seed of Abraham. You are near to [God], and near to all his holy ones. Now be pure in your flesh from all uncleanness of any man.[64]

The first requirements of priestly law thus have to do with the family purity of the priesthood. We encounter in this instruction an already familiar requirement to have endogamous marriage within one's extended family.[65] We also find here a reference to priests as the "holy seed." In *Jubilees*, it should be noted, this term applied to all patriarchs and their descendants. Now its application seems to be narrowed down to Levi and his children. The text also seems to compare the "holy seed" of Levi to the "holy place," most probably the temple. Similar to the temple that serves as a locus of holiness, the seed of the priestly family serves as a locus of holiness, preserving and transmitting it through generations. This state of holiness enables priests to maintain intimate relationships with God and the angelic hosts. The genealogical purity of the priesthood (expressed through endogamous marriages) serves to guarantee this sanctity of

---

[63] *Aram. Levi* 13–15. All translations of the *Aramaic Levi* are from Kugler, *From Patriarch to Priest*.

[64] *Aram. Levi* 16–18.

[65] Himmelfarb, "Levi, Phinehas, and the Problem of Intermarriage," 5, interprets this passage as requiring ordinary priests to marry within priesthood and prohibiting them from marrying Israelite women. This approach seems to derive from a peculiar exegesis of Lev 21:14, not shared by other Second Temple sources. Cf., for example, Philo, *Spec.* 1.110 and Josephus, *A.J.* 3.277. I would further suggest that *Aram. Levi*'s approach may reflect family halakhah of a particular priestly clan and its marriage regulations.

the seed. A properly built priestly family is essential for the adequate fulfillment of priestly tasks.

Isaac then proceeds to describe details of the sacrificial cult. He instructs Levi to wash his hands and feet before entering the temple or offering sacrifice. He further tells him to prepare wood for burning in a particular way:

> And offer split wood, but inspect it first for worms. And then offer it up, for thus I saw Abraham my father acting carefully. Of any of twelve kinds of wood he said to me that they are fitting for offering upon the altar, for their smoke rises up with a pleasant odor. These are their names: cedar, and juniper, and almond, and fir, and pine, and ash, and cypress, and fig, and oleaster, laurel, and myrtle, and asphaltos. These are those that he told me are fitting to offer up from them under the burnt offering upon the altar.[66]

This instruction tells us something about the nature of the entire "law of priesthood" transmitted by Isaac to Levi. It is an ancestral law of Levi's family transmitted and practiced from generation to generation by his forefathers. To explain his list of kinds of wood that can be burnt on the altar, Isaac cites the practice of his father Abraham, as well as his explicit instructions about what kinds of wood should be used. Both ancestral practices and ancestral instructions acquire an authoritative quality. The "true law" mentioned above emerges in this passage as the ancestral halakhah of Isaac's family, transmitted from father to son.[67] The family of patriarchs thus emerges as an embodiment of the "true law of the priesthood" just as it embodies the "holy seed" of Israel. Its practices acquire the status of the "law of the priesthood." Ancestral practice becomes the foundation of the halakhah of priestly families. In the Greek text of Mt. Athos, Isaac makes several more references to the tradition of Abraham:

> And now, my child, listen to my words and pay heed to my commandments, and let not these my words leave your heart all your days, for you are a holy priest of the Lord, and all your seed will be priests.

---

[66] *Aram. Levi* 22–25.

[67] The priestly law of *Aramaic Levi* differs in several important details from that of the Pentateuch. This may very well be a result of an independent priestly family tradition lying behind Levi's halakhah. On the differences see further Kugler, *From Patriarch to Priest*, 109–10.

And command your sons thus, so that they do according to this deter-
mination as I have shown you. For thus father Abraham commanded
me to do and to command my sons.[68]

The law of priesthood is transmitted from father to son. It is "owned"
by the seed of priests. Isaac commands Levi what his father Abraham
commanded him, and he expects Levi to impose the same requirements on his children. The transmission of ancestral halakhah takes
place through parental instruction of their children or through children's observance of their parents' practices. In both cases the family and its life serve as an embodiment of the law, lived by this
family's successive generations.[69]

On the other hand, like *Jubilees*, the *Testament of Levi* also emphasizes the importance of the written transmission of the ancestral
halakhah.[70] Later in his instruction to Levi, Isaac explains laws of
draining blood from slaughtered animals by referring to Abraham:

For thus my father Abraham commanded me, for thus he found in
the writing of the book of Noah concerning blood.[71]

As we have seen above, *Jubilees* recognizes two ways of transmission
of ancestral laws. One is the oral deathbed instruction of a patriarch to his children. The other takes place by means of ancestral
books passed down from generation to generation within the family. Indeed, in his instruction about details of the sacrificial cult in
Jub. 21, Abraham also refers to ancestral books of Enoch and Noah
as the source of his knowledge. Isaac does the same in the *Testament
of Levi*. Abraham's knowledge comes from what he has read in the
books of his forefathers. It is only logical, then, that in his own
farewell testimony, Levi instructs his children to "teach reading, and

---

[68] *Aram. Levi* 48–50.

[69] Scholars have duly noted parallels between the instruction of Isaac in *Aram.
Levi* and that of Abraham in *Jubilees* 21. Both of them deal with technical aspects
of the priesthood as well as with more general issues. For possible explanations of
this interdependence see Kugler, *From Patriarch to Priest*, 110–11. Cf. J. Kugel, "Levi's
Elevation to the Priesthood in Second Temple Writings," *HTR* 86 (1993), 17–19
and 54.

[70] Cf. Jaffee, *Torah in the Mouth*, 24: "The image of the scribal transmission of
the book from original dictation is ubiquitous. Testaments conveyed on the deathbeds
of the sons of Jacob were portrayed as having been transmitted orally to them and
preserved in scribal copies." Unfortunately, Jaffee does not sufficiently dwell on the
predominantly family setting of such transmissions.

[71] *Aram. Levi* 57.

writing, and instruction, and wisdom to your children."[72] Reading and writing are portrayed here as an essential part of one's wisdom, but the exhortation to study them appears in the form of oral testimony given by a father to his sons. Moreover, Levi appeals to the example of his brother Joseph, who "taught reading, and writing, and the instruction of wisdom" to corroborate his words.[73] The family continues to function in this instruction as a repository of wisdom. Children receive their training in wisdom from their fathers. The knowledge of wisdom is a "family business," a profession whose skills are transmitted within the household from one generation to another. In this respect, the mastery of wisdom mirrors that of priestly sacrificial skills and techniques. Both of them function as an ancestral halakhah preserved and transmitted through generations of the "holy seed" of chosen families.[74]

The Testament of Qahat discovered at Qumran reflects a very similar set of ideas:

> Now, my sons, be careful with the heritage that is handed over to you, which your fathers have given you. Do not give your heritage to strangers, and your inheritance to knaves so that you become humiliated and foolish in their eyes and they despise you, for, although sojourners among you, they will be your chiefs. So hold to the word of Jacob, your father, and seize the laws of Abraham and the righteousness of Levi and mine. And be holy and pure of all fornication in the community . . . And you will give me a good name among you, and a rejoicing to Levi, and joy to Jacob, delight to Isaac, and glory to Abraham, because you will keep and walk (in) the herit[age] which your fathers will have left you . . . and according to all that I will have taught you in truth from now until all [the age] . . .[75]

The Testament of Qahat specifically addresses priests, but it reflects the same basic set of ideas about family halakhah as *Jubilees* and the *Testament of Levi*.[76] Qahat urges his children to preserve their "her-

---

[72] *Aram. Levi* 88.

[73] *Aram. Levi* 90.

[74] Kugler, *From Patriarch to Priest*, 127 and 129–30 correctly observes that Levi praises the technical "secular" wisdom of scribes not explicitly associated with Torah. In his address, Levi emphasizes the importance of acquisition and transmission of professional skills within family.

[75] 4Q542 I, 4–II, 1. The translation is from G. Vermes, *The Complete Dead Sea Scrolls in English* (New York: Penguin Books, 1997), 532–33.

[76] On the Testament of Qahat, its date, and literary characteristics see É. Puech, "Le Testament de Qahat en araméen de la Grotte 4 (*4QTQah*)," *RevQ* 15 (1992), 23–54. The carbon 14 test places this document to as early as the third or maybe even fourth century BCE. Its composition clearly predates the Qumran sect itself.

itage" by not intermingling with strangers. In this case, however, the term "heritage" may refer not only to biological purity, but also to a body of laws and traditions that should not be disseminated among outsiders. These traditions are described as a family lore transmitted from generation to generation from the patriarchs down to Qahat and his children. They constitute the family's "heritage," a private possession not to be divulged to outsiders. After listing several moral maxims, our text continues:

> And now Amram, my son, I instruct you . . . and your sons to their sons. I instruct [you . . .] and they have given to Levi, my father, and Levi my father gave (them/it) to me . . . all my books in testimony that through them you should beware . . . [and that there should be] for you through them much merit when you walk in conformity with them.[77]

We encounter in this passage exactly the same set of ideas that we have already observed in *Jubilees* and in the *Testament of Levi*. Jewish halakhah emerges in this text as an instruction transmitted within the household from generation to generation. Similar to the two previous texts, Qahat transmits his testimony in both oral and written form. The latter comes as ancestral books received by Qahat from earlier generations of his forefathers. He instructs his son Amram to transmit them to his children as well.[78] Jewish law is thus portrayed as a family legal tradition passed down from fathers to sons and shielded from outsiders. The tradition is a "heritage," which should not be disseminated but rather kept and watched as the most valuable family property. The Testament does not mention the "holy seed" dimension of the family, but it is probably implied.

A number of Jewish texts from the Second Temple period envision family legal traditions as the prime means of transmitting halakhah. This halakhah includes various types of laws, out of which ceremonial law and family law are best attested in our sources. The law exists on two levels: the cosmic level of the heavenly tablets and the earthly level of family practices. The law practiced by pious families thus receives heavenly endorsement and the status of the universal and eternal law of the creation. On the other hand, this

---

[77] 4Q542 II, 10.

[78] According to *Jubilees* Amram taught his son Moses writing (*Jub.* 47:9). There is no explicit indication that Moses acquired his family tradition from Amram along with the art of writing, but this may be presupposed. See Najman, "Interpretation as Primordial Writing," 387–88.

heavenly law becomes embodied and ensouled in individual households through their successive generations. It can be transmitted
either in the form of written "books of the forefathers" or in the
form of oral deathbed instructions, or both. Eventually the idea of
a law being embodied in the practices of particular households contributed to the development of a priestly law transmitted within
priestly families and closed to outsiders. According to *Jubilees*, however, no distinction is made between the priestly law and a regular
law of Israel. Both traditions are transmitted through the generations of the patriarchs as part of their family halakhah. "The traditions of the forefathers" appear to be ancestral traditions preserved
and transmitted within individual families as part of their family lore.
At this stage halakhah does not exist as an abstract set of laws. It
is embodied through the everyday life of pious families in Israel.

Families and the Ancestral Law in the Epistle of Enoch

The author of *Jubilees* seems to make allusions to another pseudepigraphic text, known today as the Epistle of Enoch.[79] Indeed, the two
texts share elements of both form and content, and could be produced by like-minded groups within Judaism. That is why it would
be worthwhile to conclude our discussion of *Jubilees* by reviewing
data from the Epistle to see if it shares with *Jubilees* the same vision
of households and their role in shaping and transmitting halakhah.[80]
The Epistle of Enoch is introduced as an instruction of Enoch to
his sons in a way very similar to patriarchal instructions in *Jubilees*:

> Now, my son Methuselah, summon all your brothers on my behalf,
> and gather together to me all the sons of your mother. For a voice
> calls me, and the spirit is poured over me so that I may show you
> everything that shall happen to you forever. Then Methuselah went
> and summoned his brothers, and having summoned them to him, gath-

---

[79] See J. VanderKam, "Enoch Traditions in Jubilees and Other Second-Century
Sources," in idem, *From Revelation to Canon: Studies in the Hebrew Bible and Second Temple
Literature* (Boston: Brill, 2002), 305–31. Cf. J. Collins, *The Apocalyptic Imagination: An
Introduction to the Jewish Matrix of Christianity* (New York: Crossroad, 1984), 49, and
Nickelsburg, *Jewish Literature*, 150.

[80] On the literary structure of the Epistle and its complex editorial history see
Nickelsburg, *Jewish Literature*, 145–51, and J. VanderKam, *Enoch and the Growth of an
Apocalyptic Tradition* (Washington, D.C.: Catholic Biblical Association of America,
1984), 141–78.

ered his family together. Then he (Enoch) spoke to all of them, children of righteousness, and said, "Hear, all you children of Enoch, the talk of your father and listen to my voice in uprightness."[81]

Several other passages in the subsequent narrative indicate a family setting of Enoch's testimony, but none is more elaborate that the one just quoted. They include further elements resembling *Jubilees*. Thus, in addition to oral exhortation, Enoch is said to have written a book "for all the children that dwell upon the earth," containing "all the signs of wisdom among all the people."[82] The book may indeed be akin to the heavenly tablets, and Enoch is recounting from "books" during his review of Israelite history, known as the *Apocalypse of Weeks* and addressed, once again, to his children.[83] The theme of righteousness is equally present throughout Enoch's address. He exhorts his children to "love righteousness and walk therein."[84] In fact, his entire exhortation may be seen as an eschatological elaboration of the theme of righteousness and the respective rewards and punishments that await the righteous and the sinners after their death. As Dexinger has insightfully observed, the term "righteousness," both in the context of *Jubilees* and in the context of Enoch, has strong halakhic connotations and indeed may refer to the observance of the Jewish law, understood in a broad sense as incorporating moral righteousness as well.[85] Compared to *Jubilees*, however, the thrust of Enoch's exhortation is on eschatological reward and punishment. The Epistle shares many of *Jubilees'* literary tools but projects its message of righteousness and obedience to law forward into the eschaton, where the righteous receive their reward.[86] From our perspective, it is important to observe that both books construct their message as testimonies of patriarchs to their sons and thus firmly place them into a family setting. Religious instruction of either a halakhic or eschatological nature is passed on and received as the family lore of a righteous household.

---

[81] *1 En.* 91:1–3.
[82] *1 En.* 92:1.
[83] *1 En.* 93:1–2.
[84] *1 En.* 94:1.
[85] F. Dexinger, *Henochs Zehnwochenapokalypse und offene Probleme der Apokalyptikforschung* (Leiden: Brill, 1977), 178.
[86] See Nickelsburg, *Resurrection, Immortality, and Eternal Life*, 112–30, and "The Apocalyptic Message of 1 Enoch 92–105," *CBQ* 39 (1977), 309–28.

Unlike *Jubilees*, the Epistle of Enoch also produces a strongly articulated social message.[87] It seems to have a fairly specific group in mind, which it castigates as "sinners," although scholars have been debating the exact nature of that group. The prime characteristics of "sinners" include their conspicuous affluence, as well as their arrogance and the fact that they despise the "righteous." They "build their houses with sin" and "through the hard toil of others."[88] The building materials for their houses are "bricks and stones of sin."[89] Further accusations refer to gargantuan banquets, at which "sinners" "eat the best bread and drink wine in large bowls."[90] They have accumulated enormous riches and wear all kinds of jewelry.[91] As a whole, the Epistle repeatedly describes "sinners" as families rather than individuals. They are characterized as "houses" built with sin, which will ultimately be destroyed. Like the way in which pious households serve as embodiments of righteousness, households of sinners become embodiments of sin. In both cases the household emerges as the focus of exhortation and warning. The "sinners" are portrayed as affluent aristocratic families violating both religious law and laws of social justice. Indeed, unlike *Jubilees* with its emphasis on religious aspects of halakhah, the Epistle contains a strong social message. It almost appears that the religious transgressions of "sinners" (such as idolatry) are of secondary importance to the author.[92]

The ultimate destruction of the "sinners" is described as a fall of aristocratic families:

> In those days, the nations shall be confounded, and the families of the nations shall rise in the day of the destruction of the sinners. In those days, they (the women) shall become pregnant, but they (the sinners) shall come out and abort their infants and cast them out from their midst. They shall abandon their children, casting their infants out while

---

[87] See G. Nickelsburg, "Riches, the Rich and God's Judgement in *1 Enoch* 92–105 and the Gospel According to Luke," *NTS* 25 (1979), 324–32.

[88] *1 En.* 94:7–9 and 99:13. Nickelsburg, "Riches," 328, correctly interprets this text as referring to actual households, not allegories of general moral corruption.

[89] *1 En.* 99:13.

[90] *1 En.* 96:4–5.

[91] *1 En.* 98:1–3.

[92] Based on contemporaneous literary sources, Collins, *Jewish Wisdom*, 24–35, provides a vivid reconstruction of an affluent Jewish household and its ethos that might have served as an object of *Enoch*'s criticism. Cf. Tcherikover, *Hellenistic Civilization*, 117–51.

they are still suckling. They shall neither return to them (their babes) nor have compassion upon their beloved ones.[93]

In those days, the father will be beaten together with his sons, in one place. And brothers shall fall together with their friends in death, until a stream shall flow with their blood. For a man shall not be able to withhold his hands from his sons nor from (his) sons' sons in order to kill them. Nor is it possible for the sinner to withhold his hands from his honored brother. From dawn until the sun sets, they shall slay each other.[94]

The cosmic judgement is paralleled by catastrophic upheavals in this world. The destruction of the "sinners" is perceived as the destruction of their households. The author predicts internal strife and breakdown with the families of the "sinners" and describes them in vivid details. Only afterwards will the divine forces intervene to seal the judgement. Once again, the image of the family is crucial for the Epistle's description of the "sinners" and their fate. Just as righteousness is embodied in Enoch's family, sinfulness is embodied in the households of arrogant aristocrats. In both cases the focus is on families rather than individuals. In this respect, *Enoch* comes very close to *Jubilees*. Both texts envision the same social structure of the groups they either address or criticize. In both cases a family through its generations constitutes the prime manifestation and embodiment of either virtues or misdeeds, and it is the family as a whole that is either punished or rewarded. Indeed, similar to *Jubilees*, the Epistle at least once refers to the eternal destruction of the "seeds" of the wicked.[95]

Unlike *Jubilees*, the Epistle focuses most of its accusations on the unethical and socially oppressive behavior of its opponents. Their religious transgressions take a back seat to their social misdeeds. Still, there are indications that the families of "sinners" had their own understanding of Jewish law. At one point they are accused of "altering the words of truth and perverting the eternal law."[96] They also "invent fictitious stories and write out my (divine) Scriptures on the

---

[93] *1 En.* 99:5.

[94] *1 En.* 100:1–2.

[95] *1 En.* 108:3.

[96] *1 En.* 99:2. According to G. Nickelsburg, "The Epistle of Enoch and the Qumran Literature," *JJS* 33 (1982), 338, this polemic indicates that the opponents followed their own understanding of the Torah, not that they rejected the Law outright.

basis of their own words."[97] It looks like the "sinners" had their own halakhic traditions, which were in sharp disagreement with those of the Epistle's author.[98] The possible nature of these traditions may be gauged from the following accusation:

> Woe unto you who build your houses through the hard toil of others,
> And your building materials are bricks and stones of sin,
> I tell you, you have no peace.
> Woe unto you who reject the foundations and the eternal inheritance of your fathers!
> Who shall pursue after the wind—the idol;
> For there shall be no rest for you.[99]

The "sinners" are accused of building their houses with "bricks and stones of sin," while abandoning "foundations and the eternal inheritance of your fathers."[100] The text goes on to specify idolatry as a particular instance of such abandonment. It appears that the "sinners" substitute their own understanding of Jewish laws and practices for their ancestral traditions. The text implicitly contrasts two types of "houses:" one is built on the foundations of the "eternal inheritance of the fathers," the other is composed of "bricks and stones of sin." The "sinners" transformed their houses from one type into the other. Given the context, the text seems to be referring to the "fathers" in a sense of immediate physical ancestors. "Eternal inheritance of the fathers" probably designates here a religious tradition of a kind transmitted by Enoch to his sons. It serves to ensure their righteousness and salvation both in this world and in the eschatological future. It also has its heavenly double recorded in the heavenly tablets. As we have observed above, the "sinners" bend it to meet their ends by "inventing fictitious stories and rewriting the

---

[97] *1 En.* 104:10–11. Cf. Nickelsburg, "Epistle of Enoch," 342, for a similar interpretation of this passage as referring to "some kind of tendentious rewriting of the Torah." Contrast J. Milik, *The Books of Enoch* (Oxford: Clarendon Press, 1976), 50. He sees this passage as a reference to the Hellenistic historians tampering with biblical history.

[98] Nickelsburg, "Epistle of Enoch," 334–43, correctly emphasizes conflict between two Jewish groups and their respective interpretations of the Torah as background of the Epistle. See esp. p. 337 for parallels with groups described in the Pesher Nahum (on which see below).

[99] *1 En.* 99:13–14.

[100] Nickelsburg's interpretation of this passage emphasizes the cosmic and eternal aspect of the debate and misses its possible sociological implications. See Nickelsburg, "Epistle of Enoch," 339–40.

Scriptures on the basis of their own words." They invent their own ancestral lore for their houses, which will eventually destroy them.

The "eternal inheritance of the fathers" thus refers to family traditions transmitted through generations of physical descendants and manifested through everyday existence of righteous households. The reference to righteous individuals is noticeably absent in these descriptions. The law is embodied through the corporate life of the family in its successive generations, not through the lives of individual pietists. It is the "seed" that ultimately is either damned or saved in eternity. This understanding of the "eternal inheritance of the fathers" is remarkably similar to the concept of ancestral halakhah recorded in *Jubilees*. In both cases it provides theological background for patriarchs' testimonies to their sons as a key mode of halakhic transmission, and for the centrality of the natural family as social matrix of righteousness.

Conclusions: The Law and the Plant of Righteousness

It would be appropriate to conclude our discussion by revisiting the whole concept of the "plant of righteousness" and its use in *Jubilees*, the Epistle of Enoch, and the Damascus Document. Following an earlier discussion by Dexinger,[101] Philip Davies has persuasively argued for strong halakhic connotations of the term "plant of righteousness" and variations thereof. He observes that the way in which the term "righteousness" (*zdk*) is used in *Jubilees* and some texts from the Enochic corpus "may suggest that *zdk* by itself denotes law, having the law and (righteously) obeying it being undifferentiated."[102] The same is true for the Damascus Document. Davies further observes that "plant" in this context "denotes Israel as settled in its soil, its land." The "plant of righteousness" thus denotes Israel settled in its land and observing the law, i.e., being righteous.[103]

I would like to take Dexinger's and Davies' argument one step further and to maintain that the term "plant of righteousness" may specifically refer to pious families embodying the law of Israel through

---

[101] Dexinger, *Zehnwochenapokalypse*, 178.
[102] P. Davies, *Behind the Essenes: History and Ideology in the Dead Sea Scrolls* (Atlanta: Scholars Press, 1987), 130.
[103] Davies, *Behind the Essenes*, 131.

their practices and lives. In its review of Israelite history *Jubilees* promises to "transplant them as a righteous plant," apparently, in the sense of restoring Israel in its land.[104] A similar but somewhat more specific statement appears in CD: "He caused a plant root to spring from Israel and Aaron to inherit His land and to prosper on the good things on His earth."[105] This text can be understood in the light of the following verse from the Apocalypse of Weeks:

> And at its (sixth week's) completion the house of the kingdom shall be burnt with fire. And therein the whole clan of the chosen root shall be dispersed.[106]

Whereas the Apocalypse of Weeks talks about the destruction of the First Temple and subsequent exile of Israelites, CD appears to refer to the restoration of Israel in its land. Family connotations of "plant" and "root" are vague and implicit in CD. But they become fairly explicit in the Apocalypse of Weeks with its reference to the "clan of the chosen root." Moreover, in the Apocalypse "the clan of the chosen root" probably corresponds to the references to Abraham as "the plant of the righteous judgement" and to Jacob as "the eternal plant of righteousness" appearing in the description of the third and fourth weeks.[107] "The clan of the chosen root" thus refers to their descendants. In fact, Enoch himself begins his review of the Weeks by the following address to his children:

> Concerning the children of righteousness, concerning the elect ones of the world, and concerning the plant of truth, I will speak these things, my children.[108]

It is not immediately clear if Enoch's children and their descendants are also included in the "plant of truth," but they probably are. What Enoch tells them amounts to a history of their family for generations to come. This may explain the prominence of the "plant of righteousness" image throughout the narrative.

---

[104] *Jub.* 1:16.

[105] CD I, 7–9. Cf. 1QS VIII, 4 where the term "eternal planting" designates an eschatological community without apparent family implications. This may be later development of this term parallel to that of *bene Zadoq* in the same document. It is possible that the latter also gradually lost its family-specific connotations and came to designate communal leadership in general. See Davies, *Behind the Essenes*, 51–72.

[106] *1 En.* 93:8.

[107] *1 En.* 93:5.

[108] *1 En.* 93:2.

Jubilees further develops the family connotations of the term "plant of righteousness." Abraham concludes his exhortation to Isaac to observe the law by promising that God "will raise up from you a righteous plant in all the earth throughout all the generations of the earth."[109] The "plant" here clearly refers to Abraham's posterity and serves as a substitute for the "seed."[110] The observance of the ancestral law is the essential prerequisite for this plant to flourish. Isaac makes a similar statement in his farewell testimony:

> Remember, my sons, the Lord, the God of Abraham, your father, and (that) I subsequently worshipped and served Him in righteousness and joy so that He might multiply you and increase your seed like the stars of heaven with regard to number and (so that) He will plant you on the earth as a righteous planting which will not be uprooted for all the eternal generations.[111]

Our texts demonstrate a remarkable consistency in using the term "plant of righteousness." In all of them it seems to symbolize a righteous family embodying the law through its life and practices. The term encapsulates the intimate relationship between the law (understood as righteousness) and households fulfilling it and transmitting it through generations. It also adds a new dimension to the notion of the "holy seed" so prominent in the Second Temple literature. The holy seed of Israel is transmitted within families along with the law. In fact, the two are interrelated, and their combination constitutes the "plant of righteousness:" Jewish households embodying the cosmic law through their lives and their posterity.

---

[109] *Jub.* 21:24. Cf. Noah's address to his children: "And now, my children, hear (and) do justice and righteousness so that you might be planted in righteousness on the surface of the whole earth" (*Jub.* 7:34).

[110] Cf. *Jub.* 21:22 and 25.

[111] *Jub.* 36:6.

CHAPTER THREE

HOUSEHOLDS AND SOCIAL STRUCTURE
OF THE DEAD SEA SECT

The Dead Sea sect has long been viewed by scholars as an example of a ritual, study, and observance-centered community, which provided for its members a new corporate identity surpassing (or even supplanting) natural kinship ties. The Dead Sea sect forged a new identity based on commonality of spiritual aspirations and halakhic observances. It pushed aside the traditional framework of allegiances to the people of Israel or one's natural family. Instead, "the children of light" isolated themselves both physically (by moving into the Judaean desert) and spiritually (by lumping everyone else into the "children of Belial" category destined to eternal damnation). The new community was formed around the combination of elaborate purity laws, study of sacred texts (of which the group claimed unique understanding), and regular public gatherings for meals, decision-making, or ritual ceremonies. The entire lifestyle of the community served to actualize sanctity here and now, although its members were eagerly expecting the final days when the entire universe would be transformed in accordance with their vision of the sacred. For the meantime, however, they withdrew to the desert to embody as a community the realm of purity and true understanding otherwise abandoned by the rest of Israel.[1]

At least some rule books found at Qumran seem to corroborate this picture. The Community Rule (1QS) portrays a group of people existing in relative isolation from the surrounding world.[2] In the course of their acceptance into the community, individuals gradually merged their property with that of the community. It remains unclear

---

[1] On realized eschatology and apocalyptic expectations in the Dead Sea scrolls see John Collins, "Apocalypticsm and Literary Genre in the Dead Sea Scrolls," in P. Flint and J. VanderKam eds., *The Dead Sea Scrolls After Fifty Years: A Comprehensive Assessment* (Leiden: Brill, 1999), vol. 2, 403–30.

[2] For summary and discussion see M. Knibb, "Rule of the Community," in L. Schiffman and J. VanderKam, *Encyclopedia of the Dead Sea Scrolls* (Oxford: Oxford University Press, 2000), vol. 2, 793–97.

how much of private ownership was retained during this process, but the communal use and sharing of property was clearly perceived as the norm. The communal sharing of possessions reflected the centrality of corporate identity within the group. Shared public meals and public sessions held to study sacred writings also served to cement ties among the members of the community and to develop a common identity different from natural kinship ties. Interestingly, the Community Rule contains no references to celibacy (but neither does it mention marriage or regulate for married couples). Still, unlike other texts produced by the sect, such as Damascus Document or 1QSa Messianic Rule, 1QS does not envision the family as the basic building block within the community. Instead, as John Collins has observed, membership "is achieved by a free act of adults."[3] The community of 1QS is constituted by adult (male?) individuals, not families.

Shaye Cohen has described Second Temple sectarianism as "the culmination of the democratization of Judaism" and has connected it with "the breakdown of the belief in corporate responsibility and the emergence of a doctrine of theodicy based on the individual."[4] On the social level this process mirrored "the breakdown of the tribe into the clan and the clan into the family." It also reflected the religious doctrines of the period that "treated the individual not merely as a member of a family, clan, or nation, but as an independent being whose ultimate reward and punishment depended on his or her own deeds alone." Cohen further identifies this development with social changes in the Greek and Roman period that took place predominantly in Hellenistic urban settings.[5] In other words, he tends to see the Second Temple Jewish sect as the source of a new corporate identity for an individual surpassing (or even supplanting) that of one's natural kinship ties. The Community Rule corresponds to this picture of a Second Temple Jewish sect in many important ways. It regulates the life of a community composed of adult (male?) individuals exercising free will in joining the community and taking upon themselves obligations and restrictions that come with their choice.

---

[3] See Collins, *Apocalyptic Imagination*, 118.

[4] Cohen, *From the Maccabees to the Mishnah*, 115–16. Cf. A. Nock, *Conversion: The Old and the New in Religion from Alexander the Great to Augustine of Hippo* (Baltimore: Johns Hokins University Press, 1998), 99–121.

[5] Cohen, *From the Maccabees to the Mishnah*, 116. Cf. A. Baumgarten, "Graeco-Roman Voluntary Associations and Ancient Jewish Sects" in M. Goodman, ed., *Jews in a Graeco-Roman World* (Oxford: Clarendon Press, 1998), 93–111.

Natural kinship ties are absent throughout the document. They are replaced by ties forged and maintained among individual members of the community. These members form a new corporate entity designed to embody and preserve sanctity and true knowledge in expectation of the last days. Moshe Weinfeld correctly noticed the profoundly Hellenistic nature of the group portrayed in the Manual, when he compared its structure and functioning to those of Hellenistic voluntary associations.[6] Both types fit Cohen's description of individualized religious experience that takes over the Hellenistic world and requires new organizational forms for its expression. Thus, despite its explicit particularism, the group portrayed in 1QS represents a profoundly *Hellenistic* phenomenon.[7] In this respect it marks a new stage compared to the Damascus Document or Messianic Rule with their emphasis on the household as the prime building block within the sect.

In other words, the Dead Sea sect appears to be our first unambiguous example of the transition from family-based groups to Hellenistic associations uniting like-minded individuals. Documents produced by the sect reflect both social forms. I shall argue below that this transition was caused by a basic shift in the "holiness discourse" of the sectarians. Whereas the more traditional framework of family alliances envisioned the household and its everyday life as prime embodiments of sanctity, the new association-type movement perceived the community of adult (male?) individuals bound together by the shared notion of religious truth and salvation as the main depository of holiness. As a result, natural families were no longer part of the religiously meaningful universe. The sectarians could very well continue to marry (I shall argue that there is no evidence that 1QS envisioned an all-celibate community), but their households were

---

[6] See M. Weinfeld, *The Organizational Pattern and the Penal Code of the Qumran Sect: A Comparison with Guilds and Religious Associations of the Hellenistic-Roman World* (Fribourg: Editions Universitaires; Göttingen: Vandenhoeck & Ruprecht, 1986), 10–47. Cf. B. Dombrowski, "היחד in 1QS and τὸ κοινόν: An Instance of Early Greek and Jewish Synthesis," *HTR* 59 (1966), 293–307 and M. Klinghardt, "The Manual of Discipline in the Light of Statutes of Hellenistic Associations," in M. Wise et al., eds., *Methods of Investigation of the Dead Sea Scrolls and the Khirbet Qumran Site: Present Realities and Future Prospects* (New York: The New York Academy of Sciences, 1994), 251–67 for similar observations.

[7] On Hellenistic literary characteristics of some documents from Qumran see Shaye Cohen, "Hellenism in Unexpected Places," in J. Collins and G. Sterling, eds., *Hellenism in the Land of Israel* (Notre Dame: University of Notre Dame Press, 2001), 217–23.

no longer positively charged as religiously meaningful social units. They became religiously neutral. This shift in the perception of holiness would eventually bring about much more radical forms of non-familial piety, including probable celibacy of some groups within the larger Dead Sea movement. It is possible, as many scholars have suggested, that celibate groups within the sect represented the spiritual "elite" of the movement, whereas its other members were perceived as following less rigid rules. In this case, the crystallization of such an "elite" was part of a sociological transformation of the movement that reflected the shift in its focus from family-based to individualized spirituality and religiosity. In terms of phenomenology, however, the Dead Sea sect in its multiple forms of religious identity represents the first clear example of transition from a family-based matrix of Jewish sectarianism to a much more individualized and Hellenized type of voluntary association.[8]

Families and the Sectarian "Myth of Origins"

I shall begin our discussion by arguing that like other Jewish religious movements of the time, the Dead Sea sect started as an alliance of several households wedded to a particular interpretation of Jewish law. During the early period of its existence households constituted the main building blocks within this movement. From a sociological perspective the structure of the early Dead Sea sect was not much different from that of Ezra-Nehemiah's group or from the groups envisioned in *Jubilees* and other related texts. Only later would more utopian "association-like" elements become increasingly prominent, reflecting profound changes in the identity and mentality of the group.

The Damascus Document provides a number of clues pertaining to the way in which the Dead Sea sect perceived its own structure. The first part of this text contains a schematized history of the movement, describing its place within the larger covenantal history of the people of Israel. The latter is understood as a sequence of acts of

---

[8] On Hellenistic voluntary associations see Stephen G. Wilson, "Voluntary Associations: An Overview," in J. Kloppenborg and S. Wilson, *Voluntary Associations in the Graeco-Roman World*, 1–15.

disobedience caused by "the thoughts of a guilty inclination and eyes of lust":

> Because they walked in the stubbornness of their heart the Heavenly
> Watchers fell. They were caught because they did not keep the com-
> mandments of God. And their sons also fell who were tall as cedar
> trees and whose bodies were like mountains ... Through it, the chil-
> dren of Noah went astray, together with their kin, and were cut off.
> Abraham did not walk in it, and he was accounted a friend of God
> because he kept the commandments of God and did not choose his
> own will. And he handed them down to Isaac and Jacob, who kept
> them, and were recorded as friends of God and party to the Covenant
> for ever. The children of Jacob strayed through them and were pun-
> ished in accordance with their error. And their sons in Egypt walked
> in the stubbornness of their hearts, conspiring against the command-
> ments of God and each of them doing that which seemed right in his
> own eyes. They ate blood, and He cut off their males in the wilderness.[9]

The text depicts the covenantal history of Israel as a history of families, which either obeyed or (more often) disobeyed the covenant.
Watchers appear along with their sons. The sons of Noah and their
families went astray. Abraham, Isaac and Jacob obeyed the covenant,
whereas Jacob's sons and his grandchildren did not. The family or
clan appears to be a major subject of the covenant, and the sum
total of such clans constitutes Israel. They can either obey the covenant
or go astray, thus causing their own destruction. This story sets the
stage for the subsequent portions of the Damascus Document with
its focus on the "new covenant" and the covenant's proper observance. The story may reflect a sectarian understanding of the social
makeup of groups, which either observed or broke the covenant.
The same interest in an individual family/clan as a basic unit within
the sect repeats itself over and over again throughout the Damascus
Document.[10]

A parallel vision of Israelite history as a history of families that
either observed or broke the covenant emerges from *Jubilees*. The
Damascus Document's list of disobedient Israelite families finds its

---

[9] CD II, 18–III, 7. The translations of the Dead Sea Scrolls are from G. Vermes,
The Complete Dead Sea Scrolls in English (New York: Penguin Books, 1997) and have
been revised when necessary.

[10] P. Davies, *The Damascus Covenant* (Sheffield: JSOT Press, 1983), 76–83, notices
the centrality of genealogy for this part of the CD. He further draws a promising
parallel with the *Book of Jubilees* and its interest in genealogies as means for orga-
nizing historical narrative.

parallel in *Jubilees*' recurrent references to the families that throughout Israelite history failed to follow the covenant and were wiped out as a result. In his deathbed testimony to his children Noah explains the causes of the flood in the following way:

> For on account of these three the Flood came upon the earth. For (it was) because of the fornication with which the Watchers, apart from the mandate of their authority, fornicated with the daughters of men and took for themselves wives from all whom they chose and made a beginning of impurity. And they begat sons, the Naphidim (sic), and all of them were dissimilar. And each one ate his fellow.[11]

Noah goes on to describe all kinds of injustice and crimes committed by the giants and concludes with God's decision to "blot out everything from the face of the earth on account of the evil of their deeds."[12] The failure to observe proper marital laws led to the destruction of the offspring of the Watchers. The most heinous crime the Watchers committed was against the integrity and propriety of family life. It led to the destruction of their seed.

The improper family union also led to the destruction of Lot's posterity:

> And he and his daughters also committed sins upon the earth which were not (committed) on the earth since the days of Adam until his time because the man lay with his daughters. And behold it is commanded and it is engraved concerning all of his seed in the heavenly tablets so that that he will remove them and uproot them and execute their judgement just like the judgement of Sodom and so that he will not leave seed of man for him on the earth in the day of judgement.[13]

Illicit sexual unions and relationships within the family result in the destruction of that family's seed from the face of the earth. The story depicts Lot's family and its practices as the root cause for its ultimate failure, just as it will describe the righteous families of the patriarchs and their children as the quintessential people of Israel. The entire history of *Jubilees* is dominated by the notion that the family is the key social and religious unit within Israel. The family is indeed described as the matrix of religious life and observance of the law. Improper marriage practices destroy the very space in which

---

[11] *Jub.* 7:21–22.
[12] *Jub.* 7:25.
[13] *Jub.* 16:8–9.

the Law should be performed. This becomes especially clear from the story of Esau. When Rebecca encourages Jacob to make a proper marriage with a wife "from my father's house and my father's kin," she cites Esau as a negative example:

> My son, do not take for yourself a wife from the daughters of Canaan as (did) Esau your brother, who took for himself two wives from the daughters of Canaan. And they have embittered my soul with all their impure deeds, because all of their deeds (are) fornication and lust. And there is no righteousness with them because (their deeds are) evil.[14]

As Dexinger and Davies have convincingly demonstrated, the term "righteousness" in *Jubilees* refers specifically to the observance of Jewish law.[15] The family thus emerges as the key unit that enables one to be righteous, i.e., to fully follow halakhic requirements. Indeed, as we shall see later, according to *Jubilees* the righteous family and its life and practices ensoul and embody the Jewish law in this world. On the other hand, improper marriage destroys any hope that the law will be observed, precisely because it destroys the prime social body ensouling the law: the family. Proper family design thus acquires an almost eschatological significance. The ultimate fate of Esau's family will be eternal destruction, as his father Isaac predicts:

> And neither he nor his seed is to be saved, for they will be destroyed from the earth and they will be uprooted from under the heaven, since he has forsaken the God of Abraham and he has gone after his wives and after their defilement and after their errors, (both) he and his sons.[16]

The fate of Esau's family is going to be the same as the fate of the giants and the children of Lot. Because of their failure to construct families according to the Law, all of them are doomed. The account in *Jubilees* tends to see the entire Israelite history through the prism of whether families followed the law or did not. The historical section of CD reflects a similar approach. The history of Israel is described as a sequence of households that either followed the law or strayed and were ultimately destroyed. In both cases, the family is perceived as the main building block in the religious history of Israel.

---

[14] *Jub.* 25:1.
[15] Dexinger, *Zehnwochenapokalypse*, 178, and Davies, *Behind the Essenes*, 130.
[16] *Jub.* 35:14.

CD's historical introduction about Israel's response to the divine covenant is brought to its conclusion by the account of the origins of the sect itself:

> As God ordained for them by the hand of the Prophet Ezekiel, saying: "The Priests, the Levites, and the sons of Zadok who kept the charge of my sanctuary when the children of Israel strayed from me, they shall offer me fat and blood" (Ezek 44:15). The "Priests" are the converts of Israel who departed from the land of Judah, and [the "Levites"] are those who joined them. The "sons of Zadok" are the elect of Israel, the men called by name who shall stand at the end of days. Behold the exact list of their names according to their genealogies (הנה פרוש שמותיהם לתולדותם) and the time when they lived, and the number of their trials, and the years of their sojourn, and the exact list of their deeds.[17]

The depiction of the sect itself thus follows the same pattern: it is typologically depicted as a group of priestly and levitical families who were chosen to carry out the true covenant with God in the "age of iniquity." This group is supposed to be listed "according to its genealogies" in apparent resemblance to the genealogies of families entering the renewed covenant in the books of Ezra and Nehemiah.[18] CD III, 21–IV, 6 has been sometimes taken to indicate that the Zadokite priestly family constituted the basis of the nascent Dead Sea movement.[19] However, it can also indicate that there was a group of families (clans) that typologically associated themselves with righteous priestly families of Ezekiel (Levites, priests, and the sons

---

[17] CD III, 21–IV, 6.

[18] See Davies, *Damascus Covenant*, 93–94, for parallels between the group described in the CD and "the Congregation of the Exile" of Ezra-Nehemiah. He emphasizes the notion of exilic origins crucial for the identity of both groups as well as their Zadokite ideology. For the genealogical list see his commentaries on pp. 95–96. Davies does not associate it with the genealogies of Chronicles, Ezra and Nehemiah; moreover he explicitly claims that "the group is constituted not by descent but by membership in a covenant." Contrast J. Murphy-O'Connor, "An Essene Missionary Document? CD II,14–VI,1," *RB* 77 (1970), 201–229, and "The Damascus Document Revisited," *RB* 92 (1985), 232. He sees this list as an actual genealogy and correlates it with the genealogies of Ezra. Notice that CD XIV, 3–6 contains actual provisions for a census (mustering ceremony).

[19] See L. Schiffman, *The Halakhah at Qumran* (Leiden: Brill, 1975), 70–75, and *Reclaiming the Dead Sea Scrolls* (Philadelphia: JPS, 1994), 113–17, for summary and discussion. Cf. also F. Cross, *The Ancient Library of Qumran and Modern Biblical Studies* (Garden City: Doubleday, 1958), 95–119, and J. Liver, "The 'Sons of Zadok the Priests' in the Dead Sea Sect," *RevQ* 6 (1967), 3–30.

of Zadok).[20] In any case, the history of the sect is described as the story of righteous families joining together to perform "deeds of holiness." Genealogical lists play a key role in the self-definition of the sect.[21]

CD VI, 14–VII, 6 contains stipulations of the covenant made between God and the sect. Those include among other things the requirement "to seek the peace of his brother and not commit sin against his blood relation, to refrain from fornication in accordance with the regulation."[22] Proper relationships within one's family and more specifically conduct "in accordance with the regulation" are thus perceived as the essential part of the covenant.[23] The text picks up a couple verses later:

> And if they live in camps according to the rule of the Land,[24] marrying[25] and begetting children, they shall walk according to the Law and according to the statute concerning binding vows, according to the rule of the Law which says, "Between a man and his wife and between a father and his son" (Num 30:17). And all those who despise shall be rewarded with the retribution of the wicked when God shall visit the Land, when the saying shall come to pass which is written[26] among the words of the Prophet Isaiah son of Amoz: "He will bring upon you, and upon your people, and upon your father's house, days such as have not come since the day that Ephraim departed from Judah" (Isa 7:17).[27]

This text clearly envisions individual households as the main unit within the sect, as well as the main unit within groups opposed to it. If the life of an individual household is organized "according to

---

[20] For a more skeptical approach cf. Davies, *Behind the Essenes*, 51–72, and R. Kugler, "Priesthood at Qumran" in Flint and VanderKam, *The Dead Sea Scrolls after Fifty Years*, vol. 2, 93–116.

[21] CD XIV, 3–6 appears to be ranking members of the community according to their genealogical descent: the priests, the levites, the children of Israel, and the proselytes. Each group shall be "inscribed by their names, each one after his brother" (ויכתבו בשמותיהם איש אחר אחיהו). For a similar system of ranking in early rabbinic Judaism and its dependence upon genealogy see Satlow, *Jewish Marriage in Antiquity*, 147–56.

[22] Cf. 4Q269 4 ii.

[23] Contrast CD VIII, 5–6 (= 4Q266 3 iv) where sins against one's near kin are singled out as one of the gravest transgressions against the covenant.

[24] MS B adds: "as it was from ancient times."

[25] MS B adds: "according to the custom of the Law."

[26] MS B continues with an entirely different eschatological pronouncement based on Zech 13:7.

[27] CD VII, 6–12. See Davies, *Damascus Covenant*, 125–42, for discussion of this section of the CD.

the regulation of the teachings," it "shall live a thousand generations." If not, the household will be destroyed. Proper relationships between members of a household are seen as the essential component of the covenant. In fact, most of the covenantal regulations mentioned in CD VI, 14–VII, 6 might have had a household setting. Once again, one is reminded of the community established by Ezra and Nehemiah and the central role that individual households and their proper halakhic behavior played there. Structurally, the social makeup of the Dead Sea sect in its initial stages appears to have been very similar to that of the groups formed by Ezra and Nehemiah.[28] It would be only later that the social fabric of the sect evolved into a more "utopian" type of community, as reflected in the Community Rule and other related documents.

As a whole, the historical section of the Damascus Document provides interesting insights into the social structure of the Dead Sea sect as seen by the sectarians themselves. It also may portray the covenantal history of Israel from the perspective of a second-century BCE clan-based sectarian movement. In both cases a group of individual households/families is seen as a main operational force either in keeping or breaking the covenant. The essential part of the covenant includes regulations dealing with the internal life of these families and their proper conduct. Such a depiction perfectly corresponds to the way in which Qumran texts describe their sectarian opponents as groups of families following "wrong" interpretations of the law. It also corresponds to the description of the "proto-sectarian" group created by Ezra and Nehemiah in the fifth century BCE. In other words, the Dead Sea texts demonstrate remarkable consistency in depicting contemporaneous sects as halakhically determined alliances of families. We shall turn now to the accounts detailing the inner structure of the Dead Sea sect.

The Rule of the Congregation (the document deemed to describe the Qumran community in the eschatological times)[29] repeatedly

---

[28] For connections between the early Dead Sea movement and the Jewish community formed in the Exile see further J. Murphy-O'Connor, "The Essenes and Their History," *RB* 81 (1974), 215–44, and "The Essenes in Palestine," *BA* 40 (1977), 100–124. For more recent discussion cf. J. Campbell, "Essene-Qumran Origins in Exile: A Scriptural Basis?" *JJS* 46 (1995), 143–56. None of these studies, however, compares the social structures of the two movements.

[29] The text appears as an appendix to the *Community Rule*. It was published in D. Barthelemy and J. Milik, *Qumran Cave I* (Oxford: Clarendon Press, 1955), 107–30, and identified as a rule for the eschatological community. For the eschatological

refers to the group called "chiefs of the clans of the congregation" (שרי אבות העדה or ראשי אבות העדה).[30] They are described as judges and military commanders, participating in communal gatherings and finally attending the messianic banquet. "Clans (or families) of Israel" constitute according to this text a major component within the eschatological community. These texts indicate that the Dead Sea community was composed of individual clans and/or households. Unfortunately, nothing can be said conclusively about the social makeup of these households. Still, the reference to their heads as eschatological judges and military leaders may indicate that they possessed high status within the society of their own time as well.

In fact, the Rule of the Congregation repeatedly stresses the function of individual households as the main building blocks within the sect.[31] The document describes the sect as a community that gathers to "walk in accordance with the regulation of the sons of Zadok, the priests, and the men of the covenant, who have turned away from the path of the people."[32] The Rule sets the following procedure for the (eschatological?) public gathering of the sect:

> When they come, they shall assemble all those who come, including children and women, and they shall read into their ears all the regulations of the covenant, and shall instruct them in all its precepts, so that they do not stray in their [errors].

The text envisions a public assembly in which sectarians participate along with their families. All members of the family, including women and children, are instructed in the sectarian interpretation of the

---

nature of the document see further L. Schiffman, *The Eschatological Community of the Dead Sea Scrolls* (Atlanta: Scholars Press, 1989). In recent years, H. Stegemann has suggested to see the text as "an early rule book of the Essenes" rather than an eschatological document. See H. Stegemann, "Some Remarks to 1QSa, to 1QSb, and to Qumran Messianism," *RevQ* 17 (1996), 479–505. Cf. C. Hempel, "The Earthly (sic) Essene Nucleus of 1QSa," *DSD* 3 (1996), 253–67. According to her conclusions 1QSa represents a "piece of communal legislation that goes back to the Essene parent movement of the Qumran community." For critical discussion of this hypothesis see J. Collins, "Forms of Community in the Dead Sea Scrolls," in S. Paul et al., ed., *Emanuel: Studies in Hebrew Bible, Septuagint and Dead Sea Scrolls in Honor of Emanuel Tov* (Leiden: Brill, 2003), 107–10.

[30] 1QSa I, 16 and 23, II, 14–16.

[31] See Stegemann, "Some Remarks," 487–88, who describes 1QSa as "a third rule book copied in the same scroll as 1QS but addressed to married people like CD." Cf. Hempel, "Earthly Essene Nucleus," 262–66.

[32] 1QSa I, 1–5.

law, which is apparently referred to above as the "regulation of the sons of Zaddok." This provision is remarkably similar to the description of Nehemiah 8–10, according to which entire families participated in the covenant renewal ceremonies. The ceremonies also included public reading and interpretation of the law.[33] Thus the document takes an entire family and not just its male adult members to be members of the sect.[34] This agrees with the requirement of CD XV, 5–6 that "whoever enters the covenant, for all Israel for an eternal law, he must impose upon his sons, who belong to those who are enrolled, the oath of the covenant." The text envisions a family rather than an individual as a subject of the covenant. Such an approach imposes particular requirements on the head of the family to ensure compliance of his nearest kin with the covenant and its demands.[35]

In the subsequent description of children's education in traditions of the sect, the Rule of the Congregation spells out the crucial importance of the family as a basic social unit within this movement. When they were still young, children had to be indoctrinated in the principles of the covenant and its regulations.[36] At age of twenty a young man joins the community:

> At the age of twenty years [he shall be enrolled], that he may enter upon his allotted duties in the midst of his family (בתוך משפחתו) (and) be joined to the holy congregation. He shall not [approach] a woman to know her by lying with her before he is fully twenty years old, when he shall know [good] and evil. And thereafter, he shall be

---

[33] Schiffman, *The Eschatological Community*, 13, also draws a parallel between the gathering stipulated by 1QSa and covenant renewal ceremonies described in the Bible, including Nehemiah 9–10. However, he does not single out the latter as a special case. Cf. Weinfeld, *The Organizational Pattern and the Penal Code of the Qumran Sect*, 46–47, esp. n. 229. He observes the covenant renewal in Nehemiah 8–10 "is no different from the rite of initiation into the covenant in the Manual of Discipline."

[34] Schiffman, *The Eschatological Community*, 17, compares the structure and public status of the family in 1QSa to those of priestly families described in the Bible. He specifically mentions the laws governing the utilization of *terumot* or priestly dues. Female members of the household (and children under the age of twenty) were members of the sect by virtue of the status of their male relatives, just as women of priestly families had certain rights by virtue of belonging to a priest's household.

[35] Hempel, "Earthly Essene Nucleus," 260–69, observes that our text "shows a number of important common features with the CD which point to a similar social setting." Those include use of term עדה (congregation) and "all Israel", exclusion of physically disabled people, references to the Book of Hagu and regulations for family life.

[36] 1QSa I, 6–8.

accepted when he calls to witness the judgements of the Law, and
shall be (allowed) to assist at the hearing of judgements.[37]

The text seems to imply that the acceptance of a young man as a
full-fledged member of the congregation coincides with his becoming an independent head of his own household. The heads of households constituted the leadership of the community, and so one's status
within the communal structures corresponded to his status within a
household. A man's status in the society was conditioned upon his
marital status and his ability to establish and maintain his own family. Only the head of a household could be considered a full-fledged
member of the sect. The administrative structure of the sect was
intimately bound to the structure of the households constituting it.
The Rule of the Congregation explicitly identifies people who supervise key administrative and judicial functions within the sect as "heads
of households":

> And every head of family in the congregation (וכול רשי אבות העדה)
> who is chosen to hold office, [to go] and come before the congrega-
> tion, shall strengthen his loins that he may perform his tasks among
> his brethren in accordance with his understanding and the perfection
> of his way. According to whether this is great or little, so shall one
> man be honored more than another.[38]

Later on, the document states that in the case of a simpleton, unfit
for public service in the congregation, "his family shall inscribe him
in the army register and he shall do his service in the forced labor
to the extent of his ability."[39] He does not acquire a standing of his
own, and is still treated as a subservient member of his father's
household, just as he is considered a second-rate member of the sect.

   All these texts assign to the family a primary role within the sect
and closely bind one's status within the sect to the status within a
household. Family members must be instructed in the laws of the
sect. Special attention must be paid to children: they are supposed
to be brought up by their families fully instructed in the principles
of the sect. Finally, when young men from sectarian families formally joined the community, they themselves had to be heads of
independent households. Only this would allow them to fulfill cer-

---

[37] 1QSa I, 9–11.
[38] 1QSa I, 16.
[39] 1QSa I, 20–22.

tain administrative functions, such as participating in court sessions. As the person achieves maturity as a head of his household, he joins governing structures of the sect. In other words, families provided major identity markers within the sect. Far from destroying traditional family ties, the Dead Sea sect at least in its early stages recognized the families of its members as the main structural component.

It is against this background that we can revisit a somewhat enigmatic statement of the 4QDamascus Document about the "mothers" of the congregation. The reference to them appears in 4Q270 7 I, 13–15 and reads as follows:

> [One who murmur]s against the fathers (על האבות) [shall be expelled] from the congregation and not return. [If] it is against the mothers (על האמות), he shall be penalized for ten days, since the mothers do not have authoritative status within [the congregation].

There have been several inconclusive attempts to identify "the mothers."[40] Based on what has been discussed above, I would suggest that the "fathers" and the "mothers" of the congregation were members of families within the sect that had special authoritative status, perhaps founding families related to the priesthood. The Rule of the Congregation discussed above indicates that the "chiefs of the clans of the congregation," as well as regular family members, fulfilled important public functions within the sect. It is fully possible that "fathers" of the congregation were male heads of several leading families, whereas the word "mothers" referred to their wives.[41] If so, noticeable inequality between the two becomes understandable. "Fathers" were actual leaders of the sect, whereas "mothers" held subordinate although respected positions as their wives.[42] Similar to

---

[40] Baumgarten, *Qumran Cave 4.XIII*, 8, stops short of suggesting any specific explanation about the nature of this group. Still, he concludes that offences against the Fathers and the Mothers of the community "presuppose family life with marriage and children." It is also possible that "the Mothers of the community" should be seen in connection with *zeqenim* and *zeqenot* of 4Q502 identified by Baumgarten as "aged couples." See J. Baumgarten, "4Q502, Marriage or Golden Age Ritual?" *JJS* 43 (1983), 125–36.

[41] Cf. the suggestive discussion of "mother's house" in C. Meyers, "To Her Mother's House: Considering a Counterpart to the Israelite *Bêt 'āb*," in D. Jobling et al., eds., *The Bible and the Politics of Exegesis: Essays in Honor of Norman K. Gottwald on His Sixty-Fifth Birthday* (Cleveland: Pilgrim Press, 1991), 39–51 and 304–07.

[42] Cf. 1QS VII, 1–2, which details penalties against someone who has insulted priests. This law, however, seems to be more lenient as it does not involve expulsion from the sect without right to return.

what has been observed in the Rule of the Congregation, family
structures here overlapped with those of the sect, since families constituted the main structural units within the community. Leadership
of the sect was also concentrated within particular families, rather
than individuals.[43]

Legal Texts, Families, and the Structure of the Sect

To illustrate these conclusions about the role of traditional households in shaping Jewish sectarian movements of the Second Temple
period, we have to review some of the halakhic or legal compositions produced by the Dead Sea sect.[44] Many of these texts reflect
the social structure of the sect and aspects of its membership. All of
them explicitly envision the traditional household as a basic building block within the sect. These legal sectarian compositions illustrate in a more technical way the centrality of the family for a Jewish
sectarian movement of the Second Temple period, hinted at in our
previous discussion. Most informative in this respect are various legal
compositions of the Dead Sea sect.

4Q270 6 V of the 4QDamascus Document contains a regulation
which prohibits a nurse from carrying an infant on the Sabbath. It
also contains a prohibition against contending with one's slave or
maidservant on the Sabbath (את עבדו ואת אמתו).[45] Together with
other regulations addressing the management of various parts of one's
private business during the Sabbath, these laws presuppose an audience that consists of members of households who could afford to
have various groups of slaves and servants, as well as livestock at

---

[43] The sect probably recognized an enormous importance of women for the
proper conduct of family life according to halakhah. As Baumgarten observes,
"women were evaluated within the Qumran community in accordance with their
'intelligence and understanding' as 'daughters of truth.'" See Baumgarten, *Qumran
Cave 4.XIII*, 144, as well as his "4Q502, Marriage or Golden Age Ritual," 125–36.
Baumgarten, *Qumran Cave 4.XIII*, 165, observes that the wife had important responsibilities to "admonish her husband about the laws concerning sexual intercourse,
with which she is to familiarize herself by learning them and fulfilling them."

[44] I will particularly focus on the texts included in the so-called Damascus
Document and fragments from cave 4 related to it. See J. Baumgarten, *Qumran Cave
4.XIII: The Damascus Document (4Q266–273)* (Oxford: Clarendon Press, 1996).

[45] 4Q270 6 V, 16–17 (= 4Q271 5 I, 6–8). Cf. CD XI, 10–14 for a different
version of this law. See Schiffman, *Halakhah at Qumran*, 119–20, for discussion.

their disposal. Other regulations concerning the Sabbath include the prohibition against demanding payment from a neighbor or litigation "concerning property and gain."[46] A parallel excerpt from 4Q271 5 I prohibits a man from grazing an animal outside his town, as well as from delivering the newborn of an animal on the Sabbath. It also prohibits the raising of an animal that has fallen into a pit.[47] In addition, carrying spices, opening sealed vessels, and carrying items outside one's house are strictly prohibited.[48] As a whole, a man is prohibited from desecrating the Sabbath "for the sake of property and profit."[49] Overall, a "typical" household envisioned by the Sabbath law of CD is relatively well to do and has the social attributes of an aristocratic household. The household is presumed to possess servants (slaves?) along with cattle. Its members are expected to be involved in transactions "for the sake of property and profit," including lending money to their neighbors.[50] Other texts from CD address the possibility of a man having intercourse with his slave-woman, something not unexpected in an aristocratic household of the time.[51]

The family law attested in CD includes regulations pertaining to menstrual impurity, the laws of *sotah* (the unfaithful wife), and rules of marriage and divorce.[52] All three categories of law apparently envision a household (or group of households) of the type discussed above as their setting. All three of them indicate that family life and its associated halakhic practices constituted an important part of the Dead Sea sect's existence. The laws of *sotah*, although fairly fragmentary, reflect an elaborate procedure of testing a wife suspected of unfaithfulness to her husband. It basically agrees with similar laws

---

[46] 4Q270 6 V, 4.

[47] 4Q271 5 I, 2–4 and 8–9 (cf. 4Q270 6 V, 12–13 and 17–18, and CD XI, 5 and 11–14). See Schiffman, *Halakhah at Qumran*, 111–13 and 121–22, for discussion.

[48] 4Q271 5 I, 5–6 (cf. 4Q270 6 V, 14–15 and CD XI, 6–9). See Schiffman, *Halakhah at Qumran*, 113–17, for discussion.

[49] 4Q271 5 I, 10 (= 4Q270 6 V, 18–19 and CD XI, 15). For possible connotations of this prohibition see discussion below.

[50] Cf. F. Cross and E. Eshel, "Ostraca from Khirbet Qumran," *IEJ* 47 (1997), 17–28, for an ostracon interpreted to contain a deed of gift, in which one Honi transfers his estate and his slave to a person named Elazar. The editors suggested that the ostracon describes the transfer of the property of a member of the community into the communal ownership.

[51] 4Q266 XII, 7 (= 4Q270 IV, 14).

[52] For the most recent summary and bibliographic references see E. Schuller, "Women in the Dead Sea Scrolls," in Flint and VanderKam, *The Dead Sea Scrolls after Fifty Years*, vol. 2, 117–44.

attested in biblical and later rabbinic writings.[53] It also appears to
be followed by laws addressing a man's sexual relationships, including his relationship with his slave-woman.[54]

Regulations pertaining to menstrual impurity and birth-related
impurity likewise envision a household of means as their setting.[55]
The laws address the issue of a woman's ability to partake of clean
food as well as her "liminal" status within her family and the community at large during her menstruation periods and after childbirth.
Despite the lack of more specific information about their social setting, the laws of menstrual purity support what has been previously
observed about the setting of the Dead Sea sect's family law. Individual
households and relationships among their members appear to be at
the center of this type of sectarian legislation.

The rules of marriage and divorce preserved in the 4QDamascus
Document reflect a similar picture. According to the 4Q266 9 III:

> Let no man do anything involving buying or selling unless he informs
> the Overseer who is in the camp (מבקר אשר במחנה). He shall do it
> with counsel so that they don't err. Likewise for anyone who takes a
> wife (לבול לוקח אשה), let it be with counsel, and so shall he guide one
> who divorces. He shall instruct their sons and daughters and their chil-
> dren in a spirit of humility and loving-kindness.[56]

The text refers to the enigmatic figure of the "Overseer who is in the
camp" as supervising various daily activities of the members of the
sect, including their marriage and divorce.[57] The degree of supervision, however, remains unclear, as well as the nature of the position of the overseer itself. The term "camp" used in the excerpt
most probably refers to the sum total of the sectarians living in a
particular Jewish town or city.[58] Did the *mevaqqer* fulfill functions as

---

[53] 4Q270 IV, 1–8. See Baumgarten, *Qumran Cave 4.XIII*, 153–54, for commentary and parallels with later rabbinic texts.

[54] 4Q270 IV, 13–21.

[55] 4Q266 6 II (cf. 4Q272 1 II and 4Q273 5). See Baumgarten, *Qumran Cave
4.XIII*, 56–57, for commentary. For other examples of the law of purification after
childbirth in the Second Temple literature see J. Baumgarten, "Purification after
Childbirth and the Sacred Garden in 4Q265 and Jubilees," in G. Brooke, ed., *New
Qumran Texts and Studies* (Leiden: Brill, 1994), 3–10.

[56] Cf. CD XIII, 15–19.

[57] On the *mevaqqer*, his role and functions see J. Milik, *Ten Years of Discovery in the
Wilderness of Judaea* (London: SCM, 1959), 99, and Schiffman, *Reclaiming the Dead
Sea Scrolls*, 121–23. The functions of the overseer primarily included admission into
the community, supervision of finances and trade and judicial proceedings.

[58] 4QMMT B 29–31 uses the term "camps" in exactly this sense. See L. Schiffman,

the leader of a local community?[59] Given the paucity of data at our disposal, a final assessment would be very difficult indeed. Still, two things are clear. First, individual households and/or families are envisioned in this text as the basic building block within the sect. Second, because of this the sectarian leadership is expected to actively participate in shaping and defining the nature of these families.[60]

The degree of sectarian involvement in household life as attested in 4Q266 9 provides a close parallel to some themes in the Rule of the Congregation discussed above. In both cases the sectarian indoctrination of children appears to be of prime importance. In both cases it takes place within the family, but the sect's leadership demonstrates a keen interest in keeping a close eye on the entire process. A special provision to bring up children in the spirit of the sect is repeatedly stressed in both documents. The sectarian leadership gets even more actively involved in one's decision about taking a wife. Community law explicitly states that one has to marry "with counsel." The same is true for divorce. Overall, the text reflects a situation within a group of households, united by the same interpretation of Jewish law and distancing themselves from the larger community. Households constituting this group voluntarily allowed external supervision of their affairs by the leadership of the sect to ensure compliance with sectarian laws and regulations. As a result, the leaders of the sect were increasingly perceived as legal experts whose knowledge and expertise were seen as authoritative by the households that constituted the sect.

Families that for some reason no longer followed the sectarian interpretation of the law were automatically excluded from the sect. Several excerpts from the 4QDamascus Document state that "one who comes near to fornicate with his wife contrary to the law shall

---

"The Place of 4QMMT in the Corpus of Qumran Manuscripts," in J. Kampen and M. Bernstein, eds., *Reading 4QMMT* (Atlanta: Scholars Press, 1996), 89, for discussion.

[59] *The Damascus Document* often associates *mevaqqer* with the camps. See for example CD XV, 14, XIII, 7, 13, 16 and XIV, 89. On the other hand, he is occasionally mentioned as an authority in the community of "the many" (הרבים). See C. Hempel, "Community Structures in the Dead Sea Scrolls," in Flint and VanderKam, *The Dead Sea Scrolls after Fifty Years*, vol. 2, 80–81.

[60] A similar situation of communal control over individual members, their families, and their assets emerges from Ezra 10:8. See Hoglund, *Achaemenid Imperial Administration*, 234, for discussion.

depart and return no more."[61] Joseph Baumgarten has correctly observed that the crucial word within this phrase is "contrary to the law." However, he tends to find here references to specific transgressions committed by a man in violation of the law.[62] I would suggest that any relationship carried out "contrary to the law," i.e., contrary to the sectarian understanding of the law, was perceived as fornication and led to expulsion from the sect. In other words, once the family (or the head of the family) was no longer prepared to accept the sectarian interpretation of the law as authoritative it automatically detached itself from the sect. "Fornication with one's wife contrary to the law" indicates that one no longer conducts his family life according to the law of the sect. Interestingly enough, at least in one case this regulation is immediately followed by a statement that one murmuring against the "fathers" has likewise to be permanently excluded from the sect.[63] It appears that in both instances we are dealing with conflicts between the sectarian leadership and rank-and-file members of the sect. In both instances the failure to accept the sectarian leadership as authoritative led to an immediate and permanent break with the group.

4Q271 3 provides another important insight into the individual household as the basic unit of the Dead Sea sect. According to this text:

> If a man gives his daughter to a man, let him disclose all her blemishes to him, lest he bring upon himself the judgement of the curse which is said of the one who that 'makes the blind to wander out of the way.' Moreover, he should not give her to one unfit for her, for that is *kil'ayim*, plowing with ox and ass and wearing wool and linen together. Let no man bring a woman into the holy covenant (בברית הקודש) who has had sexual experience, whether she had it in the home of her father or as a widow who had intercourse after she was widowed. And any woman upon whom there is a bad name in her maidenhood in her father's home (בבית אביה), let no man take her except upon examination by trustworthy women of repute (נשים נאמנות וידעות) selected by the command of the overseer over the many. Afterward he may take her, and when he takes her he shall act in accordance with the law.[64]

---

[61] 4Q270 7 I, 12–13 (cf. 4Q267 9 VI, 4–5).
[62] Such as "unnatural intercourse"; see Baumgarten, *Qumran Cave 4.XIII*, 164–65.
[63] 4Q270 7 I 13.
[64] Cf. 4Q269 9 and 4Q270 5.

This text specifies various rules of proper engagement and marriage as seen by the sectarians. Several items call for our attention. First, the main social unit described by the text appears to be one's "house" (*bayit*) or rather the household. Second, and similar to other Second Temple Jewish sources, this text may be addressing the problem of preservation of the "holy seed" through a marriage between "proper" houses.[65] The text seeks to preserve the "holy seed" of Israel through prohibition of betrothing one's daughter to a person who is "unfit for her," as well as through the requirement of disclosing all blemishes of one's daughter prior to her marriage.[66]

On the other hand, unlike 4QMMT, which uses the same notion of *kil'ayim* to outlaw mixed marriages in priestly families, this passage does not have explicit priestly connotations.[67] In fact, it almost certainly legislates for the lay Israelite families comprising the sect. CD as a whole takes a somewhat ambiguous view toward priesthood and its role in the community, often choosing to sideline priests in favor of lay officials.[68] The focus of CD's legislation seems to be on Israelite non-priestly households and their halakhic practices rather than on the household halakhah of priestly families, as in the case of 4QMMT. In this respect, CD comes closer to the traditions of Ezra, Nehemiah, and *Jubilees*, which also address lay Israelite households rather than priestly families.[69] Like *Jubilees*, CD also seeks to

---

[65] The improper marriage with the "one unfit for her" is described here as *kil'ayim*, "mixing of seeds and kinds" prohibited by Jewish law. See Baumgarten, *Qumran Cave 4.XIII*, 177, for other contemporaneous and later rabbinic parallels. A similar reference appears in 4QMMT. See E. Qimron and J. Baumgarten, *Qumran Cave 4.V*, 171–75, and our discussion above. All these texts seem to be concerned with preservation and transmission of the "holy seed" through pure family lineage.

[66] I have problems accepting Baumgarten's interpretation of the *kil'ayim* in this particular case as "the metaphor describing sexual promiscuity." The text appears to be specifically referring to the unfit marriage. In 4QMMT an analogous passage implied either priests marrying lay Israelites or possibly, Israelites marrying non-Jews. See E. Qimron and J. Baumgarten, *Qumran Cave 4.V*, 171–75. Cf. Schiffman, "The Place of 4QMMT in the Corpus of Qumran Manuscripts," 91–92. See also the discussion above about preferable marriage within one's own clan.

[67] On 4QMMT and its use of *kil'ayim* to describe forbidden marriages see Hayes, *Gentile Impurities*, 82–89, and Satlow, *Jewish Marriage*, 142–43.

[68] See for example CD XIII, 1–13. Schiffman, *Reclaiming the Dead Sea Scrolls*, 125–26, talks about possible transition of authority within the sect from priestly to lay officials.

[69] Cf. M. Himmelfarb, "'A Kingdom of Priests': The Democratization of the Priesthood in the Literature of Second Temple Judaism," *Journal of Jewish Thought and Philosophy* 6 (1997), 89–104. She suggests that *Jubilees* and other Second Temple texts develop an idea of the "priesthood of all Israel." As a result, they apply the priestly notion of family lineage to the entire people of Israel.

restrict some forms of endogamous marriage, most noticeably marriages between a niece and an uncle.[70]

This text perceives the authoritative structures of a traditional Jewish household as the system allowing for the transmission and preservation of the holy seed. The head of the household plays a crucial role in his daughter's marriage. It is his responsibility to assure that the marriage leads to a proper marital union and proper family life. He must disclose all blemishes of a prospective bride and to make sure that she marries a person who is "fit" for her. The last requirement is sufficiently vague to imply restrictions on marriage not only with non-Jews but particular categories among Jews as well. Overall, this text is remarkably conservative in terms of its social ideals. The household and its traditional patriarchal leadership become a crucial element in assuring the purity and integrity of Israel. An individual household is portrayed as a central element in a system designed to fulfill the religious ideal of this group.[71]

This understanding of social reality finds a close parallel in *Jubilees* and its vision of the traditional patriarchal family. The latter plays a crucial role in the religious program of the book:

> And if there is any man in Israel who wishes to give his daughter or his sister to any man who is from the seed of the gentiles, let him surely die, and let him be stoned because he has caused shame in Israel. And also the woman will be burned with fire because she has defiled the name of her father's house and so she will be uprooted from Israel.[72]
>
> And there is no remission or forgiveness except that the man who caused defilement of his daughter will be rooted out from the midst of all Israel because he has given some of his seed to Moloch and sinned so as to defile it.[73]

These two passages emphasize the responsibility of the head of the family for the proper marriage of his daughter in a way similar to that of CD. It is the father who is responsible for preserving of the holy seed within his family. If he gives his daughter or his sister to

---

[70] CD V, 8–11.
[71] Cf. Berquist, *Controlling Corporeality*, 51–79, for discussion of the central role of the Ancient Israelite household in controlling interpersonal relations in general and sexuality in particular. This paradigm is fully suitable to describe the Dead Sea movement as well.
[72] *Jub.* 30:7.
[73] *Jub.* 30:10.

a gentile, he commits a grave sin and should be "rooted out from the midst of Israel." The woman who marries a gentile defiles "the name of her father's house" and should be burned with fire. The text is explicit in describing intermarriage as a sin against one's family. By marrying a gentile, the person effectively causes a contamination (if not destruction) of his family's holy seed, not just the holy seed of Israel.[74] According to *Jubilees* improper marriages resulted in the destruction of families throughout the entire history of Israel.[75] The only stable and lasting family is the one that has been created as a result of a proper marriage and thus serves to preserve the ancestral holy seed. An almost exact parallel to *Jubilees* comes from the *Aramaic Levi* document:

> And she profanes her name and the name of her father. . . husband(s?) to bu[r]n her . . . and (the?) shame. And every virgin who ruins her name, and the name of her fathers, she also causes shame for all her brothers [and for] her father. And the reputation of her revilement will not be wiped out from among all the people forever.[76]

This passage condemns illicit marriages in exactly the same terms as *Jubilees* does.[77] By contracting an improper marriage, a daughter defiles her father's house and even "ruins the name of her fathers."[78] Similar to *Jubilees*, *Aramaic Levi* advocates endogamous marriages. Both documents (similar to a number of other Second Temple texts) see endogamous marriage as the safest way to ensure preservation and transmission of the ancestral "holy seed."[79]

In social terms, *Jubilees* and *Aramaic Levi* construct their religious ideals within the framework of a traditional patriarchal family, where

---

[74] See Hayes, *Gentile Impurities*, 73–81, and Satlow, *Jewish Marriage*, 141–43.

[75] See for example *Jub.* 35:14, where Rebecca predicts the destruction of Esau and his seed because he "has forsaken the God of Abraham and he has gone after his wives and after their defilement and after their errors, (both) he and his sons."

[76] *Aram. Levi* 24–26. The translation is from Kugler, *From Patriarch to Priest: The Levi-Priestly Tradition from Aramaic Levi to Testament of Levi* (Atlanta: Scholars Press, 1996).

[77] On a common source possibly underlying both texts see Kugler, *From Patriarch to Priest*, 82–87.

[78] Women's prominence in preservation and transmission of the "holy seed" can explain their importance in genealogical lists of Jubilees (as opposed to their relative insignificance in the Pentateuch). See B. Halpern-Amaru, "First Woman, Wives, and Mothers in *Jubilees*," *JBL* 113 (1994), 609–26.

[79] The same tendency manifests itself in genealogical lists of the *Genesis Apocryphon*, where the granddaughters of Noah receive prominence, which they lack in the Pentateuch. See J. VanderKam, "Granddaughters and Grandsons of Noah," *RevQ* 16 (1994), 457–61.

the head of the family is responsible for the marriage of the female members of his household and, as a result, for the preservation of the holy seed within his house. This approach is remarkably similar to what we have observed in CD. All these texts seem to reflect the same social reality and ideals. The sectarian ideology in each case becomes intimately intertwined with the traditional familial moral code, and it is difficult to distinguish between the two. The traditional institution of the patriarchal household is perceived as responsible for embodying and transmitting norms of religious behavior. It serves as a major bulwark ensuring Israel's life in accordance with the laws of Torah. Household halakhah becomes a prime manifestation of the Law of Israel. The texts clearly attest that households constituted the religiously significant building blocks and social units within Jewish movements of the Second Temple period, including the Dead Sea sect.[80]

The books of Ezra and Nehemiah provide another parallel to the Dead Sea sect, as it emerges from the documents discussed.[81] There, the so-called "congregation of the exile," the group of Jewish clans that returned from the Babylonian exile, is depicted along very similar lines. The author sees it as an organized and disciplined group, following a specific set of laws and embodying authentic Judaism.[82] The congregation is directed by a body of official interpreters of the Jewish Law, including Ezra (and Nehemiah?) himself.[83] Still, the individual clan or family remains the main unit within the "congregation of the exile."[84] It is probably due to the importance of this unit that intermarriages become such an issue within the congregation

---

[80] 4Q271 4 II, 10–12 deals with the right of the husband/father to annul the oath of his wife/daughter. The law integrates the traditional right of the *paterfamilias*, to control oaths taken by other members of his house into the sectarian halakhah. If the oath transgresses the covenant it has to be annulled. See Baumgarten, *Qumran Cave 4.XIII*, 180, for parallels with biblical and later rabbinic texts.

[81] See esp. Ezra 6–10 and Nehemiah 9–10.

[82] See M. Smith, "The Dead Sea Sect in Relation to Ancient Judaism," 347–60, for parallels between the "Congregation of the Exile" of Ezra-Nehemiah and the Dead Sea Sect. Cohen, *From the Maccabees to the Mishnah*, 140–41, further elaborates on this topic.

[83] Neh 8:1–8 and 13–18.

[84] Neh 8:2 and 10:29–30 specifically refer to families participating in the covenant renewal ceremony. According to Neh 8:13 "the heads of the clans of all the people" (ראשי אבות לכל העם) participate in the special session with Ezra, at which they interpret the law as to its meaning.

itself as well as its leadership.[85] In any case, the hands-on involvement of the leaders of this congregation with the problem of intermarriages and the forcible divorce of foreign wives provides a clear parallel to what we encounter in CD.[86]

In addition to the family (and specifically, marriage) law, the Damascus Document shares with Ezra and Nehemiah its interest in properly paid tithes as well as restrictions imposed on private business transactions with outsiders. According to 4Q270 2 II, one has to be very meticulous about giving to the sons of Aaron tithes "from the cattle and the sheep" along with various types of redemption donations and first fruits. Laws of tithing are further elaborated in 4Q271 2 with specific directions regarding the amount of tithes paid "from the threshing floor and from the garden."[87] These regulations are very similar in nature to the elaborate procedures envisioned by the laws of Ezra and (especially) Nehemiah to establish material support for the priesthood. In both cases donations by individual households were deemed to be an essential part of the renewed covenant and its economic backbone.[88]

The same can be said about regulations limiting economic interaction with gentiles. Similar to Nehemiah's laws, CD XII, 8–11 prohibits a member of the sect from selling animals, clean birds or "anything from his granary or his press" to gentiles. Somewhat earlier, the same text states that "no one should stay in a place close to gentiles on the Sabbath." It further requires that "no one shall violate the Sabbath for the sake of wealth or profit on the Sabbath."[89] This regulation may be similar in nature to Nehemiah's prohibition of selling and buying from gentiles on the Sabbath.[90] On a larger scale, the laws promulgated by Ezra and Nehemiah and the laws of

---

[85] Ezra 9–10, Neh 9:2, 13:1–3 and 23–31. Williamson, *Ezra and Nehemiah*, 96, interprets the prohibition of intermarriages in Ezra 9:2 in the light of Lev 19:19 prohibiting mixture of unlike animals, crops and material. If so, we have another parallel to the family law of the early Dead Sea sect.

[86] The title *mevaqqer* appears to have biblical roots. A similar official has been also mentioned in Nabatean inscriptions. See Weinfeld, *The Organizational Pattern and the Penal Code of the Qumran Sect*, 19–21.

[87] These laws further demonstrate that the community hardly saw itself as being cut off from the temple. See Baumgarten, *Qumran Cave 4.XIII*, 145–46 and 174, for commentaries. Notice especially parallels between these texts and 4QMMT.

[88] Neh 10:33–40.

[89] CD XI, 14–15.

[90] Neh 10:32 and 13:15–22. Cf. Schiffman, *Halakhah at Qumran*, 124–25, for a similar observation.

the Damascus Document have the same social setting. They try to regulate the everyday life of Jewish households that formed a religious alliance and agreed to practice the Jewish law in a particular way. Both collections of regulations focus on such issues as family law, tithing and interaction with gentiles, as these issues were of prime interest to groups consisting of reasonably affluent households, with their social and economic concerns.

Overall, this analysis of halakhic documents produced by the Dead Sea sect tends to corroborate the earlier observations about traditional Jewish households as the major social unit within religious movements of Second Temple Judaism. Most of these laws address issues that could emerge only within a household of certain means. They also tend to allocate considerable importance to the "proper" family behavior and traditional family values of honor and propriety. The hands-on involvement of the sectarian official (*mevaqqer*) in what appears to us as private family business indicates the importance of the individual household within the sectarian system of values. This involvement appears to closely resemble the policy pursued by the leaders of the "congregation of exile" in the books of Ezra and Nehemiah, and later in the *Book of Jubilees*.

Opponents of the Dead Sea Sect and "Splinter Groups"

As I have observed above, the Damascus Document starts with a detailed, albeit somewhat enigmatic, description of the history of the Dead Sea sect. This description, which tells about the early stages of the sect's history and places those within the larger history of the people of Israel, contains a number of allusions to the nature of the sect itself, as well as to that of its opponents. Whereas I have discussed texts addressing the sect itself earlier in this chapter, the focus of the present section is going to be on the excerpts from the Damascus Document that seek to characterize the Dead Sea group's opponents. One needs to assess what the sectarians deemed sufficiently important about their opponents to be included in brief symbolic descriptions of their quintessential characteristics. The first detailed description of the opponents of the sect appears in CD IV, 12–V, 11 and runs as follows:

> And during these years Belial will be sent against Israel, as God has said by means of the prophet Isaiah, son of Amoz, saying: "Panic, pit

and net are against you, earth-dweller." Its explanation: They are Belial's three nets about which Levi, son of Jacob, spoke, in which he catches Israel and makes them appear before them like three types of justice. The first is fornication. The second, wealth. The third, defilement of the temple. He who eludes one is caught in another and he who is freed from that, is caught in another. The builders of the wall who go after Zaw—Zaw is a preacher as it is said, "Assuredly he will preach"—are caught twice in fornication: by taking two wives in their lives, even though the principle of creation is "male and female he created them." And the ones who went into the ark "went in by two into the ark." And about the prince it is written: "He should not multiply wives to himself." [. . .] And they also defiled the temple, for they did not keep apart in accordance with the law, but instead lay with her who sees the blood of her menstrual flow. And each man takes as a wife the daughter of his brother and the daughter of his sister. But Moses said: "Do not approach your mother's sister, she is a blood relation of your mother." The law of incest, written for males, applies equally for females, and therefore to the daughter of a brother who uncovers the nakedness of the brother of her father, for he is a blood relation. And also they defile His holy spirit, for with blasphemous tongue they have opened their mouth against the statutes of God's covenant, saying: "they are unfounded." They speak abomination against them. They are all igniters of fire, kindlers of blazes. Webs of a spider are their webs, and their eggs are viper's eggs. Whoever is close to them will not be unpunished. The more he does it, the guiltier he shall be, unless he has been compelled.

This text describes opponents of the author(s) of the Damascus Document. They are called here "builders of the wall."[91] The "builders of the wall" found themselves entrapped in three nets spread by Belial: fornication, wealth and defilement of the temple. As the text goes on, it focuses specifically on fornication and illicit marital relationships.[92] The sect's opponents are accused of "taking two wives in their lives," having sexual relationships with a menstruating woman and marrying their nieces. It is precisely because of this misbehavior

---

[91] See Davies, *The Damascus Covenant*, 111–12, for discussion of this term. He identifies "builders of the wall" with the entire community of Israel outside the sectarian movement, not with a particular rival group.

[92] Davies, *The Damascus Covenant*, 115–16, discusses the relationship between sexual offences enumerated in this section of the document and temple defilement. His conclusions are ambiguous since he tends to downplay the importance of the theme of temple defilement in the CD. But he is correct to observe that "the issue of Temple defilement does not indicate any formal breach with the sanctuary" on the part of authors of the Damascus Covenant. In this respect they would also resemble earlier Second Temple movements.

that they eventually "defile the temple," in other words their family practices render them impure and unfit to come in contact with the temple. A reference to "viper's eggs" may symbolize teachings of the "builders of the wall" as well as their offspring from "unlawful" marriages.[93] As a whole, the description amounts to a consistent (if somewhat baroque) image of the opponents of the Dead Sea sect.

The Damascus Document characterizes these people by their wealth, family practices and their relation to the temple. In fact, all three of these characteristics are interconnected. The "builders of the wall" defile the temple precisely because of their family law, which renders them and their offspring ritually impure. The most essential characteristic of this group is based on its family law and marital practices. The "builders of the wall" appear in this text as a group of heads of influential households, who do not follow proper family law by marrying their close relatives, by not observing menstrual impurity laws and by taking more than one wife. As a result of that, they "defile the temple." Thus, the participation in temple life is intrinsically interwoven with the proper conduct of family life, and both practices serve as prime characteristics of the "builders of the wall." They are also wealthy, although the text does not elaborate on this aspect of their existence.

In addition to its wealth, family practices and relation to the temple, the group in question is also characterized by its peculiar legal teachings, or rather by the ways in which it practices the law. They are said to have rejected the "statutes of God's covenant" by stating that "they are unfounded."[94] This phrase apparently refers to their rejection of the law as understood and interpreted by the Dead Sea sect. The symbolism of fire, blazes, spider's webs and viper's eggs may actually refer to the group's teachings.[95] In fact, the entire passage contains repeated legal argumentation against specific teachings/practices of this group. This argument is based on quotations from biblical texts and their interpretation. In other words, the law followed by the "builders of the wall" seems to constitute another important part of their definition.

---

[93] CD V, 13–15.
[94] CD V, 12–13.
[95] Although, reference to viper's eggs may also imply an offspring from illicit marriages made within that group. See above.

It is equally significant that when the Damascus Document talks about the halakhic dimension of the "builders of the wall," it seems to imply their practices rather than their teachings (in fact, the two can hardly be distinguished). The law of the "builders of the wall" is the law as it is practiced by households whose sum total constitutes this group. As mentioned above, it includes permission to take more than one wife and to marry one's niece, as well as to disregard menstrual impurity. The following of these (and probably other) practices of the "builders of the wall" makes anyone who joins them ever guiltier, "unless he has been compelled."[96] As we can see, the law of the "builders of the wall" is limited in this description to the family law as practiced within their families. In other words, this excerpt from the Damascus Document tends to identify the law of its opponents with halakhic practices of their households, specifically in the realm of family law. The practices of the households constituting the "builders of the wall" amount to the quintessential halakhah of this group. It is these practices that defile their followers as well as the temple in which they serve. That is why these practices are deemed so dangerous.[97]

As a whole, CD IV, 12–V, 15 draws a relatively comprehensive portrait of the opposing group, which it labels "builders of the wall." The categories used to describe this group include its wealth, its relation to the temple, its particular halakhic practices and the centrality of the household for its structure. The text attacks the way in which "builders of the wall" practice the law within their households. It does not distinguish between public and private legal realms, or between legal teachings and legal practices. The family law followed by the "builders of the wall" defiles the temple. It is also seen as a quintessential sample of their halakhah and halakhic mistakes. Anyone who accepts the practices of this group as authoritative is guilty of transgression. The text seems to understand the "builders of the wall" as a network of households practicing the law in a particular way. The Dead Sea group perceived this way as halakhically wrong and dangerous.

---

[96] CD V, 15.

[97] See below on the polemics in 4QMMT, which also seem to be centered on the halakhic practices of priestly families. In both cases it is priestly family law and practices that come under attack. They were considered crucial for maintaining the purity of the temple.

A similar picture emerges from the analysis of another document
reflecting the early history of the Dead Sea sect. The Halakhic Letter
(4QMMT) contains a list of legal disagreements between the sect
and its unnamed opponents.[98] These disagreements apparently caused
the sectarians to detach themselves from the religious establishment
in Jerusalem. The central portion of this letter is organized as an
enumeration of the sect's legal opinions, often contrasted with the
halakhic practices of its opponents. The disagreement reflected here
tends to focus on temple worship and purity laws. Among other
problems the letter mentions improper marriage practices among the
Jewish elite:

> And concerning the fornication carried out in the midst of the peo-
> ple: they are members of the congregation of perfect holiness, as it is
> written: "Holy is Israel." And concerning his pure animal it is writ-
> ten that he shall not pair off two species. And concerning clothing, it
> is written that no materials are to be mixed. And he will not sow his
> field or his vineyard with two species because they are holy. And the
> sons of Aaron are the holiest of holy, but you know that a part of the
> priests and of the people mingle and they squeeze each other and
> defile the holy seed and also their own seed with fornication, because
> the sons of Aaron [. . .] who will come and who [...] And concern-
> ing women: [. . .] and betrayal [. . .] for in this matters [...] for vio-
> lence and fornication several places have been ruined.[99]

The text criticizes the marriage practices of an opposing group.
Indeed, it may contain criticism of priests marrying lay Israelites.[100]

---

[98] 4QMMT apparently belongs to the earlier stages in the history of the sect
and may reflect its pre-Qumranic period. It appears to reflect disputes (among
priestly families?) about the interpretation of the Torah and proper conduct of the
temple ritual. These disputes eventually resulted in the split between the sect and
its opponents. See J. Baumgarten, "The Pharisaic-Sadducean Controversies about
Purity, and the Qumran Texts," *JJS* 31 (1980), 157–70. Cf. L. Schiffman, "The
New Halakhic Letter (4QMMT) and the Origins of the Dead Sea Sect," *BA* 53
(1990), 64–73.

[99] 4Q396 1–2 IV and 4Q397 6–21. Cf. the requirement of the *Testament of Levi*
34:14–21 that one has to take a wife from his own family. The holy seed should
not be defiled with outsiders. See further commentary in E. Qimron and
J. Baumgarten, *Qumran Cave 4.V: Miqsat Ma'aseh Ha-Torah*, 174–75, which puts the
restriction into a broader Second Temple context. In fact, many non-priestly families of that time preferred to marry women from their own clan. See Tob. 1:9 and
4:12.

[100] Qimron and Strugnell interpreted 4QMMT to prohibit marriages specifically
between lay and priestly families within Israel (see *DJD* vol. 10, 171–72). For a
similar view cf. Himmelfarb, "Levi, Phinehas, and the Problem of Intermarriage,"

From the point of view of its author, by doing so both sides violate the law of forbidden mixture of diverse kinds and thus defile their own respective seeds.[101] Because of this practice, along with other illicit practices that defile the temple and the people of Israel, the sect is forced to withdraw itself from the larger Jewish society.

This text shows some clear similarities with the Damascus Document. In both cases the opponents of the sect are criticized for their incorrect halakhic practices. In both cases these practices involve family law as well as laws pertaining to the temple's sacredness.[102] Both texts appear to portray households whose halakhic practices encompass various realms of law especially family law and temple worship. Finally, both texts are phrased as polemics against these practices. They first denote the actual practice and then criticize it either by quoting relevant passages from the Torah or by logically deriving the correct ordinance from other legal precedents. In both cases the sectarian legal polemic specifically targets the halakhic practices of the sect's opponents. The main debate here is about the legal validity and authority of practical halakhah followed by particular Jewish groups. Both the Damascus Document and 4QMMT share the same understanding of the nature of halakhic debates among Jews and such debates' social underpinnings.[103]

The early documents produced by the Dead Sea sect reflect a consistent perception of the opponents of this sect. These opponents

---

1–24, and Satlow, *Jewish Marriage*, 142. For an opposite view, namely that the prohibition deals with marrying non-Jews, see Hayes, *Gentile Impurities*, 82–89.

[101] Cf. 4Q271 3 8–10 for a similar argument against improper marriages. See commentary in J. Baumgarten, *Qumran Cave 4.XIII: The Damascus Document*, 177 for parallels in Josephus and later rabbinic texts. Cf. Hayes, *Gentile Impurities*, 82–89, and Satlow, *Jewish Marriage*, 142–43.

[102] In fact, the two were often interrelated. 4QMMT tends to associate the preservation of the family's sanctity with that of the temple. See E. Qimron and J. Baumgarten, *Qumran Cave 4.V: Miqsat Maʿaseh Ha-Torah*, 158–60, for the double meaning of "those forbidden to enter the congregation" in 4QMMT. Cf. Baumgarten, *Qumran Law*, 39–49, and Schiffman, "The Place of 4QMMT in the Corpus of Qumran Manuscripts," 94. Contrast, however, M. Bernstein, "The Employment and Interpretation of Scripture in 4QMMT," in Kampen and Bernstein, *Reading 4QMMT*, 37–38, who interprets the phrase as referring only to marriage.

[103] Both texts also reflect an early stage in the development of the sect and may be seen as portraying the social roots of the group that would later become the Dead Sea sect. See J. VanderKam, "Identity and History of the Community" in Flint and VanderKam, *The Dead Sea Scrolls after Fifty Years*, vol. 2, 487–531 (esp. 524–31), for the most recent discussion and summary of previous discussion. For further parallels between the two see L. Schiffman, "The Place of 4QMMT in the Corpus of Qumran Manuscripts," 90–94.

are depicted as groups practicing Jewish law in a way different from
that of the sectarians. Households following specific halakhic practices seem to constitute the main units within the groups opposed
to the Dead Sea sect. Our sources direct most of their criticism
against "incorrect" family law followed by these households. But their
halakhic practices are not limited to family law. They also include
sacrificial and purity laws related to the temple. In both the Damascus
Document and 4QMMT there is a clear understanding that the
households rendering themselves impure by practicing incorrect family law also stand in special relationship to the temple and temple
law. Sometimes they are clearly identified as priestly families, sometimes not. In either case there is an overwhelming perception of
these groups as networks of aristocratic households following particular halakhic practices and interpreting the Jewish law according to
these practices. The debate between them and the founders of the
Dead Sea sect seems to be centered around the question of whose
understanding of the law should be deemed authoritative and legally
binding. In many respects, the social setting of this debate is similar to that of Ezra and Nehemiah. It appears that the roots of the
Dead Sea sect as described in 4QMMT and the Damascus Document
are indeed similar to those of the "congregation of the exile." I now
turn to other references to the groups opposed to the Dead Sea sect
in the somewhat later Pesharim literature.

A number of scholars have argued that the two groups designated
in the Pesher Nahum as Ephraim and Manasseh can be identified
with Pharisees and Sadducees of Josephus respectively.[104] Even if the
precise identification is no longer possible, both groups seem to rep-

---

[104] See J. Amoussine, "Éphraïm et Manassé dans le Pesher de Nahum," *RevQ* 4
(1963), 389–96, and D. Flusser, "Pharisäer, Sadduzäer und Essener im Pescher
Nahum," in Grözinger et al., eds., *Qumran: Wege der Forschung* (Darmstadt, 1981),
121–66. For more recent discussion, see L. Schiffman, "Pharisees and Sadducees
in *Pesher Nahum*," in M. Brettler and M. Fishbane, eds., *Minhah le-Nahum: Biblical
and Other Studies Presented to N.M. Sarna* (Sheffield: JSOT Press, 1993), 272–90, and
A. Baumgarten, "Seekers after Smooth Things," in Schiffman and VanderKam,
Encyclopedia of the Dead Sea Scrolls, vol. 2, 857–59. On the other hand, G. Stemberger,
Jewish Contemporaries of Jesus: Pharisees, Sadducees, Essenes (Minneapolis: Fortress Press,
1995), 111–13, offers a much more cautious assessment of our sources. See also G.
Doudna, *4Q Pesher Nahum: A Critical Edition* (London: Sheffield Academic Press, 2001),
577–99. He identifies Manasseh with a "Jerusalem-based oppressive regime which
oppresses Ephraim" but rejects the notion that either Manasseh or Ephraim stands
for any specific Jewish sect of the time.

resent factions opposed to the Dead Sea sect. Let us take a closer look at how these groups are described. Commenting on Nahum 3:8 "Do you act better than Ammon seated between the Niles?" Pesher Nahum III, 9 says that Ammon "is Manasseh and the Niles are the important people of Manasseh, the nobles of . . . (נדולי מנשה נכבדי)" The verse goes on to say: "Water surrounds the one whose rampart was the sea, and the water is her walls." Pesher Nahum comments: "Its interpretation: they are her men at arms, her mighty warriors." Somewhat later, commenting on Nahum 3:10 ("she too fled to exile, her children were dashed to pieces at every crossroad and for their nobles they cast lots and all important people [were loaded] with chains") the Pesher says:

> Its interpretation concerns Manasseh, in the last time, since his control over Israel was weakened . . . his women, his children and his babies (נשיו עילוליו וטפו) will go into captivity, his warriors and his nobles (נבוריו ונכבדיו) [will fall] by the sword.[105]

None of these passages identifies Manasseh as a particular religious group, something that we would call a "sect". Only in the Pesher to Psalm 37 I, 18–19 is Manasseh identified as one of the adversaries of the Qumran community and its leader ("the priest"), which may imply (although not necessarily so) its religious character. So, what are the most important characteristics of Manasseh according to the Pesher Nahum?

Members of the group labeled "Manasseh" are said to consist of two main types. They include, on the one hand, "important people of Manasseh," "nobles," "men at arms," "mighty warriors," in other words, those whom we would call "military aristocracy." On the other hand, this group includes "women, children and babies" who are said to have been destroyed along with the warriors and nobles of Manasseh. What social category does this description fit the best? Probably, the families and clans of the Jewish military aristocracy provide the best match. Manasseh is defined in the Pesher Nahum as a group composed of aristocratic families, which include the military aristocracy on the one extreme and women and children on the other. This combined reference to warriors along with women

---

[105] 4Q169 IV, 3–4.

and children best characterizes the aristocratic clans of the Hasmonean military elite.[106]

Josephus provides an interesting parallel to this description in his story about the Pharisaic rebellion against Alexander Jannaeus and its consequences (*A.J.* 13.379–380). Here too, the Pharisees who fought against Alexander are described as warriors accompanied by their children and wives. The bloodbath perpetrated by Jannaeus in the wake of the rebellion immediately calls to mind the vague allusions of Pesher Nahum to the destruction of the "warriors and wives and children" of Manasseh. Jannaeus attacked Pharisees, whereas Pesher Nahum seems to imply Sadducees, but the social structure of both groups appears to be the same. This may indicate common social characteristics that existed across the board of Jewish sectarian movements of the Second Temple period. Similar to the movement of Ezra and Nehemiah, these sectarian movements also consisted of aristocratic families following a particular understanding of Jewish law. In both cases individual clans constituted the backbone of the movement, just as they constituted the backbone of the contemporaneous society in general.[107]

Whereas the description of Manasseh provided by Pesher Nahum omits any reference to the religious identity of this group, passages from the same text dealing with Ephraim contain allusions to its ideological differences with Qumranites. Commenting on Nahum 3:4 the text says:

---

[106] Cf. Doudna, *4Q Pesher Nahum*, 577–99. The best parallel would be that of Onias, who established a Jewish military colony as well as the temple in Egypt. His family and friends apparently constituted the core of this settlement (see discussion above). For an early and somewhat simplistic attempt to find parallels between the two groups see S. Steckoll, "Qumran Sect in Relationship to the Temple of Leontopolis," *RevQ* 6 (1967–69), 55–69. Cf. the criticism in M. Delcor, "Le temple d'Onias en Egypte," *RB* 75 (1968), 188–205. A more sophisticated suggestion about possible parallels appears in Hayward, "Jewish Temple at Leontopolis," 441–43. Cf. also R. White, "The House of Peleg in the Dead Sea Scrolls," in P. Davies, ed., *A Tribute to Geza Vermes* (Sheffield: JSOT, 1990), 67–98, for an attempt to identify the House of Peleg and the movement of Onias.

[107] Murphy-O'Connor, "The Essenes and Their History," 225, makes an interesting connection between the group described in the Damascus Document and Jewish military colonists of Antiochus III (*A.J.* 12.119–121). He speculates that some of the "Essenes" could have come from there. Although this connection is far from obvious, the social structure of both groups may indeed be similar in that both of them had Jewish aristocratic clans as their basis. On the sectarian group described in the Damascus Document and its social structure, see discussion above.

Its interpretation concerns those who misdirect Ephraim, who with their fraudulent teaching and lying tongue and perfidious lip misdirect many; kings, priests and people together with the proselyte attached to them. Cities and families (ערים ומשפחות) will perish through his advice, nobles and leaders (נכבדים ומושלים) will fall because of their tongues.[108]

The last sentence of this excerpt defines Ephraim in terms of his "nobles and leaders." Moreover, the text contains explicit reference to the "clans/families" of Ephraim, thus confirming the observations above about the social makeup of sectarian movements. The text also makes it clear that the "clans/families, nobles and leaders" of Ephraim follow particular religious ideas different from those of the author(s) of Pesher Nahum. Someone "misdirects" them, apparently, into a particular religious doctrine. In other words, in addition to confirming the social information of the previous texts, Pesher Nahum ii.9–10 adds a religious dimension, thus putting the groups under discussion closer to the "philosophical schools" of Josephus.[109]

Pesher Nahum depicts two groups (Ephraim and Manasseh) that can be identified as Jewish factions of the Second Temple period. Both of them are described as composed of aristocratic clans (households) that follow a particular approach to Judaism. This description closely resembles the one of the Pharisees provided by Josephus in his story about the reign of Alexander Jannaeus. Still, unlike Josephus, who prefers to describe the sects as "parties" or "schools," Pesher Nahum portrays them by using family and clan-based terminology. As a whole this description is consistent with the way in which the Damascus Document and 4QMMT describe the opponents of the sect. Both texts can shed light on the social and religious mode of functioning of the Second Temple Jewish sects. In both cases those sects appear to be networks of Jewish households sharing particular halakhic practices as publicly binding and manifesting the correct interpretation of Jewish law.

We get additional information about the possible structure of the Dead Sea sect from the accounts of the house of Absalom and the house of Peleg, whose members were related to but not identical

---

[108] 4Q169 II, 9–10.
[109] Cf. CD XX, 14–15 referring to "men of war" who "walked with the Man of Lies." The identification of this group is hardly possible, but the text seems to contain another reference to military aristocracy in the context of sectarian strife within Judaism.

with those of the Dead Sea sect. We learn from Pesher Habakkuk
V, 9–10 about the house of Absalom. This passage interprets Habakkuk
1:13, "Why are you staring, traitors, and you maintain your silence
when a wicked priest consumes someone more upright than himself?" According to the pesher:

> Its interpretation concerns the house of Absalom and the members of
> his council (בית אבשלום ואנשי עצתם), who kept silent at the time of the
> reproach of the Teacher of Righteousness and did not help him against
> the Man of Lies, who rejected the law in the midst of their whole
> comm[unity].

Here "the house of Absalom and the members of his council" constitute the background against which the conflict between the Teacher
of Righteousness and the Man of Lies takes place. The exact nature
of the house of Absalom eludes us, although this group seems to
have been originally related to the Teacher of Righteousness but
later rejected him.[110] Was this house one of the clans whose sum
total constituted the community according to the Rule of the
Congregation? The house of Absalom appears in the pesher as a
setting for the religious debate, reminiscent of the Ephraim in Pesher
Nahum. Still, there is not much we can say about this group's social
makeup.

The situation is somewhat better with the so-called house of Peleg,
which appears in both Pesher Nahum and the Damascus Document.
In the Damascus Document XX, 22–23, we read about "the house
of Peleg (בית פלג), who left the holy city and leaned on God in the
age of Israel's unfaithfulness; but they defiled the temple and turned
back to the path of the people in some things." There is not much
we can say about the house of Peleg based on this excerpt, other
than that it had joined the Dead Sea group at a certain point but
later split away from it (hence, its coded name "the house of division or separation").[111]

---

[110] Murphy-O'Connor, "The Essenes and their History," 234–35, identifies the
house of Absalom as "part of the original community that didn't support the Teacher
of Righteousness against the Man of Lies." Cf. B. Nitzan, "Absalom, House of,"
in L. Schiffman and J. VanderKam, eds., *Encyclopedia of the Dead Sea Scrolls*, vol. 1,
4–5.

[111] Davies, *The Damascus Covenant*, 190–94, concludes that the CD does not portray the house of Peleg as part of the Dead Sea sect. The Damascus Document
sees the house of Peleg as another (sectarian?) group sharing some of its ideals but
at the same time suspicious in other matters. Its members can be accepted into the

We can glean more adequate information about the possible social structure of the house of Peleg from the Pesher Nahum IV, 1, which interprets Nahum 3:9: "Put and Lybia were her guards" by identifying them with "the house of Peleg (בית פלג), which joined themselves to Manasseh." This phrase comes as part of the larger discussion of Manasseh referred to above. It appears to deal with a clan that originally had allied itself with the Dead Sea sect but later changed its allegiance and joined aristocratic clans whose sum total composed the group called "Manasseh" in Pesher Nahum.[112]

In other words, we can say that similarly to Ephraim and Manasseh, the Dead Sea sect itself consisted of a number of clans which agreed to follow a particular understanding of Judaism. CD XX, 12–13, which immediately precedes the information about the house of Peleg, shows that both the house of Peleg and the house of Absalom are indeed clan- or family-based groups and not symbolic figures of speech for uncertain social entities.[113] This passage deals with a person "who enters the congregation of the men of perfect holiness and is slack in the fulfillment of the instructions of the upright." Such men:

> Should be judged according to the judgment of their companions, who turned back with insolent men, for they spoke falsehood about the holy congregation and despised the covenant and the pact which they established in the land of Damascus, [which is the first covenant]. And neither for them, nor their families (משפחותיהם) there shall be a part in the house of the law (בבית התורה).[114]

community on a case by case basis. But the movement itself is not part of the Dead Sea sect. Davies also observes that "the 'house of Peleg' paragraph permits us some speculation about the origins of the community of the 'new covenant' itself." It may reflect ideas of the "parent community" of the Dead Sea sect which, unlike the Dead Sea sect, was not prepared to cut itself off the temple. Although it believed that current temple practices resulted in its defilement, its reaction to this defilement was more measured. Once again, we can find here parallels with the group of Ezra and Nehemiah, whose rejection of certain priestly practices did not result in their withdrawal into the wilderness. Cf. Murphy-O'Connor, "The Essenes and their History," 239 and 241, who sees the house of Peleg as reference to non-Qumran Judaism in general.

[112] White, "The House of Peleg in the Dead Sea Scrolls," 67–98, arrives at the conclusion that Bet Peleg refers to Onias and his temple. Although this particular conclusion is open to debate, the clan-based structure of Onias' movement seems remarkably similar to that of the early Dead Sea sect.

[113] See J. Murphy-O'Connor, "A Literary Analysis of Damascus Document XIX,33–XX,34," *RB* 79 (1972), 544–64, for critical analysis of this section and its sources. He maintains that originally CD XX, 22c–34 was a separate document not connected with the preceding section. Cf. Davies, *The Damascus Covenant*, 173–97.

[114] "House of the law" refers here to the sectarian community. For parallels and

In this passage the person who violates the precepts of the sect must be excluded from it. Interestingly enough, the exclusion is not limited to him alone but rather includes his family as well. The passage talks specifically about their participation in "the covenant and the pact, which they established in the land of Damascus, which is the first covenant." It implies that the covenant was made with individual families and their heads and they are its main subjects. The household-based structure of the sect thus becomes clear. The example of the house of Peleg that follows immediately afterwards may serve to provide an illustration of this general rule. In other words, the terms "the house of Peleg" and "the house of Absalom" appear to refer to actual clans rather than to general symbols of some social groups.[115]

To summarize: similarly to the accounts describing early stages in the development of the Dead Sea sect itself, descriptions of its opponents identify households and clans as essential blocks within Jewish religious movements of the time. There are reasons to believe that the clans which composed the Dead Sea sect were not substantially different from those which constituted other movements. This allowed such groups as the house of Peleg and the house of Absalom to switch sides relatively easily and to choose among the various ideologies present within Second Temple Judaism.

Hellenistic Associations and the Community of 1QS

Despite the centrality of traditional patriarchal households for preservation, transmission, and development of the Law, early Second Temple movements also featured what may be called "supra-familial" structures, i.e., organizational communal structures surpassing the level of individual families. It was because of these structures that alliances of families could occasionally function as religious move-

---

discussion see Murphy-O'Connor, "A Literary Analysis of Damascus Document XIX,33–XX,34," 549–50.

[115] Davies, *The Damascus Covenant*, 182–86, sees the entire admonition of CD XX, 8–13 as a warning to people who tend to abandon the Dead Sea sect for its parent community. It is thus directly related to the following passage on the house of Peleg. If we accept this explanation as a working hypothesis, we can talk about the household-based organization of the parent community and its similarity to the organization of the "Congregation of the Exile" in Ezra-Nehemiah.

ments ("sects") within Judaism. Such structures became visible as early as the time of Ezra and Nehemiah and were essentially identical with the assemblies of the heads of households constituting the community. We have already discussed the gathering of Neh 8:13–15, at which the "heads of the clans of all the people" joined Ezra to interpret the Torah. The result of this meeting was their decision to celebrate the festival of the seventh month in a particular way. The decision was made obligatory for their respective families, and so a new way of celebrating the holiday was established.

CD XIII, 2–3 probably attests similar practices of regulative gatherings when it requires that "where the ten are, there shall never be lacking a priest learned in the Book of Meditation. They all shall be ruled by him." Similar to Nehemiah 8, CD sees the study of religious texts as crucial for the movement's identity. In fact, CD V, 20–VII, 8 explicitly recognizes the interpretation of the Law by "the Interpreter of the Law" and "the members of the new covenant in the land of Damascus" as the central element in the life of the new community. Although CD does not specify who exactly took part in such study sessions, we may speculate that in this case they were also the heads of the households constituting the sect.[116] Just as was the case with Nehemiah himself, CD is perfectly comfortable with having a non-priestly official (mevaqqer) running the affairs of the community. The document attests a wide range of supervisory privileges for this official. He interprets the law for the community and controls its everyday affairs, including trade practices and marriages.[117] Overall, as we have already indicated above, his powers are remarkably similar to those claimed by Nehemiah. Finally, in both cases large public assemblies (called "the assembly of all the camps" in CD) play a crucial role in controlling and directing activities of individual families within the movement.[118]

---

[116] Consider the prohibition of sinning against one's "near kin" and the requirement "to keep from fornication according to the statute" in CD VII, 1. Schremer, "[T]he[y] did not Read," 105–26, argues that the emergence of the written text as the main source of religious authority in Second Temple Judaism marginalized family-based ancestral traditions of earlier times. Still, "the Congregation of the Exile" of Ezra-Nehemiah, the early Dead Sea sect, and other related movements seem to prove that families continued to remain basic social and religious units within early Second Temple sectarian groups even when these groups built their identity around sacred texts.

[117] CD XIII, 7–19.

[118] See CD XIV, 3–12, 4Q 266 10 I, 1–10 and 4Q 267 9 V, 6–14. Cf. Nehemiah 9–10.

Still, the existence of such supra-familial communal structures should not be seen as curtailing the centrality of families for the religious projects of these groups. In all of the abovementioned cases there remained a clear understanding that the traditional patriarchal family constituted the prime locus of holiness within the movement and thus served as the true embodiment of either observance or non-observance of the Law. This holiness had to be preserved by all means necessary against pollution and violation. As a result, the family constituted the prime object of legislation in earlier halakhic rules of the Second Commonwealth. The community and its officials sought to regulate family life precisely because it was deemed so central for their religious aspirations. Far from denying the religious value of traditional households, supra-familial structures of early Second Temple movements treated families as central for their religious discourse. In this situation, the larger community (such as the "congregation of the exile" in Ezra-Nehemiah or the "community of the renewed covenant" in CD) structured itself as an alliance of families intended to preserve themselves as loci of sanctity by practicing Jewish law in a particular way. Although supra-familial communal structures were becoming increasingly influential starting with Ezra-Nehemiah, there is no evidence that the basic centrality of household (and its everyday functions) as the prime building block of the community was ever questioned.[119]

The real change in the nature of the community came with the shift in basic perception of what constitutes the embodiment of holiness in Judaism. This change occurred when the community of like-minded individuals gradually replaced the family as the prime locus of sanctity in Judaism. As a result, the focus of religious discourse shifted from sanctifying one's everyday family life in accordance with particular halakhic norms to joining a new community of righteous individuals. The latter served as a religious substitute for the notion

---

[119] CD VI, 11–VII, 6 contains a list of rules for the group of sectarians identified as "those who walk in perfect holiness." It is possible (although not certain) that our text contrasts this group with "those who live in camps according to the order of the land and marry," addressed in subsequent passages of CD. If so, the former may (but again, not necessarily) represent a celibate "elite" movement within the sect. See J. Baumgarten, "The Qumran-Essene Restraints on Marriage" in L. Schiffman, ed., *Archaeology and History in the Dead Sea Scrolls: The New York University Conference in Memory of Yigael Yadin* (Sheffield: JSOT Press, 1990), 18–20. Depending on one's interpretation of this passage, CD VI, 11–VII, 6 may be indicative of the shift toward new religious consciousness taking place within the sect.

of familial holiness advocated in earlier texts. It was this new entity that embodied sanctity and led to ultimate salvation, not the traditional patriarchal family. The Community Rule expresses this new vision of holiness in vivid terms:

> When these become members of the Community in Israel according to all these rules, they shall establish the spirit of holiness according to everlasting truth. They shall atone for guilty rebellion and for sins of unfaithfulness, that they may obtain loving-kindness for the Land without the flesh of holocausts and the fat of sacrifice. And prayer rightly offered shall be as an acceptable fragrance of righteousness, and perfection of way as a delectable free-will offering. At that time, the men of the Community shall set apart a House of Holiness in order that it may be united to the most holy things and a House of Community for Israel, for those who walk in perfection.[120]

The community emerges from this description as the prime setting of holiness and sanctity destined to replace the Temple in carrying out atonement for Israel. There is nothing in this particular text that would indicate that the community in question no longer binds together families but rather individual followers. Still, other sections of the Community Rule indicate that this indeed is the case:

> No man shall be in the community of His truth who refuses to enter the Covenant of God so that he may walk in the stubbornness of his heart, for his soul detests the wise teaching of just laws. He shall not be counted among the upright for he has not persisted in the conversion of his life. His knowledge, powers, and possessions shall not enter the Council of the Community . . . He shall not be justified by that which his stubborn heart declares lawful, for seeking the ways of light he looks towards darkness. He shall not be reckoned among the perfect. He shall neither be purified by atonement, nor cleansed by purifying waters, nor sanctified by seas and rivers, nor washed clean with any ablution. Unclean, unclean shall he be. For as long as he despises the precepts of God he shall receive no instruction in the Community of His counsel.[121]

This exhortation addresses an individual. It castigates such personal characteristics as "stubbornness of the heart" and misplaced freedom of making choices. Thus, it is an individual based on his own merits who either gets accepted to or rejected from the community "of the perfect." As Lawrence Schiffman has observed, there is "an

---

[120] 1QS VIII, 4–10.
[121] 1QS II, 25–III, 6.

understanding of the unique relationship between repentance, initiation into the sect, and ritual purification."[122] The act of joining the community comes as a result of one's repentance and the decision to transform one's inner self. It is meant to be deeply personal.[123] The family and family-centered halakhic observances no longer play any significant role in paving one's way toward righteousness. A person's lot is determined within his heart and expressed by his decision to join the community of Truth or leave it. Upon joining the community, he is examined "with respect to his understanding and practice of the Law."[124] Afterwards he undergoes annual examinations of "spirit and deeds" to determine his spiritual advancement.[125] Overall, individual spirituality and piety play a central role in the religious discourse of the Community Rule (culminating in the famous "Tractate on Two Spirits"). Throughout the document the community is described as the depository of holiness on earth built around pure lifestyles of its individual members.

If we compare specific regulations recorded in the Community Rule to those of CD, we see how much the paradigm of a sacred community consisting of individual adult devotees replaced that of the alliance of households.[126] The bulk of laws preserved in the Rule deal with two types of relationships. First, they seek to regulate routine interaction among individual members of the group. Offenses against fellow sectarians, such as gossiping, cursing, insulting, and cheating, are singled out and punished with various degrees of severity.[127] Second, they address relationships between an individual member and the community as a corporate entity. These include offenses against the community and its officials, disturbing behavior during public gatherings, lying about one's property, etc.[128] The family, which played such a role in CD, is virtually non-existent in the Rule. It is no longer part of its discourse of sanctity. What matters is how an individual community member positions himself vis-à-vis other

---

[122] Schiffman, *Reclaiming the Dead Sea Scrolls*, 103.
[123] 1QS III, 6–12 and V, 8–10. Cf. the blessing formula of the purification ritual in 4Q512. See Schiffman, *Reclaiming the Dead Sea Scrolls*, 299.
[124] 1QS V, 20–22.
[125] 1QS V, 24.
[126] Cf. discussion of these laws in L. Schiffman, *Sectarian Law in the Dead Sea Scrolls: Courts, Testimony and the Penal Code* (Chico: Scholars Press, 1983), 155–90.
[127] See 1QS VI, 25–27 and VII, 4–6, 8–9, 15–16.
[128] See 1QS VI, 24–25 and VII, 1–3, 6–8, 9–15, 17, 18–21.

members or vis-à-vis the community as a whole. It is these norms of behavior, not regulations pertaining to everyday life of households, that allow the group to preserve itself as an embodiment of holiness in this world. The change of the legal subject of regulations vividly underscores this transformation of religious mentality.

This new type of the community also structures itself around a particular set of rituals underscoring its uniqueness and holiness, as well as reinforcing common bonds among people assembled in it. The Community Rule focuses specifically on various types of ritualized gatherings creating a new identity in the group's members. Those include common meals, communal assemblies, and discussion of sacred texts within study circles. They all seek to strengthen the self-perception of the community as the true embodiment of sanctity and knowledge within Israel:

> They shall eat in common, and bless in common, and deliberate in common.
>
> Wherever there are ten men of the Council of the Community there shall not lack a priest among them. And they shall all sit before him according to their rank and shall be asked their counsel in all things in that order. And when the table has been prepared for eating, and the new wine for drinking, the priest shall be the first to stretch out his hand to bless the first fruits of bread and new wine.
>
> And where the ten are, there shall never lack a man among them who shall study the Law continually, day and night, concerning the right conduct of a man with his companion. And the congregation shall watch in community for a third of every night of the year, to read the Book and to study the Law and to bless together.[129]

The combination of communal study, communal liturgy, and communal meals was a potent tool of forging new identity for community members, surpassing and sidelining that of their natural kinship bonds. Parts of this passage from the Community Rule bear strong resemblance to the already quoted section from CD that requires the presence of "a priest learned in the Book of Meditation" among any ten men of the community, who "shall be ruled by him."[130] Indeed, the two of them may describe the same practice of the communal study of the Law. But their present contextual settings are different. Whereas CD seeks to legislate for a community in which

---

[129] 1QS VI, 2–8.
[130] CD XIII, 2–3.

family life constitutes the centerpiece of religious experience, the Rule
provides guidance for a religious community that creates a new identity for its members. This identity is built around common practices
and rituals, which sanctify and give religious meaning to the life of
the individual as part of the sectarian community, not as part of a
family.[131]

Two additional rules of shared possessions and shared "pure meal
of the Congregation" further emphasized the uniqueness of the group.
Both practices reflected complete absorption of a new member into
the community. Once the person had been accepted, his property
was "merged" with that of the Congregation and he was allowed to
partake of the "pure meal" (meaning both food and liquids) of its
members.[132] At the same time, he was prohibited from sharing his
possessions and his meal with non-members.[133] It remains unclear
just how much of the communal ownership of goods is presupposed
by the term "merger." Most scholars today would probably agree
that the text refers to the communal use of private possessions rather
than their complete appropriation by the community.[134] The permission to eat "pure meal" also does not necessarily refer to ceno-
bite-style common meals but rather to the foodstuffs of the network
of people whose meals were deemed pure and thus were allowed to
be shared. Despite similarities in language, there is little indication
that we are dealing here with the direct forerunner of cenobite
monasticism. It is unlikely that upon joining the community envisioned by the Community Rule everyone would merge his possessions in a common ownership pool and withdraw into the Judaean
desert to live the life of "ascetic scholasticism" and shared communal meals. In reality, people probably continued to live in their

---

[131] On the central role of ritualized study in Qumran community and its discourse of holiness see S. Fraade, "Interpretive Authority in the Studying Community
of Qumran," *JJS* 44 (1993), 46–69. He does not distinguish, however, between
different ways in which the practice of study might have worked at different stages
of the group's history.

[132] See 1QS VI, 13–23 on different stages of this process. On possible meanings
of ritualized meals at Qumran see, most recently, Hempel, "Community Structures,"
84–86, and D. Smith, "Meals," in Schiffman and VanderKam, *Encyclopedia of the
Dead Sea Scrolls*, vol. 1, 530–32.

[133] 1QS V, 14–15 and IX, 8–9.

[134] See, for example, Hempel, "Community Structures," 74–75, Schiffman, *Reclaiming
the Dead Sea Scrolls*, 106–110, and J. VanderKam, *The Dead Sea Scrolls Today* (Grand
Rapids: Eerdmans, 1994), 82–84. Cf. Collins, "Forms of Community," 102–103,
for a more cautious assessment.

homes, but their possessions (and their meals) were supposed to be readily available to their fellow-sectarians.[135]

One cannot miss, however, that the holiness discourse of the Community Rule lacks any reference to one's household. This does not mean that families themselves disappeared from the life of individual sectarians, only that they were no longer part of the religiously meaningful universe. They no longer constituted the loci of sanctity and holiness. Properly regulated family life was no longer seen as the way to achieve purity and salvation. Instead, the Rule focused on the religious community of like-minded adults and portrayed it as the only religiously significant social space of life and interpersonal relationships. Only as part of the community could people achieve their religious goals. Once again, all this does not imply that sectarians no longer had families. It implies that these families lost their religious value to the new type of sacred community and were no longer part of one's religious experience.[136]

Hellenistic associations provide the closest contemporaneous parallel to this phenomenon. They also did not necessarily abrogate family lives of their members. But Hellenistic associations, as a gathering of like-minded and professionally related individuals, created a new, religiously meaningful space.[137] This new identity was forged around commonly held rituals and practices, such as common meals, sacrificial offerings, and celebrations. Moshe Weinfeld was certainly correct when he observed remarkable similarities between the Community Rule and statutes of Hellenistic associations. In fact, both of them shared the same idea of what constituted the properly functioning community and its governing structures.[138] In both cases

---

[135] 1QS VI, 2–3 implies that sectarians continued to reside in communities across the land. As John Collins has observed, "The *yahad* is not a single community, but an association of people who live in many communities." See J. Collins, "Forms of Community," 97–111, for further discussion. Cf. H. Stegemann, *The Library of Qumran: On the Essenes, Qumran, John the Baptist and Jesus* (Grand Rapids: Eerdmans, 1998), 142. This, of course, does not automatically mean that they had families, but the likelihood of such a scenario becomes considerably higher.

[136] The question of celibacy in the yahad remains highly controversial. See most recently J. Baumgarten, "Celibacy," in Schiffman and VanderKam, *Encyclopedia of the Dead Sea Scrolls*, vol. 1, 122–24, and Schuller, "Women in the Dead Sea Scrolls," 117–44. Cf. Collins, "Forms of Community," 104.

[137] See Nock, *Conversion*, 99–121, and Wilson, "Voluntary Associations," 1–15.

[138] Weinfeld, *Organizational Pattern*, 10–21. Cf. Dombrowski, "היחד in 1QS and τὸ κοινόν," 293–307. On similarities and differences between Hellenistic associations and the Qumran group see further E. Larson, "Greco-Roman Guilds," in Schiffman and VanderKam, *Encyclopedia of the Dead Sea Scrolls*, vol. 1, 321–23.

we find the same attempt to create new forms of religious and social identities that could surpass and sideline traditional kinship loyalties.[139] In the case of Hellenistic associations this process would often result in the emergence of multiple religious identities. Members of an association participated in the newly created religious space of their common gathering but at the same time did not abandon traditional family-based observances. The same scenario is possible for those who followed the Community Rule, although there is little explicit evidence to prove that. As it stands now, the Community Rule is absolutely silent about any religious value of one's family life and thus appears to be more exclusive in its demands than Hellenistic associations would usually be. Just how much the congregation envisioned by 1QS was receptive to multiple religious identities of its members must remain an open question.

Weinfeld's analysis of similarities between the Community Rule and statutes of Hellenistic associations focused on their respective penal codes. We have argued above that the Rule's penal regulations predominantly deal with two types of relationships: those among individual members of the community and those between individual members and the community as a whole. Weinfeld's discussion proves that in this respect they were virtually identical with regulations of a typical Hellenistic association of the time. In both cases individual relationships among the members and members' behavior vis-à-vis the community become the prime subject of legislation. Transgressions against the community in both cases include infidelity to the group, disturbing behavior during public gatherings or repeated failure to attend them. The requirement of fixed sitting order based on rigid internal ranking within the community and related demands of orderly participation in public deliberations also play a crucial role in both instances. Additional laws regulate issues related to members' property, which in both cases has to be readily available for communal use.[140]

Laws regulating the relationships among individual followers of the sect are equally similar. They seek to restrain such everyday vices as gossiping, cursing, getting angry at one another, and cheating. All

---

[139] Cf. Cohen, *From the Maccabees to the Mishnah*, 115–16.
[140] Weinfeld, *Organizational Pattern*, 24–34.

interpersonal conflicts within the group have to be settled internally by using an elaborate system of witnesses and communal courts. The use of an outside court to settle internal disputes is considered a particularly grave offense in the Rule as well as in regulatory statutes of Hellenistic associations.[141] In addition to Weinfeld's observations, one also has to notice the paucity of legislation regulating one's behavior within the family. In both cases a member's family is put outside the scope of regulations. Both the Rule and Hellenistic statutes seek to create a new space for their members, in which traditional families play no role. As far as these groups are concerned, the household space loses its social and religious significance.

While providing a thorough comparison of legislative aspects of 1QS and Hellenistic associations, Weinfeld stops short of addressing their religious similarities. In fact, he tries to argue that religion is precisely the area in which the two differed.[142] Matthias Klinghardt has rightly criticized this inconsistency, arguing that parallels between the movements also included matters of ritual and piety.[143] Weinfeld himself maintains that rituals of acceptance for new members, their examination, and required periods of probation for candidates are similar in both cases.[144] In both cases the emphasis is put on individual piety required for membership and tested through a multistage acceptance process. But ritual similarities went much further than that. For example, ritualized communal meals that were so central for forging common identity in the community of 1QS were equally central in many (if not most) Hellenistic associations of the time.[145] Both types of movements constructed new religiously and socially meaningful space around common rituals that sanctified the existence of members within the groups. In the process both of them were creating a new discourse of holiness centered on the community of like-minded individuals.

Overall, there are serious reasons to believe that transition from the family-centered community of CD and 4QMMT to the com-

---

[141] Weinfeld, *Organizational Pattern*, 34–41.
[142] Weinfeld, *Organizational Pattern*, 46–47.
[143] See M. Klinghardt, "The Manual of Discipline in the Light of Statutes of Hellenistic Associations," in M. Wise et al., eds., *Methods of Investigation of the Dead Sea Scrolls and the Khirbet Qumran Site: Present Realities and Future Prospects* (New York: The New York Academy of Sciences, 1994), 251–67. Cf. Collins, "Forms of Community," 100–104.
[144] Weinfeld, *Organizational Pattern*, 21–23 and 43–44.
[145] See Klinghardt, "Manual of Discipline," 253–54 and 261–62.

munity of like-minded individuals of 1QS was a result of profound Hellenization of the contemporaneous Jewish society. This process obviously did not occur overnight. In fact, its exact chronological parameters are fairly difficult to ascertain. It would be prudent to maintain that in the first century BCE this process was well under way. At the same time, the early paradigm of family-based community probably continued to exist, as can be concluded from the ongoing copying of CD. It is once again necessary to emphasize that the new religious ethos of 1QS did not negate the existence of the family (just as the latter was not negated by Hellenistic associations). All it did was to marginalize the family's role in the grand project of an individual's salvation. But this marginalization would have long-lasting effects on the entire fabric of Jewish and Christian religiosity in centuries to come.

The religious discourse of 1QS provided two possible venues for future development. On the one hand, it could be combined with that of CD and other earlier texts to produce a balanced community, which tried to integrate family into its space of holiness.[146] On the other hand, the holiness project of 1QS could potentially become increasingly more "utopian" by severing natural ties with the outside world and replacing them with a newly constructed sacred realm of its own. This process might have given birth to the celibate Essenes of Josephus and Pliny.[147] It may also account for the existence of "the men of perfect holiness," an elite within the *yahad* of 1QS who underwent especially rigorous spiritual training. The latter might have involved the withdrawal into the desert and prolonged periods of abstinence, as well as instructions in "esoteric" doctrines of the sect.[148] It is possible that the Qumran settlement played the role of a "training center" for such an elite. In each of these cases the utopian vision of a sacred community composed of uniquely pious individuals clearly dominates religious discourse.

Overall, the transformation of Jewish sectarianism from a family-based to an association-type enterprise marked the turning point in the religious history of the Second Commonwealth. Different stages in the development of the Dead Sea sect provide us with the first clear example of such change.

---

[146] As probably "the married Essenes" of Josephus did. See *B.J.* 2.160–161.

[147] *B.J.* 2.120–121 and Pliny, *Nat.*, 5.17.4 (73).

[148] 1QS VIII, 5–16. See Collins, "Forms of Community," 105–107, for further discussion of this passage and its implications.

Conclusions

In recent years, scholars have focused on the earlier stages in the history of the Dead Sea sect. J. Murphy-O'Connor and Philip Davies have proposed looking for the origins of the movement in the period of the Babylonian Exile.[149] Florentino García Martínez and other proponents of the "Groningen Hypothesis" have looked into the apocalyptic movements of early Hellenistic Judaea for possible roots of the Dead Sea sect.[150] Although the specific details of any of these theories are open to debate, there is an increasing consensus among scholars that the Dead Sea sect came into existence as a fairly typical movement within early Second Temple Judaism.

It comes as no surprise, then, that the social structure of the Dead Sea sect resembled, at a certain stage of its history, the social structure of Ezra-Nehemiah's movement(s). It would be logical to suggest that such a resemblance was strongest at the early stages of the sect's history. In this respect, the theory about the "Babylonian" origins of the movement possesses clear merits. Even if we disagree with an attempt to actually trace sectarian origins back to the Exile, its social structure appears to be close to the social structure of other Jewish movements that emerged in Babylonia. In other words, it would be fair to speak of a particular social type of Jewish religious movement stretching from the times of Ezra and Nehemiah through the early Hellenistic period and maybe even beyond it. Whether or not we should label it "Babylonian" or "exilic" is open to further debate.

The Dead Sea scrolls use a remarkably consistent language and system of images to depict what are otherwise known as "sects" of the Second Temple period. Unlike Josephus, who tends to phrase his description in a way suitable for his Roman readers, the documents from Qumran describe the sects as alliances of families following a specific interpretation of the Law. On a larger scale, such a social structure perfectly fits into the overall social and political system of the Persian, Hellenistic and Roman Near East, aptly described by

---

[149] See references to their works throughout this chapter.

[150] See F. García Martínez, "Qumran Origins and Early History: A Groningen Hypothesis," *Folia Orientalia* 25 (1988), 113–36, and F. García Martínez and A. van der Woude, "A 'Groningen' Hypothesis of Qumran Origins and Early History," *RevQ* 14 (1990), 521–41. Cf. G. Boccaccini, *Beyond the Essene Hypothesis: The Parting of the Ways between Qumran and Enochic Judaism* (Grand Rapids: Eerdmans, 1998), 81–117.

Rostovtzeff as "oriental feudalism," and provides a promising correction to the traditional description of sects as Hellenistic voluntary associations.[151]

On the other hand, the Dead Sea sect provides the earliest unambiguous example of gradual transition from the household-based matrix of Jewish sectarianism to a community that encompassed adult male individuals. In the process it surpassed and sidelined natural kinship ties. The new community was formed and sustained by a free act of its adult members. In the case of the Dead Sea sect, the two stages did not exist in strict chronological sequence, although the "family-dominated" stage was probably a more archaic one. In reality, the two stages overlapped, producing by the first century CE different types within the same movement. A new group that emerged within the movement resembled in its structure Hellenistic associations and probably came into existence as a result of gradual Hellenization of Jewish society. Similar to the associations, it provided its members with a new sense of religious and social identity. Families would no longer play any role within its discourse of holiness. Instead, the holiness was preserved and transmitted in the community comprised of like-minded individuals who followed particular rules of personal piety. This form of religious organization would eventually win the day in Jewish Palestine and reach its fruition in the disciple circles of early Christians and rabbis. And it is to Rabbinic Judaism that we shall turn in the second part of this work.

[151] See M. Rostovtzeff, *The Social and Economic History of the Roman Empire* (Oxford: Clarendon Press, 1966), vol. 1, 269.

PART TWO

RABBIS AND HOUSEHOLDS: NEGOTIATING HOLINESS

CHAPTER FOUR

PHARISAIC TRADITIONS IN JOSEPHUS AND THE NEW TESTAMENT

The writings of Flavius Josephus and the New Testament represent our main Greek sources on Second Temple Jewish sectarianism. In particular, both of them contain detailed descriptions of the Pharisees and unique "traditions of the fathers" (*paradosis tōn paterōn*) that distinguished the Pharisees from other contemporaneous Jewish groups. In this chapter I shall take a closer look at what these traditions might have been. I shall argue that rather than designating halakhic teachings transmitted within disciple circles, the term "traditions of the fathers" referred to practices, beliefs, and halakhic norms developed and transmitted from generation to generation within Pharisaic households. These households produced and embodied Pharisaic "traditions of the fathers" just as priestly families embodied priestly halakhah and knowledge of the temple law and lore. The purpose of these household practices was to sanctify the everyday routine of those who practiced them and to transform the everyday lives of patriarchal Jewish families into religiously meaningful activities. Such practices fit perfectly well into the cultural and religious context of their times. As archaeological evidence seems to suggest, familial customs, cultural tastes and commitments can hardly be separated from Jewish religious practices at the turn of the Common Era.[1] Around the same time domestic cults and devotion had also become prominent manifestations of local religiosities across the Roman East.[2]

---

[1] Ritual pools (*miqva'ot*) unearthed in large numbers in and around Jerusalem provide an excellent example of how much individual tastes could be a factor. Were these pools used specifically and exclusively for ritual immersion purposes? Were they just regular bath tubs of affluent citizens? Perhaps, both? For a good summary of ambiguities and uncertainties involved see B. Wright, "Jewish Ritual Baths—Interpreting the Digs and the Texts: Some Issues in the Social History of Second Temple Judaism," in N. Silberman and D. Small, eds., *The Archaeology of Israel: Constructing the Past, Interpreting the Present* (Sheffield: Sheffield Academic, 1997), 190–214. Marriage practices were equally dictated by private customs and cultural preferences. See Satlow, *Jewish Marriage*, 93–132 and 162–81.

[2] On the role of domestic religion in Roman Egypt see D. Frankfurter, *Religion in Roman Egypt: Assimilation and Resistance* (Princeton: Princeton University Press, 1998), 131–42.

Finally, contemporaneous Greco-Roman ideology of familial virtue and piety might have provided a cultural vocabulary for at least some Greek-speaking Jewish authors, most noticeably, Josephus and Philo. Both of them routinely portray family as the backbone of Jewish religious observance by using Greco-Roman rhetoric that praises family as an embodiment of social virtues.[3]

On the other hand, Pharisaic families now operated within the civil environment of the Roman province of Palestine. This environment, among other things, introduced important changes into how religious knowledge was perceived and transmitted.[4] Both Josephus and the New Testament reflect the gradual emergence of disciple circles as the main setting for the formation and dissemination of teachings during the first century BCE and first century CE. This transition would eventually result in the formation of mature Rabbinic Judaism. Pharisaic masters are increasingly portrayed as surrounded by their disciples, not their families. Even John Hyrcanus emerges in these stories as a "disciple" of the Pharisees. When put together, Josephan accounts of Pharisees reflect this transition from a household-centered society of Hellenistic Judah to the civil society of urbanized and profoundly Hellenized Roman Palestine. The emergence of Rabbinic Judaism was one of the most long-lasting results of this transition.

Pharisaic "Ancestral Traditions" in Josephus

The problem of the Pharisaic "traditions of the fathers" has traditionally received much scholarly attention.[5] Recently, there has been

---

[3] On the importance of family values for Jewish Greek writers and their Roman imperial context see M.R. D'Angelo, "Εὐσέβεια: Roman Imperial Family Values and the Sexual Politics of 4 Maccabees and the Pastorals," *Biblical Interpretation* 11/2 (2003), 139–64. Cf. C. Osiek and D. Balch, *Families in the New Testament World: Households and House Churches* (Louisville: Westminster John Knox Press, 1997), 118–21. For a specific example of *dextrarum iunctio* in Roman iconography see G. Davies, "The Significance of the Handshake Motif in Classical Funerary Art," *AJA* 89 (1985), 638–39 (and literature cited there).

[4] Baumgarten, *Flourishing of Jewish Sects*, 137–51, correctly stresses the role of urbanization and urban culture in the transformation of Second Temple Judaism, although this process of urbanization probably started later than he thinks (Roman rather than Hellenistic period). See Jones, "Urbanization of Palestine," *JRS* 21 (1931), 78–85.

[5] For various meanings of term *paradosis* in Josephus see A. Baumgarten, "The Pharisaic *Paradosis*," *HTR* 80 (1987), 64. Its most relevant meaning in our case is "history" or "tradition."

a gradual shift from a tendency to explain the Pharisaic traditions of the fathers from the perspective of the Oral Law of later Rabbinic Judaism to judging them on their own merit and without superimposing on them later theological and halakhic constructs.[6] When seen from this angle, the Pharisees appear much more "normal" in their Second Temple setting. They differed from other groups in respect to specific laws that they followed, but their social structure was probably similar to that of other religious groups of the time. In a brief but very insightful note on the Pharisaic ancestral tradition, Martin Goodman states that "for most individuals in most societies religion is caught, through imitation of parental customs, rather than taught, whether through writings or verbal instruction."[7] He further observes that "Pharisees encouraged ordinary Jews to keep ancestral customs common to all Jews." In other words, it was their strict adherence and propagation of devotion to ancestral customs that made Pharisees distinct. Unfortunately, the brief nature of the note did not allow Goodman to further elaborate his statement. Still, one can reasonably guess that it presupposes the centrality of family and family-based religious customs for the Pharisaic movement and its halakhic identity.

In this section I shall focus on possible implications of the term "ancestral tradition" as it appears in Josephus, in connection with

---

[6] Most important in this respect is a gradual abandonment (or, at least. questioning) of an old view that what distinguished Pharisees as a religious group was the oral nature of their traditions. This view ultimately derives from the identification of the Pharisaic "traditions of the fathers" with the Oral Law of later Rabbinic Judaism. Recently, scholars have argued that our sources do not indicate that transmission of Pharisaic traditions was any different from that in other contemporaneous Jewish sects. It could be oral, written, or, most often, both. See J. Neusner, "The Written Tradition in the Pre-Rabbinic Period," *JSJ* 4 (1973), 56–65, and "Oral Torah and Oral Tradition: Defining the Problematic," in idem, ed., *Method and Meaning in Ancient Judaism* (Missoula: Scholars Press, 1979), 59–75. Cf. also E. P. Sanders, *Jewish Law from Jesus to the Mishnah: Five Studies* (London: SCM Press, 1990), 99–130, S. Mason, *Flavius Josephus on the Pharisees: A Composition-Critical Study* (Leiden: Brill, 1991), 240–45, and Jaffee, *Torah in the Mouth*, 39–61, esp. 50–52, for similar conclusions. For critical response to this approach see J. Baumgarten, "Form Criticism and the Oral Law," *JSJ* 4 (1974), 34–40 (cf. Neusner's response in "Exegesis and the Written Law," *JSJ* 5 [1974], 176–78), and M. Hengel, and R. Deines, "E.P. Sanders' 'Common Judaism,' Jesus and the Pharisees: A Review Essay," *JTS* 46 (1995), 29–32.

[7] M. Goodman, "A Note on Josephus, the Pharisees and Ancestral Tradition," *JJS* 50 (1999), 18. Cf. Schremer, "[T]he[y] Did not Read in the Sealed Book," 105–26, for further elaboration of Goodman's thesis.

my broader discussion of the social structure of the Pharisaic movement. Before I proceed further, however, several general observations have to be made. All Josephan texts that contain references to the unique Pharisaic *paradosis* seem to belong to the later period of his writings. All of them occur in *Antiquitates*. The passages in which they occur apparently come from the same editorial layer.[8] In many respects, this layer has clear similarities with later rabbinic writings and is remarkably different from earlier descriptions of Pharisees by Josephus. It tends to transmit semi-legendary stories about named pharisaic masters or historical figures, who allegedly came into close contact with the Pharisees. It also tends to emphasize the social influence of the Pharisees as a group and their potential role in maintaining civil peace and stability in Roman Palestine. As a whole, these texts seem to reflect the self-understanding of particular Pharisaic (proto-rabbinic?) groups in the late first century CE. I shall argue that the picture of Pharisaic "ancestral traditions" portrayed in these texts reflects the transition from household halakhic traditions of particular families to the classical rabbinic law of study circles. This transition corresponded to the social transformation of the "proto-rabbinic" movement itself: from Second Temple-style networks of families embodying practices of the Jewish law to study circles studying and transmitting these practices in the form of the "Oral Law" of later Rabbinic Judaism.

The first reference to the Pharisees in *Antiquitates* occurs in the context of Jonathan's reign and appears to be a summary of *Bellum*'s account of three Jewish sects.[9] Josephus inserts it, quite artificially, into the otherwise smoothly running narrative of Jonathan's affairs. The passage does not supply any new information compared to its *Bellum* prototype and thus is of relatively little interest to us.[10] The next time we encounter Pharisees is in the account of John Hyrcanus' reign. There, Josephus performs another artificial insertion of external material into an otherwise consistent and literarily smooth account of *Bellum*, which merely mentions civil disturbances in Judaea without detailing the nature of his opponents.[11] According to *Bellum* the

---

[8] For detailed terminological and linguistic analysis of these references see Mason, *Flavius Josephus*, 230–40. He also stresses their uniqueness within the larger text of Josephus.

[9] *A.J.* 13.171–173.

[10] For discussion of this passage see Mason, *Flavius Josephus*, 196–212.

[11] *B.J.* 1.67. Most scholars agree that style-wise the corresponding section of

sedition happened out of the "envy" of "his countrymen" toward the "prosperous state of affairs" under Hyrcanus. After reproducing almost verbatim the account of *Bellum* in the first sentence of *A.J.* 13.288, Josephus suddenly mentions the Pharisees as prime culprits:

> Particularly hostile to him were the Pharisees, who are one of the Jewish schools (*hairesis ontes mia tōn Ioudaiōn*), as we have related above. And so great is their influence with the masses that even when they speak against a king or high priest, they immediately gain credence.

Although there has been a widely shared opinion that this section comes from the original version of Nicolaus of Damascus somehow omitted by *Bellum*, I tend to agree with Mason that it was written by Josephus and corresponds to his overall picture of the Pharisees in *Antiquitates*.[12] The story serves as a (somewhat clumsy) transition from *Bellum*'s (Nicolaus'?) account to the new material about to be inserted by Josephus. In addition to the linguistic parallels detailed by Mason, the story features rhetorical commonplaces typical of *Antiquitates*' treatment of the Pharisees. The latter include, first and foremost, popular support of the Pharisees and their teachings, something that accords well with the provincial society of the Roman Empire but not with the authoritarian regime of either Herod or his Hasmonean predecessors. Josephus then proceeds to the actual narrative that introduces Pharisees feasting together with John Hyrcanus. This narrative has been widely recognized as borrowed by Josephus from an external source. There are several opinions about the exact nature of this source.[13] For many scholars its Talmudic

---

Antiquitates is mechanically inserted into an otherwise smoothly running narrative that parallels *Bellum*. See D. Schwartz, "Josephus and Nicolaus on the Pharisees," *JSJ* 14 (1983), 158–59, and Stemberger, *Jewish Contemporaries of Jesus*, 104–110. Cf. S. Schwartz, *Josephus and Judaean Politics* (Leiden: Brill, 1990), 173–74.

[12] Schwartz, "Josephus and Nicolaus," 158, argues that whereas *A.J.* 13.288 is favorably disposed toward Hyrcanus and unfavorable toward Pharisees the main body of subsequent narrative is pro-Pharisaic. Hence, they come from different sources (Nicolaus and Josephus, respectively). See also Stemberger, *Jewish Contemporaries*, 111–12. I do not find any unambiguous negativity toward Pharisees in *A.J.* 13.288. Their description corresponds nicely to other passages in *Antiquitates*, which portray them as a powerful and politically active group. I thus agree with Mason, *Flavius Josephus*, 213–45, who attributes the entire section of *A.J.* 13.288–298 to Josephus (albeit on somewhat different grounds).

[13] H. Bloch, *Die Quellen des Flavius Josephus in seiner Archäologie* (Leipzig: Teubner, 1879), 90–92, identifies it as a chronicle of Hyrcanus' reign. J. Destionon, *Die Quellen des Flavius Josephus* (Kiel: Lipsius & Tischer, 1882), vol. 1, 41–44, is more unspecific and refers to it as merely a written narrative. Finally, G. Hölscher, "Josephus," PW, vol. 9:2, 1974–75, sees it as an oral legend.

parallel and details of the narrative itself suggest some sort of a proto-rabbinic tradition, which Josephus chose to insert into the main body of his *Bellum* text:[14]

> Hyrcanus too was a disciple of theirs (*mathētēs de autōn*), and was greatly loved by them. And once he invited them to a feast and entertained them hospitably, and when he saw that they were having a very good time, he began by saying that they knew he wished to be righteous and in everything he did try to please God and them—for the Pharisees profess such beliefs. At the same time he begged them, if they observed him doing anything wrong or straying from the right path, to lead him back to it and correct him. But they testified to his being altogether virtuous, and he was delighted with their praise.

The story further describes how one of Hyrcanus' guests, by name Eleazar, remarked in response that if Hyrcanus wanted to be truly virtuous he had to give up the high priesthood and remain merely a king. He explains his opinion by referring to the tradition of the elders:

> We have heard from the elders (*akouɔmen para tōn presbuterōn*) that your mother was a captive in the reign oɔ Antiochus Epiphanes.

The accusation implied that the purity of Hyrcanus' priestly genealogy was in doubt. Several aspects of this story require our attention. First, the Pharisees emerge in it as a group of Hyrcanus' friends. They spend time together and maintain common social space.[15] The Pharisaic teaching is not an abstract doctrine, which one has to learn, but a way of life, which one has to live. The Pharisees are portrayed

---

[14] Josephus may have borrowed it from the late first century sources related to rabbinic accounts about Alexander Jannaeus (TB Qid. 66a). For detailed discussion see Stemberger, *Jewish Contemporaries of Jesus*, 104–114. See also G. Hölscher, *Die Quellen des Josephus für die Zeit vom Exil bis zum jüdischen Kriege* (Leipzig: Teubner, 1904), 81–84, and Neusner, *From Politics to Piety*, 57–60. The latter prudently observes that "the relationships between the two versions are not clear." S. Zeitlin, *The Rise and Fall of the Judaean State* (Philadelphia: JPS, 1964), vol. 1, 168–70, maintains that the talmudic version of the tradition is older. But cf. S. Cohen, "Parallel Historical Tradition in Josephus and Rabbinic Literature," *Proceedings of the Ninth World Congress of Jewish Studies* (Jerusalem, 1986), vol. 1, 7–14.

[15] Cf. A. Saldarini, *Pharisees, Scribes and Sadducees in Palestinian Society: A Sociological Approach* (Wilmington: Glazier, 1988), 87: "Hyrcanus is the Pharisees' political ruler and patron; the Pharisees are clients dependent on him and act accordingly by not criticizing him." He also emphasizes the importance of the banquet setting of the entire scene.

as participating in banquets, not study sessions.[16] They emerge from this description as a network of people who follow common halakhic practices and are famous for their righteousness. Being their disciple means sharing in their practices and worldviews.[17] Such a description corresponds to what is otherwise known about the early rabbinic movement and its social structure.[18] There too a network of like-minded people played a central role. Discussions often took place in an informal setting of banquets held in rabbinic households. The role of Hyrcanus in this story is somewhat close to that of Rabban Gamaliel in early rabbinic narratives: he is a recognized public leader, but this does not shield him from occasional criticism from his rabbinic colleagues.[19] In both cases we find the same idealized picture of the relationship between power and piety in the emerging rabbinic subculture.

The Pharisees of this story share traditions unique to themselves.[20] The one which surfaces in this story has to do with the genealogical purity of a high priest and Hyrcanus' unsuitability for this position. The tradition is introduced by the phrase, "we have heard it from the elders." Following a thorough discussion of this term by Alastair Campbell, I tend to assume that the "elders" in question are the actual ancestors of the Pharisaic families, who had transmitted critical traditions about the genealogical unfitness of the Hasmonean family to their children.[21] As Catherine Hezser has demonstrated, even during the early rabbinic period this "patriarchal" meaning of the term "elder" was very much alive. Only later on will it be phased out by

---

[16] Although the text refers to Hyrcanus as their "disciple" (*mathētēs*). This may reflect the increasing importance of discipleship in proto-rabbinic circles during this period.

[17] In the *Antiquitates'* version of the story about the Pharisees' refusal to take an oath of allegiance to Herod, Josephus refers to the followers of Samaias and Pollio as *sundiatribontōn autois*. See *A.J.* 15.370. This Greek phrase, customarily rendered as "their disciples," is more general in nature and should rather be translated as "those spending time with them" or "their associates." It thus reflects a similar view of the Pharisaic movement as the story of Hyrcanus.

[18] See Hezser, *Social Structure*, 228–39, and Sivertsev, *Private Households*, 117–39 and 169–83.

[19] Cf. for example M Rosh Hashanah 2:8–9.

[20] As can be inferred from Josephus' claim that Eleazar's story was false. Not everyone accepted the tradition as authentic.

[21] A. Campbell, *The Elders: Seniority within Earliest Christianity* (Edinburgh: T&T Clark, 1994), 20–66.

"elder" in the sense of "teacher."[22] In this context the term "elders" most probably referred to heads of particular households controlling the social, economic, and religious life of their families. The genealogy-related nature of the tradition transmitted by Eleazar in the name of "elders" only confirms this theory. The preservation of the purity of one's stock dominated the Jewish family lore of both priestly and non-priestly families throughout the Second Temple period and well into rabbinic times.[23] Eleazar's tradition would fit perfectly into the larger pattern of contemporaneous Jewish traditions preserved and transmitted by families.

What had begun as a symposium conversation gone sour developed into a full-blown confrontation between Hyrcanus and his former friends, thanks to the intervention of another friend of Hyrcanus, Jonathan. Josephus identifies him as a Sadducee, who masterfully steers Hyrcanus away from the Pharisees.[24] Once again, the halakhic traditions of the Pharisees irritate Hyrcanus, this time when they tell him that Eleazar deserves lashes and imprisonment but not execution for his speech. Once again, the decision seems to have come from the Pharisaic ancestral traditions, not necessarily shared by other groups.[25] As a result, Hyrcanus leaves "the party of the Pharisees" and joins "the Saducean party." Presumably, the legal traditions and norms of the latter began to look more appealing to him. When Hyrcanus abandoned the Pharisees for the Sadducees, he also "abolished the decrees they had imposed on the people, and punished those who observed them."[26] Later, when the Pharisees were back in power under Salome Alexandra, she "restored those practices which the Pharisees had introduced according to the traditions of their forefathers which her father-in-law, Hyrcanus, had abrogated."[27] The story implies that Pharisaic laws were imposed upon most of the Judaean population as early as the reign of John Hyrcanus. All this may be considered part of the glorification of the Pharisees that

---

[22] Hezser, *Social Structure*, 277–86.

[23] Satlow, *Jewish Marriage*, 147–56, correctly emphasizes the importance of genealogical purity traditions for rabbis.

[24] Cf. Saldarini, *Pharisees, Scribes and Sadducees*, 88. He also sees the conflict between Pharisees and Sadducees as rivalry between two groups of influential retainers.

[25] As implied by Josephus in his digression on pharisaic "traditions of the fathers" right after the story (*A.J.* 13.297–298).

[26] *A.J.* 13.296.

[27] *A.J.* 13.408.

characterizes *Antiquitates* as a whole and probably reflects the post-70 reality of social and political life in Judaea.[28] The narrative reflects an idiosyncratic perspective on Jewish history, which views Pharisees and their legal traditions as dominating pre-70 Jewish history.

Josephus concludes his account of Hyrcanus' break with the Pharisees by providing a brief description of the Pharisaic *paradosis* and contrasting it with the Sadducean approach to Judaism:

> For the present I wish merely to explain that the Pharisees had passed on to the people certain regulations handed down by the fathers and not recorded in the Laws of Moses (*nomima tina paredosan tō dēmō hoi Pharisaioi ek paterōn diadochēs, haper ouk anagegraptai en tois Mōuseōs nomois*), for which reason they are rejected by the Sadducean group (*to tōn Saddoukaiōn genos*), who hold that only those regulations should be considered valid which were written down, and that those which had been handed down by the fathers (*ta d' ek paradoseōs tōn paterōn*) need not be observed. And concerning these matters the two parties came to have controversies and serious differences, the Sadducees having the confidence of the wealthy alone but no following among the populace, while the Pharisees have the support of the masses. But of these two [groups] and of the Essenes a detailed account has been given in the second book of my *Judaica*.[29]

Despite the concluding statement referring the reader back to *Bellum*, this description is totally without parallel in *Bellum*'s account of the sects. Similar to the story it purports to clarify, the account appears to be a product of Josephus' attempt to use in his narrative materials favorable to the Pharisees. Moreover, just like Hyrcanus' tale, this description may actually reflect the views of the proto-rabbinic movement about itself, its place in life, and its opponents.[30] The statement about the popularity of the Pharisees among the masses clearly reflects the pro-Pharisaic bias of the entire account and could be borrowed by Josephus from the Pharisees themselves. Similar to a later account of Salome Alexandra in *A.J.* 13.406 and the description of three Jewish sects in *A.J.* 18.12–17, it reflects the political climate of an

---

[28] On the pro-Pharisaic bias in *Antiquities* and its connection with the new distribution of power in post-70 Judaea, see most recently Schwartz, *Josephus and Judaean Politics*, 170–208. For earlier observations to this effect, cf. M. Smith, "Palestinian Judaism in the First Century," in M. Davis, ed., *Israel: Its Role in Civilization* (New York: JTSA, 1956), 67–81, and Neusner, *From Politics to Piety*, 54–64. See also Cohen, *Josephus in Galilee and Rome*, 144–51, who provides a similar argument based on *Vita*.

[29] *A.J.* 13.297–298.

[30] Cf. Mason, *Flavius Josephus*, 230–45.

eastern Roman province. All of them regard the ability of local civil elites to control the local *dēmos* as a big political advantage worth emphasizing over and over again. Be that as it may, the entire section of *Antiquitates* including the story of Hyrcanus' confrontation with the Pharisees, as well as the subsequent review of Pharisaic and Sadducean beliefs, seems to be informed by Pharisaic (or proto-rabbinic) traditions. In this context we need to determine the precise meaning of the term "traditions of the fathers" as it appears here and in other *Antiquitates* passages.

We have already observed above that, according to Josephus, the Pharisees have passed on "a great many observances handed down by their forefathers." Nothing prevents us from understanding this phrase in its literal sense: the Pharisees have passed on halakhic observances practiced in their families but not recorded in the Law of Moses. In this case the Sadducean rejection of such practices would become more understandable, since it was not *their* forefathers who practiced them. Josephus seems to imply a plain meaning of "fathers" in a sense of physical "ancestors" rather than in the sense of the later rabbinic *ʾavot ha-ʿolam* ("fathers of the world"). When Eleazar accuses John Hyrcanus of violating the genealogical rules of priesthood, he refers to something that he has heard from "elders." This tradition probably had a relatively limited circulation, since not even all Pharisees agreed with him. Sadducees definitely did not share it. The "elders" in this context, as we have observed above, probably refer to heads of households possessing and transmitting halakhic traditions. Hyrcanus abandons the Pharisees and punishes those who follow Pharisaic practices. During her reign Salome Alexandra "restored those practices which the Pharisees had introduced according to the traditions of their forefathers." In both cases the text emphasizes specific ancestral halakhic practices followed by the Pharisees, which were either allowed or not allowed to influence the public observance of Jewish law. The Pharisees emerge from these accounts as actively advocating and disseminating familial halakhic traditions. The latter are based on the interpretation of Jewish law produced and recognized as normative within their families. The dissemination of these traditions takes place through informal channels of patronage and interaction with influential households. Under favorable circumstances the ancestral law of Pharisaic households acquires the status of the "law of the land." When the political tide turns against them, it loses this status.

On another occasion Josephus provides a much less flattering description of the Pharisees in their confrontation with Herod, which seems to confirm our conclusions about Pharisaic "traditions of the fathers":

> There was also a group of Jews (*morion ti Ioudaikōn anthrōpōn*) priding itself on its adherence to ancestral custom (*ep' exakribōsei mega phronoun tou patriou*) and claiming to observe the laws of which the Deity approves, and by these men, called Pharisees, the women [of the court] were ruled.[31]

This account reflects an animosity toward Pharisees otherwise uncharacteristic of Josephus at this stage of his writing career. It has been suggested that Josephus might have directly borrowed here from the historical account of Herod's reign by Nicolaus of Damascus.[32] The description implicitly distinguishes between "the ancestral custom" of the Pharisees, on adhering to which they pride themselves, and "the laws of which the Deity approves."[33] The Pharisees "claim" to observe the latter, apparently because they adhere to their ancestral custom, but do they? The two types of the law are by no means the same in this description, although the author recognizes that the Pharisees identified them. The implications of the phrase are that the Pharisees were scrupulous in observing their "ancestral traditions," which they also saw as the true manifestation of the Law of Moses. The author, however, remains unconvinced.

This statement appears in a context that reflects patronage-based relationships between the Pharisees and various members of Herod's household.[34] The Pharisees function as private figures following a

---

[31] *A.J.* 17.41.

[32] See Bloch, *Quellen*, 169, Destinon, *Quellen*, 120, Schürer-Vermes, *History*, vol. 2, 383, n. 1, and G. Alon, *Jews, Judaism, and the Classical World* (Jerusalem: Magnes Press, 1977), 41, n. 61. For a more recent treatment cf. Schwartz, "Josephus and Nicolaus," 159–60, and A. Baumgarten, "The Name of the Pharisees," *JBL* 102 (1983), 414–16. For a summary of their arguments and their critique see Mason, *Flavius Josephus*, 274–80. He maintains that the story comes from Josephus himself. He also demonstrates that the language of this account is consistent with that of other authentically Josephan passages. But this does not necessarily prove Josephan authorship, only that he "has made the passage his own." See S. Cohen, *Josephus in Galilee and Rome: His Vita and Development as a Historian* (Leiden: Brill, 1979), 232–33. Saldarini, *Pharisees*, 99, n. 52 also argues for Josephan authorship.

[33] See Baumgarten, "Name of the Pharisees," 415, for a close reading and analysis of the Greek text. He fully appreciates its ambiguity and negative connotations. Cf. Mason, *Flavius Josephus*, 263–67.

[34] *A.J.* 17.41–43 (cf. *B.J.* 1.571). See Saldarini, *Pharisees, Scribes and Sadducees*, 56–59.

particular set of beliefs and practices. Their influence consists of
informal contacts maintained with members of the royal household
who accept the Pharisaic claims of proper observance of the divine
laws and having foreknowledge of future events. In other words, the
ancestral customs of the Pharisees are their private lore, which people
are free either to follow or disregard. And the author of our passage seems to imply that the people would be better off disregarding
it. Overall, this story corroborates in its own way my earlier observations about the private nature of Pharisaic ancestral halakhah.
Unlike the previous account, however, it evaluates these traditions from
the critical perspective of someone not sharing the Pharisaic worldview.

When Josephus finally summarizes the teachings of the Pharisees
in his description of the three "philosophical schools" in *Antiquitates*,
he combines a review of their teachings about fate and immortality
of the soul from *Bellum* with additional remarks unique to *Antiquitates*.
These remarks, in agreement with the earlier description of the
Pharisees in *Antiquitates*, tend to focus on halakhic aspects of their
lifestyle, although they do not refer directly to the "traditions of the
fathers." Thus in *A.J.* 18:12 Josephus observes that "the Jews, from
the most ancient times, had three philosophies pertaining to their
traditions." Speaking of the Pharisees, Josephus continues:

> The Pharisees simplify their standard of living, making no concessions
> to luxury. They follow the guidance of that which their doctrine has
> selected and transmitted as good, attaching the chief importance to
> the observance of those commandments which it has seen fit to dic-
> tate to them. They show respect and deference to their elders (*tois
> hēlikia*), nor do they rashly presume to contradict their proposals (*tōn
> eisēgēthentōn*).

Josephus then proceeds to what amounts to a rephrased summary
of Pharisaic doctrines from *Bellum*. He concludes his description of
the Pharisees by mentioning their influence on the urban population of Judaea. In this account we encounter a remarkable example
of a thoroughly hellenized presentation of the Pharisaic halakhah.
Josephus finds a way to stress the importance of practical law without offending the philosophical sensibilities of his Greco-Roman readers. After all, philosophy was also a way of life and not just a
teaching.[35] The reference to "those advanced in years" seems to

---

[35] Cohen, *From the Maccabees to the Mishnah*, 146, understands Josephus in precisely this sense.

imply "the fathers" of other texts by Josephus. There is nothing in this particular phrase that would make us read it any differently from other excerpts dealing with "the fathers," i.e., as a reference to familial ancestors of Pharisaic households. A somewhat murky reference to "the guidance of that which their doctrine has selected" also implies the profoundly private and subjective nature of Pharisaic halakhah. In a sense, all this stands in contrast with later claims of public clout wielded by Pharisees. In other words, despite the thoroughly hellenized nature of this description, it may reflect the centrality of private halakhic traditions for the Pharisaic movement. Similar to the story about John Hyrcanus, it may reflect the desire of households adhering to Pharisaic halakhah to play a bigger public role in the post-70 provincial society of Judaea.

Pharisaic Traditions in Context

Against this background it would be reasonable to suggest that the "traditions of the fathers," in which Pharisees were experts, were indeed customs of their fathers, i.e., legal traditions shaped and transmitted within their families but also sometimes deemed authoritative by broader society. In this case the reference to the priestly families becomes especially important. Elias Bickerman and Albert Baumgarten have insightfully suggested that the Pharisees tried to pattern the presentation of their *paradosis* after that of the priests.[36] Steve Mason, on the other hand, has argued that Josephus' interest in the genealogical succession of high priests has to do with his concern about the preservation and accurate transmission of the Law, entrusted by Moses to priests.[37] The priests thus formed a chain of tradition resembling that of the Pharisees, albeit based on the genealogical principle. I would like to suggest that in fact, there was not much difference between the two chains of tradition to begin with. In other words, like most priestly traditions, those of the Pharisees evolved and were transmitted within the familial halakhic lore, but at the same time significant numbers of "common" Jews recognized some of these traditions as religiously authoritative.

---

[36] Bickerman, "Chaîne de la tradition pharisienne," 266–68, and Baumgarten, "Pharisaic *Paradosis*," 72–74.

[37] *A.J.* 20.224–51. See Mason, *Flavius Josephus*, 236.

Josephus several times refers to ancestral priestly traditions, preserved and transmitted within priestly families but at the same exercising enormous public authority.[38] For him, the preservation and
transmission of traditions within priestly families vouchsafed their
accuracy and reliability above anything else. Moreover, the genealogical
purity of priestly families is exactly what guarantees this accuracy:

> Not only did our ancestors in the first instance set over this business
> men of the highest character, devoted to the service of God, but they
> took precautions to ensure that the priests' lineage should be kept
> unadulterated and pure. A member of the priestly order must, to beget
> a family, marry a woman of his own race, without regard to her wealth
> or other distinctions. But he must investigate her pedigree, obtaining
> the genealogy from the archives and producing a number of witnesses.[39]
>
> [In the case of war] they also pass scrutiny upon the remaining
> women, and disallow marriage with any who have been taken cap-
> tive, suspecting them of having had frequent intercourse with foreign-
> ers. But the most convincing proof of our accuracy in this matter is
> that our records contain the names of our high priests, with the suc-
> cession from father to son for the last two thousand years.[40]

This description comes in the context of Josephus' argument about
the trustworthiness and historical reliability of Jewish traditions.[41]
He further proceeds to talk about biblical accounts of history and
contrasts them with Greek historical accounts, which he deems too
fanciful to be true.[42] The central role of the genealogical purity of
priestly families for the faithful transmission of traditions is thus
unmistakable. Only a genealogically pure family line (or succession)
can adequately transmit the truth about the past, as well as religious
truth. The knowledge is not yet alienated from its carriers. Rather,
it is embodied through their families stretching back through their
generations for thousands of years.[43]

---

[38] Cf. R. Gray, *Prophetic Figures in Late Second Temple Jewish Palestine* (New York:
Oxford University Press, 1993), 53–58, for similar conclusions. She stresses, however, that according to Josephus, "it was not priestly status or descent as such that
made one an expert in the interpretation of scripture, but rather the kind of training and education that were common among priests." I would argue that this kind
of education was precisely part of priestly descent and stemmed from familiarity
with family traditions.

[39] *C. Ap.* 1.30–32.

[40] *C. Ap.* 1.35–36.

[41] *C. Ap.* 1.28–29.

[42] *C. Ap.* 1.37–46.

[43] Satlow, *Jewish Marriage in Antiquity*, 147–51, argues that early rabbis tried to

Much of this knowledge had to do with the authentication of proper priestly pedigrees. It ensured that no priest of doubtful background would be allowed to officiate in the temple. Sometimes it was used for political purposes. When Jews tried to prove that the temple in Jerusalem is more legitimate than that on Mount Gerizim, they sought to demonstrate:

> From the law and the succession of the high priests, how each had become head of the temple by receiving that office from his father.[44]

The latter argument could be based on family traditions of the high priests, although not necessarily.[45] But the legal traditions of priestly families known to Josephus were not limited to genealogies. When the leaders of Jerusalem tried to avert the rebellion against Rome in 66 CE by persuading the people to resume sacrifices received from the Emperor, they "produced priestly experts on the traditions of their country (*tous empeirous tōn patriōn hiereis*), who reported that all their forefathers (*pantes hoi progonoi*) had received sacrifices from foreign nations."[46] The "traditions of their country" mentioned here apparently amounted to the practices of the priests' forefathers, who used to accept sacrifices from foreigners. This practice was deemed publicly authoritative. The priests testified based on the "customs of the forefathers," just as the Pharisees used to do. Technically speaking, there was no difference between the legal customs of Pharisaic families and those of priestly clans. Both originated as part of family lore and became publicly recognized as binding legal traditions. In his writings Josephus hardly implies any distinction between the two. When in *Vita* Josephus tries to legitimize his own accuracy as a historian, he once again starts by referring to his family's pedigree (both priestly and Hasmonean).[47] He then makes a direct connection between this pedigree and his own knowledge:

---

demonstrate their knowledge of and control over priestly genealogies. They claimed to "control information that could be highly damaging to 'powerful' men and priests, the two groups with whom they also appear to be competing with for authority at this time." It is possible that the true power of flawed genealogies had to do with their ability to invalidate the priestly knowledge and priestly traditions.

[44] *A.J.* 13.78.

[45] See Bickerman, "Chaîne de la Tradition," 267, and Baumgarten, "Pharisaic *Paradosis*," 72, for this interpretation.

[46] *B.J.* 2.417.

[47] *Vita* 1.

> Distinguished as he was by his noble birth, my father Matthias was
> even more esteemed for his upright character, being among the most
> notable men in Jerusalem, our greatest city. Brought up with Matthias,
> my own brother by both parents, I made great progress in my edu-
> cation, gaining a reputation for an excellent memory and understanding.
> While still a mere boy, about fourteen years old, I won universal
> applause for my love of letters; insomuch that the chief priests and
> the leading men of the city used constantly to come to me for pre-
> cise information on some particular in our ordinances.[48]

Josephus' own knowledge is part of his upbringing in a noble (priestly)
family. Although the section about chief priests dropping by to get
an insight from a fourteen year old boy may seem like a tall tale,
it actually agrees with a number of early rabbinic accounts. They
portray various members of rabbinic households (servants, daughters,
and minors) as knowledgeable about points of law precisely by virtue
of belonging to such households and thus sharing in their corporate
knowledge of halakhah.[49] An entire household can serve as the embodiment of traditional knowledge and practice.

Josephus does not limit family-based transmission of religious traditions to priests alone. Rather, every Jewish family is supposed to
serve as the prime source of religious knowledge to a child:

> [The law] orders that they shall be taught to read, and shall learn
> both the laws and the deeds of their forefathers (*tōn progonōn tas pra-*
> *xeis*), in order that they may imitate the latter, and, being grounded
> in the former, may neither transgress nor have any excuse for being
> ignorant in them.[50]

The average Jewish family emerges from this discourse as the prime
source of a child's religious knowledge and observance. The context
of this statement is Josephus' summary of different types of Jewish
law (most immediately, Jewish family law). It appears that one acquires

---

[48] *Vita* 2. The story of the embassy sent to depose Josephus in *Vita* 197–198 provides another illustration that proper genealogy and knowledge were inseparable in
Jewish tradition. The description characterizes all members of the delegation by
their knowledge and their birth.

[49] See the next chapter for detailed discussion.

[50] *C. Ap.* 2.204. Cf. *C. Ap.* 2.173–178. See discussion in J. Barclay, "The Family
as the Bearer of Religion in Judaism and Early Christianity," in H. Moxnes, ed.,
Constructing Early Christian Families: Family as Social Reality and Metaphor (London:
Routledge, 1997), 68–72, for similar conclusions. Cf. Barclay, *Jews in the Mediterranean
Diaspora: From Alexander to Trajan (323 BCE–117 CE)* (Edinburgh: T&T Clark, 1996),
402–13. Barclay discusses relevant texts in the broader context of the ethnicity-
based nature of Diaspora Judaism.

familiarity with this law first and foremost by learning its principles and following its requirements within one's own family. The latter becomes a depository of religious knowledge and practice transmitted from one generation to the next. Although the reference to "the deeds of their forefathers" probably indicates the study of biblical history and its exemplary figures, the setting of this study is once again within one's family. It results in acquisition of familial virtue and religious piety along the lines recognized in the contemporary Roman society.[51]

This notion of the family as the prime setting of Torah instruction finds parallels in several other Jewish sources from the first century CE. For Philo family also constituted an important setting for the transmission of traditional knowledge. Explaining the commandment of Deut 19:14 that "thou shalt not remove thy neighbor's landmarks which thy forerunners have set up," he observes:

> Now this law, we may consider, applies not merely to allotments and boundaries of land in order to eliminate covetousness but also to the safeguarding of ancient customs. For customs are unwritten laws, the decisions of men of old (*ethē gar agraphoi nomoi, dogmata palaiōn andrōn*), not inscribed on monuments nor on leaves of paper which the moth destroys, but on the souls of those who are partners in the same citizenship. For children ought to inherit from their parents, besides their property, ancestral customs (*ethē patria*) which they were reared in and have lived with even from the cradle, and not despise them because they have been handed down without written record.[52]

In other words, for Philo, one's household constitutes the prime setting where children receive instruction in Jewish law and "ancestral customs."[53] The latter are passed down within the families from

---

[51] The idea of family-centered transmission of the Torah should probably be seen within the larger context of family values and family piety emphasized during this period by Jewish Greek writers and their Roman contemporaries. See J. Crouch, *The Origin and Intention of the Colossian Haustafel* (Göttingen: Vandenhoeck & Ruprecht, 1972), 74–101, and D'Angelo, "Εὐσέβεια," 141–47. On "the deeds of their forefathers" cf. 4 Macc 18:10–19 (see below).

[52] Philo, *Spec.*, 4.149–150. Cf. 1.314 and 2.88. See also *Leg.* 115 and 210. The translations are from the Loeb edition of Philo and have been amended when necessary.

[53] See Goodman, "Note on Josephus," 18, for a similar interpretation of this passage. N.G. Cohen, "The Jewish Dimension of Philo's Judaism—An Elucidation of *de Spec. Leg.* IV 132–150," *JJS* 38 (1987), 165–86, provides the most recent argument that this passage implies specifically Jewish practices and Jewish piety. Cf., however, J. Martens, "Unwritten Law in Philo: A Response to Naomi G. Cohen," *JJS* 93 (1992), 38–45. He agrees that the "unwritten law" here means custom, but insists that it is used in a Greek sense of unwritten customary practices. I do not find these two approaches mutually exclusive.

parents to children. It is precisely the family that constitutes the main
depository of Jewish halakhic knowledge of both written and unwritten laws. The "ancestral customs" or "unwritten laws" are as important in his discourse as the written law. By identifying the two, Philo
uses the language of his Stoic contemporaries to describe the patriarchal Jewish household as an embodiment of the Law, preserved
and transmitted from one generation to another.[54] This corresponds
to his (and Josephus') use of Greco-Roman models of family life and
"household management" to justify Jewish religious life and practices. In Philo's (and Josephus') writings the household looms large
as the centerpiece of Jewish society, just as it does among contemporaneous Greco-Roman thinkers.[55]

For Philo the danger of Jewish assimilation in the non-Jewish
Hellenistic milieu has precisely to do with abandonment of "the
teaching of their race and of their fathers, in which they were trained
from the earliest years" (*tēs suggenous kai patriou didaskalias, hēn ek prōtēs
hēlikias epaideuthēsan*).[56] Such people "look down on their relations and
friends and set at naught the laws under which they were born and
bred, and subvert the ancestral customs" (*huperoptai men oikeiōn kai
philōn eisi, nomous de parabainousi, kath' hous egenēthēsan kai etraphēsan, ethē
de patria . . . kinousin*).[57] On occasion, Philo contrasts this behavior with
that of Moses, who while being brought up in the Pharaoh's household "was zealous for the discipline of his kinsmen and ancestors"
(*tēn suggenikēn kai progonikēn edzēlōse paideian*) and preferred "the good
fortune" (*ta agatha*) of his "natural parents" (*tōn physei goneōn*) to that
of his adopted family.[58] Throughout his works Philo consistently portrays one's household as an embodiment of religious laws and ideas.
The commitment to Judaism is virtually indistinguishable from the
commitment to one's family and its values.

---

[54] For a recent discussion of "unwritten laws" in Philo and summary of earlier
opinions see H. Najman, "The Law of Nature and the Authority of Mosaic Law,"
The Studia Philonica Annual 11 (1999), 65–72.

[55] See detailed discussion and literature in D. Balch, "Household Codes," in
D. Aune, ed., *Greco-Roman Literature and the New Testament: Selected Forms and Genres*
(Atlanta: Scholars Press, 1988), 25–50. For comprehensive treatment of Greco-
Roman and Jewish authors see Crouch, *Origin and Intention of the Colossian Haustafel*,
37–101, and Balch, *Let Wives Be Submissive: The Domestic Code in I Peter* (Atlanta:
Scholars Press, 1981), 21–62.

[56] *Praem.*, 162.

[57] *Mos.*, 1.31.

[58] *Mos.*, 1.32–33.

Philo is not the only first century author who asserts an intimate relationship between the Jewish family and preservation of the Law. Fourth Maccabees recasts several accounts of martyrdom under Antiochus Epiphanes found in Second Maccabees into a single account of the priest Eleazar, his seven sons and their mother, who are tortured and killed by Antiochus for their refusal to abandon the Law.[59] The entire narrative serves as a stage for a Stoic-like philosophical exhortation (a diatribe) to remain faithful to the Law and to suffer martyrdom if necessary. It contains elaborate dialogues in which members of Eleazar's family defend their choice with Stoic-like philosophy. In addition to the philosophical argument, Fourth Maccabees promises vindication for a righteous death in the form of the resurrection of the righteous and the ultimate punishment of the wicked.[60] The story focuses on a pious Jewish family that confronts a tyrant and chooses martyrdom. In doing so, its author blends together two originally independent accounts from Second Maccabees, the martyrdom of a pious man Eleazar (not identified as a priest) and the martyrdom of a mother and her seven sons. The pious family of Eleazar thus appears to be a literary construct of the author, but its centrality to the narrative is indicative of the role that patriarchal households and their family values might have played in the contemporaneous Jewish society.[61] The tyrant Antiochus is confronted not by individuals but by the righteous family embodying the highest values of Jewish Law to the point of death. The story concludes with the mother's speech addressed to her children. She starts by describing her life first in "her father's house" and then with her husband in accordance with the laws of chastity. The righteous family life culminates in the birth of seven sons, who receive instruction in the Law from their father:

---

[59] For literary characteristics of Fourth Maccabees see J. Collins, *Between Athens and Jerusalem: Jewish Identity in the Hellenistic Dispora* (New York: Crossroad, 1983), 187–91, and Nickelsburg, *Jewish Literature*, 223–27. The book was possibly written in the city of Antioch.

[60] See Nickelsburg, *Resurrection, Immortality, and Eternal Vita*, 109–11. Cf. Van Henten, *Maccabean Martyrs*, 270–94.

[61] For a superb discussion of family values and family piety in 4 Maccabees see D'Angelo, "Εὐσέβεια," 147–57. The work correctly emphasizes the Roman setting of these ideals but is somewhat mute about their possible implications for Judaism and the Jewish understanding of the Torah.

He, while he was still with you, taught you the Law and the Prophets. He read to you of Abel, slain by Cain, of Isaac, offered as a burnt offering, and of Joseph, in prison. He spoke to you of the zeal of Phineas, and taught you about Hananiah, Azariah, and Mishael in the fire. He sang the praises of Daniel in the lions' den and called him blessed. He reminded you of the scripture of Isaiah which says, "Even though you walk through the fire, the flame shall not burn you" (Isa 43:2). He sang to you the psalm of David which says, "Many are the afflictions of the righteous" (Ps 34:19). He recited the proverb of Solomon which says, "He is a tree of life to those who do his will" (Prov 3:18). He affirmed the word of Ezekiel "Shall these dry bones live?" (Ezek 37:3). Nor did he forget the song that Moses taught which says, "I kill and make alive" (Deut 32:39), for this is your life and length of days.[62]

This speech comprises a collection of scriptural passages validating the practice of martyrdom. It follows a well-known midrashic (exegetical) principle of the enumeration of appropriate biblical passages to justify a particular idea or set of ideas. Fourth Maccabees, however, presents this well-known principle as a family tradition passed on by a father to his sons and now interpreted by their mother as to its meaning. The righteous family thus serves as an embodiment of the divine Law in several ways. First, it transmits the Law (in this case, the Torah and the Prophets) from generation to generation by means of parental instruction and teaching. Second, it lives a righteous life in accordance with the Law. This righteous life embodies traditional patriarchal family values, as the life of the mother first in her father's house and then with her husband amply demonstrates. Third, the members of the family are ready to sacrifice their own lives rather than transgress this Law. Martyrdom serves as an ultimate proof of the family's devotion to the Law and eventually leads to resurrection and post-mortem vindication. The embodiment of the Law culminates in the resurrection of the righteous family.

The centrality of the family for the Fourth Maccabees' discourse is remarkable. Similar to Philo, the book envisions the traditional household as the main social unit responsible for the adequate preservation and transmission of Jewish tradition. This tradition is de facto identified with the ideal of family piety that dominated the contemporaneous Roman society. Because of its prime focus on mar-

---

[62] 4 Macc 18:10–19. The translation is from H. Andersen, "4 Maccabees," in James Charlesworth, *Old Testament Pseudepigrapha*, vol. 2, 531–64.

tyrdom and its justification, Fourth Maccabees uses the image of a righteous family to advance this particular vision of Judaism. The family of Eleazar ensouls the halakhah of martyrdom both through its life and its death and resurrection. Philo is less radical and specific. Similar to Josephus, he talks about Jewish traditions in general. But in Philo, as well as in Fourth Maccabees, we find valid parallels to the "traditions of the fathers" of the Josephan Pharisees. In each case these traditions emerge as household ancestral laws, consciously transmitted and preserved by Jewish families.

As a whole, Josephus presents a consistent picture of what he calls "traditions of the fathers." In their essence such traditions were similar to the halakhic traditions passed down in priestly families and associated with the temple cult and priestly purity. "Traditions of the fathers" originated in the family lore of individual households, and it was up to the individual tastes and inclinations of other Jews whether to follow them or not. In this respect, Josephus comes remarkably close to other first century Jewish authors, such as Philo and the anonymous author of Fourth Maccabees. He also displays similarities with rabbinic traditions about the Pharisees, which we shall discuss in the next chapter. In each of these cases one can find clear parallels between early Pharisaic and priestly halakhic traditions, both developing within individual households.

At the same time, some circles among the Pharisees might have contemplated an expansion and elaboration of the chain of transmission similar to the way in which Ben Sira expanded and elaborated the chain of exemplary leaders to include all the main characters of Israelite history from Aaron to Simeon the Just.[63] There began to emerge an etiological myth justifying the traditions of households by using the Hellenistic concept of the philosophical chain of tradition. Elias Bickerman has convincingly argued that the rabbinic chain of transmission in M 'Abot is patterned after analogous chains of transmission in Hellenistic philosophical schools.[64] In both cases they

---

[63] Sir 44:1–50:24. See Collins, *Jewish Wisdom*, 97–108, for discussion.

[64] Bickerman, "Chaîne de la tradition," 256–69. Cf. most recently Tropper, *Wisdom, Politics, and Historiography*, 158–72. For a detailed discussion of "succession" in Greek philosophical schools and early Christianity, see W. von Keinle, *Die Berichte über die Sukzessionen der Philosophen* (Berlin, 1961), and A. Brent, "Diogenes Laertius and the Apostolic Succession," *JEH* 44 (1993), 367–89. Josephan accounts of the Pharisees may already be reflecting this trend. Notice his use of the term *diadochē*. See further Mason, *Flavius Josephus*, 231–40 and Baumgarten, "Pharisaic Paradosis," 63–77.

served to certify the faithful transmission of teachings of the school's founder by successive generations of his disciples. The earliest tendency to ground rabbinic (Pharisaic?) traditions in "halakhah given to Moses from Sinai" may be traceable to the late Second Temple period, although such a tendency becomes unambiguously articulated only after the destruction of the Temple in 70 CE.[65]

Other attempts to present the history of Jewish Law in the form of "succession" had emerged earlier during the Hellenistic period. In addition to Ben Sira's list, Eupolemus, writing around 150 BCE, seems to have entertained the idea of prophetic "succession."[66] Josephus might have shared similar ideas about the chain of prophecy, which guaranteed the accurate transmission of religious tradition.[67] The prophecy ceases when the chain is no longer reliable. All these texts come from an unambiguously Hellenistic background and present Judaism in terms which are fully at home with Hellenistic cultural and intellectual tastes. The transition from the "traditions of the fathers" as household practices to the "traditions of the fathers" as the Oral Law passed down through generations of disciples reflected a profound and subtle Hellenization of the Jewish tradition. This transition occurred about the same time as disciple circles and formal oral instruction began to gradually replace households as prime vehicles of transmission (as we shall see in the next chapter). Rabbinic Judaism was about to be born.

The "Fourth Philosophy"

In addition to his descriptions of the Pharisees proper, Josephus provides several accounts of what he calls "the fourth philosophy" founded by Judah the Galilean.[68] I shall briefly consider this movement; first,

---

[65] See Schäfer, "Das Dogma von der Mündlichen Torah," 183–85 and M. Hengel and R. Deines, "E.P. Sanders' 'Common Judaism', Jesus and the Pharisees," 17–29 and 36–39. Hengel and Deines observe that various Jewish practices and customs were traced back not only to Moses but to other biblical characters as well (n. 93). Cf. also J. Neusner, "The Formation of Rabbinic Judaism: Yavneh (Jamnia) from AD 70 to 100," in *ANRW* 19.2 (1979), 3–42. He contrasts a "scribal" component in the early rabbinic movement (represented primarily by R. Yohanan ben Zakkai and his disciples) with more traditional Pharisaic circles (represented by R. Eliezer).

[66] Eusebius, *Praeparatio Evangelica* 9.30.1–2. See Bickerman, "Chaîne de la tradition," 264.

[67] *C. Ap.* 1:41.

[68] My understanding of this movement as a small tightly-knit group that formed

because Josephus himself asserts its affinity with the Pharisees, and second, because Josephus relates some interesting details about its structure and functioning. In *Bellum* Josephus mentions Judah for the first time when he describes the procuratorship of Coponius (6–9 CE):

> Under his [Coponius'] administration, a Galilean named Judah incited his countrymen to revolt, upbraiding them as cowards for consenting to pay tribute to the Romans and tolerating mortal masters, after having God for their lord. This man was a sophist who founded a sect (*hairesis*) of his own, having nothing in common with the others.[69]

Josephus describes Judah as an innovating sophist, who breaks with the tradition by founding his own teaching. Josephus immediately proceeds with his famous description of the three Jewish sects, which are implicitly contrasted with Judas' movement. Branding Jewish revolutionaries as innovators and thus exonerating the traditional Jewish establishment is a common literary device in *Bellum*. As we shall see below, Judah was probably much less innovative than this description would like us to believe. In *Antiquitates* the story about Judah appears in the description of the census taken by the legate of Syria Quirinus:

> But a certain Judas, a Gaulanite from a city named Gamala, who had enlisted the aid of Saddok, a Pharisee, threw himself into the cause of rebellion. They said that the assessment carried with it a status amounting to downright slavery, no less, and appealed to the nation to make a bid for independence.[70]
>
> In this case certainly, Judas and Saddok started among us an intrusive fourth school of philosophy. And when they had won an abundance of devotees, they filled the body politic immediately with tumult, also planting the seeds of those troubles which subsequently overtook it, all because of the novelty of this hitherto unknown philosophy that I shall now describe.[71]

---

around a particular family and its ideals develops the line of argument suggested by M. Smith, "Zealots and Sicarii, Their Origins and Relations," *HTR* 64 (1971), 1–19, and D. Rhoads, *Israel in Revolution* (Philadelphia: Fortress Press, 1976), 47–60 and 111–22. The exact relationship between the "Fourth Philosophy" and the larger *Sicarii* movement remains unclear. On some occasions Josephus might have used this term in a very general sense, not as a group-specific designation. See Smith, "Zealots," 18–19.

[69] *B.J.* 2.118.
[70] *A.J.* 18.4.
[71] *A.J.* 18.9.

Josephus once again emphasizes the novelty of the movement founded by Judah and Saddok. Still, he makes a brief mention of the Pharisees, by saying that one of the founders of the sect, namely Saddok, was a Pharisee. We do not know whether Judah also adhered to their teachings or not.[72] However, later in *Antiquitates* Josephus provides a more specific description of the Pharisaic connection of the Fourth Philosphy:

> As for the fourth of the philosophies, Judas the Galilean set himself up as leader of it. This school agrees with in all other respects with the opinions of the Pharisees, except that they have a passion for liberty that is almost unconquerable, since they are convinced that God alone is their leader and master. They think little of submitting to death in unusual forms and permitting vengeance to fall on kinsmen and friends if only they may avoid calling any man master.[73]

Here Josephus explicitly states that the Fourth Philosophy is an offshoot of the Pharisees but has more radical political claims.[74] It probably would be fair to suggest that the social structure of these two movements (at least on the earlier stages) was somewhat similar. In other words, the information we get on the organization of Judah's movement can be applied to the mainstream Pharisees as well. Unfortunately, Josephus does not specify if "all other respects" in which the Fourth Philosophy agreed with the opinions of the Pharisees included halakhic practices or theological teachings. Still, he probably meant both.[75]

Josephus' reference to "kinsmen and friends" is also significant, as it may be a different way of describing the composition of the movement. In other words, two categories of people, kinsmen and friends,

---

[72] Rhoads, *Israel in Revolution*, 54, observes that "to distinguish Saddok as a Pharisee may indicate that Judas himself was not one."

[73] *A.J.* 18.23.

[74] I do not find Rhoads' argument that the connection made between Judas' sect and the Pharisees was influenced by Josephus' "later apologetic tendency to exaggerate the historical significance of the Pharisees" convincing. See Rhoads, *Israel in Revolution*, 54, and his references to earlier literature in n. 15. M. Hengel, *The Zealots* (Edinburgh: T&T Clark, 1989), 86–88, correctly observes that the "Fourth Philosophy" developed new and revolutionary ideas within the framework of the more traditional Pharisaic movement. Cf. also R. Horsley, "The Sicarii: Ancient Jewish Terrorists," *JR* 59 (1979), 442–45 and 447–48.

[75] For a summary of Judas' teaching and its theological roots see Hengel, *Zealots*, 90–145. Cf. Rhoads, *Israel in Revolution*, 48–51. Josephus stresses the fact that Judas was a "sophist," i.e. a religious teacher.

constituted the bulk of followers of Judah, or at least the core of his group. Further information about this movement and its social makeup provided by Josephus tends to corroborate this hypothesis. Josephus does not say what the results of the original unrest initiated by Judah and Saddok were (if there were any to speak of).[76] He also does not specify whether any of them met with a violent end or not. The next time he mentions the Fourth Philosophy was during the procuratorial tenure of Tiberius Alexander (46–48 CE):

> And besides this, the sons of Judas of Galilee were now slain. I mean of that Judas who caused the people to revolt, when Cyrenius [Quirinus] came to take an account of the estates of the Jews, as we have shown in a foregoing book. The names of those sons were James and Simon, whom Alexander commanded to be crucified.[77]

In his first reference to the movement after the death (?) of its founder, Josephus discloses one characteristic that persists throughout its history: the leaders of the Fourth Philosophy come from the family (perhaps, the extended family) of Judah the Galilean. The movement was thus founded and led by members of the same family. It was almost a family business. Apparently, the teaching of the Fourth Philosophy became associated with the family tradition of Judah's clan and as such it became accepted by some Jews.[78] Judah was an innovator because he added a revolutionary agenda to the otherwise perfectly Pharisaic lore of his family. It was only natural that Judah's "kinsmen and friends" became the core group within the new movement, as hinted by Josephus. The "no lord but God" theology became recognized as part of the ancestral tradition of Judah's descendants, part of the "tradition of their forefathers."[79]

With the death of the two sons of Judah, the Fourth Philosophy disappears from the scene, only to reemerge in the time of the Great Revolt of 66–73 CE. During this time, the movement was led by Menahem (the son [grandson?] of Judah the Galilean) and Eleazar, the son of Yair (a relative of Menahem). According to *Bellum* Menahem

---

[76] See discussion in Rhoads, *Israel in Revolution*, 55–60.

[77] *A.J.* 20.102.

[78] Cf. Rhoads, *Israel in Revolution*, 54–55, for similar observations.

[79] At least one other contemporaneous revolutionary movement was led by a household, that of Athronges and his seven brothers. See *B.J.* 2.60–65 and *A.J.* 17.278–84. M. Hengel, *The Charismatic Leader and His Followers* (New York: Crossroad, 1981), 72, interprets them as a "royal, 'messianic' household."

appeared in Jerusalem in the first days of the revolt and wreaked havoc on both Romans and the high priests:

> At this period a certain Menahem, the son of Judas, surnamed the Galilean . . . took his intimate friends off with him to Masada, where he broke into king Herod's armory and provided arms both for his fellow people (*tois dēmotais*) and for other brigands. Then, with these men for his bodyguard, he returned like a veritable king to Jerusalem, became the leader of the revolution, and directed the siege of the palace.[80]

The core of Menahem's followers consisted of a clearly identifiable group, referred to here as "intimate friends." In what follows, Josephus refers to this group on a number of occasions. To describe the movement he uses a term "those around Menahem" (*hoi de peri ton Manaēmon*).[81] Martin Goodman has already observed that Josephus uses a very similar terminology when he describes priestly gangs that ravaged Jerusalem prior to the revolt.[82] It is also possible that these groups consisted primarily of priests' servants, members of their households and some hired hands, and should be seen as "private troopers" of high priestly clans.[83] It appears that the movement of Menahem would fit the same description.[84] Some of his followers were clearly his relatives (Eleazar the son of Yair) or his friends. These apparently constituted the core of his movement. The majority of his followers, however, consisted of various trouble seekers and other discontented elements of the contemporaneous Judaean society.

After Menahem's death at the hands of Eleazar b. Ananias and "those around him," his relative Eleazar b. Yair retreated to Masada, taking some of his followers along.[85] The family disappears from Josephus' story until the siege of Masada, where Eleazar b. Yair took his last stand against the Romans. Josephus characterizes him as a "potent man" as well as a "descendant from Judas."[86] Josephus also

---

[80] *B.J.* 2.433–434.

[81] *B.J.* 2.440 and 446.

[82] M. Goodman, *The Ruling Class of Judaea: The Origins of the Jewish Revolt against Rome* (Cambridge: Cambridge University Press, 1987), 146–47. Cf. Horsley, "Sicarii," 450–55.

[83] See Sivertsev, *Private Households*, 97–107, for further discussion.

[84] Menahem's chief opponent, the priest Eleazar, is also accompanied by his own retinue. See *B.J.* 2.443 and 445. On the possibility of an original alliance between Menahem and the priestly oligarchy see Smith, "Zealots and Sicarii," 18–19.

[85] *B.J.* 2.447.

[86] *B.J.* 7.253.

describes the garrison of Masada as consisting of "Eleazar's companions," along with "their children and their wives."[87] In fact, the presence of the defenders' families in Masada becomes a central point in the entire narrative. The story's plot repeatedly comes back to this issue. The preservation of family honor becomes one of the key justifications for suicide in Eleazar's speech, whereas pity to one's family is seen as the main obstacle for the implementation of this plan.[88] The defenders of Masada are described as "laying themselves down by their wives and children on the ground" to be murdered in this posture.[89] Finally, "an old woman, and another who was of kin to Eleazar, and superior to most women in prudence and learning, with five children" escape death by concealing themselves in caverns.[90] Overall, the presence of families plays a crucial role in shaping the story about the mass suicide at Masada. The question is whether this description can be trusted.

Scholars have long since questioned the historical reliability of what Josephus tells us about the siege of Masada. The accuracy of his story about the mass suicide committed by the Jewish defenders of the fortress is very much open to doubt.[91] As far as our discussion is concerned, we need to know whether the central role of families repeatedly emphasized in Eleazar's speech is merely a rhetorical trick, or whether it reflects a particular historical reality. Unfortunately, even an educated guess is impossible. On the one hand, Josephus could be correct in grasping the importance of the presence of rebels' families in Masada. Indeed, there is nothing inherently implausible about this piece of evidence even if the rest of the story is merely a rhetorical fantasy. After all, it fits nicely into the family-based nature of the "Fourth Philosophy" reflected throughout Josephus'

---

[87] *B.J.* 7.321.

[88] See *B.J.* 7.334 and 380–382 (preservation of family honor and freedom), and 7.338 (pity for one's family).

[89] *B.J.* 7.389–395. In this passage Josephus moralizes extensively about the unacceptability of such behavior.

[90] *B.J.* 7.399.

[91] For a critical review of earlier historiography see L. Feldman, "Masada: A Critique of Recent Scholarship," in J. Neusner, ed., *Christianity, Judaism and Other Graeco-Roman Cults* (Leiden: Brill, 1975), vol. 3, 218–48. The nature of a more recent debate can be gleaned from comparing S. Cohen, "Masada: Literary Tradition, Archaeological Remains, and the Credibility of Josephus," *JJS* 33 (1982), 385–405, and D. Ladouceur, "Masada: A Consideration of the Literary Evidence," *Greek, Roman, and Byzantine Studies* 21 (1980), 245–60. Cf. also Rhoads, *Israel in Revolution*, 118–19.

accounts. On the other hand, the dramatic significance of rebels slaughtering their loved ones makes families central to the *rhetorical plot* of Josephus' description.[92] Their visible presence in the Masada narrative constitutes an essential part of this narrative and the rhetorical zenith of its drama. As they appear in story, the families fulfill an important literary function, which totally overshadows their true historical role. Despite overwhelming evidence for the family-based structure of the "Fourth Philosophy," the most glowing piece of evidence must remain at best inconclusive. The Masada story belongs outside the realm of historical fact.

Pharisaic Traditions in the New Testament

In spite of the seeming importance of the New Testament in general and of the Gospels in particular for our discussion, the usable information which they can provide is relatively limited. Over the past several decades there have been growing concerns among scholars as to the reliability of the information on Jewish sects contained in this literature.[93] The post-70 CE dating for Luke, Matthew and John makes any attempt to use their material for the analysis of the pre-70 CE situation vulnerable to criticism. Indeed, there has been substantial evidence that the description of the pre-70 Jewish social groups provided by each of these Gospels reflects worldviews and agendas of the time when the Gospel was composed. In a sense, material provided by Matthew, Luke and John can be better used to describe the trends in the early rabbinic society than in the society of the late Second Temple period.[94]

On the other hand, scholars have singled out a number of the New Testament texts that indeed might have predated the destruction of the Temple. Those include several Pauline epistles, possibly

---

[92] Cf. Josephus' rhetoric in *B.J.* 7.266, where he accuses the sicarii of sacrificing family ties for the cause.

[93] For a helpful review of relevant sources and basic methodological issues see L. Grabbe, "Sadducees and Pharisees," in J. Neusner and A. Avery-Peck, eds., *Judaism in Late Antiquity* (Leiden: Brill, 1999), part 3, vol. 1, 46–52 and 57–58.

[94] For a word of caution about the attributions of various statements to specific Jewish groups mentioned in the Gospels see R. Bultmann, *The History of the Synoptic Tradition* (New York: Harper & Row, 1963), 52–54. M. Smith, *Jesus the Magician* (New York: Harper & Row, 1978), 153–57, takes a hypercritical approach by denying the validity of most references to the Pharisees in the Gospels.

the Gospel of Mark (or at least its sources) and the so-called "Q," a saying-source behind the information shared by Matthew and Luke but absent in Mark. Although the exact nature and composition of these sources remains a matter of heated debates, it would be worth-while to review the information that they provide on the Jewish sects of the Second Temple period. Still, one has to be constantly mind-ful of uncertainties surrounding even this corpus of "early" docu-ments. Out of all the texts discussed so far, the New Testament data must be taken with the biggest grain of salt.[95]

In the epistles firmly attributed to Paul himself, he mentions the Pharisees only twice. In Gal 1:14–16 he states describing his life prior to conversion:

> I was advancing in Judaism beyond many Jews of my age and was extremely zealous for the traditions of my fathers (*tōn patrikōn mou para-doseōn*). But when it pleased God, who separated me from my mother's womb (*ek koilias mētros mou*) and called me through His grace, to reveal his son in me, that I might preach him among the gentiles, I did not immediately confer with flesh and blood (*sarki kai haimati*).

Paul goes on to distinguish between his preaching and that of the immediate disciples and relatives of Jesus.[96] Paul contrasts his knowl-edge of Christ received as a result of direct experience and revela-tion with that taught and transmitted by human teachers and within human chains of tradition.[97] As Daniel Boyarin has observed, "the precise claim that Peter and James had made against him is, in effect, that they have a *paradosis* of Jesus which Paul does not."[98] One of the prime objects of Paul's attack seems to be James, "the Lord's brother" (*ton adelphon tou kuriou*).[99] And it is within this con-

---

[95] For two of the most recent attempts to use these texts as reliable historical sources see Saldarini, *Pharisees, Scribes and Sadducees*, 134–98, and Stemberger, *Jewish Contemporaries of Jesus*, 21–37. Both authors recognize often insurmountable obsta-cles that emerge in this kind of analysis. Neusner, *From Politics to Piety*, 67–80, and Jaffee, *Torah in the Mouth*, 44–50, assume that the New Testament writings are basi-cally reliable sources of information for pre-70 Pharisaic practices.

[96] Jaffee, *Torah in the Mouth*, 45, makes an insightful remark that in this passage "Paul subsumes the Judaic 'traditions of my fathers' under a larger category of humanly generated tradition that includes the teachings of other apostles about Christ." Unfortunately, he does not further develop this observation.

[97] Gal 1:11–12.

[98] D. Boyarin, *A Radical Jew: Paul and the Politics of Identity* (Berkeley: University of California Press, 1994), 110.

[99] Gal 1:19. Cf. Gal 2:12.

text of his polemics against "flesh and blood" that Paul further develops his idea of spiritual kinship as opposed to carnal relation. Israel becomes associated with the "Law" transmitted by means of natural ("fleshly") kinship, whereas Paul establishes "the household of faith" (*tous oikeious tēs pisteōs*) by spiritual preaching.[100] The overall context of this apologetic discourse indicates that for Paul "traditions of the fathers" are associated with "natural" transmission of the religious lore, perhaps, within one's own family. The divine revelation separates Paul from his "mother's womb." When Paul encounters the resurrected Christ, he detaches himself from any "tradition of the fathers," including those preached by James and his associates. The tradition of spirit must permanently sideline that of flesh and blood.[101]

It seems that Paul's reference to his Pharisaic past has similar connotations in Phil 3:5–6. There, Paul summarizes his Jewish credentials as follows:

> Circumcised on the eighth day, of the people of Israel, of the tribe of Benjamin, a Hebrew of Hebrews, in regard to the law, a Pharisee (*kata nomon Pharisaios*), as for zeal, persecuting the church, as for righteousness in the law (*kata dikaiosunēn tēn en nomō*)—faultless.

The context of this speech is, once again, to warn against the "confidence in flesh" and circumcision.[102] Being a Pharisee is part of Paul's genealogy: he comes from the people of Israel and tribe of Benjamin.[103] He follows a Pharisaic understanding of the law. He is flawless in regard of his natural pedigree, yet he deems all this

---

[100] Gal 6:10. Gal 3:16 attacks the exclusiveness of "Abraham's seed" by interpreting it as a reference to Christ and Christians. Gal 3:26–4:7 uses household imagery to describe the election of the Christians as "Abraham's seed." Finally, Gal 4:22–31 interprets the story of Ishmael and Isaac as a symbol of the rejection of that "born according to the flesh" in favor of the one "born according to the promise." Notice the praise of a barren woman in contrast to a married one in Gal 4:27. Paul's discourse concludes with a scathing critique of flesh and praise of spirit in Gal 5:16–25 and 6:8.

[101] Boyarin, *Radical Jew*, 57–85, and Schwartz, *Studies in the Jewish Background of Christianity*, 1–26, convincingly argue that Paul fits into a larger trend of attempts to "spiritualize" Judaism during the Hellenistic period. The latter came as a result of the new distinction between spirit and body introduced by Hellenism and previously unknown in Judaism. Schwartz also emphasizes the centrality of family and "seed" for Jewish religious identity and practices at the earlier stages. As soon as the new distinction between body and spirit had been introduced, the traditional system began to fall apart.

[102] See Phil 3:2–3.

[103] Cf. similar genealogical self-references in 2 Cor 11:22 and Rom 11:1.

unworthy in comparison with his experience of the resurrected Christ. Only the latter provides true knowledge and salvation.[104] Both passages in Philippians and Galatians seem to reflect a shared view of what it meant to be a Pharisee. In both cases the "natural" (within one's family?) transmission of religious knowledge appears to be emphasized and eventually rejected. The Pharisaic "traditions of the fathers" serve to illustrate such a transmission. Paul abandons them in favor of direct and personal religious experience.[105]

In the Gospel of Mark the Pharisees are part of the narrative background and serve as literary antagonists for Jesus' preaching. As a result, their representation often becomes highly schematic.[106] Similar to some texts of Josephus, the Gospels provide the Pharisees with a highly anonymous corporate identity, often losing sight of the particular reality behind it. One can find examples of such usage in Mk 2:18–20 and 23–28, 3:1–6, 8:11–12, and 12:13–17. In other instances, however, we can get some additional glimpses into the structure of the Jewish sects and into the nature of their teachings. Mk 7:1–13 provides one of the most detailed and realistic descriptions of the Pharisees in the entire New Testament corpus of texts. More importantly, it contains an elaborate (albeit highly negative) discussion of the "traditions of the fathers" advocated by the Pharisees. The text of this story runs as following:

> Now when the Pharisees gathered together to him, with some of the scribes, who had come from Jerusalem, they saw that some of his disciples ate with hands defiled, that is, unwashed. For the Pharisees, and all the Jews, do not eat unless they wash their hands, observing the tradition of the elders (tēn paradosin tōn presbyterōn). And when they come from the market place, they do not eat unless they purify themselves,

---

[104] Cf. Boyarin, *Radical Jew*, 82: "These literal and physical marks of status—this commitment to the corporeal as locus of meaning and value—become mere dung in Paul's eyes in the light of Christ's invitation to all people to join the spiritual circumcision."

[105] My friend and colleague Christopher Mount has called my attention to Rom 16:7, which seems to imply that some of Paul's relatives converted to Christianity prior to him. The entire story of Paul's conversion may have to be reexamined in light of this evidence.

[106] On the Mark's portrayal of the Pharisees (and other opponents of Jesus) see most recently Malbon, "The Jewish Leaders in the Gospel of Mark: A Literary Study of Markan Characterization," *JBL* 108 (1989), 259–81, and Saldarini, *Pharisees, Scribes and Sadducees*, 146–57. Both authors recognize the historical value of Mark's references in spite of all uncertainties involved. For a much more skeptical assessment cf. M. Cook, *Mark's Treatment of the Jewish Leaders* (Leiden: Brill, 1978).

and there are many other traditions which they observe, the washing
of cups and pots and vessels of bronze. And the Pharisees and the
scribes asked him, "Why do your disciples not live according to the
tradition of the elders, but eat with hands defiled?" And he said to
them, "Well did Isaiah prophesy of you hypocrites, as it is written:
'This people honors me with their lips, but their heart is far from me.
In vain do they worship me, teaching as doctrine the precepts of men
(*didaskontes didaskalias entalmata anthrōpōn*).' You leave the commandment
of God, and hold fast the tradition of men (*tēn paradosin tōn anthrōpōn*)."
And he said to them, "You have a fine way of setting aside the commandments of God in order to observe your own traditions (*paradosei
hymōn*). For Moses said, 'Honor your father and your mother,' and
'Anyone who curses his mother or his father should be put to death.'
But you say that if a man says to his father or mother, 'Whatever
help you might otherwise have received from me is a Corban' (that
is, a gift devoted to God), then you no longer let him do anything for
his father or mother. Thus you nullify the word of God by your tradition that you have handed down (*paradosei hymōn hē paredōkate*). And
you do many things like that."

In this story the Pharisees are once again mentioned along with
scribes, although the two are now distinguished. Overall, the relationship
between the two groups remains murky throughout the Gospels,
which keep using them interchangeably.[107] At any rate, the text seems
once again to depict the Pharisees as an anonymous and shadowy
group lacking any individuality. The particular significance of Mk
7:1–13, however, has to do with its elaborate discussion of the "tradition of the elders." In his response Jesus gives two characteristics
of this tradition. First, he calls it the "tradition of men." Second, he
characterizes it as "your own traditions" and "your tradition that
you have handed down."[108] The latter definition resembles the "traditions of their fathers" of Josephus almost verbatim. Both texts imply
that the traditions in question are of a subjective and private nature.
Unlike Josephus, however, Mk 7:1–13 is much more critically disposed toward the ultimate validity of these traditions and their religious authority.

To illustrate his point, Jesus brings an example from family law:
whoever sets aside a portion of his income as a sacrificial gift is no
longer obliged to spend it in order to sustain his parents. Does this
example taken from family law reflect the family-based nature of the

---

[107] See Saldarini, *Pharisees, Scribes and Sadducees*, 144–98, esp. 144–57 (on the Gospel
of Mark).
[108] Cf. Baumgarten, "Pharisaic *Paradosis*," 66–67, and Jaffee, *Torah in the Mouth*, 47–49.

"tradition of the elders" as understood by Mk 7:1–13? The evidence is too scanty for a decisive answer. Still, it is remarkable that the example does not directly address the problem of purity, which otherwise constitutes the background of the entire debate. Instead, it addresses relations within the family, and specifically the obligation of children to sustain their parents. We may be dealing here with a subtle attack against the Pharisaic household and its norms of behavior.

At least two more debates between Jesus and representatives of various Jewish sects in Mark have similar family settings. First, in Mk 10:2–9 the Pharisees test Jesus by asking if it is lawful for a man to divorce his wife. Second, Mk 12:18–25 contains a dispute with the Sadducees:

> Then the Sadducees, who say there is no resurrection, came to him with a question. "Teacher," they said, "Moses wrote for us that if a man's brother dies and leaves a wife but no children, the man must marry the widow and have children for his brother. Now there were seven brothers. The first one married and died without leaving any children. The second one married the widow, but he also died, leaving no child. It was the same with the third. In fact, none of the seven left any children. Last of all, the woman died too. At the resurrection whose wife will she be, since the seven were married to her?" Jesus replied, "Are you not in error because you do not know the Scriptures or the power of God? When the dead rise, they will neither marry nor be given in marriage. They will be like the angels in heaven."

The debate concerns the Sadducean view that there is no resurrection, but it is specifically centered around the halakhic requirement to marry one's brother's widow and its possible implementation after the resurrection. Once again, the family setting is central for an entire debate. It seems that in addition to purity laws, family laws played an important part in controversies between Jesus and members of other sectarian movements. Does this tell us something about the household-based nature of sectarian legal traditions? The evidence is too circumstantial, but it manifests a certain consistency that should not be neglected. Several recent studies have emphasized the importance of traditional households in the early Jesus movement (as opposed to more egalitarian and itinerant groups).[109] It is possible

---

[109] See most recently J. Elliott, "The Jesus Movement Was Not Egalitarian but Family-Oriented," and A. Destro and M. Pesco, "Fathers and Householders in the Jesus Movement: The Perspective of the Gospel of Luke," *Biblical Interpretation* 11 (2003), 173–210 and 211–238.

that both Jesus and his opponents operated within a context of Jewish families adhering to certain understandings of the Torah and its authoritative interpretation.

Overall, the New Testament texts at our disposal tend to be too ambiguous and imprecise. Most of them contain layers of later editing, adjusting the material to more contemporaneous tastes. Often, the depiction of Second Temple Jewish groups becomes too schematic and literary. On the other hand, both the Pauline letters and the Gospels provide occasional insights into how the early Christian authors perceived the makeup and the nature of the Pharisees and some other Jewish groups. These insights tend to corroborate what has been said above about the social structure of Jewish sects and their legal traditions. The early New Testament texts imagine the Jewish sects (primarily, the Pharisees) as close-knit and sometimes, family-based groups. The "traditions of the fathers" are perceived as evolving within the hereditary family lore of such groups. The debates reflected in the Gospels often emerge over the question of the public religious authority of such traditions. As a whole, this picture agrees remarkably well with what Josephus and the non-Greek sources have to say about the Jewish sects of the Second Temple period.

Conclusions

The Pharisaic "traditions of the fathers" mentioned by Josephus and the New Testament appear to refer to the halakhic practices of Pharisaic households. They constitute the customary law (and lore) of individual families and groups of families. Within Pharisaic circles these laws were considered religiously authoritative and binding. Other Jewish groups of the time would not necessarily agree with that. At the same time, the contemporaneous Greco-Roman ideology of familial piety added a new sense of significance and legitimacy to familial customs. I shall now take a closer look at how early rabbinic documents (Mishnah, Tosefta, and Tannaitic midrashim) portray historical predecessors of the sages and their practices. I shall argue that the latter confirm and amplify our observations about the household setting of the Pharisaic "traditions of the fathers" in Greek sources.

CHAPTER FIVE

PHARISAIC TRADITIONS IN TANNAITIC TEXTS

The Mishnaic tractate *'Abot* opens with a statement about the famous rabbinic chain of tradition stretching back to Moses and finding its culmination in the study circle of R. Yohanan b. Zakkai and his disciples. It is through this chain of transmission that the Oral Law is handed down from one generation to another. The law is "owned" and preserved, not within biological families (as we would expect in priestly tradition) but within disciple circles. It is passed down from a master to his students, not from a father to his sons. Priests, as a separate group, are noticeably absent in this tradition. *'Abot* encapsulates in this description some of the basic beliefs and values of Rabbinic Judaism that would characterize it as a system ever since. The centrality of a disciple circle for the preservation, study, and transmission of Torah is one such value. The concept of the Oral Torah, preserved, studied, and transmitted within such a circle, is another. The two of them constitute a single matrix that character-izes the very essence of Rabbinic Judaism.[1]

But the very same text of *'Abot* also incorporates a slightly different vision of the prime social unit within Judaism. M 'Abot 1:4–5 attrib-utes the following statements to the first of the so-called "pairs" (groups of two scholars in each generation that received and passed down the Oral Law until the time of Hillel and Shammai):

> Yose b. Yoezer of Seredah and Yose b. Yohanan of Jerusalem received [the Law] from them. Yose b. Yoezer said:
> "Let your house be a meeting house for sages (יהי ביתך בית ועד לחכמים), and sit in the dust of their feet and drink in their words with thirst."

---

[1] See Fraade, *From Tradition to Commentary*, 69–72, for important observations about the rabbinic concept of Torah in M 'Abot. On the literary and editorial characteristics of this text see A. Saldarini, *Scholastic Rabbinism: A Literary Study of the Fathers according to Rabbi Nathan* (Chico: Scholars Press, 1982), 9–23, and Tropper, *Wisdom, Politics, and Historiography*, 17–107. H. Strack and G. Stemberger, *Introduction to the Talmud and Midrash* (Edinburgh: T&T Clark, 1991), 120–21, contains a com-prehensive bibliography on the subject.

Yose b. Yohanan of Jerusalem said:
"Let your house be wide open, and let the poor be members of
your household (בני ביתך), and do not talk much with women."[2]

According to this text, it is one's house, not a disciple circle, that
serves as a place for studying the Law.[3] The two Yoses provide two
different views on what constitutes a pious household. According to
Yose b. Yoezer, one has to bring in sages and participate in their
discussions. According to Yose b. Yohanan, one has to reach out to
destitute members of the community by making the "poor" (as opposite to the "sages" in the previous clause) "members of your household." Still, both Yoses share a common perspective on one's household
as the basic social unit within which the person operates. Their
advice does not address masters and their disciple circles. It addresses
a householder (presumably of considerable means) who seeks to conduct a righteous life in accordance with the law. According to the
first "pair" of sages, the Law is preserved, studied, and transmitted
within one's household, not a disciple circle.

We know preciously little about either one of the Yoses.[4] Yose of
Seredah was most probably a priest. At least some of the traditions
transmitted in his name may indeed be authentic, and those indicate his priestly background.[5] Thus according to Sifra, "Yose ben
Seredah (sic) gave testimony concerning the waters of the slaughter-
house, that they are clean."[6] In Sifra's setting this testimony serves
as a proof for R. Eliezer's apodictic statement regarding the uncleanness of liquids. This sequence may be an example of how a particular legal precedent was reshaped first as a testimony and then as
an apodictic statement. Furthermore, according to M 'Eduyot 8:4:

---

[2] I have used the following translations of early rabbinic texts, reworking them as
necessary to clarify points critical to the discussion: H. Danby, *The Mishnah* (London:
Oxford University Press, 1938); J. Neusner, *The Mishnah: A New Translation* (New Haven:
Yale University Press, 1988); J Neusner, *The Rabbinic Traditions about the Pharisees* (Leiden:
E.J. Brill, 1971), vol. 1–3; J. Neusner, *The Tosefta* (New York: Ktav, 1977–1986),
vol. 1–6; J. Gereboff, *Rabbi Tarfon: The Tradition, the Man, and Early Rabbinic Judaism*
(Missoula: Scholars Press, 1979); S. Kanter, *Rabban Gamaliel II: The Legal Traditions*
(Chico: Scholars Press, 1980); J. Lightstone, "Sadoq the Yavnean," in W. Green, ed.,
Persons and Institutions in Early Rabbinic Judaism (Missoula: Scholars Press, 1977), 49–147.

[3] On this text and its manuscript versions see detailed discussion in Goldin, *Studies
in Midrash and Related Literature*, 39–56. He also emphasizes the centrality of one's
household and its mores for this discourse.

[4] See Neusner, *Rabbinic Traditions about the Pharisees*, vol. 1, 61–81, for a critical
review of relevant traditions.

[5] Only M Hag. 2:7 explicitly identifies him as a priest.

[6] Sifra Shemini 8:5 (Weiss, 55a).

R. Yose b. Yoezer of Seredah testified that the Ayil-locust is clean and that the liquids in the [temple] shambles are clean, and that he who touches the corpse becomes unclean. And they called him, "Yose the permitter."

The setting of Yose's testimony remains unclear.[7] The same is true for a group that labeled him "Yose the permitter." They could be priests or Pharisees, or both. But the laws themselves clearly pertain to purity laws as well as temple practice. Does Yose defend here ritual practices of his own family dealing with basic household purity and technical temple halakhah? Given the family-based structure of the priesthood, this conclusion seems likely, although we have no explicit statement in this respect. In other words, in his testimonies Yose may be transmitting his own family lore and its regulations regarding the temple cult.[8]

The figure of Yose of Seredah thus raises interesting questions about the origins of Rabbinic Judaism. He is a priest, who explicitly sees one's household as a prime setting for Torah study. His own statements are transmitted in tannaitic texts as individual testimonies, not necessarily accepted by others either in his own lifetime or later. Still, they serve as valid precedents, or at least, they have to be taken into account. One's household and household legal traditions loom large in the tannaitic portrayal of Yose, whatever its historical value may be. These traditions appear as a starting point of the development that would eventually lead to the emergence of the study circle of R. Yohanan b. Zakkai and the "classical" form of Rabbinic Judaism, focused on the preservation and transmission of the Torah within disciple circles. We have to take a closer look at this original stage of Rabbinic Judaism and its connection with earlier movements of the Second Temple period.[9]

---

[7] See Neusner, *Rabbinic Traditions*, vol. 1, 64–65.

[8] On the other hand, a number of scholars have argued that the entire "he testified" formula is a later editorial device used to arrange individual halakhic opinions. In connection with Yose's testimony see J. Epstein, *Mevo'ot le-Sifrut ha-Tanaim: Mishnah, Tosefta, u-Midreshe-Halakhah* (Jerusalem: Magnes, 1957), 505–06, and Neusner, *Rabbinic Traditions*, vol. 1, 64–66.

[9] There is surprisingly little research on possible Second Temple sources within the Mishnah and other early rabbinic texts. For promising observations in need of further elaboration see Cohen, "Parallel Historical Tradition in Josephus and Rabbinic Literature," 7–14, and G. Stemberger, "Narrative Baraitot in the Yerushalmi," in P. Schäfer, ed., *The Talmud Yerushalmi and Graeco-Roman Culture* (Tübingen: Mohr Siebeck, 1998), vol. 1, 63–81.

"Traditions of the Fathers" in Tannaitic Writings

In his discussion of rabbinic traditions about the Pharisees before 70 CE, Jacob Neusner distinguishes between the traditions transmitted in the name of the Houses (*Bet Shammai* and *Bet Hillel*) and those of the named masters. He observes that whereas the former traditions come in the form of "brief, abstract lemmas and debates," the latter are precedent-based narratives:

> These may be brief or long. In the former category are one-sentenced references to something a master had said, done, or decreed as precedent. In the latter category are fully developed stories of legal interest, which cannot be formally distinguished from equivalent stories of non-legal interest.[10]

Most of the Houses' debates are arranged according to what Neusner calls "standard legal form." This usually follows the formula "Authority X + says + opinion, in direct discourse," which can easily be augmented to produce the simple debate form.[11] The legal opinions transmitted in such a way tend to be abstract generalizing statements devoid of references to specific precedents and/or legal cases. Whereas Neusner maintains that this is a predominant way of arranging early material in the Mishnah, he also considers it to be relatively late.[12]

On the other hand, Neusner observes that "the redaction of the Houses-material followed literary and formal conventions not brought to bear upon the sayings of the named pre-70 masters."[13] As a result, unlike most laws assigned to the Houses, "all laws attributed to all named pre-70 masters are narratives of one kind or another."[14] Elsewhere, Neusner refers to narrative style and tale telling as characteristic of the "priestly source of the Mishnah," i.e., sections of the Mishnah that might have originated in halakhic traditions of the Second Temple priesthood. According to Neusner these passages "diverge from the standard formal and analytical style" of the Mishnah. Rather, "to describe cultic procedures, they resort to narrative style, telling what someone does or did, with a minimum of interruption

---

[10] Neusner, *Rabbinic Traditions*, vol. 3, 23–24.
[11] Neusner, *Rabbinic Traditions*, vol. 3, 5–6.
[12] Neusner, *Rabbinic Traditions*, vol. 3, 93.
[13] Neusner, *Rabbinic Traditions*, vol. 3, 14.
[14] Neusner, *Rabbinic Traditions*, vol. 3, 23.

for the familiar exercises of analytic and problem solving."[15] In this section I shall argue that many of the precedents singled out by Neusner originated within the practices of households (either priestly or lay) and were recognized as binding by other Jewish groups and/or families. Such a situation would perfectly agree with what has been said above about the household-based structure of at least some of the Second Commonwealth sectarian movements. The discussion will allow us a glimpse into how the sectarian understanding of Jewish law took shape by the late first century CE. It will also establish a connection between post-70 Rabbinic Judaism and pre-70 "traditions of the fathers." As we shall see in the subsequent chapters, a substantial body of halakhic traditions of early rabbinic masters follows the same form of precedent-based *ma'asim*. Only later does a more standard Mishnaic form of sayings take over, thus marking a new stage in the development of Rabbinic Judaism.[16]

Catherine Hezser has observed in her discussion of rabbinic houses that "just as the non-rabbinic houses, the rabbinic houses mentioned in the Mishnah and Tosefta are mentioned in connection with particular practices." She further distinguishes between these types of houses and the "houses" of Hillel and Shammai that transmit teachings and disputes in their masters' names.[17] This distinction comes close to that of Neusner and merits further attention. Hezser enumerates three types of houses mentioned in the Mishnah and Tosefta in connection with their practices: priestly houses, houses of private individuals, who are identified neither as priests nor as rabbis, and finally the rabbinic "houses" attached to a particular rabbi other than

---

[15] Neusner, *Judaism*, 248–50. It is interesting to compare Neusner's list of examples of the texts constituting the "priestly source of the Mishnah," with that in Epstein, *Mevo'ot le-Sifrut ha-Tanaim*, 25–58 (which Epstein suggests to be the earliest documentary stratum of the collection). There are some remarkable overlaps as well as differences. The source-critical approach to the Mishnah is by no means dead, despite all the difficulties involved.

[16] This comes as a logical conclusion from Neusner's conclusions about the history of the Oral Law. He correctly observes that the notion of the Oral Law, transmitted from master to his disciples by means of recitation, emerged in the academic setting of bet midrash. It probably reflects the teaching environment of the rabbinic academy more than anything else. The formation of Rabbinic Judaism is closely related with the beginning of academic study of the Oral Law. See further Neusner, *Rabbinic Traditions about the Pharisees*, vol. 3, 143–79. Cf. Schäfer, "Das Dogma von der Mündlichen Torah," 153–97, and (most recently) Jaffee, *Torah in the Mouth*, 65–152.

[17] Hezser, *Social Structure of the Rabbinic Movement*, 309.

Hillel and Shammai. The latter include the houses of R. Gamaliel,
R. Shimon b. Gamaliel, and R. Hananiah, prefect of the priests. In
connection with all three of them the Mishnah and Tosefta always
refer to their practices but not to their teachings.[18] As a whole, Hezser's
observation about the nature and functions of the "Mishnaic" houses
serves as an important addition and correction to the views of Jacob
Neusner. A household setting appears to have been an important
feature of early halakhic legislation, and halakhic practices of individual households were deemed worthy of transmission. Stories about
such practices fit into the pattern of precedent-oriented narratives as
the main form of transmitting laws in the name of pre-70 masters.
In other words, stories about household practices may very well
belong to the same category of tradition as narratives about individual
masters. One has to consider this type of legal narrative more closely.

Tannaitic texts contain occasional references to priestly practices
and duties associated with particular individuals or priestly families
in the Second Temple. In many cases early rabbinic sources attest
that the distinction between the "private" practices of priestly households and their "public" role remained blurred at best. According
to M Yoma 3:11:

> Those of the House of Garmu would not teach how to prepare the
> Shewbread. Those of the House of Abtinas would not teach how to
> prepare the incense. Higros b. Levi had a special art in singing, but he
> would not teach it. Ben Kamtsar would not teach the craft of writing.[19]

This is a list of priestly individuals and families that choose to keep
to themselves their professional secrets instead of teaching them to
a broad audience. According to the list of temple officials in M
Sheqalim 5:1, each of them fulfilled particular technical functions in
the temple: "Higros b. Levi was over singing, the House of Garmu
was over the preparation of the Shewbread, the House of Abtinas
was over the preparation of the incense." Each of these groups and
individuals "owned" certain technical skills that insured their position
within the temple establishment. At least, the House of Garmu and
the House of Abtinas appear to refer to priestly families that transmitted
the knowledge of preparing the Shewbread and incense only to family
members, thus insuring their social status. The same may apply to

---

[18] Hezser, *Social Structure*, 309–11.
[19] Cf. M Sheqal. 5:1, T Kipp. 2:6, and T Sheqal. 2:6.

other names as well.[20] In other words, it was a technical knowledge
of certain practices that characterized these priestly families. This
knowledge included particular professional skills, but also, no doubt,
legal traditions pertaining to the matter. These practices and legal
knowledge could also be referred to as "traditions of the forefathers."

The acquisition of necessary skills and knowledge in such cases
would most often come as a result of observing one's close relatives
performing their professional duties. As a result, precedent-based
opinions played a crucial role in pre-70 traditions. To give an example, Tannaitic texts transmitted in the name of Hananiah, Prefect
of the Priests (סגן הכהנים) consist almost exclusively of precedent-
based traditions.[21] When the Mishnah discusses the sacrificial validity of a blemished animal, it quotes Hananiah as referring to the
practice of his father: "Hananiah, Prefect of the Priests, said, 'Father
would reject the blemished [animals] from the altar.'"[22] In other
words, Hananiah derives his halakhic statement from the legal practice of his father. His own legal opinion is firmly rooted in and
halakhicly justified by the ancestral practice. Hananiah presents a
similar argument, based now on his own experience as member of
the priestly clan, when he says, "I have never seen a hide taken out
to the place of burning."[23] Hananiah justifies his legal opinion by
appealing to priestly practices. It remains unclear if, like in the first
case, he is referring here specifically to the practices of his family
or not. At any rate, Hananiah's testimony emphasizes his unique
position to observe priestly practices and transmit them. His own
experience as an officiating priest plays a crucial role in his reasoning. In a subsequent debate R. Aqiva and anonymous sages discuss
whether or not these practices (or rather lack thereof) can be taken
as a valid argument for a halakhic decision. Their responses reflect
two ways of integrating the practice-based family lore of Hananiah
into the academic setting of the Mishnah. R. Aqiva preserves the

---

[20] T Menah. 13:21 describes priestly houses as typical households including children, sons-in-law, and slaves. These households are actively involved in public politics (albeit in a pretty heavy-handed way). See Hezser, *Social Structure*, 308–09 and
Sivertsev, *Private Households*, 101–07.

[21] See Neusner, *Rabbinic Traditions*, vol. 1, 400–413, for a review of Hananiah's
traditions. He essentially accepts their authenticity and pre-70 dating.

[22] M Zebah. 9:3. Cf. Sifra Tsaw 1:9 (Weiss, 29a) and T Zebah. 9:5.

[23] M Zebah. 12:4. Cf. M 'Ed. 2:1–3. Epstein, *Mevo'ot*, 84, sees the Zebahim version of the story as an original one. The list of testimonies attributed to Hananiah
Segan ha-Kohanim in 'Eduyot looks like a later editorial exercise.

overall validity of Hananiah's testimony by suggesting that it be *interpreted* in a particular way. By doing so, however, he shifts the emphasis from the testimony and its underlying practice to its scholarly interpretation. The relative value of the family halakhah of Hananiah and his claims to its unique ownership are thus significantly diminished. But R. Aqiva at least recognizes the validity of Hananiah's testimony. His anonymous colleagues reject the testimony altogether, stating that "we have not seen" is not a valid proof.[24]

Similar to Hananiah, his son R. Simeon serves as a tradent for several traditions about the temple practice. Although it is nowhere stated that he derives them from the halakhic knowledge of his family, this can be reasonably assumed. Thus Rabban Simeon b. Gamaliel transmits in his name a detailed description of the temple veil, which seems to be inserted into the standard halakhic discussion of the Mishnah almost as a side note.[25] Rabban Simeon b. Gamaliel also transmits R. Simeon's opinion regarding the preparation of the Shewbread on a festival day.[26] The latter disagrees with an anonymous mishnah about the preparation of the Shewbread in the temple. This tradition appears in the standard Mishnaic form of an individual lemma, but it also may ultimately derive from R. Simeon's family lore that disagrees with another tradition (or later conjecture?) transmitted as an anonymous mishnah.

Hananiah, Prefect of the Priests, and his son R. Simeon thus serve to introduce bits and pieces of their priestly family lore into the Mishnaic discussion. Moreover, R. Simeon always appears in connection with Rabban Simeon b. Gamaliel, who transmits his traditions. The two families are also mentioned together in another Mishnaic description of the temple ritual. A general statement in M Sheqalim 6:1 about the thirteen prostrations that had to be made in the temple is qualified by a reference to the House of R. Gamaliel and the House of R. Hananiah, which used to make fourteen prostrations, adding one prostration opposite the wood-store. This prac-

---

[24] This discussion is absent in the 'Eduyot version, which can be seen as a perfect example of the more academic and detached approach taken to Second Temple traditions by later generations of rabbis. The law is no longer embodied in practices of particular priestly households. It becomes an abstract category of scholarly debate. For the Aqivan redaction of this passage see further Epstein, *Mevo'ot*, 84 and 431. Cf. Neusner, *Rabbinic Traditions*, vol. 1, 403–04.

[25] M Sheqal. 8:5.

[26] M Menah. 11:9.

tice is explained by "the tradition among them from their forefathers, that there the ark lay hidden" (שכן מסורת בידם מאבותיהם).[27] The text seems to refer to the physical parents of R. Gamaliel and R. Hananiah and their ancestral traditions (lore) about the location of the ark within the temple precincts. These traditions determined the liturgical practices of the houses of R. Gamaliel and Hananiah in the temple. In this case the term "traditions of the forefathers" clearly refers to halakhic rulings passed down within a family. They constitute the ancestral lore of both lay (R. Gamaliel) and priestly (Hananiah) families combining halakhic and non-halakhic traditions. Moreover, these traditions were not limited to household space but defined such public spheres as temple ceremonial law.[28] Another passage describes the particular way in which "those of the house of Rabban Gamaliel" (שלבית רבן נמליאל) paid their shekel dues to ensure that they would be used directly to purchase the sacrifice.[29] Overall, several mishnaic texts contain traditions originating in the household practices of R. Hananiah the Prefect of the Priests and Rabban Gamaliel. Both families seem to have maintained close relationships, since the son of Rabban Gamaliel would occasionally transmit traditions in the name of R. Hananiah's son. In both cases we find no distinction between the private practices of family members and "public" halakhah. In fact, the former shaped the latter. Finally, in both cases household practices and rituals seem to have been informed by ancestral family traditions of both halakhic and aggadic nature. Both families lived their lives and performed their duties according to their respective "traditions of the fathers."

Similar to Hananiah, Prefect of the Priests, Yohanan b. Gudgada is repeatedly mentioned in tannaitic texts in connection with practices of his family.[30] Thus in the Toseftan version of the list of priestly groups and families appointed over different services in the temple, Yohanan b. Gudgada is mentioned as appointed over the locking of

---

[27] M Sheqal. 6:1.

[28] I think that Neusner is overcautious in his assessment that "it is difficult to say whether their immediate parents or their masters are meant." See Neusner, *Rabbinic Traditions*, vol. 1, 346. The text specifically implies physical ancestors of both families rather than "fathers of the world."

[29] M Sheqal. 3:3. Epstein, *Mevo'ot*, 26, assigns this tradition to the same source as M Sheqal. 6:1. His attribution of this source to Abba Yose b. Hannan is obviously very questionable.

[30] See Neusner, *Rabbinic Traditions*, vol. 1, 417–19.

the gates in the sanctuary.[31] Sifre Numbers elaborates the same subject by providing a (real? fictitious?) dialogue between R. Joshua b.
Hananiah and Yohanan b. Gudgada. The former is said to have
gone to assist Yohanan with fastening the temple gates. Yohanan,
however, told him to turn back and not to endanger himself, "for
I am of the gate-keepers and you are of the singers" (שאני מן השוערים
ואתה מן המשוררים).[32] This dialogue corresponds to what the Mishnah
has noted about the "professional jealousy" between various priestly
families regarding their professional status, skills and place within the
temple's hierarchy. In this case, however, the point is driven home
even more strongly by observing that the breach of hierarchy may
result in the miraculous death of an offender. A similar chord is
touched in another narrative, according to which "Yohanan b. Gudgada
always ate [his common food] in accordance with [the rules of]
cleanness of Hallowed things, yet for them that occupied themselves
with sin-offering water his apron counted as suffering *midras*-unclean-
ness."[33] Apparently this text reflects yet another stratification that
existed among priestly families. It also puts into due perspective the
dialogue between Yohanan and R. Joshua. Different tasks fulfilled
by different priestly clans apparently corresponded to different degrees
of intrinsic purity. Finally, according to the Tosefta R. Judah transmitted a story "of the sons of Rabbi Yohanan b. Gudgada that they
were deaf and dumb, and all the purities of Jerusalem were done

---

[31] T Sheqal. 2:14. Epstein, *Mevo'ot*, 27, sees this addition as coming from a tradition different from that of the Mishnah. Unlike the Mishnah, the Toseftan tradition focuses on low-rank functionaries from the Levites. I would add that it is
quite possible that we are dealing with two family traditions here: one comes from
a priestly family and focuses on priestly arrangements, whereas the other (the
Toseftan) comes from a Levite family.

[32] Sifre Num. 116 (Horovitz, 132). Epstein, *Mevo'ot*, 27, correctly notices how
specific this tradition is. It focuses on a particular person, although we know that
there were scores of priests and Levites manning the temple gates. This focus on
a particular person may be an indication of the family tradition serving as a basis
for this story. As a whole, tannaitic traditions about Second Temple personnel tend
to refer to particular people, some of whom are not known otherwise and probably did not play any significant role in the temple administration. However, they,
their relatives, or their friends could be responsible for transmitting traditions now
in the Mishnah and other tannaitic texts. As a result, these traditions would contain a very subjective assessment of whom among temple officials deserved to be
mentioned. If at least some of the Mishnaic temple-related traditions come from
family halakhot of priestly and levitical households, then this preponderance of seemingly insignificant personalities and events becomes understandable.

[33] M Hag. 2:7.

under their supervision."[34] Despite its relatively late attestation and clearly anecdotal characteristics, this story develops the notion that the priestly family of Yohanan b. Gudgada was responsible for specific temple activities.[35] Moreover, the reference to the "supervision" of the sons of Yohanan b. Gaba over "all the purities of Jerusalem" may imply the notion of legislative (halakhic) activity carried out within a particular family but still perceived as publicly binding. It reflects the understanding of halakhah as transmitted within Yohanan's family but also accepted as publicly authoritative. This lack of distinction between the private lore of priestly families and rules that governed their public performance seems to have characterized the entire realm of priestly halakhah, especially as it emerges from the Mishnah and related tannaitic texts.

In this context it should come as no surprise that the practices of priestly households are sometimes (but not too often) related in connection with their female family members. Tannaitic stories associated with Martha bat Boethus are remarkable in this respect. M Yebamot 6:4 tells about her marriage with Joshua ben Gamla as a legal precedent, which serves to determine the priestly marriage law:

> A high priest shall not marry a widow . . . but if he had betrothed a widow and was nominated high priest—he may marry her. There was the case of Joshua ben Gamla who had betrothed Martha bat Boethus and the king nominated him high priest and he took her as a wife.

The Mishnah discusses the possibility of a high priest marrying a widow. Although the general rule prohibits such a marriage, there may be exceptions. If the betrothal took place prior to one's nomination as a high priest, it is deemed valid. The case of Joshua ben Gamla, who had betrothed Martha bat Boethus (presumably, a widow) and then was nominated to become a high priest, serves as a legal precedent for this exception. Here, once again, the practice of a priestly household serves as a basis for public halakhah. Moreover, the focus on the narrative is not on Joshua ben Gamla himself but rather on

---

[34] T Ter. 1:1.

[35] The family of Yohanan b. Gudgada occupied a relatively modest position in the temple hierarchy. As can be concluded from the reviewed passages, they were Levites responsible for specific technical tasks (operating the gates) and apparently were barred from more prestigious functions in the temple. The claim that Gudgada's sons controlled "all the purities of Jerusalem" is clearly a fantasy. On the implications and limitations of his levitical status see further Epstein, *Mevo'ot*, 27.

his household.[36] The latter also includes his wife Martha, who was
a scion of another leading priestly family of Boethus.[37] According to
this account it is their joint practice that serves as a valid halakhic
source of Jewish law.

One more time Martha appears in connection with her children
and the particular way in which they offered sacrifices:

> Twenty four sacrifice an ox . . . [in which case] two hold the foot and
> bring it to the altar . . . This is in the case of public sacrifices, but in
> the case of private sacrifices anyone who wants to sacrifice may sacrifice.
> It once happened with the sons of Martha bat Boethus, one of whom
> would hold two thighs of an ox bought at one thousand dinari in his
> two fingers walking heel to toe to bring them to the altar.[38]

The story serves to distinguish between the manner in which public
and private sacrifices were brought. In the latter case people had
more freedom to perform the ceremony according to their own tastes
(or lack thereof). The example of Martha's sons serves to illustrate
this point (perhaps in an exaggerated way). It is remarkable that this
story uses Martha's name to identify her children, while they themselves
remain anonymous. It is the ceremonial practices of Martha's household (her ancestral law) which are deemed important in this account.
Her children serve as mere performers of their ancestral halakhah.
The centrality of Martha's family entails the centrality of her name
as an identification marker in this account.

Priestly halakhic practices were not necessarily limited to the realm
of Temple ceremonial law. A legendary account shows that even the
private piety of individual priestly households, not directly connected
with temple procedures, could be taken as halakhically authoritative
by the Jewish public:

> Joseph the Priest brought his first fruits of wine and oil, and they
> would not accept them. He also brought his sons and the men of his

---

[36] T. Ilan, *Mine and Yours are Hers: Retrieving Women's History from Rabbinic Literature*
(Leiden: Brill, 1997), 89, correctly observes that whereas Josephus mentions Joshua
ben Gamla on numerous occasions but never mentions his wife, rabbinic texts "seem
much more interested in Martha than in her husband." I would add that they are
probably more interested in the family than in its individual members.

[37] See M. Stern, "Aspects of Jewish Society: The Priesthood and Other Classes,"
in S. Safrai et al., eds., *The Jewish People in the First Century* (Philadelphia: Fortress,
1976), 604–06.

[38] T Kipp. 1:13–14.

household (את בניו ואת בני ביתו) to keep the Lesser Passover in Jerusalem, but they turned him back lest it should be established as an obligation (שלא יקבע הדבר חובה).[39]

The story asserts that anonymous "they" (priestly authorities in the temple?) did not allow Joseph the Priest to bring his household to Jerusalem to celebrate the Second Passover there. This was done out of suspicion that such a celebration, instead of being perceived just as a pious act of an individual priest and his family, could have been perceived as a halakhic requirement by other people. The story specifically identifies Joseph's household as the prime setting of his halakhic practice. The pious behavior of this household could have been mistakenly taken to be paradigmatic by other people, and so it had to be cancelled. It is unclear if Joseph's priestly status had anything to do with the paradigmatic significance of his household's behavior. Still, it indicates that the halakhah of priestly households played an important role in defining public religious observances. In another case Joseph the Priest's practice of making a hole in the side of his inkwell is mentioned to illustrate an anonymous statement that "an inkpot of an ordinary person is not clean until one will make a hole in its side."[40] Thus the Mishnah repeatedly uses Joseph's household halakhic practices as valid precedents in the realm of "public" Jewish law.[41]

Mishnaic references to the temple-related traditions of R. Eliezer b. Jacob illustrate how priestly household lore could be integrated into post-70 rabbinic tradition. In M Mid. 1:2 he quotes an unfortunate experience of his maternal uncle as an illustration of a particular temple practice: "They once found my mother's brother asleep and burnt his raiment." The story appears as part of a largely anonymous description of temple practices and measurements featuring from time to time other remarks by R. Eliezer.[42] On several occasions

---

[39] M Hallah 4:11.
[40] M Miqwa'ot 10:1.
[41] T 'Abod. Zar. 1:8 tells how Joseph the Priest chose to defile himself by going abroad (to Sidon) in order to study there with R. Yose. The story serves to illustrate R. Yose's opinion that a priest may contract uncleanness to go to study Torah with a particular master.
[42] M Mid. 1:9 and 2:6. The combination of technical data and legendary lore in the anonymous description of the temple precincts may partially come from priestly family traditions. On early layers of M Middot see further Epstein, *Mevo'ot*, 31–36. Epstein credits R. Eliezer with the authorship of the entire mishnah, which

the Mishnah makes him report a practice, the meaning and/or details
of which he no longer remembers. Thus in the anonymous description of buildings occupying the Court of Women, R. Eliezer suddenly remarks about a southwest chamber: "I forget for what it was
used" (שכחתי מה היתה משמשת). The Mishnah then quotes one Abba
Saul, who explains the purpose of the chamber.[43] The same happens
further in the description of the Temple Court, when R. Eliezer for-
gets the purpose of the "Wood Chamber." Once again Abba Saul
comes to the rescue and supplies an appropriate tradition.[44] The
Mishnah portrays R. Eliezer's knowledge of the temple as deriving
from his ancestral tradition. The incident with his maternal uncle
serves as an important source of information about temple practices.
In his testimonies R. Eliezer has to rely on his memory, which is
not always impeccable. He is a transmitter of family (or professional
priestly) lore about the temple, but he is not a scholar who arrives
at conclusions by means of logical syllogisms. He either remembers
his traditions or he does not. His testimonies have to be integrated
into the academic setting of rabbinic Torah. The testimonies function as raw material to be molded at will by subsequent generations
of rabbis. This seems to reflect a predominant rabbinic approach
toward halakhic traditions of pre-70 authorities. These traditions are
reshaped in accordance with the new intellectual environment of *bet
midrash*, where the prime focus dwells on one's ability to interpret
the law, not on the accurate transmission of one's household lore.

Sometimes rabbis chose to emphasize the fact that priests do not
in fact possess sufficient knowledge of their own traditions. We have
seen that already in the accounts of R. Eliezer's "forgetfulness." In
another story the statement attributed to one Simeon HaTsanua
("the Modest") is brought up to refute the opinion of R. Meir that
those who do not wash their hands and feet do not enter the temple area leading to the altar.[45] Simeon quotes his own experience of
entering this area without having washed hands and feet. In what
follows, however, R. Eliezer b. Hyrcanus sharply rebukes and insults

---

is clearly an exaggeration. It appears that the early stratum of M Middot has
emerged out of the conflation of several priestly traditions, edited and organized
by later redactors.
  [43] M Mid. 2:5.
  [44] M Mid. 5:4.
  [45] T Kelim B. Qam. 1:6.

him, referring to a tradition, attested elsewhere in the Mishnah, that if the high priest enters the area in front of the altar without washing hands and feet his fellow priests kill him with clubs.[46] By doing so, R. Eliezer once again asserts the supremacy of rabbinic knowledge over the practical halakhah of priests. He shows that the priests do not sufficiently know their own traditions. It is remarkable, however, that R. Eliezer chooses to refute Simeon by referring to another priestly practice, not to an intellectual syllogism of a rabbinic study circle. He thus tacitly accepts and confirms the halakhic validity of priestly lore, but claims that priests do not know their own traditions well enough and that rabbis constitute better tradents of priestly halakhah. The legal authority of priestly practices goes unchallenged. What is questioned is the ability of priests to accurately transmit and comprehend their own traditions.

As a whole, the Mishnah explicitly presents some of its traditions as deriving from priestly practices and the practice-based lore of priestly families. It also unambiguously distinguishes them from "standard" rabbinic traditions and seeks to correlate the two. Priestly traditions are usually perceived as halakhically valid but requiring further elaboration by rabbis. They supply halakhic material to be molded at will by successive generations of *talmide hakhamim*. Mishnaic editors are conscious of the changing settings in which these traditions are transmitted as well as of the changing authority patterns that are associated with the transmission. Some pre-70 traditions originate as part of the ancestral family lore of particular households. They represent the unique hereditary possession of these households, which "own" them just as they "own" the unique technical skills required to perform duties in the temple. The halakhic practices of individual members of any given household are important because they contribute to and interpret the household's ancestral lore. They also represent a unique way of public dissemination of these practices. The latter, indeed, are deemed publicly authoritative both within the temple precincts and sometimes outside of them. The temple halakhah emerges as the sum total of priestly household traditions, not as an anonymous set of laws and precepts regulating temple procedures.

---

[46] See M Sanh. 9:6. Epstein, *Mevo'ot*, 56, takes it to be an early tradition, mostly because it is quoted by R. Eliezer in the Tosefta. I do not find this argument particularly convincing, but the mishnah may indeed belong to early priestly lore. The Tosefta definitely uses it as a veritable priestly tradition about temple procedures.

In this respect, tannaitic texts possess an acute awareness that the "traditions of the fathers" are the prime building blocks of pre-Destruction halakhah. They seek to integrate them, whenever appropriate, into an entirely new intellectual universe based on the study of abstract legislation within disciple circles. The household-owned "traditions of the fathers" had to be transformed into the Oral Law of the rabbinic *bet midrash*.

Pharisees and Sadducees in Rabbinic Sources

In addition to legal traditions attributed to individuals, statements attributed to Pharisees and Sadducees constitute another source of possibly pre-70 material in tannaitic literature. The historical value of these texts has been sometimes questioned, and as a whole it remains uncertain. Earlier scholars tended to accept traditions transmitted in the form of debates between *Perushim* and *Tsaddukim* as historically accurate.[47] Jack Lightstone, in agreement with the methodological presuppositions of Jacob Neusner's school, has challenged this approach and suggested that the traditions in question could very well be a literary construct.[48] The discussion acquired a new dimension after the publication of the 4QMMT (*Miktsat Ma'aseh ha-Torah*) from Qumran. This text reflects an early halakhic controversy in which some of the opinions represented are attributed in the Mishnaic corpus to Pharisees and Sadducees, respectively. It thus may corroborate the historical accuracy of the Mishnaic collection, or at least some of its elements.[49] All things considered, I tend to accept the tannaitic versions of the *Perushim/Tsaddukim* collection as

---

[47] See, for example, Finkelstein, *Pharisees*, vol. 2, 637–753. Cf. Guttman, *Rabbinic Judaism in the Making*, 136–61.

[48] See J. Lightstone, "Sadducees *versus* Pharisees," in J. Neusner, ed., *Christianity, Judaism and Other Greco-Roman Cults* (Leiden: Brill, 1975), vol. 3, 206–17. Neusner addressed several of these traditions and treated them as later literary constructs. See, for example, J. Neusner, *A History of the Mishnaic Law of Purities* (Leiden: Brill, 1974), vol. 22, 244–50. Cf. J. Neusner, *Development of a Legend: Studies on the Traditions concerning Yohanan ben Zakkai* (Leiden: Brill, 1970), 60–61.

[49] See Baumgarten, "Pharisaic-Sadducean Controversies," 157–70. Cf. Schiffman, "New Halakhic Letter," 64–73, and "Pharisaic and Sadducean Halakhah in Light of the Dead Sea Scrolls," *DSD* 1 (1994), 285–99. Cf., however, L. Grabbe, "4QMMT and Second Temple Jewish Society," in M. Bernstein et al., eds., *Legal Texts and Legal Issues: Proceedings of the Second Meeting of the International Organization for Qumran Studies* (Leiden: Brill, 1997), 89–108, for criticism of this hypothesis.

containing material which dates to the pre-destruction period but may also reflect the reality of early post-destruction times (late first and second centuries CE).[50] It is, moreover, possible that tannaitic criticism of the "Sadducean" lore reflects the emergence of mature rabbinic discourse along with its attempt to replace relatively amorphous "ancestral traditions" with clearly defined and universally authoritative halakhah of rabbinic schools. In this case the *Tsaddukim* become less associated with a particular group within Judaism than with a specific way of practicing Torah that has to be abrogated by new forms of emerging rabbinic legislation. Our sources repeatedly identify the "Sadducean" teachings with family-based halakhic practices and seek to replace them with laws designed within disciple circles.[51]

M Yadaim 4:6–9 contains a cluster of traditions organized in the form of a debate between Pharisees and Sadducees. M Yadaim 4:7 reads as follows:

> Say the Sadducees, "We cry out against you Pharisees, for you say, 'If my ox or my ass have done an injury they are culpable, but if my manservant or maidservant (ועבדי ואמתי) have done an injury they are not culpable.' If, in the case on my ox or my ass, concerning which no commandment is laid upon me, I am responsible for the injury that they do, how much more so in the case of my manservant or my maidservant, concerning whom commandments are laid on me, must I be responsible for the injury that they do."
>
> They said to them, "No! As you argue concerning my ox or my ass which have no understanding, would you likewise argue concerning my manservant and my maidservant which have understanding? For if I provoke him to anger he may go and set fire to another's stack of corn, and I will be responsible to make restitution.

This debate deals with a civil law, but more specifically it deals with the accountability of one's household for the damage done by its animals or by its servants. The Sadducean approach tends to strengthen the legal bond between a master and his/her servants, seeing the former as being fully responsible for the misdemeanors of the latter,

---

[50] See Stemberger, *Jewish Contemporaries of Jesus*, 38–66, for discussion of available evidence. Cf. Jaffee, *Torah in the Mouth*, 52–60. On the possibility of continuous existence of the Sadducees in post-Destruction times see M. Goodman, "Sadducees and Essenes after 70 CE," in S. Porter, et al., eds., *Crossing the Boundaries: Essays in Biblical Interpretation in Honour of Michael D. Goulder* (Leiden: Brill, 1994), 347–56.
[51] Cf. Boyarin, *Border Lines*, 44–45 and 54–67. He sees the first post-Destruction centuries as crucial in the development of rabbinic heresiological discourse and puts the debate against the "Sadducees" in this context.

the same way he is responsible for the misdemeanor of his cattle. From a legal perspective Sadducees tended to view servants as possessing a kind of corporate identity with the household of their masters. As servants are recognized as sharing the corporate identity of their master's house in respect to their circumcision and participation in the Passover celebration, so they are recognized in respect to their crimes.[52] On the other hand, the Pharisees recognize servants as independent legal subjects. Only when a servant is explicitly commanded by his master to inflict damage is the master culpable. In other words, Pharisees tended to emphasize the individual responsibility of the servant at the expense of his/her household identity and corporate legal responsibility.[53] Although this debate may in and of itself be reflective of important social trends within Jewish households, our prime interest has to do with its setting. The debate is centered around the halakhic practices of groups of individual aristocratic households referred to as *Perushim* and *Tsaddukim*, one of which must be recognized as publicly authoritative.

The debate attested in T Yadaim 2:20 appears to be directly related in form and content to the debate of M Yadaim 4:7.[54] The beginning of the Tosefta text clearly alludes to the Mishnah and would be totally incomprehensible without prior knowledge of the Mishnah's

---

[52] H. Albeck, *Shishah Sidre Mishnah: Seder Tohorot* (Jerusalem: Bialik, 1959), 609, indicates parallels between the Sadducean approach and Hellenistic legislation. The latter held a master culpable for damage caused by his slave.

[53] The distinction reflects an ambiguity of a slave's legal status. On the one hand, he is classified as *res* (an object) or a chattel that does not possess an independent human status and has to be perceived along with other household implements. On the other hand, he is *persona* (a human being), possessing his own volition and thus capable of acting independently. This problem of the dual status of a slave was recognized in both Roman law and Near Eastern (including Jewish) laws. On the former see A. Kirschenbaum, *Sons, Slaves, and Freedmen in Roman Commerce* (Washington, D.C.: Catholic University of America Press, 1987), 15–16, n. 48. On the latter cf. G. Feeley-Harnik, "Is Historical Anthropology Possible? The Case of the Runaway Slave," in G. Tucker and D. Knight, eds., *Humanizing America's Iconic Book* (Chico: Scholars Press, 1982), 95–126, and D. Martin, "Slavery and the Ancient Jewish Family," in S. Cohen, ed., *The Jewish Family in Antiquity* (Atlanta: Scholars Press, 1993), 117–18. P. Flesher, *Oxen, Women, or Citizens? Slaves in the System of the Mishnah* (Atlanta: Scholars Press, 1988), 67–90, discusses how rabbinic tradition tries to accommodate both aspects of a slave's legal status.

[54] See Lightstone, "Sadducees *versus* Pharisees," 211. As Stemberger, *Jewish Contemporaries*, 52, observes: "The text functions as a variation of the Mishnah text, summarizing a developed state of affairs and completing other things that are only suggested." In both cases we find a case from civil law inserted into an otherwise fairly uniform legal collection dealing with purity laws.

parallel.[55] Although the Tosefta refers to the opponents of the Pharisees as Boethusians rather than Sadducees, the two groups appear to be related.[56] T Yadaim 2:20 thus merits attention in the light of what has been said about M Yadaim 4:7, especially if the two of them are to be viewed as parts of the same unit. The text in question runs as follows:

> Say the Boethusians: "We cry out against you Pharisees! If the daughter of my son, who came from the strength of my son who came from my strength, inherits me, all the more so my daughter who came from my strength should inherit me." Say the Pharisees, "No! If you say thus in the case of a daughter who shares with the brothers, then will you say thus in the case of a daughter who does not share with the brothers?"

One finds in this narrative a clash of family laws as practiced by two groups of households. According to the Boethusians the daughter of the head of the family has at least the same right of inheriting from him as the daughter of his son. Their argument is based on the respective degrees of closeness between various members of the kin.[57] According to the Pharisees the daughter's rights cannot be argued from those of a granddaughter since the two of them belong to different legal categories.[58] Important for the present discussion is the fact that the debate between the Pharisees and the Boethusians has a household setting. The argument is about whose practice of family law is more adequate. The Mishnah chooses to identify these two groups by their family practices and their respective laws based on such practices. It portrays two types of households following

---

[55] Still, it is hard to say whether this implies that the Tosefta's passage is secondary to that of the Mishnah. They may very well be contemporaneous, despite the fact that the Tosefta's *edition* is clearly later than that of the Mishnah and depends on it.

[56] On Boethusians and their connection with Sadducees see J. LeMoyne, *Les Sadducéens* (Paris: Lecoffre, 1972). Cf. further G. Stemberger, "The Sadducees— Their History and Doctrines," in W. Horbury et al., *Cambridge History of Judaism*, vol. 3, 434. Boethusians are mentioned only in rabbinic texts, and those tend to be of Amoraic rather than Tannaitic provenance. Often, different versions of rabbinic narratives use them and "Sadducees" interchangeably. Stemberger identifies them as "a group around the dynasty of Boethius, invested by Herod with the high-priestly dignity" (cf. LeMoyne, 336–37). He also sees them as "the kernel of the larger Sadducean group." For a more cautious approach cf. Saldarini, *Pharisees, Scribes and Sadducees*, 228.

[57] As Lightstone, "Sadducees," 211, observes, the Sadducean halakhah seems to be closer to the plain meaning of Num. 27:8 than the Pharisaic one. For an opposite view cf. Finkelstein, *Pharisees*, vol. 2, 694–96.

[58] Cf. M B. Bat. 8:2 for a plain statement of the Pharisaic/rabbinic law.

different notions of family law. Along with the formal characteristics of T Yadaim 2:20, this description of the two groups shows the affinity between this passage and the one in M Yadaim 4:7.[59]

Mishnah and Tosefta Niddah constitute another major cluster of tannaitic texts reflecting the centrality of households and their respective practices for the identity of the *Perushim* and *Tsaddukim*. According to M Niddah 4:2:

> The daughters of the Sadducees, if they follow the ways of their fathers (שנהגו ללכת בדרכי אבותיהן), are like Samaritan women. If they separated themselves to follow the ways of Israel, they are like Israelites. Rabbi Yose says: "They are always considered like Israel unless they separate themselves so as to follow the ways of their fathers."

Here the *Tsaddukim* are once again defined in terms of their family law and practices. The daughters of the Sadducees are said to follow "ways of their fathers" thus separating themselves from "Israel." Given the one-sidedness of this report, one obviously wonders what the Sadducean definition of "following the ways of Israel" might have been. We are immediately reminded of Josephus' description of the "traditions of the forefathers" accepted by the Pharisees but rejected by the Sadducees.[60] The main question shared by both texts might have been: "The ways of *whose* forefathers amounted to those of Israel?" Thus both texts presuppose the notion that the "traditions of the fathers" are indeed the household halakhic lore of individual families. It is only logical that the Mishanh identifies the *Tsaddukim* by specific practices followed in the families belonging to this group. T Niddah 5:3 may provide further illustration of the same point:

> A story about a certain Sadducee, who was conversing with the High Priest, and some spittle squirted from his mouth and fell upon the garments of the High Priest. And the face of the High Priest turned greenish. And they came and asked his wife and she said: "Sir High Priest, although we are Sadducean women, they all inquire of a sage." Said R. Yose: "We are more familiar with the Sadducean women than with all others, for they all inquire of a sage, except for one who was among them, and she died."[61]

---

[59] Finkelstein, *Pharisees*, vol. 1, 138–42, argues that the two different approaches to inheritance derived from the different social status of Pharisaic and Sadducean households ("plebeian" vs. "patrician"). This explanation seems simplistic, but it correctly reflects the household setting of the disagreement.

[60] *A.J.* 13.297.

[61] The text of the Tosefta is problematic in many respects and needs emenda-

The Tosefta's story serves as an illustration of the Mishnah. Its anecdotal nature notwithstanding, the story communicates the same message as the Mishnah about defining characteristics of the group called *Tsaddukim*. What characterizes the Sadducees are the particular purity laws practiced within their families and not necessarily shared by other Jews. Moreover, both stories share the same tendency to integrate members of the Sadducean families into what they perceive as mainstream Judaism. The daughters of the Sadducees tend to abandon the "ways of their fathers" and to follow those of the sages. Finally, R. Yose features prominently in both compositions.[62]

These two texts are visibly shaped by interests and concerns of later rabbinic editors. As such, they reflect a shift from the household piety to the piety shaped, interpreted, and transmitted within disciple circles. As both Charlotte Fonrobert and Daniel Boyarin have observed, we are dealing here with a new type of totalizing discourse that distinguishes between the "ways of the fathers" and "the ways of Israel."[63] Such a discourse reflects the quest for authority and control (both halakhic and intellectual) on the part of rabbis. According to Boyarin:

> In this text, women's bodies and sexuality are made an instrument in the struggle for power between the men of the rabbinic group and their rivals (the "fathers" of the Sadducean women). Other Jews, presumably behaving in accordance with ancient Jewish practice or with the ways of their fathers—a highly positively coded term when it is "our" fathers who are being invoked—are read out of Israel because they refuse the control of the rabbinic party.[64]

But there is more than just a clash of two competing traditions of Jewish law going on here. We witness here a transition from family-based Jewish halakhic traditions centered around the ritualized ancestral (family) lore to the abstract and totalizing reasoning of rabbinic disciple circles. As we shall see below, rabbinic claims for authority

---

tions. See S. Lieberman, *Tosefet Rishonim* (Jerusalem: Bamberger & Wahrmann, 1939), vol. 3, 268.

[62] I cannot agree with Lightstone's observation that "Yose's statement as it appears here is totally autonomous" and does not require the previous passage for its context. See Lightstone, "Sadducees," 215.

[63] See C. Fonrobert, "When Women Walk in the Ways of Their Fathers: On Gendering the Rabbinic Claim for Authority," *Journal of the History of Sexuality* 10, no. 3/4 (2001), 398–415, and D. Boyarin, *Border Lines*, 58–63.

[64] Boyarin, *Border Lines*, 62.

had a lot to do with rabbis' ability to control the familial practices of other Jews. In this situation the authority of rabbis and traditional practices of families could sometimes coexist but often did not. These texts transform conflicts between Sadducees and Pharisees over the "ways of their fathers" into the clash over whose practices are those of "Israel," i.e., constitute the "true" halakhah. The texts accomplish their task by showing that no matter what theoretical opinions might have been, in *practice* everyone followed the ways of rabbis.

T Kippurim 1:8 follows a similar approach by trying to smooth out disagreements between the Boethusians and the sages, and to demonstrate that they had a purely academic nature, whereas both groups followed the *practice* of the sages. The text runs as follows:

> A certain Boethusian prepared his incense while he was outside [the Holy of Holies] and the cloud of incense went forth and shook the temple. For the Boethusians say, "He shall prepare the incense while he is outside [the Holy of Holies], as it is said: "And the cloud of incense shall cover the ark-cover" (Lev 17:13). The sages said to them: "Has it not already been said, 'And he shall put the incense upon the fire before the Lord' (Lev 17:13). If so, why is it said: 'And the cloud of incense shall cover?' It teaches that he puts in them a smoke producing substance. If he did not put in them a smoke producing substance he is deserving of death." When he emerged he said to his father: "All of your days you interpreted and you did not do [thus] until I came and did [so] myself." [His father] said to him: "Although we interpret, we do not do [thus]. We obey the words of the sages. You will astonish me if you last [more than a few] days." It was not but three days until they placed him in his grave.[65]

According to the story the Boethusians and sages advocated different procedures of entering the Holy of Holies and presenting incense offering before the ark. The Boethusians held that the High Priest had to throw incense on the coals of a fire-pan prior to entering the Holy of Holies. He would thus enter the most sacred part of the temple with his offering already smoking and enveloping him in a cloud of incense. According to the sages the High Priest was supposed to throw incense on the fire once he has already entered the

---

[65] The story serves to illustrate M Yoma 1:5. According to the Mishnah the elders of the court used to instruct the High Priest how to carry out the service on the Day of Atonement. The Tosefta provides a legendary illustration of this statement. Still, parallels in Philo, *Spec.* 1.72, show that the story reflects historical reality. See further Stemberger, *Jewish Contemporaries*, 57–58.

Holy of Holies, but not prior to that.[66] The Tosefta presents the Sadducean opinion as essentially a family tradition passed from father to son. The son's mistake is that he takes this tradition in good faith to be a practical guidance for his performance in the temple, whereas in truth it is an intellectual exercise of his father. The practical halakhah agrees with that of the sages.

This story has a number of similarities with T Niddah 5:3. Both of them contrast the halakhic opinions of Second Temple groups (Sadducees and Boethusians) with those of the sages rather than the Pharisees. Both claim that disagreements between the sages, on the one hand, and either the Sadducees or Boethusians, on the other, were of a purely theoretical nature. In *practice* everyone followed rulings of the sages. Finally, those rare individuals who happened not to follow the practices of the sages tended to die out. Both stories appear to belong to the same editorial stratum and to further the same ideological agenda. They try to drive home the notion that no matter what theoretical disagreements there might have been, all Jewish groups *practiced* the law according to the opinion of the sages.[67] In both cases we find blatant attempts by the rabbis to control the realm of Jewish law by controlling family practices. The power of family traditions has to take a back seat to the power of rabbinic reasoning. Despite their apparent anachronism these stories emphasize the centrality of household halakhic practices by singling them out as the prime focus of rabbinic attack.

At the same time, these texts also share common assumptions that may reflect pre-70 reality. According to these texts the halakhah of the Sadducees and the Boethusians is shaped within the individual families that compose these groups. In T Kippurim 1:5 the Boethusian High Priest follows regulations of his father in performing the ritual of the Day of Atonement.[68] Tosefta's attempt to demonstrate that

---

[66] Cf. M Yoma 5:1.

[67] For an application of this notion to particular rabbinic masters see discussion below.

[68] J. Lauterbach, "A Significant Controversy between the Sadducees and the Pharisees," in idem, *Rabbinic Essays* (Cincinnati: Hebrew Union College Press, 1951), 51–83, insightfully observes that the Boethusian practice makes sense only if we consider it as part of a larger priestly lore presupposing the numinous physical presence of God in the Holy of Holies. Although he draws most of his evidence for this lore from later Amoraic sources, his conjecture is very interesting. In a similar way M Sheqal. 6:1 explains particular liturgical practices of the households of Rabban Gamaliel and Hananiah Prefect of the Priests by their family lore locating

he mistook his father's theoretical speculations for a practical halakhah is clearly anachronistic. Moreover it appears to precisely counter the notion that in earlier times practical halakhah was dominated by family traditions.[69] In this respect T Kippurim's text (along with that of T Niddah) constitutes an interesting example of transition from the sectarian Judaism of the Second Temple period to the more uniform Rabbinic Judaism. Whereas during the Second Temple period different Jewish groups not only expounded scriptures in different ways but also followed different halakhic practices, Rabbinic Judaism allowed theoretical disagreements as long as they did not result in different systems of practical halakhah.[70] The anachronistic nature of both stories has precisely to do with the fact that they shifted the focus of disagreement from legal practices to theoretical legal interpretation. In practice, however, all competing Jewish groups followed the halakhah of the sages, at least according to the claim of the rabbinic editor.

The importance of these testimonies is precisely in their attempt to smooth out differences in the halakhic practices of individual households. Both stories recognize the family-based social structure of the Sadducees and the Boethusians. Both stories admit that there were particular regulations transmitted within those families from parents to children. T Kippurim 1:8 argues that those regulations were of a purely theoretical nature, whereas T Niddah 5:3 (in conjunction with M Niddah 4:2) claims that all Sadducean women follow the practical regulations of the sages and not "the ways of their fathers."

---

the Ark of the Covenant beneath the Temple mount. Cf. a slightly different explanation by E.P. Sanders, *Judaism: Practice and Belief, 63 BCE–66 CE* (London: SCM Press, 1992), 335. According to him, Boethusian halakhah simply made better practical sense and reflected their actual involvement with temple practices, whereas rabbinic suggestions were purely theoretical and exegesis-driven in nature. Both authors, however, agree that the rabbinic approach is closer to the plain sense of Lev 16:12–13 regulating the ritual of the Day of Atonement. The Sadduceans appear to have followed their own family customs, which in this case superseded the plain message of the Scriptures.

[69] Finkelstein, *Pharisees*, vol. 2, 655, points out that the Boethusian halakhah could reflect a particular way in which affluent households of the time burnt spices at the end of the meal. The Boethusians merely applied logic of their household practices to the temple.

[70] For operational principles behind Rabbinic Judaism see S. Cohen, "The Significance of Yavneh: Pharisees, Rabbis, and the End of Jewish Sectarianism," *HUCA* 55 (1984), 27–53. But cf. Goodman, "Sadducees and Essenes after 70 CE," 347–56, and Boyarin, *Border Lines*, 44–45 and 54–67.

In either case the pre-70 historical reality is twisted to illustrate a new ideological agenda of the single binding halakhah, instead of the diverse halakhic practices of individual households. Still, both texts recognize that individual families with their legal traditions constituted the basis of groups called "Sadducees" and "Boethusians." These legal traditions embraced ritual law of the temple as well as purity aspects of family law.

Several case stories may provide indirect evidence that tannaitic texts perceived individual families as the main building blocks of the group called *Perushim*. M 'Erubin 6:2 transmits the following account:

> Rabban Gamaliel said: "Once a Sadducee lived with us, adjoining the same alley in Jerusalem, and my father told us: 'Hurry and take all the vessels out to the alley before he takes things there and makes it forbidden for you.'" Rabbi Judah says this in different words: "Hurry and do all you have to do in the alley so that he does not take something there and make it unlawful to you."

Here we have a case story about two families sharing an alley in Jerusalem. One family is identified as Sadducean, whereas another, being that of Rabban Gamaliel, is presumably Pharisaic. The two of them follow different practices in respect to 'eruv (the creation of a common domain by joining several houses to allow carrying items during the Sabbath).[71] The story gives a snapshot of the nature of relationships between the two groups, their modes of coexistence and their social structure.[72] It also shows how a Pharisaic halakhic practice could be modified in an ad hoc manner within a particular family and then transmitted by the members of the family as authoritative law. The story clearly envisions neighboring households and their halakhic practices as an important setting of the legal controversies between *Tsaddukim* and *Perushim*.

A similar story (although it does not mention either Sadducees or Pharisees by name) may appear in T 'Abodah Zarah 3:10. According to this text:

---

[71] On 'eruv as a Pharisaic legal invention deemed to simplify celebration of the Sabbath among neighboring households see Sanders, *Judaism*, 335 and 425. Sadducees rejected it because "it had not a particle of biblical support." The law of 'eruv may, perhaps, serve as an example of halakhic tradition that evolved out of household practices.

[72] See, however, Neusner, *Rabbinic Traditions about the Pharisees*, vol. 1, 379–80, for his opinion that the entire story is a later editorial construct. Cf. J. Epstein, *Mavo le-Nusah ha-Mishnah* (Jerusalem, 1965), 1200.

> A story is told of Rabban Gamaliel the Elder, who gave his daughter in marriage to Simeon b. Netanel the Priest, and agreed with him on the condition that she should not prepare clean things with him.

Whether or not Simeon was a Sadducee is unclear.[73] Still, it is likely that he was not a Pharisee, or at least that he did not follow Rabban Gamaliel's purity practices. Nevertheless, the two families found a way to marry into one another after stipulating rules so as to avoid violating halakhic regulations accepted by each of them. Once again, individual households constitute here the prime setting for the halakhic disagreement, whereas the halakhah itself is implicitly identified with particular practices followed by households. The story also shows (perhaps somewhat idealistically) that there were ways to smooth out halakhic differences between different families if there was a need to do so.

The Second Temple Havurot

In his famous article on the fellowship (*havurah*) in the Second Temple Judaism, Jacob Neusner has made the following observation regarding its social structure: "The fellowship cut across family ties. Wives might become members without their husbands, and children without their parents, though if a child was a born into a family known to adhere to the rule, he was assumed to be observant until he indicated otherwise."[74] A little bit further, he continued: "By transcending family, class, and caste distinctions, the order established a new, if limited polity in the old society of village and town." This view of the Second Temple *havurah* as transcending "natural" social bonds is fairly common in modern scholarship.[75] Saul Lieberman has identified the *havurah* with the *yahad* of the Manual of Discipline from Qumran. According to him both institutions shared a number of common characteristics including formal admission into their ranks, hatred to outsiders and the recognition of different levels of sanctity. Both groups represented a new type of social body formally

---

[73] Based on its context, the story seems to identify him as merely *'am ha-'arets*. See Neusner, *Rabbinic Traditions about the Pharisees*, vol. 2, 358–59.

[74] Neusner, "The Fellowship (*havurah*) in the Second Jewish Commonwealth," 128.

[75] See also Cohen, "Rabbi in Second-Century Jewish Society," 957.

overcoming traditional boundaries and creating new social structures.[76]

On the other hand, Aharon Oppenheimer sounds a dissenting note in this almost unanimous evaluation of the *havurah*. He is careful to stress the importance of traditional family structures in the formation of *havurah* and insightfully observes, "The association was generally guided by a preference to maintain the family framework rather than achieve greater scrupulousness in those areas around which the life of the association centered."[77] In addition to Oppenheimer, E.P. Sanders makes several similar observations about the centrality of traditional family structures in what he calls "Pharisaic associations."[78] It remains unclear, however, if he specifically talks about *havurot* or a broader Pharisaic movement.[79] In this section, I shall focus on the problem of the social structure of the Jewish *havurah* and ask the same questions I asked before: is it possible to see the *havurah* as a network of households whose heads agreed to practice the halakhah in a particular way? Or, was it indeed a completely new structure that cut across all traditional boundaries of "family, class and caste distinctions?"[80]

T Demai 2:14 gives the following description of the relationship between a *haver* and members of his household:

---

[76] S. Lieberman, "The Discipline in the So-Called Dead Sea Manual of Discipline," *JBL* 71 (1951), 199–206. Cf. C. Rabin, *Qumran Studies* (Oxford: Oxford University Press, 1957), 11–21, and Cohen, "Rabbi," 957, n. 159. For a more cautious assessment see A. Oppenheimer, *The ʿAm Ha-Aretz: A Study in the Social History of the Jewish People in the Hellenistic-Roman Period* (Leiden: Brill, 1977), 147–51.

[77] Oppenheimer, *ʿAm Ha-aretz*, 139. Cf. further his discussion of family and social connections between *haverim* and *ʿamme ha-ʾarets* on pp. 161–69.

[78] Sanders, *Judaism*, 440–43.

[79] The exact relationship between *haverim* mentioned in the early rabbinic literature and the Pharisees remains an enigma. Earlier scholars tended to identify the two, whereas more recent studies demonstrate increasing caution on this question. Neusner, "Fellowship," 125, and Oppenheimer, *ʿAm Ha-Aretz*, 118–19, see the two groups as overlapping although not exactly identical. E. Rivkin, "Defining the Pharisees: The Tannaitic Sources," *HUCA* 43 (1972), 234–38, and *Hidden Revolution*, 173–75, followed by E.P. Sanders, *Paul and Palestinian Judaism: A Comparison of Patterns of Religion* (Philadelphia: Fortress Press, 1977), 154–57, rejects any connection between them. Saldarini, *Pharisees, Scribes, and Sadducees*, 216–20, and Hezser, *Social Structure*, 74–75 and 315, are equally skeptical.

[80] Just how much in early rabbinic descriptions of the *havurah* reflects the reality of Second Temple times must remain an open question. Recently, several scholars have observed that the Tannaitic picture of a *haver* might have been purely rabbinic and not inherited from earlier times. See A. Avery-Peck, *Mishnah's Division of Agriculture: A History and Theology of Seder Zeraim* (Chico: Scholars Press, 1985), 84, and Stemberger, *Jewish Contemporaries*, 84.

> He who takes [upon himself the obligations] before a *havurah*—his sons
> and servants (עבדיו) do not have to take [upon themselves the oblig-
> ations] before a *havurah*. But they take [upon themselves the obliga-
> tions] before him. R. Simeon b. Gamaliel said, "A *haver* who has gone
> astray is not like the son of a *haver* who has gone astray."

This text envisions an entire *haver*'s family as participating in the
havurah. Rather than "cutting across family ties" the *havurah* seems
to embrace them as the essential part of its structure. The head of
the household preserves his traditional status even within the fellowship: his sons and servants take upon themselves the obligations
of *haverut* before him, not before other members of the *havurah*. In
other words, the prestige and authority of traditional social structures is not only preserved, but also enhanced within the fellowship.[81]

Subsequent sections of T Demai contain further details in respect
to the status of one's household within the *havurah*. T Demai 2:16
deals with the case of the daughter and the wife of an *'am ha-'arets*
who married a *haver*, as well as with the servant of an *'am ha-'arets* who
was sold to a *haver*. All of them are expected to take upon themselves
the obligations of *haverut*. The same is true for the son and the servant
of an *'am ha-'arets* who are apprentices to a *haver*.[82] It is explicitly
stated for the last two categories that "while they are in his domain
they are assumed to behave like a *haver*, when they leave his domain
they are assumed to behave like an *'am ha-'arets*." In other words,
the text singles out the household of a *haver* as a domain in which
rules of *haverut* are fully observed. Anyone who enters such a domain
is by definition expected to take upon him (her)self these obligations.
Belonging to the fellowship is not a matter of individual piety. It
rather embraces an entire household, perceived as an extension of
its head.

Special rules governed relationships between the members of *haver*'s
household and households of their relatives, especially if the latter
were not members of the fellowship. A number of laws referred to
the "son of a *haver* who went to the home of his maternal grandfather, an *'am ha-'arets*."[83] In particular, these laws addressed the issue
of improperly tithed and unclean food given to the son of a *haver*
by his grandfather. The household remains the most important social

---

[81] Cf. Oppenheimer, *'Am Ha-Aretz*, 139.
[82] T Demai 2:19.
[83] T Demai 2:15 and 3:5.

entity in all these requirements. They envision the interaction not between an individual *haver* and an individual *'am ha-'arets* but rather between their families. As observed above, the transition from the family of an *'am ha-'arets* to that of a *haver* presupposed taking upon oneself special obligations. It was one's household and not an individual that was perceived as the main unit within the fellowship. In this situation the relationships between the old family and the new one required special supervision. At the same time, family bonds were considered sufficiently important to produce relatively lenient regulations.[84] The laws dealing with a problem of a *haver*'s son visiting his maternal grandfather begin with the words that "his father does not worry lest he [the grandfather] feed him [the son] food." The relationships between the families have to be preserved.[85] Another law envisions the situation when a *haver* and his son attend the banquet of an *'am ha-'arets* (their relative?) and contains provisions for tithing their food under these circumstances.[86]

The regulations also envision the situation in which a member of the *haver*'s family enters the household of an *'am ha-'arets*:

> The daughter of a *haver* who married an *'am ha-'arets*, the wife of a *haver* who married an *'am ha-'arets*, the servant of a *haver* who was sold to an *'am ha-'arets*—behold, these remain in their presumed status until they are suspected. [R. Simeon b. Eleazar says, "They must take upon themselves (the obligations of *haverut*) anew." And thus][87] did R. Eleazar say in the name of R. Meir, "It once happened that a certain woman was married to a *haver* and fastened tefillin-straps for him. She married a customs-collector and knotted customs seals for him."[88]

Similarly, the son of a *haver* or his servant who were apprenticed to an *'am ha-'arets* were assumed to remain observant until they indicated otherwise.[89] In all these cases members of a *haver*'s household were seen as members of the fellowship simply by virtue of their

---

[84] Cf. Oppenheimer, *'Am Ha-Aretz*, 162–63.

[85] Special laws regulated hospitality toward outsiders, probably including family members, who were not *haverim*. Usually, an outsider was believed to be careful not to defile the house of a *haver*. See Neusner, "The Fellowship." 139–40. These rules regulated relationships with relatives and other people not belonging to *havurah*; they did not outlaw them.

[86] T Demai 3:7.

[87] Not in MS Vienna.

[88] T Demai 2:17.

[89] T Demai 2:18. Cf. T Demai 3:6, regulating duties of a *haver*, who serves as a waiter at the banquet of *'am ha-'arets*.

belonging to his household. Once again, the household was perceived as fully participating in *havurah*. Its members were presumed to remain in their status of *haverim* until proven otherwise. At the same time, as the position of R. Simeon shows, the integration of members of the *haver*'s household into households of *'amme ha-'arets* was perceived as endangering their status as *haverim*. He assumes that they are likely to change their ways of life to those of their new family.[90] All this further underscores the centrality of a household rather than an individual as the main building block of the *havurah*. It was particular households rather than their individual members that undertook the obligations of *haverut* and built their lives according to them.

These texts take a similar approach to being *ne'eman*: a person who is trustworthy with respect to tithing his food. Once again they focus on a household rather than on an individual:

> "He who undertakes to be trustworthy (נאמן) tithes what he eats and what he sells and what he purchases, and he does not accept the hospitality of *'am ha-'arets*,"—the words of R. Meir. And the sages say, "One who accepts the hospitality of an *'am ha-'arets* is trustworthy. Said to them R. Meir, "If he is not trustworthy concerning himself, should he be trustworthy concerning me?" They said to him, "Householders (בעלי בתים) have never refrained from eating with one another, nonetheless the produce in their own homes is properly tithed."[91]

Tithing takes place within one's household, and the person who takes upon himself to observe it is considered *ne'eman*. Still, this observance does not bar him from maintaining relationships with other households that do not follow the same rules. The last sentence of our excerpt makes it very clear that individual households constituted the main social units within the structure envisioned by rabbis. Either fulfillment or non-fulfillment of laws and regulations takes place within them.

T Demai 3:9 provides a similar picture of a household as the main subject of legislation dealing with one's trustworthiness:

> If he [i.e., a husband] was trustworthy and his wife was not trustworthy, they purchase from him but do not accept his hospitality. Nonetheless they have said, "It is as if he dwells in the same cage with a serpent." If his wife is trustworthy and he is not trustworthy, they accept his hospitality but do not purchase from him. If he is not

---

[90] Cf. S. Lieberman, *Tosefta Ki-fshutah: A Comprehensive Commentary on the Tosefta* (New York: JTSA, 1955), vol. 1 (Order Zera'im), 214.

[91] T Demai 2:2.

trustworthy but one of his sons is trustworthy, or one of his servants is trustworthy, or one of his maidservants (משפחותיו) is trustworthy, they purchase and eat relying on them, and they prepare [food] for him and he eats. With regard to seventh-year produce and food requiring conditions of cleanness, they are not allowed to do so.

The text envisions a household as the main participant in social transactions involving the purchase of foodstuffs and hospitality. Unlike previous examples, this law addresses the situation when not all members of the household are equally trustworthy. Still, the household remains the main subject of social interactions. *Haverim* have to decide in what ways they can interact with the household which is partially trustworthy. The degrees and modes of interaction between the household and *haverim* will differ depending on which member of the household is trustworthy and which is not. But all the same, the household will remain the main subject of such an interaction. It will also constitute the prime realm in which laws advocated by *haverim* are either followed or neglected.

Conclusions

Overall, rabbinic texts about the pre-70 CE religious groups and their legal traditions consistently emphasize households as the main building block within this system. Such households followed particular halakhic practices, which were shaped and transmitted as part of their family lore. It was the peculiarity of familial halakhic traditions that divided households from one another. On the other hand, occasionally, the broader Jewish population perceived some families as "role models" of piety and recognized their practices as religiously authoritative and binding. In this respect, the *Perushim* and *Tsaddukim* of rabbinic sources were not significantly different from the priestly households described in the same texts. A similar picture emerges when we consider the structure of *havurot* described in the Tannaitic literature. The pre-Destruction (and early post-Destruction?) *havurah* appears to have had the household as its major unit. Far from abrogating traditional family structures, the fellowship used them as a basis for its own existence. The proper observance of most of the obligations of *haverut* would have been impossible without the full involvement of households. It also would have been impossible without the obligations of *haverut* becoming an essential part of family halakhah.

As familial piety narratives were becoming part of the grand discourse of mature Rabbinic Judaism there emerged a complex web
of relationships between the two of them, ranging from careful acceptance to outright rejection of earlier forms by the new intellectual
tradition. The value of abstract reasoning as the ultimate source of
religious knowledge and piety gradually replaced the value of carefully following ritualized ways of everyday life regulated by ancestral
practices. In the following chapter I shall examine to what degree
family-based halakhic traditions continued to shape early rabbinic
halakhah in the first two centuries after the destruction of the temple.

CHAPTER SIX

RABBINIC HOUSEHOLDS AND THEIR TRADITIONS IN THE LATE FIRST AND SECOND CENTURIES

A number of scholars have argued over the past several decades that "body"-centered imagery and language played a crucial role in rabbinic discourse. As Daniel Boyarin has observed: "The Rabbis insisted on the corporeality of human essence and on the centrality of physical filiation and concrete historical memory as supreme values."[1] In this respect they differed significantly from Hellenistic philosophical anthropology that tended to prioritize the soul over the body. Subsequent research has demonstrated that the body-centered discourse of the rabbis perceived the household as a natural extension of individual human bodies. The notion of the family as a living corporeal organism whose daily functions need to be regulated and sanctified permeates most of the Tannaitic literature. Moreover, Cynthia Baker has convincingly demonstrated that the architectural remains of Jewish houses from the same period (late first through early third centuries CE) provide social grounding for this mode of discourse. Early Rabbinic Judaism seeks to sanctify the body of the household, not just the bodies of its individual members (in fact, the very distinction between the two may be misleading).[2]

On the other hand, it has been noticed that rabbinic discourse in its mishnaic form seeks to actively control the corporeal functions of the household. As Charlotte Fonrobert observes, it achieves this goal by creating a "rabbinic science" of bodily functions (such as menstruation) that both constructs and controls the body through the objectifying hermeneutics of its life cycles.[3] In the rabbinic discourse of the body scholastic fantasy and reality are blended together and become virtually indistinguishable. It is often impossible to determine where one ends and the other begins. The rabbinic construct of the household owes at least as much to the rabbinic hermeneutics of

---

[1] See Boyarin, *Carnal Israel*, 235.
[2] Baker, *Rebuilding the House of Israel*, 34–76.
[3] Fonrobert, *Menstrual Purity*, 103–27.

bodily sanctity as it does to the historical reality of late antique Jewish society in Galilee.[4]

A growing number of scholars tend to agree that the household legislation of early rabbinic texts (predominantly, that of the Mishnah) tells us more about an idealized legal fiction of rabbinic intellectuals than about the real state of a contemporaneous Jewish family (rabbinic or not). In the Mishnah rabbis construct an imagined household in conformity with their halakhic and cultural ideals, just as Plato's *Republic* constructs an imagined state in conformity with the philosopher's idealistic vision. Shaye Cohen has persuasively argued that the matrilineal principle of descent originated as a rabbinic intellectual construct with little precedent in earlier Jewish practice.[5] Miriam Peskowitz has further suggested that gender roles proposed by rabbinic constructs of the household are just that: fantasies about an orderly and male-dominated reality of the family.[6] Rabbinic texts imagine relationships between husband and wife in accordance with an intellectual discourse quite detached from the contemporaneous reality and common practices. More recently, Michael Satlow has proposed that the rabbinic *ketubbah* (marriage contract) "was a tannaitic fantasy, instituted by logical and legal necessity and perhaps also as a response to a sense of crisis."[7]

To continue this line of argument, one can reason that at least some parts of the Mishnah may represent a rabbinic version of slightly earlier household codes. As we have observed above, the latter are well attested for both Greco-Roman and Christian settings of the first and second centuries CE.[8] It is, moreover, possible that both

---

[4] See Fonrobert, *Menstrual Purity*, 40–67, for discussion of rabbinic metaphorical constructs of women's corporeality as "house." Cf. Baker, *Rebuilding the House of Israel*, 48–70. Together they provide a good example of how social reality and fantasy may mix together in the rabbinic discourse.

[5] Cohen, *Beginnings of Jewishness*, 263–307. Notice especially pp. 293–98 where he discusses the possible impact of the Roman law.

[6] See M. Peskowitz, *Spinning Fantasies: Rabbis, Gender, and History* (Berkeley: University of California Press, 1997), 27–108. Cf. also Baker, *Rebuilding the House of Israel*, 77–112 and 122–35, for examples of "self-generated Talmudic discourse" driven by contemporaneous cultural concerns and anxieties.

[7] Satlow, *Jewish Marriage*, 216. In a subsequent paragraph Satlow nuances this radical formulation. He also convincingly argues that rabbis artificially constructed their system of marital casts by using earlier priestly traditions and applying them more broadly (pp. 147–55).

[8] See J. Crouch, *The Origin and Intention of the Colossian Haustafel* (Göttingen: Vandenhoeck & Ruprecht, 1972), as well as Balch, *Let Wives Be Submissive: The Domestic Code in I Peter* (Atlanta: Scholars Press, 1981) and "Household Codes,"

Josephus and Philo were considerably indebted to them for their pre-sentations of Judaism. In household codes, just as in the Mishnah, philosophical visions of an ideal family life formed the foundation of regulative and doctrinal legislation detailing how things ought to be conducted in order to ensure the pious and righteous lifestyle of households (and, by extension, that of the larger community/state).[9] In both cases the philosophical constructs of male intellectuals were utilized to shape the reality of family life or, perhaps, to create an alternative reality unconcerned with the actual state of affairs.

All this, however, does not necessarily rule out that actual house-holds might have played a crucial role in transmitting early rabbinic traditions just as they played a central role in transmitting and dis-seminating other teachings of the time (including Christianity). In fact, just as the production of pagan and Christian household codes was motivated by concerns about real families and their lifestyles, so was the production of their rabbinic counterparts. Similar to house-hold codes in philosophical paganism and Christianity, rabbinic instructions were produced in order to sanctify conventional patterns of family life. In each of these cases idealized intellectual fictions were constructed to transform the everyday lives of ordinary house-holds. Cynthia Baker's recent work fully appreciates the complexity of relationships between real-life Jewish families and "rabinically imag-ined" households. There is no simple answer to the question as to where historically accurate descriptions of Jewish households end and the "self-generated Talmudic discourse" begins.[10] Studies by Hayim Lapin and Jacob Neusner have further emphasized the importance of real households in shaping at least some of the Mishnaic texts. According to them, early rabbinic texts repeatedly address the concerns of relatively prosperous householders, who either engage themselves

---

25–50. Cf. M. MacDonald, *Pauline Churches: Socio-Historical Study of Institutionalization in the Pauline and Deutero-Pauline Writings* (Cambridge: Cambridge University Press, 1988), 102–20 and 184–202. For a more recent summary of the discussion see MacDonald, *Colossians and Ephesians* (Collegeville: Liturgical Press, 2000), 152–70 and 324–42.

[9] MacDonald, *Pauline Churches*, 136–37 and 207–14, demonstrates how patriar-chal skills of household management served as a prerequisite for communal lead-ership in at least some Christian groups. On family as a metaphor for political leadership in the time of Principate see E. Lassen, "The Roman Family: Ideal and Metaphor," in H. Moxnes ed., *Constructing Early Christian Families: Family as Social Reality and Metaphor* (London: Routledge, 1997), 103–20.

[10] See Baker, *Rebuilding the House of Israel*, 34–76, esp. 70–75.

in agricultural production or lease their land to others. Rabbinic traditions seek to regulate the everyday lives of such householders in accordance with a set of halakhic norms.[11]

Sociologically, the development of the rabbinic movement demonstrates some important parallels with that of the Dead Sea sect.[12] In both cases we witness the transition from networks of families wedded to a particular understanding of Torah to communities of like-minded adult individuals creating a new "utopian" identity around specific sets of practices, rituals, and beliefs. But there is at least one important difference: whereas 1QS totally excludes the household from its discourse of holiness, rabbis continue to recognize it as a crucially important locus of sanctity. To be sure, they deny the household a number of important religious functions that it traditionally played, most importantly, its role as the setting of halakhic learning and transmission of religious knowledge. Still, rabbis explicitly need the household for their construct of sacred space. The household's everyday functioning has to be meticulously regulated to assure that Israel continues to live a religiously meaningful life. That is why, unlike 1QS, they spend so much energy legislating for family needs whether real or imagined. Far from denying the household any religious value, rabbis constantly try to integrate its life into their discourse of sanctity. Rabbinic "household codes" represent a complex mix of fantasy and reality precisely because they seek to project non-familial holiness constructs back onto real families. In this respect they too come remarkably close to contemporaneous pagan and Christian "household codes."[13]

To complicate things even further, early rabbinic literature is, at least partially, aware of the familial halakhic practices and their legitimacy. While legislating for families, rabbis recognized that their ideals did not necessarily correspond to historical ancestral practices. The rabbinic holiness project had to be correlated with that of the traditional lore. Its supremacy had to be argued. Finally, households continued to play a crucial role in the formation of Rabbinic Judaism

---

[11] See Neusner, *Judaism*, 250–56, and *Economics of the Mishnah*, 50–71, and Lapin, *Early Rabbinic Civil Law*, 119–241.

[12] Cf. Schiffman, *Reclaiming the Dead Sea Scrolls*, 125–26, and Fraade, "Interpretive Authority," 46–69.

[13] See C. Fonrobert, "The Didascalia Apostolorum: A Mishnah for the Disciples of Jesus," *Journal of Early Christian Studies* 9:4 (2001), 483–509, for suggestive parallels between rabbinic and early Christian traditions.

itself. The social setting in which rabbinic halakhah developed was by no means limited to disciple circles. The households continued to exert considerable influence by either patronizing individual rabbinic schools or simply by serving as role models of piety well into the Amoraic period (third through fifth centuries).[14] In this chapter I shall discuss how early rabbinic texts portrayed household traditions of individual rabbinic masters. I shall, first of all, observe that there was a basic continuity between Jewish household traditions of the late Second Temple period and those of early rabbis both in terms of their form and their substance. But I shall also argue that early rabbinic texts present these traditions as part of the elaborate and complex dialogue with halakhic norms produced within disciple circles. As a result, some of the familial teachings become detached from their (original?) household setting and reformulated as abstract legal principles and guidelines to be studied and transmitted within disciple circles. Others are simply discarded and glossed over as non-binding practices of individual pietists. Overall, the new rabbinic philosophy of the household and its halakhic management reflects a changing and increasingly scholastic mindset, which would eventually bring about a mature rabbinic Judaism.

Finally, one has to make a methodological observation about our sources. The discussion in this chapter will be primarily based on the analysis of early rabbinic *ma'asim*, i.e., brief accounts or case stories about rabbis making halakhic decisions in real life situations. However, as recent studies have shown, it remains unclear if these accounts record actual events or rather represent literary constructs designed to illustrate rabbinic discussions and create an illusion of reality behind the rabbinic legal fiction.[15] In fact they could do both. These stories are rabbinic narrative and self-representation, which may or may not reflect the historical reality of the early rabbinic movement. They show how rabbis saw themselves and their traditions. I shall argue that in the rabbinic *self-portrayal*, the halakhic lore of individual households occupied a noticeable, although somewhat marginalized position, being increasingly sidelined in favor of teachings

---

[14] See Sivertsev, *Private Households*, 117–83, for detailed discussion.

[15] On case stories in the Mishnah and their literary characteristics see A. Goldberg, "Form und Funktion des Ma'ase in der Mischna," *FJB* 2 (1974), 1–38. Cf. C. Hezser, *Form, Function and Historical Significance of the Rabbinic Story in Yerushalmi Neziqin* (Tübingen: Mohr Siebeck, 1993), 283–92.

transmitted within disciple circles. This self-portrayal is remarkably
similar to Philo's and Josephus' descriptions of Judaism and reflects the
same tendencies taking place within the Jewish society of the time.

Before a discussion of halakhic practices of post-70 rabbinic households, it would be worthwhile to review tannaitic references to halakhic
practices of pre-70 lay families. They are not as numerous as those
attributed to priestly households, but some of them are sufficiently
important to merit our attention. They demonstrate, among other
things, that from the tannaitic perspective the phenomenon of ancestral household halakhah was not confined to priestly families. Early
tannaitic texts mention several Second Temple lay households that
were remembered for their ancestral halakhic traditions. These traditions usually emerge from household settings of named masters and
reflect their personal practices, taken to be halakhically authoritative.
The famous story about Hillel the Elder, who would celebrate the
Passover by folding unleavened bread and bitter herbs together and
eating them, may serve as an example of authoritative individual
practice recognized as a mizvah, if not as a requirement.[16] Several
precedent-based narratives are associated with Hillel's famous opponent Shammai. Thus M Sukkah 2:8 starts with an abstract and
anonymous legal statement that "women, slaves, and minors are
exempt from the Sukkah. And every minor that no longer needs his
mother must fulfill [the law] of the Sukkah." This statement is
qualified by a story about (ma'aseh be-) the daughter in law of Shammai
the Elder who bore a child during the festival of Sukkot. Shammai
"broke away roof-plaster and made a Sukkah-roofing over the bed
for the sake of the infant." Here the practice of Shammai and his
household is contrasted with an apodictic legal statement of the
Mishnah, which appears to be the norm. It is interesting, however,
that an individual practice of Shammai appears to merit the same
attention as a more general and legally binding anonymous ruling.
Its position here is ambiguous. It is not clear if it qualifies the pre-

---

[16] T Pisha 2:22 (cf. Mekhilta de-Rabbi Shimon b. Yohai 1:12, where the story
serves to illustrate an interpretation of Exod 12:8). Neusner identifies this passage
as an early example of Hillel's traditions. He calls it "a legal teaching in narrative
style" perceiving Hillel's actions as paradigmatic. On the other hand, he maintains
that originally the entire story was deemed to illustrate the exegesis of Exod 12:8,
and so he takes the exegetical setting of the Mekhilta to be an original one. I cannot agree with this part of his assessment. See Neusner, *Rabbinic Traditions*, vol. 1,
212 and 231.

ceding statement or is taken to be a pious exception. Indeed the anonymous statement may serve to soften the early halakhah based on the practice of Shammai's household. In this case, it indicates that the practice of Shammai is not legally binding.[17]

Another example of Shammai's household practice contrasted with an apodictic legal ruling comes from the Mekhilta. The passage discusses how often an individual has to examine his tefillin. According to the words of the House of Hillel this should take place once a year, and then the Mekhilta provides the opinion of the House of Shammai in the following form:

> The House of Shammai says, "One need never examine them."
> Shammai the Elder (שמאי הזקן) said, "These are the tefillin of my mother's father אבי אימא)."[18]

The statement of Shammai clearly serves to qualify the halakhic opinion of an entity, referred to as the "House of Shammai." It also demonstrates that one cannot generalize from this particular practice of Shammai's household, as the case was quite exceptional. In other words, the practice of Shammai's household is called upon to specifically demonstrate that it cannot be used as a basis for general halakhic regulation, as the "House of Shammai" tried to do.[19] In both cases involving Shammai there is an attempt to correlate between authoritative practices of an individual and his household on the one hand, and an anonymous and abstract legal statement on the other. Moreover, at least in the second case the latter seems to be (mistakenly?) derived from the former.

Whereas rabbis tried to find an agreement between earlier practices of Shammai's household and later apodictic halakhah, in other cases they would state clearly that individual halakhic practices did not bear on later apodictic legislation. According to T Makhshirim 3:3–4, Hilfata b. Qavinah and Joshua b. Perahiah pronounced certain types of food coming from abroad to be unclean because of

---

[17] See Neusner, *Rabbinic Traditions*, vol. 1, 193–94, for further discussion of this passage. He notices that the 'Aqiban editors would occasionally present practices of individual households as manifestations of individual piety, thus putting them outside of the public Jewish law binding for everyone. This approach was often taken in respect to Shammaitic traditions including those of Rabban Gamaliel. Cf. Epstein, *Mavo le-Nusah ha-Mishnah*, 605.

[18] Mek. Pisha 17 (Lauterbach, 157).

[19] Cf. Neusner, *Rabbinic Traditions*, vol. 1, 188–89.

methods used in their preparation. But both of their statements are
followed by a qualifying remark that "the sages said, 'if so, let it be
unclean for Hilfata b. Qavinah (or Joshua b. Perahiah) and clean
for all Israel.'" The second statement may indicate that a private
practice of these two named authorities is just that: a private practice of private individuals and it does not reflect the standard rabbinic halakhah (quoted here as an apodictic statement of anonymous
sages).[20] This clause is somewhat similar to what we have observed
before in the case of Shammai's family practices. In both cases sages
draw a boundary between private halakhah of pious individuals and
public halakhah of Israel. As we shall see, the Mishnah treats halakhic
traditions of rabbinic households in a similar way.[21]

Ancestral Traditions of Rabban Gamaliel

Among legal materials attributed to the early generations of tannaitic
masters, case stories occupy a prominent, although not a leading
position. Some masters tend to have more case stories associated
with their names, while others have almost none. Among the former, the figure of Rabban Gamaliel clearly stands out. His legal traditions are often presented in the form of case stories and legal
precedents, which serve as a basis for official rabbinic halakhah.
Shamai Kanter has rightly stressed the role that narratives play in
the transmission of Rabban Gamaliel's halakhic legacy. He has also
correctly observed that most of these stories "do not appear to have
been created as illustrations for the laws they often accompany."
Rather, "the stories are used within their respective contexts as if
they are legal lemmas. *Rabban Gamaliel did x* is treated the same way

---

[20] Epstein, *Mevo'ot*, 510, maintains that this passage is authentic and very old.
See also Epstein, *Mavo le-Nusah ha-Mishnah*, 1153–54. Cf. Neusner, *Rabbinic Traditions*,
vol. 1, 82, for a more reserved assessment. I tend to agree with him that the passage as a whole reflects later editing. Among other things, an editor distinguished
between private halakhah of Joshua and public halakhah of Israel.
[21] A story about the excommunication of Akabya ben Mahalaleel in M 'Ed. 5:6
provides another example of the same trend to incorporate individual halakhic traditions into the grand edifice of the later rabbinic law. See A. Saldarini, "The
Adoption of a Dissident: Akabya ben Mahalaleel in Rabbinic Tradition," *JJS* 33
(1982), 547–56. Certain elements within the story (such as the sages' appeal to a
precedent in order to counter Akabya's argument and his deathbed instruction to
his son) may imply that the story deals with another example of household halakhah
being integrated into rabbinic tradition. Cf. Boyarin, *Border Lines*, 64–65.

as if it were *Rabban Gamaliel says x*." Kanter further concludes that in the case of Rabban Gamaliel "legal narratives expressed paradigmatic actions for those who formulated and circulated them. They are the equivalent of other forms of legal statement."[22]

Kanter also observes that "the Gamaliel narratives share their narrative form with the pre-70 pharisaic masters (aside from the Houses)."[23] This conclusion agrees very well with what has emerged from our earlier discussion: rabbinic traditions about the named pre-Destruction masters tend to derive their halakhah from precedent and the authoritative practices of masters and their households, rather than from abstract legal principles and explicit legal exegesis. The traditions of Rabban Gamaliel (unlike those of many other tannaitic masters) were preserved and transmitted in exactly the same form as traditions of the pre-70 Pharisees. This may indicate a continuity of halakhic transmission that persisted in at least some rabbinic circles. Rabban Gamaliel is one of very few post-Destruction rabbis for whom we can ascertain pre-Destruction history. He comes from an influential pharisaic family of the first century aristocrats. For at least several generations before him, his family played a crucial role of shaping social, political, and religious life in Jerusalem. Rabban Gamaliel's family is one of the few vestiges of the pre-Destruction Jewish elite in the new religious elite of the post-Destruction period. This family and status continuity can perhaps account for the form in which Rabban Gamaliel's traditions are transmitted. He marks a transition from precedent-oriented halakhah of the Second Temple Pharisees to the abstract and apodictic law of the rabbinic bet midrash. Rabban Gamaliel's legal traditions managed to preserve their uniqueness not only in content but also in form. They became integrated into the rabbinic halakhah without giving up their original practice-oriented form.[24]

---

[22] Kanter, *Rabban Gamaliel*, 247.

[23] Kanter, *Rabban Gamaliel*, 247–49. Cf. Lightstone, "Sadoq the Yavnean," 134–35. Both authors seem to explain the importance of *maʿasim* for halakhic traditions of Rabban Gamaliel by his status as *nasi*. Precisely because of that his halakhic actions had paradigmatic importance. However, the nature of Rabban Gamaliel's formal authority remains unclear, as does the status of the *nasi* in general. See M. Jacobs, *Die Institution des jüdischen Patriarchen: Eine quellen- und traditionskritische Studie zur Geschichte der Juden in der Spatantike* (Tübingen: Mohr Siebeck, 1995), 124–205.

[24] Kanter correctly observes that "the legal narrative form looks back towards the pre-70 Pharisees." But I cannot agree with him that the reason for this similarity was R. Gamaliel's attempt to find "Jewish validation of the patriarch as *nasi*"

Kanter's explanation that Rabban Gamaliel's halakhic actions had paradigmatic significance as practices of a highly respected individual follows earlier theories about the halakhic value of rabbinic *ma'asim*. In particular, it comes close to Birger Gerhardsson's earlier discussion.[25] He correctly singles out individual practices of rabbinic teachers as one of the main sources of mishnaic and later talmudic halakhah. He further refers to several examples where the way in which individual rabbis would go about their daily routine would set authoritative halakhic precedents for their students. In this respect, behavior of a teacher would have the same halakahic value as his teachings. Both students and teachers knew that and acted accordingly. The following story from T Demai 5:24 illustrates this approach:

> It once happened that our masters came to the towns of the Samaritans [which were] by the road. They brought before them greens [to eat]. R. Aqiva jumped up and tithed them as untithed produce.
>
> Said Rabban Gamaliel to him, "How is it that your heart made you transgress the words of your colleagues? Or who gave you permission to tithe?"
>
> He replied to him, "Did I establish halakhah in Israel?" He said to him, "I did tithe my greens."
>
> He said to him, "Know that you have established halakhah in Israel by tithing your own greens!"

This story demonstrates that tannaim recognized individual halakhic practices as valid sources of public legislation. It attributes this view to Rabban Gamaliel without, however, further explaining it. The story does not tell why an individual practice was considered as halakhically binding. Moreover, it portrays R. Aqiva as being unaware of this principle. In other words, although this story (which reflects later editing and transmission by disciples of R. Aqiva) clearly attests the public importance of a sage's behavior, it does not provide any explanation for it. As a result, modern scholars tend to interpret it as emphasizing the authoritative value of an individual's behavior (and this is probably how students of R. Aqiva interpreted it as

---

by making a connection with pre-70 halakhic authorities. I also agree with Kanter's observation that the use of a standard rabbinic dispute form in some of R. Gamaliel's traditions "records the 'rabbinization' of the patriarch." I would only add that this use reflects in general a transition from the pre-70 format of the "traditions of the fathers" to rabbinic apodictic format. See Kanter, *Rabban Gamaliel*, 248–49.

[25] See Gerhardsson, *Memory and Manuscript*, 181–89.

well).[26] In reality, however, the individual's practice could be seen as a valid precedent because it reflected his household halakhah. It was perceived as an accurate and legitimate manifestation of the ancestral traditions of one's family and the "interpretation" of these traditions by actions of the legitimate offspring. The ultimate authority of one's actions derived not so much from his own position in the society as from the respect accorded to his family and its practices. By performing specific actions, he either enacted or "interpreted" his familial halakhah. The increased role of personal knowledge and individual authority of the rabbi, reflected in R. Aqiva's transmission of the story, represented a major shift from "traditions of the fathers" to a rabbinic study-based approach.[27]

Thus, authoritative practices attributed to Rabban Gamaliel should be considered within the context of authoritative practices attributed to his household. In other words, very often it is not Rabban Gamaliel himself whose actions are deemed halakhically authoritative but rather his or even "his father's" household.[28] Rabban Gamaliel's halakhah should be seen as a specific example of his household halakhah. Perhaps it was precisely the respect and recognition accorded to his household that made his own behavior as paradigmatic as it appears in tannaitic texts. The personality of Rabban Gamaliel should not overshadow the family tradition, which he represented. In several cases, Rabban Gamaliel explicitly justifies his opinion with practices of his father's house:

---

[26] In addition to Gerhardsson's discussion of this passage, see Safrai, *Literature of the Sages*, 178–80.

[27] T Ber. 1:4 (cf. Sifre Deut. 24 [Finkelstein, 62–63]) likewise interprets the individual ways that R. Ishmael and R. Eleazar b. Azariah said the Shema as potentially authoritative for their students. Here, again, the individual master's behavior is perceived as paradigmatic and authoritative. R. Ishmael acts contrary to R. Eleazar, "so that the students should not see and establish the law according to your words." He also identifies R. Eleazar's practice as that of the House of Shammai and his own practice as that of the House of Hillel (cf. M Ber. 1:3). This part of the narrative clearly presupposes a disciple circle as its setting. But it most probably constitutes a later redaction of the original story about two sages reading the Shema in two different ways. See T. Zahavy, *The Traditions of Eleazar ben Azariah* (Missoula: Scholars Press, 1977), 17–18 for discussion.

[28] Cf. Kanter's thesis that it is the authoritative practice of R. Gamaliel himself that matters as paradigmatic (*Rabban Gamaliel*, 250–51).

In three things Rabban Gamaliel gives the more stringent ruling, according to the words of the House of Shammai,

"They do not cover up hot food on a festival day for the Sabbath; and they do not put together a candlestick on a festival; and they do not bake bread in [the form of] large loaves but only in [the form of] thin wafers."

Said Rabban Gamaliel, "Never did my father's household (שלבית אבא) bake bread in [the form of] large loaves but only in [the form of] thin wafers."

They said to him, "What shall we make of your father's household? For they imposed a stringent rule on themselves, while imposing a lenient rule on all Israel, so that they [Israel] may bake large loaves and cakes."

Moreover, he said three things [which are more] lenient, "They sweep between the couches, and put spices on the fire on a festival; and they prepare a kid roasted whole for Passover evening."

And Sages prohibit.[29]

The debate between Rabban Gamaliel and the sages concerns several issues on which Rabban Gamaliel's rulings are either more stringent or more lenient than those of the sages.[30] In the case of the three strict rulings Rabban Gamaliel explicitly appeals to the authority of his father's household's practice. In the case of the more lenient ruling such an appeal is absent but probably presumed by editors. Both groups of rulings address the celebration of a holiday (Sabbath or Passover) within a household space and thus represent perfect examples of halakhah that has evolved within a family as family lore but then enters the rabbinic halakhic realm as an authoritative ruling.[31]

---

[29] M Betsah 2:6–7 (= M 'Ed. 3:10–11).

[30] Cf. M Shabb. 1:9 and T Shabb. 1:22, where people of the house of Rabban Gamaliel follow a more stringent (Shammaite) view by giving white garments to the gentile laundryman three days before the Sabbath to make sure that the work on them would not be done during the holiday. Whereas the Mishnah transmits this account as R. Simeon b. Gamaliel's recollection of practices of his father's house, the Tosefta presents it as R. Eleazar b. Tsadoq's account of Rabban Gamaliel's household practices. Do we have here two independent accounts of the same practice or does one of them derive from the other? According to Neusner, *Rabbinic Traditions*, vol. 2, 130, the Tosefta version may be an original one.

[31] Individual ways of celebrating the Passover could vary significantly from one household to another. The Passover Haggadah describes R. Aqiva and his fellow-rabbis talking about the Exodus from Egypt for the entire Passover night. T Pisha 10:12, on the other hand, mentions Rabban Gamaliel and his friends discussing the laws of the Passover sacrifices throughout the night. It does not mention the Exodus at all. See Boyarin, *Border Lines*, 83–84. He identifies Rabban Gamaliel's practice as "the Pharisaic tradition" and that of Aqiva and his associates as the "Scribal" one.

In fact, the opponents of Rabban Gamaliel explicitly draw a distinction between the private practices of his father's household and authoritative rabbinic halakhah that can be derived from them. As Jacob Neusner correctly observes, this response reflects a more general rabbinic approach toward the teachings of Shammai. They "are made to apply to the authority himself, but the rule for the people is different."[32] This tendency may be a direct result of individual household halakhot entering the public realm as authoritative Jewish law. Some of them become fully recognized as standard laws, while others are adjusted and changed. At these earlier stages of adjustment the explicit distinction between private norms of respectable households and rabbinic Jewish law still can be observed. With standardization and codification of the Mishnah, rhetorical smoothing of the text will all but eliminate any vestige of this process.

The halakhic stringencies of Rabban Gamaliel's family are handled in precisely this way. They remain confined to the private realm of his household, whereas more lenient (and thus more democratic) rulings are applied to "all Israel." On the other hand, the more lenient rulings of Rabban Gamaliel's family may be seen as direct consequences of its patrician status and thus are unwarranted in more modest households. Having servants sweep between the couches can be explained as the household practice of a prosperous family reclining at a Roman style banquet.[33] The burning of incense during festive meals could be another attribute of an affluent household. Finally, the roasting whole of a kid on the Passover could be an explicit attempt to indicate connection between the household meal and the Temple with its sacrificial Passover ritual.[34] Although this

---

[32] Neusner, *Rabbinic Traditions*, vol. 1, 380. Cf. Kanter, *Rabban Gamaliel*, 98–99. M Betsah 2:1–5 contains several apodictic legal statements arranged in the dispute form between the House of Shammai and the House of Hillel. Our passage serves as a direct continuation and illustration of these statements. I am wondering if the reference to Shammaitic practices of Rabban Gamaliel is not a later editorial construct deemed to integrate halakhic practice of Rabban Gamaliel's household into formal categories of the House of Hillel vs. the House of Shammai dispute form.

[33] As Cohen observes, "The etiquette to be followed at a rabbinic symposium mimics that of the Graeco-Roman." See Cohen, "The Rabbi in Second-Century Jewish Society," 931.

[34] Cf. M Pesah. 7:2, where Rabban Gamaliel orders his slave Tabi to roast a kid for Passover. Apparently, some households retained this practice long after the destruction of the Temple as a pious attempt to preserve as much of the original Passover ritual as possible. See G. Alon, *Toldot ha-Yehudim be-Erets-Yisrael bi-tekufat ha-Mishnah veha-Talmud* (Tel Aviv: Ha-Kibuts Ha-Meuhad, 1967), vol. 1, 165, and

practice might have been appropriate as household lore of an aristocratic family from the Jerusalem establishment, its acceptance as
a law for "all Israel" was questionable.[35] Overall, the text of our
mishnah reflects how the ancestral halakhah of Rabban Gamaliel's
household was adjusted in the process of acceptance as rabbinic ritual law. It was significantly "democratized" by leaving its aristocratic
characteristics (both in the realm of strictness and leniency) in the
private realm and accepting the rest as a law for "all Israel."[36]

Rabban Gamaliel cites the practices of his "father's house" in one
more case. The question concerns whether fruits of carob trees from
different fields can be donated as Pe'ah for each other. According
to an anonymous ruling in the beginning of the mishnah, fruits from
carob trees in one field may be donated as Pe'ah for trees in another
field, as long as the two are within sight of each other. Rabban
Gamaliel's testimony follows this ruling:

A. Guttman, "The End of the Jewish Sacrificial Cult," *HUCA* 38 (1967), 137–48.
The story provides another example of continuity between halakhic practices of the
household of Rabban Gamaliel and pre-70 Jewish traditions. It is, furthermore, possible that some Jewish households in the Greco-Roman Diaspora practiced the
sacrificing of a Passover kid at home. See Sanders, *Judaism*, 133–34, for evidence
and discussion. In other words, Rabban Gamaliel's practice might have reflected
traditions current among some upper-scale circles in the Diaspora. It is remarkable
that the Tosefta's account of Rabban Gamaliel's practices (T Yom Tov 2:15) amplifies
it by referring to one Todos of Rome, who used to do (and instructed others to
do) the same thing. For discussion of this story and its subsequent development in
rabbinic literature see B. Bokser, "Todos and Rabbinic Authority in Rome," in
J. Neusner et al., eds., *New Perspectives on Ancient Judaism* (Lanham: University Press
of America, 1987), vol. 1, 117–30.

[35] T Shabb. 12:6 reports another practice of "those of the house of Rabban
Gamaliel," which singles them out as a particularly affluent household. They did
not have to fold white garments, which they wore on the Sabbath, because they
would wear another set of garments next time. The text illustrates an exception to
the anonymous ruling of M Shabb. 15:3. Special practice of Rabban Gamaliel's
household seems to be explained by their exceptional wealth. See Kanter, *Rabban
Gamaliel*, 54.

[36] T Sotah 15:8 tells about anonymous "them" permitting "those of the house
of Rabban Gamaliel" to learn Greek "because they are close to the government."
T 'Abod. Zar. 3:5 contains a similar account of "them" permitting "the house of
Rabban Gamaliel" to look in the mirror while getting a haircut. In both cases we
may be dealing with a tacit acceptance by sages of the unique household practices
of Rabban Gamaliel's family. In both cases, these practices are phrased as exceptions to a general rule and explained by the unique social status of Rabban Gamaliel's
household. Similar to the traditions in M Betsah, these stories may reflect the
influence of one's social standing and cultural exposure to Hellenism on his/her
family halakhah.

Said Rabban Gamliel, "In my father's house they used (נוהנין היו בית אבא)
to give a single Pe'ah for the olive trees that belonged to them in each
quarter [of the city], and for carob trees [a single Pe'ah for] all that
were within sight of each other.

R. Eleazer b. Tsadoq says in his name, "[The give a single Pe'ah]
also for the carob trees that belonged to them throughout the city.[37]

As Kanter observes, given the slight discrepancy in subject, the testimony of Rabban Gamaliel was not originally intended as an illustration of the anonymous rule. It was put into the mishnah to serve
as such.[38] The testimony appears to confirm the anonymous ruling
in the beginning of the mishnah, but R. Eleazar's revision makes
them contradict each other. Both the beginning of the mishnah and
R. Eleazar's amendment appear to represent stages of an editorial
process that integrated Rabban Gamaliel's testimony into the standard
mishnaic format of legal debate. The testimony is important as
another example of Rabban Gamaliel's ancestral halakhah taken to
produce authoritative public legislation.[39]

The Tosefta makes further steps toward the reconciliation between
the practices of Rabban Gamaliel's ancestral halakhah as reported
in the Mishnah Betsah and standard rabbinic law. It starts an entire
section about practices of Rabban Gamaliel's household reported in
the Mishnah with the following story:

In Rabban Gamaliel's household (של בית רבן נמליאל) they did not put
together a candlestick on the festival night.

It once happened that Rabban Gamaliel and elders were reclining
together in Rome, and a candlestick fell down on the night of a festival. R. Aqiva got up and put it together.

---

[37] M Pe'ah 2:4 (= Sifra Qed. 2:4).
[38] Kanter, *Rabban Gamaliel*, 25–26.
[39] M Pe'ah 2:5–6 contains another story that mentions Rabban Gamaliel (presumably, the Elder). R. Simeon of Mitspah approaches him to inquire about a particular case of granting *pe'ah* from the field sown with two kinds of wheat. Rabban
Gamaliel apparently does not have an answer, and the two of them go to the
Chamber of Hewn Stone to make further inquiry. There, Nahum the Scribe tells
them a family tradition of R. Measha about this case. This story presents R. Measha's
family halakhah as the last link in the classical rabbinic chain of transmission going
back to Moses. It probably represents another example of rabbinic "domestication"
of the "traditions of the fathers." Neusner convincingly shows that the entire rabbinic chain of transmission of the Oral Law is a relatively late tannaitic invention,
reflecting the academic reality of the study house. See Neusner, *Rabbinic Traditions*,
vol. 3, 143–179. Rabban Gamaliel is somewhat out of place in the story, unless
we connect his presence with M Pe'ah 2:4.

> Said to him Rabban Gamaliel, "Aqiva! Why do you poke your head into the dispute?"
>
> He said to him, "You have taught us, 'Follow the majority [Ex 32:2].' So even though you prohibit and they permit, the law is in accord with the majority."
>
> R. Judah says in the name of Rabban Gamaliel, "They handle the candlestick on the festival, but they do not put it together."[40]

The passage begins with a subtle change of "my father's house" of Rabban Gamaliel in the Mishnah to "Rabban Gamaliel's house." I shall discuss the significance of this substitution later. The subsequent story about R. Aqiva is designed to present a household ancestral practice of Rabban Gamaliel as just another legal opinion in a scholarly dispute among rabbis. The story eventually rejects it as it would reject any other legal tradition not followed by the majority of sages. Whereas the Mishnah takes halakhic traditions of Rabban Gamaliel's household to be examples of a pious family practice not binding upon "all Israel," the Tosefta treats them as a minority opinion in a halakhic debate. Rabban Gamaliel's family tradition becomes "rabbinized" by its inclusion into the framework of rabbinic Oral Law governed by such abstract legal principles as majority rule. The tradition moves from the realm of household to the realm of the house of study. R. Judah's interpretive lemma quoted at the end of the passage serves to narrow the apparent gap between Rabban Gamaliel's tradition and the majority opinion of the sages. It represents another step toward the complete absorption of Rabban Gamaliel's ancestral halakhah into the rabbinic legal edifice. Rabban Gamaliel represents a minority opinion, but in the end of the day it is not all that different from the majority view.[41]

But in the next passage, the Tosefta makes an even more radical step as it observes that in reality Rabban Gamaliel never practiced either sweeping between the couches or burning the incense on holidays:

---

[40] T Yom Tov 2:12.

[41] T Ber. 4:15 contains a similar story regarding a number of blessings one has to say after eating certain kinds of food. There the story does not explicitly refer to the practice of Rabban Gamaliel's household but it may imply such a practice. That the household of Rabban Gamaliel had its own liturgical lore can be seen from M Ber. 1:1. If this is the case, T Ber. 4:15 represents another attempt to reconcile the household halakhah of Rabban Gamaliel and the law of the sages. It also takes the former to be a minority legal opinion of Rabban Gamaliel, rather than his unique ancestral tradition, and treats it according to standard procedures of the rabbinic debate. Cf. M Ber. 6:8 (on which T Ber. 4:15 comments). The mishnah is organized in a classical rabbinic dispute-form.

In Rabban Gamaliel's household they used to sweep between the couches on a festival.

Said R. Eleazar b. R. Tsadoq, "We ate many times at Rabban Gamaliel's house, and I never saw them sweep between the couches on the festival. Rather they used to spread out sheets on the eve of the festival. When the guests entered, they would remove them."

They said to him, "If so, it is permitted to do the same even on the Sabbath."

In Rabban Gamaliel's house they used to bring [burning] incense [into the dining room, on a holiday] in an airtight vessel.

Said R. Eleazar b. R. Tsadoq, "We ate many times at Rabban Gamaliel's house, and I never saw them bring incense in an airtight vessel. Rather they used to [fill] casks [with the] smoke [of spices] on the eve of the holiday, and when guests entered they would open them."

They said to him, "If so, it is permitted to do the same on the Sabbath."[42]

The Tosefta here tries to smooth out differences between alleged household practices of Rabban Gamaliel and the standard halakhah of the sages. It does so by quoting R. Eleazar b. R. Tsadoq's testimony about the household practices of Rabban Gamaliel that he witnessed while visiting Gamaliel's house. Similar to the previous story, the Tosefta subtly shifts emphasis from the ancestral practices of Rabban Gamaliel's family ("never in my father's house"), as the Mishnah presents them, to the practices of Rabban Gamaliel himself. The latter are found to be in full compliance with the standard halakhah of the sages. Thus the Tosefta puts final touches on the process of transformation of household halakhic practices of Gamaliel's family into rabbinic ritual law. It does so by implying that even though Rabban Gamaliel's ancestral halakhah differed from that of the sages, he himself did not follow it. It is interesting, however, that an argument from one's household practices is still deemed to be valid. To counter testimony of Rabban Gamaliel about practices of his father's house, the Tosefta has to bring somebody else's testimony about practices of Rabban Gamaliel himself. One legal precedent is thus countered with another legal precedent from a later generation of the same household. The text never questions family halakhah as a valid source of Jewish law.[43]

---

[42] T Yom Tov 2:13–14.
[43] Cf. the couple of occasions on which Rabban Gamaliel follows rulings of the House of Hillel. In M Ma'as Sh. 2:7 he changes silver coins of Second Tithe money into golden dinars.

The Tosefta further amplifies the Mishnah by bringing another example of Rabban Gamaliel's apparent leniency (not attested in the Mishnah) only to reject it once again:

> In Rabban Gamaliel's household they used to grind pepper in their mills [on holiday].
>
> Said R. Eleazar b. R. Zaddok, "Once father was reclining [at dinner] before Rabban Gamaliel, and they brought before him *elaiogaron* and *oxygaron* sauce with ground pepper on it. And father withdrew his hand from them.
>
> Said [Rabban Gamaliel] to him, 'Do not worry about them. They were ground on the eve of the festival.' "[44]

This account does not have any precedent in the Mishnah, but it tries to prove the same point with the previous passage: no matter what his ancestral halakhah was, Rabban Gamaliel followed a majority view in his household practice. The testimony is presented as an account of the clash of two families' legal traditions: that of R. Eleazar b. R. Tsadoq's family and that of Rabban Gamaliel's. The tradition of R. Eleazar b. R. Tsadoq's family is presumably the same as that of the sages. Rabban Gamaliel assures R. Tsadoq that he in fact follows the same tradition as R. Tsadoq does, no matter what the assumptions about his household's halakhah might be. Given the uncertainty about the relationship between the materials preserved in the Mishnah and in the Tosefta, it is difficult to ascertain if this story represents an apologetic construct or a true account of historical events. In either case it would illustrate the importance of family practices in constructing the tannaitic legal system.[45]

These passages from the Tosefta see the changes introduced by Rabban Gamaliel to his family halakhah in a positive light. They serve to integrate the latter into the mainstream rabbinic legal tradition. But this is not always the case. The Tosefta on at least one occasion chooses to discredit Rabban Gamliel's own practices as contrary to his family halakhah:

---

[44] T Yom Tov 2:16.

[45] T Yom Tov 1:22 refers to a practice of "Rabban Gamaliel's household" to illustrate Rabban Gamaliel's compliance with the Hillelite view regarding preparation of certain types of food on the holiday. Similar to the previous accounts, this one is transmitted by R. Eleazar b. Tsadoq. It serves to illustrate Rabban Gamaliel's apodictic statement in M Bets. 1:8, which is placed in the context of the dispute between the Houses.

Said R. Yose, "It once happened that R. Halafta went to Rabban Gamaliel in Tiberias and found him sitting at the table of Ychanan b. Nazif with a targum of the book of Job in his hand, and he was reading it.

R. Halafta said to him, 'I used to remember that Rabban Gamaliel the Elder, your father's father (רבן גמליאל הזקן אבי אביך), was sitting at the top of the stairs on the Temple Mount. They brought before him a targum of the book of Job. He told his sons[46] and they hid it under a layer of stones.' "[47]

R. Yose quotes a story about R. Halafta reprimanding Rabban Gamaliel for reading the targum of the book of Job contrary to the decision of his own grandfather, who ordered it to be stored away. In the end of the story, the Vienna manuscript of the Tosefta asserts that Rabban Gamaliel the Elder specifically instructed his sons to do so. It thus emphasizes the family aspect of this law even stronger. The authenticity and historical validity of this story is clearly open to doubt.[48] What remains important, however, is the angle from which it chooses to criticize Rabban Gamaliel's behavior. By reading the targum he violates his own ancestral halakhah. The text thus views the halakhic lore of Rabban Gamaliel's family as a valid tradition, against which it judges actions of the nasi. Rabban Gamaliel's own actions are acceptable as long as they follow his family's halakhah. Once he changes it, he has to carry the burden of proof.[49]

On occasion Rabban Gamaliel needs to be reminded of his own family tradition as in the following story:

> R. Aqiva said, "When I went down to Nehardea to ordain a leap-year, I met Nehemiah of Bet Deli. He said to me, 'I have heard that in the land of Israel they do not allow a woman to remarry on the evidence of one witness, except for R. Judah b. Baba.' I answered, 'It is so.'
>
> He said to me, 'Tell them in my name: You know that this land is in turmoil because of the marauding troops. I have received [a tradition] from Rabban Gamaliel the Elder that they allow a woman to remarry on the evidence of one witness.'

---

[46] Following Vienna MS: אמר לבניו. Erfurt MS has "he told a builder:" אמר לבנאי.

[47] T Shabb. 13:2.

[48] But cf. Neusner, *Rabbinic Traditions*, vol. 1, 356. He seems to accept the basic authenticity of the story. Cf. further Epstein, *Mavo le-Nusah ha-Mishnah*, 649.

[49] Cf. Kanter, *Rabban Gamaliel*, 54–55, for a similar observation. He suggests that this pericope might have been composed in Aqivan circles.

And when I came and recounted the matter before Rabban Gamaliel, he rejoiced at my words and said, 'We have now found a fellow for R. Judah b. Baba.'

Through these words Rabban Gamaliel remembered that certain men were killed at Tel Arza, and Rabban Gamaliel the elder allowed their wives to remarry on the evidence of one witness."[50]

The ancestral halakhah of Rabban Gamaliel's family is transmitted here not by Rabban Gamaliel himself, but by R. Nehemiah. Once he has heard this tradition, Rabban Gamaliel recalls a specific precedent when his father rendered his decision in accordance with it. The story emphasizes the importance of the ancestral halakhah of Rabban Gamaliel but also claims that he himself is not necessarily the most reliable tradent of it. Another rabbi from as far as Nehardea in Mesopotamia can more accurately transmit his ancestral traditions. Still, the story does not question the halakhic validity of Rabban Gamaliel's ancestral law. The only thing it questions is the chain of transmission.[51]

Overall, early rabbinic traditions about R. Gamaliel reflect the importance of household "traditions of the fathers" for the nascent rabbinic movement as well as persistent attempts to integrate these traditions into new halakhic teachings originating within disciple circles. This integration was achieved in a number of ways. Occasionally the household halakhah of R. Gamaliel was dismissed as pietism of an exceptionally righteous family unsuitable for "all Israel." The rhetorical contrast between "Israel" and individual halakhic practices resembles the distinction between "the ways of Israel" and "the ways of their fathers" practiced by Sadducean daughters. Moreover, the Tosefta claims that (just like the Sadducean daughters) R. Gamaliel in his private practices was following "the ways of Israel" after all. In both cases the totalizing discourse of disciple circles attempted to construct, organize, transform, and ultimately control unsystematic, diverse, and often ad hoc "ancestral traditions." Moreover, rabbis would often claim that it was they, not R. Gamaliel or other members of his household, who possessed the authentic knowledge of

---

[50] M Yebam. 16:7.

[51] See Neusner, *Rabbinic Traditions*, vol. 1, 348–50, for further discussion of this story and its formal characteristic. Neusner accepts its authenticity. Kanter, *Rabban Gamaliel*, 133–34, notices that our story demonstrates Rabban Gamaliel's dependence upon Aqiva "for the actual decision of the law, and even for information concerning the patriarchal house itself."

what R. Gamaliel's ancestral traditions *really* meant. Such an approach reflected the profoundly ambiguous attitude of rabbinic scholars to household traditions of earlier generations. Their validity as well as their role in the rabbinic "holiness project" was upheld, but the authority associated with them no longer dwelt with a *paterfamilias* and members of his household. Rather, this authority belonged to the sages who sought to regulate familial practices with new types of scholarly halakhic discourse generated within disciple circles.

In all examples discussed so far, the importance of Rabban Gamaliel's practices is derived not from him personally but rather from his family. In other words, we can hardly speak here of paradigmatic actions of an individual determining Jewish law. Rather, precedent-based traditions of Rabban Gamaliel's family appear to be a perfect example of the "traditions of the fathers" characteristic of the Second Temple Pharisees. The Mishnah incorporates them in precisely this capacity: authoritative ancestral halakhah of a trustworthy family. Even when Rabban Gamaliel introduces changes to the halakhic practices of his family, they are presented as practiced by "Rabban Gamaliel's house" not just by him. He appears in this reference as a *paterfamilias* transmitting and changing his family's ancestral law, not just as an individual rabbi holding a particular halakhic opinion. The idea of the family as the matrix of halakhah dominates the traditions of Rabban Gamaliel. In accordance with this tendency, halakhic practices ascribed to other members of Rabban Gamaliel's household acquire particular significance.

Rabbinic Families as the Source of Halakhic Authority

As Shaye Cohen has correctly observed, Tannaitic texts contain very little information about typical Roman-type slavery employing slave labor in large-scale commercial or agricultural operations.[52] Instead, in those few cases when they mention slaves, tannaim almost exclusively deal with household slaves and servants. This focus of tannaitic halakhah provides another piece of evidence for the centrality of the household and its institutions for the rabbinic worldview.[53]

---

[52] See S. Cohen, "The Rabbi in Second-Century Jewish Society," 945–46.
[53] See for example M Ketub. 5:5 (bondwomen brought by a wife as part of her *ketubbah*).

Household slaves and their practices occasionally serve as important
sources of household halakhah. Rabban Gamaliel's slave Tabi is especially prominent in this respect:

> A man who sleeps under a bed in the sukkah, has not fulfilled his
> obligation . . .
>   Said R. Simeon, "It once happened that Tabi, the slave of Rabban
> Gamaliel, slept under the bed. And Rabban Gamaliel said to the elders,
> 'You have seen Tabi, my slave. He is a student of the wise (תלמיד חכם)
> and knows that slaves are exempt from the obligation of the sukkah.
> That is why he sleeps under the bed.'
>   So, incidentally, (ולפי דרכנו) we learn that [a man] who sleeps under
> a bed has not fulfilled his obligation."[54]

The Mishnah quotes the practice of Tabi, Rabban Gamaliel's slave,
as proof for the anonymous view that sleeping under a bed in the
sukkah does not fulfill the obligation of sleeping in the sukkah. Tabi
slept under the bed precisely because he knew that slaves were exempt
from the obligation to dwell in the sukkah. Significantly, Rabban
Gamaliel refers to him as *talmid hakham*. This term is traditionally
associated with a rabbinic student who studies Torah with his master. In this case, the term is applied to a household slave who has
mastery of the practical household halakhah and acts accordingly.
Such a peculiar usage of *talmid hakham* indicates a much broader
range of meaning for the term than is usually assumed. The emphasis is not so much on study as on the faithful observance of a specific
set of halakhic norms. A household slave can be called *talmid hakham*
if he knows and follows the household halakhah ("traditions of the
fathers") of his master.[55] In another tradition Tabi's practice of wearing tefillin is cited as an exception to the rule that slaves and women
(notice, again, two household categories of people) are exempt from
wearing tefillin.[56] The halakhah of Rabban Gamaliel's family could
be learned not only from his statements but even from the behavior of his household slaves (or at least some of them).[57]

---

[54] M Sukkah 2:1.

[55] During the Tannaitic and Amoraic periods, disciples were often perceived as
subservient members of their master's household. Their education was based on
observation and participation in their master's everyday practices. The distinction
between disciples and household slaves was not always clear. See further M. Aberbach,
"The Relations between Master and Disciple in the Talmudic Age," in H. Dimitrovsky,
ed., *Exploring the Talmud* (New York, 1976), 202–225. Cf. Hezser, *Social Structure of
the Rabbinic Movement*, 332–46, and Sivertsev, *Private Households*, 117–31.

[56] Mek. Pisha 17 (Lauterbach, vol. 1, 153–54).

[57] In M Ber. 2:5–7 Rabban Gamaliel's students learn halakhah by observing their

Another household-related social group mentioned in connection with Rabban Gamaliel is his tenant farmers. In this case the Mishnah distinguishes between his private practice and the halakhah:

> A man lends his tenant farmers wheat in return for repayment with wheat, for seed but not for eating.
>
> For Rabban Gamaliel used to lend his tenant farmers wheat in return for wheat for seed.
>
> [If he lent it when the price was] expensive, and it became cheap, or [if he lent it when it was] cheap, and it became expensive, he would take it from them at the cheaper price.
>
> Not because the halakhah is that way, but because he wished to be more stringent with himself.[58]

It is not immediately clear what the text means by "halakhah." Apparently, it tries to explain that Rabban Gamaliel's practice in this case should not be taken as binding. The text stresses the difference between private practice of a pious and compassionate individual (Rabban Gamaliel) and the law.[59] Still, the actions of Rabban Gamaliel as *paterfamilias* are once again taken into account in the discussion of Jewish law. A related example comes up in the discussion of doubtfully tithed produce (Demai). An anonymous mishnah states that "they feed Demai produce to the poor and [they feed] Demai to transient guests." It further adds as a precedent of sorts that "Rabban Gamaliel used to feed Demai to his workers."[60] The practices of Rabban Gamaliel's household in this case serve to illustrate an anonymous apodictic law. As a whole, Rabban Gamaliel's practices in respect to his tenant farmers and servants constitute an important part of his functions as *paterfamilias* and also an important source for his household halakhah. Along with the stories about Tabi, they report Rabban Gamaliel's household practices as a set of valid precedents for Jewish law.

On at least one occasion Rabban Gamaliel is portrayed as making halakhic decision for his sons. The Mishnah records the following debate about the time of reciting the Shema:

---

master's behavior. Rabban Gamaliel's actions, which appear to be contrary to his own teaching, prompt his disciples' questions. One such action involves acceptance of condolences over the death of his slave Tabi. Rabban Gamaliel explains this by the exceptional qualities of Tabi. See also M Pesah. 7:2, which presents a law about the roasting of a Passover kid, based on instructions given by Rabban Gamaliel to Tabi.

[58] M B. Metsiʻa 5:8.

[59] See discussion above.

[60] M Demai 3:1. Cf. T Demai 3:15.

And sages say, "Until midnight."

Rabban Gamaliel says, "Until the dawn comes up."

It once happened that his sons came from a feast (בית המשתה). They said to him, "We have not recited the Shema." He said to them, "If the dawn has not come up, you are required to recite it."

And not just this, but in every case concerning which sages said, "Until midnight," the obligation lasts until the dawn comes up. [In case of] burning the fat pieces and limbs [of the sacrifices], the obligation lasts until the dawn comes up. [And for] all [offerings] that must be eaten on the same day, the obligation lasts until the dawn comes up. If so, why did sages say, "Until midnight"? In order to keep man far from transgression.[61]

The Mishnah quotes a liturgical practice of Rabban Gamaliel's household that stands in apparent disagreement with the opinion of the sages. It then seeks to reconcile the two by interpreting the sages to *mean* exactly what Rabban Gamaliel ordered his sons to do. In the story, Rabban Gamaliel acts as a *paterfamilias* legislating for his own household. We do not know if he merely states his ancestral halakhah or introduces a new rule. In either case he acts in the capacity of the head of his household, and it is in this capacity that the Mishnah accepts his ruling as a valid precedent. The ruling emerges in the family setting of Rabban Gamaliel's interaction with his sons and provides a good example of household halakhah.

In addition, the Tosefta records a series of conflicts between household practices of Rabban Gamaliel and his children on the one hand and local Jewish traditions on the other:

It once happened that Rabban Gamaliel was sitting on a bench belonging to gentiles on the Sabbath, in Akko. They said to him, "It is not customary here (לא היו נוהגין כן להיות), to sit on a bench belonging to gentiles on the Sabbath." He did not want to tell them, "You are permitted to do so." Rather, he got up and went away.

It once happened that Judah and Hillel, sons of Rabban Gamaliel, went in to bathe, in Kabul. They said to them, "It is not customary here, for two brothers to bathe at the same time." They did not want to tell them, "You are permitted to do so." Rather, they entered and bathed one after the other.

Again, it once happened that Judah and Hillel, sons of Rabban Gamaliel, went out wearing gold slippers on the Sabbath in Biri. They said to them, "It is not customary here to go out wearing gold slippers on the Sabbath." They did not want to tell them, "You are permitted to do so." Rather, they sent them with their servants.[62]

---

[61] M Ber. 1:1.
[62] T Mo'ed Qat. 2:14–16.

This narrative consists of three accounts. Each of them illustrates a conflict between halakhic practices of Rabban Gamaliel and his two sons, and local practices of Jews living in Akko and Kabul. The story seeks to emphasize unique characteristics of some halakhic practices of Rabban Gamaliel's household and that both Rabban Gamaliel and his sons recognized their uniqueness. Most of the practices mentioned in this passage reflect particular affluence and cultural assimilation of Rabban Gamaliel's household. Its members find it halakhically appropriate to sit on benches belonging to gentiles on the Sabbath, wear gold slippers on the Sabbath or bathe together. The story raises a broader issue of how much halakhic practices of an individual household could be influenced by external cultural realities of the time. Given the all-embracing nature of Jewish law, it was very difficult to determine where cultural conventions ended and halakhic observances began. As a result, the two were often intertwined in everyday practices of individual households.[63] These stories demonstrate the self-restraint and discretion of R. Gamaliel and his sons, who chose to follow local practices and not to enforce their own (culturally and socially determined) understanding of Jewish law. The stories also show that halakhic practices of Rabban Gamaliel's children could be perceived as legally authoritative no matter what, presumably because they were part of ancestral traditions of their household. Similar to Rabban Gamaliel himself, his children were perceived as bearers of valid familial halakhic tradition, which they sometimes had to adjust to local traditions of other Jews.

Occasionally, children of Rabban Gamaliel emerge as tradents of his household halakhah, which they learn precisely by virtue of being members of the household:

---

[63] Stories about Rabban Gamaliel visiting a bathhouse provide perfect examples of halakhically ambiguous and potentially provocative situations. See M 'Abod. Zar. 3:4 and T Miqw. 6:3. Rabban Gamaliel's private actions have public significance in both cases, since whatever he does automatically enters the realm of the ancestral halakhah of his family. In M 'Abodah Zarah this leads to a dialogue in which Rabban Gamaliel has to defend his visit to Aphrodite's bathhouse in Acco. T Miqwa'ot questions the halakhic validity of his ritual immersion in bath instead of the sea. Both stories reflect a situation when cultural conventions of the larger Greco-Roman society practiced by members of Jewish households become part of their household halakhic lore and have to be addressed accordingly. On the M 'Abodah Zarah story and its cultural and social implications see further Schwartz, *Imperialism and Jewish Society*, 162–76.

> Said Rabban Simeon b. Gamaliel, "It once happened that a woman came before father. She said to him, 'My hands entered the air-space of an earthenware vessel.'
>
> He said to her, 'My daughter, from what [source] was its uncleanness?'
>
> And I did not hear what she said to him."[64]

This story serves to illustrate a legal debate about what degrees of uncleanness of a vessel make hands unclean. Rabban Simeon b. Gamaliel appeals to his father's decision, which he witnessed. As in other precedent-based scenarios, we find here an example of the publicly authoritative family halakhah of Gamaliel's household cited to argue for an abstract ruling. The story deals with an anonymous woman who asks R. Gamaliel for advice because she is concerned about her purity status. The context of this concern is almost certainly her household activities that could potentially render her unclean. In other words, the story addresses purity laws specifically in their household context. The legal decision of R. Gamaliel has all the attributes of an informally communicated halakhic opinion. The setting of his encounter with the woman was most probably his own house, with members of his family (his son) present nearby. His son apparently just happened to overhear his father's conversation and then failed to remember all of its details. What is significant is that the halakhic knowledge the son of Rabban Gamaliel demonstrates in this story comes from his being a member of Rabban Gamaliel's family. He acquires halakhic knowledge almost by accident. His importance as a tradent fully rests on his belonging to an inner circle of Rabban Gamaliel's family and hence his direct (but sometimes incidental) exposure to his family traditions.

The centrality of household practices and their transmission allows us a fresh look at the problem of women's knowledge of halakhah, exemplified by the figure of Beruria but not confined to her.[65] The Tosefta contains two traditions associated with exceptional knowledge of halakhah by female members of rabbinic households:

> If one plastered [an oven] in a state of purity and it became impure— from what time can it be purified? R. Halafta of Kefar Hananiah

---

[64] M Yad. 3:1.

[65] See D. Goodblatt, "The Beruriah Traditions," *JJS* 26 (1975), 68–85, for detailed analysis of relevant traditions. He convincingly argues that one should not confuse the traditions about Beruria and those about the daughter of R. Hananiah b. Teradyon.

said, "I asked Shim'on ben Hananiah who asked the son of R. Hananiah ben Teradyon, and he said, 'When they move it from its place.' But his daughter said, 'When they disassemble its parts.'" When this was told to R. Yehudah ben Babba, he said, "His daughter said better than his son."[66]

The passage deals with a household-related purity issue: how one purifies an oven, which was plastered in purity but then became impure. The tradition cited originates in the family halakhah of R. Hananiah ben Teradyon. His son and his daughter give different responses to the question, and R. Yehudah ben Babba commends the response of R. Hananiah's daughter over that of his son. There is no indication that the knowledge of either of R. Hananiah's children comes from their formal education in Jewish law.[67] It would be more natural to assume that they both render their decisions in accordance with their understanding of family halakhah. Apparently the latter did not contain any specific regulation for this particular case (hence, their disagreement). Both the son and the daughter had to arrive at their decision based on their knowledge of other household practices. Alternatively, it is possible that the daughter indeed was aware of aspects of family halakhah, which the son did not know about.[68]

The second story in the Tosefta specifically refers to a woman called Beruria:

A *claustra* (door-bolt)—R. Tarfon declares it impure, but the sages declare it pure. And Beruria says, "One removes it from the door and hangs it on another on the Sabbath." When this was told to R. Yehoshua, he said, "Beruria said well."[69]

---

[66] T Kelim B.Qam. 4:17.

[67] Cf. Boyarin, *Carnal Israel*, 183, n. 16. He asks, "If the daughter were simply reporting the practice in her household, why did her brother have a different suggestion?" According to Boyarin the story suggests "that the woman (or girl) in question had an understanding of principles of religious law that she could apply to specific hypothetical situations." But such an understanding could be acquired as a result of in-depth exposure to household halakhah. Moreover, I do not think that both responses addressed a "hypothetical situation." The question was very much a real and practical one.

[68] Tannaitic tradition portrays the family of R. Hananiah b. Teradyon as a righteous family *par excellence*. Sifre Deut. 307 (Finkelstein, 346) narrates a martyrdom story about R. Hananiah and his family. According to this story the behavior of Hananiah, his wife, and his daughter in the time of persecution manifested both their piety and their knowledge of law. The story seems to partially reflect a righteous family motif so prominent in Second Temple Judaism. The halakhic expertise of R. Hananiah's daughter may be part of this image.

[69] T Kelim B. Metsi'a 1:6.

Unlike the previous tradition, this one is phrased as a classical rabbinic debate. It does not contain any explicit references to a household setting or family halakhah. As far as tannatic tradition is concerned, we know next to nothing about Beruria or her family.[70] R. Tarfon, however, is occasionally portrayed as transmitting his family halakhah in a way similar to that of Rabban Gamaliel.[71] It remains unclear whether or not our text draws on this difference between two family traditions exemplified by R. Tarfon and Beruria, but it is not impossible. The two of them are then presented in a classical rabbinic format of opposing legal views with anonymous sages and R. Yehoshua siding with Beruria (probably the only reason why her name made it into this text). At any rate, any reconstruction of family halakhah behind this text would be totally speculative. The issue addressed clearly belongs to the realm of household law, but this is as much as we can tell.

In certain ways halakhic knowledge ascribed to female members of rabbinic households belongs in the same category as halakhic knowledge ascribed to household slaves. Both of them acquire it because they are part of rabbinic households. Both of them acquire it not as knowledge of abstract legal principles but as knowledge of the "traditions of the fathers," the ancestral lore of their family. On the other hand, unlike household slaves, female members of rabbinic families exercised considerable authority in running everyday affairs of the household both in economic and religious realms. In this respect their role in preservation and application of halakhah was much more central than that of household slaves. The education in halakhah as ancestral lore would be naturally open to both men and women. It is furthermore possible to imagine that women would be much more knowledgeable about certain areas of family halakhah than men.[72] As we shall see later in this chapter, a considerable proportion of case stories involving early rabbis have to do with women's concerns about various matters of family law (including purity law). It is women who are depicted as approaching rabbis on a regular basis to inquire about specific halakhic issues. This very fact demonstrates that they were sufficiently knowledgeable in the realm of

---

[70] See Goodblatt, "Beruriah Traditions," 81–82.
[71] See below.
[72] Cf. T. Ilan, *Jewish Women in Greco-Roman Palestine* (Peabody: Hendrickson, 1996), 194–200, for similar observations.

halakhah to make a proper inquiry and to follow advice. In most cases they would address a rabbi when the halakhic decision was far from certain. In more regular cases, we may assume, they made their own decisions.[73] Overall, I tend to agree with David Goodblatt's argument that the stories about women's knowledge of halakhah do not necessarily imply any formal education. They learned it by virtue of belonging to a rabbinic household. But the same is true of a rabbi's sons. Here I strongly disagree with Goodblatt's distinction between the "practical, informally acquired knowledge of a house-wife" and the "academic knowledge of the master."[74] Similar to a rabbi's daughters, his sons received their halakhic knowledge not as an abstract set of laws, but as the "traditions of their fathers": their ancestral family halakhah embodied in everyday practices of their household. In many areas of family halakhah, both men and women had equal authority. Once Jewish law moved from the realm of fam-ily lore to the realm of academic study, it also moved into the pre-dominantly male sphere of responsibility, as later talmudic and post-talmudic interpretations of the figure of Beruria demonstrate.[75]

An example of this process can be found in the development of the Tosefta's tradition that "all those women that should be exam-ined are only examined by women." An initial commentary on this statement refers to the practice of R. Eliezer who "used to transfer [physical examinations of women] to his wife" and R. Ishmael who "transferred them to his mother."[76] In other words, at earlier stages reflected by the tradition, family members of rabbinic households were actively involved in assisting their *paterfamilias* with implementa-tion of the Jewish law. Not only rabbis but their mothers and spouses were trusted with halakhic expertise precisely because it was the household and not an individual sage that served as the depository of knowledge. In this situation the head of the household could be fully expected to solicit help from female members of his family when he

---

[73] Cf. J. Wegner, *Chattel or Person? The Status of Women in the Mishnah* (New York: Oxford University Press, 1988), 163–165, for similar conclusions regarding the laws of menstrual purity.

[74] Goodblatt, "Beruriah Traditions," 83. Boyarin, *Carnal Israel*, 183, n. 16, rejects Goodblatt's idea, that women in T Kelim B. Qam. 4:17 and B. Metsi'a 1:6 acquired their knowledge by virtue of being part of a rabbinic household. I find his argument unconvincing for reasons partially suggested above, but I agree with his criticism of Goodblatt's dichtonomy between "male" and "female" types of halakhic knowledge.

[75] See Boyarin, *Carnal Israel*, 181–96.

[76] T Nid. 6:8.

had to perform examinations of other women. However, as Charlotte
Fonrobert has convincingly demonstrated, subsequent development
of this tradition in rabbinic literature gradually (but persistently)
restricts the actual legal relevance of the examination by women.[77]
Instead, as the baraita evolves, it creates "more access for the rabbis' control into this relatively autonomous space for women." As
halakhic traditions pass from the realm of households into that of
disciple circles, scholastic constructs of rabbis begin to play an increasingly dominant role. The halakhic control shifts from the realm of
families into that of (male) legal experts and their analytical discourse.

   We can now revisit traditions in which some early rabbinic masters encouraged teaching one's daughter Torah. In the context of
household-embodied piety of the early rabbinic movement this probably meant giving her an in-depth understanding of the family law
to allow her conscious participation in family life:

> If she had any merit, it suspends her punishment.
>   On this basis Ben-Azzai said, "A man should teach his daughter
> Torah, so that if she drinks [the bitter water], she will know that merit
> suspends her punishment."
>   Rabbi Eliezer says, "Anyone who teaches his daughter Torah teaches
> her lasciviousness."[78]

The Mishnah deals with the trial by ordeal of a suspected adulteress
by making her drink "bitter waters." This paragraph concludes a
detailed list of provisions of how the "bitter waters" should be admin-
istered and what the consequences are. Ben Azzai observes that
knowledge of Torah would allow a woman informed participation
in family life. There are two possible explanations of what this
informed participation exactly means. First, since the woman knows
what the ritual of Sotah is, as well as its implications,[79] her knowledge of the ritual and its consequences may prevent her from com-
mitting adultery. It will serve as a forewarning for her. In this case,
Ben-Azzai emphasizes the pedagogical significance of the ordeal in
preventing the adultery rather than the ordeal itself. It has to be
studied as part of family halakhah in order to prevent possible mis-
conduct.[80] But it is also possible that in a semi-magical way other

---

[77] See Fonrobert, *Menstrual Purity*, 144–47.
[78] M Sotah 3:4.
[79] Cf. Wegner, *Chattel or Person*, 161–62. She understands the knowledge of "Torah"
in this case to refer specifically to the knowledge of the laws of ordeal.
[80] Several other early rabbinic regulations also imply that women were full-fledged

merits that this woman has might suspend her punishment. Once again, her knowledge of this fact comes as a result of studying Torah. In either case a woman's knowledge of Torah's norms and pre- scriptions makes her a full-fledged participant in family life regulated by these norms.

R. Eliezer's opposition to teaching Torah to one's daughter is somewhat enigmatic. It can be explained by his concern that her knowledge can potentially help her escape the punishment. It may result from his concern about increased independence of educated and informed women.[81] Or it may come from an idea that the study about lasciviousness will produce the lasciviousness itself. In any case, the prime concern of this passage is whether one's daughter should be educated in details of family law apparently transmitted as part of household halakhah or should this part of the law be left as an exclusive realm of judges administering the Sotah. The debate is about how well informed a participant in the transmission of the "traditions of the fathers" a woman should be. Does she have the same access to family law as males or not? Later this debate will lead to a larger question about whether or not women are allowed to study Torah. Palestinian Amoraic texts seem to presuppose that this was always an option, while the Babylonian rabbinic tradition is much more restrictive.[82] On the one hand, this disagreement could simply reflect a Palestinian Jewish practice of allowing women to study. Perhaps, such a practice reflected a sympathetic attitude of the provincial Greco-Roman culture toward educated women.[83] On the other hand, the Palestinian rabbinic tradition that permitted

---

and conscious participants in household halakhic practices as well as public cere- monies (which involved households). For relevant texts and their discussion see Ilan, *Jewish Women*, 176–84, and *Mine and Yours are Hers*, 159–90.

[81] So Wegner, *Chattel or Person*, 162.

[82] See Boyarin, *Carnal Israel*, 170–80, for comparative analysis of Palestinian and Babylonian interpretations of this mishnah. Both Talmuds seem to address the issue of formal study and its availability to women. We are in an entirely different con- ceptual universe there, as we move from the realm of household-based "traditions of the fathers" into the realm of formal rabbinic study of Torah.

[83] See Boyarin, *Carnal Israel*, 167–96, for the consistently positive attitude of Pales- tinian Amoraim toward women studying the Torah. He contrasts it with the Baby- lonian attitude and partially explains the difference by different cultural environments. Cf. Ilan, *Jewish Women*, 190–97. For the relative freedom and financial indepen- dence of Palestinian Jewish women see Satlow, *Jewish Marriage in Antiquity*, 199–224. W. Meeks, *The First Urban Christians: The Social World of the Apostle Paul* (New Haven: Yale University Press, 1983), 23–25, provides parallel insights into the phenome- non of educated women of means in the ancient urban Mediterranean society.

women to study Torah could reflect a much larger role that women would originally play in preservation and transmission of family halakhah or the "traditions of the fathers." In this case, vestiges of the traditional household-based transmission of religious knowledge continued to play an important role in Palestinian rabbinic circles but not in Babylonian ones.[84]

Priestly Rabbis and Household Halakhah

Rabban Gamaliel is not the only rabbi for whom we have a large volume of precedent- and practice-based traditions. We know about a number of his colleagues primarily because of the reports about their practices and the practices of their families. Some of them are described as close friends of Rabban Gamaliel, and most of them are priests. Most of the practice-based halakhah appears in tannaitic texts in connection with rabbis who are known to belong to priestly families. Like Rabban Gamaliel and his family, they have strong ties with the pre-Destruction Jewish establishment. Whereas Rabban Gamaliel comes from a patrician Jerusalem family, they come from a priestly background, although details about their priestly pedigrees are largely unknown. We have argued above that the priestly halakhah of the Second Temple period was essentially a family lore of priestly families, just as pharisaic "traditions of the fathers" were family lore of pharisaic households. The same type of halakhah appears in tannaitic traditions associated with Rabban Gamaliel and rabbis of priestly stock. Both of them belong in the same category with the named pre-70 masters of tannaitic texts. They constitute a transition from Second Temple Judaism and its "traditions of the fathers" to Rabbinic Judaism and the Mishnah.

We have observed above that a number of traditions about the

---

[84] Indeed, Palestinian Amoraim continue to mention female members of rabbinic households possessing advanced knowledge of household halakhah. See for example J Betsah 4:4 (62c) and J Shabb. 4:2 (6d) (= J Shabb. 13:7 [14b]). In the last case the sister of R. Shimon transmits to him a tradition of his father, which he did not know. Ilan, *Mine and Yours*, 51–84, has convincingly demonstrated that as we move further into the Amoraic period, women tend to fade away from rabbinic traditions. Even the traditions that originally mentioned women in halakhically-prominent roles tend to "lose" them. This process may be connected with the transformation of Rabbinic Judaism and its traditions from a household-based entity to a teaching shaped and determined within male-dominated study circles.

household of Rabban Gamaliel and its halakhic practices are transmitted in the name of R. Tsadoq and his son R. Eleazar ben Tsadoq. Their family is repeatedly portrayed as having a close relationship with the family of Rabban Gamaliel.[85] R. Tsadoq attends banquets of the latter[86] and sits on what appears to be a consilium-type court of Rabban Gamaliel.[87] The relationships between the two families are built on the basis of friendship and mutual respect. They belong to a network of provincial aristocratic households of late first century Palestine. As such they share lifestyles typical of provincial aristocracies of the Roman Empire. It is only natural that members of R. Tsadoq's family transmit several traditions about the practices of Rabban Gamaliel's household. They know them and have authority to transmit them precisely because of this close social interaction between the two families. One's household halakhah can be transmitted not only by the immediate members of his household but also by friends and clients having first-hand familiarity with the household practices and in a sense belonging to an extended household. Like the Second Temple sects, groups within the early rabbinic movement were essentially clusters of families sharing common halakhic practices.[88] Finally, some of R. Tsadoq's own practices are transmitted in connection with those of Rabban Gamaliel:

> They eat as a snack both food and drink outside the sukkah.
> Once they brought cooked food to Rabban Yohanan b. Zakkai to taste, and two dates, and a bucket of water to Rabban Gamaliel, and they said, "Bring them up to the sukkah."
> And when they gave R. Tsadoq less than an egg's bulk of food, he took it in a towel and ate it outside the sukkah and did not say the Benediction after it.[89]

The mishnah deals with the question of whether snacks which do not constitute a meal in a strict sense of the word should also be

---

[85] See Lightstone, "Sadoq the Yavnean," 133–35.

[86] Mekhilta Amaleq (Horovitz, 195–196) and probably M Pes. 7:2. R. Eleazar b. Tsadoq mentions his father dining in the house of Rabban Gamaliel on a number of occasions (see above). Cf. Sifre Deut. 38:1 (Finkelstein, 74), which mentions R. Tsadoq and other sages reclining in the banquet hall of the son of Rabban Gamaliel.

[87] T Sanh. 8:1. On the consilium-like nature of the nasi's court see Sivertsev, *Private Households*, 143–60.

[88] On the rabbinic movement as an informal network of relationships see Hezser, *Social Structure*, 228–39. She, however, does not emphasize the family-based nature of this network.

[89] M Sukkah 2:4–5.

eaten inside the sukkah. It brings two examples: Rabban Yohanan b. Zakkai and Rabban Gamaliel follow a strict rule by consuming any food inside the sukkah. R. Tsadoq is more lenient, and his practice supports the mainline anonymous opinion stated in the beginning. The entire mishnah is based on individual household practices of three early rabbinic masters, which either agree or disagree with a general anonymous rule representing a later editorial construct of the Mishnah.[90]

The traditions of R. Tsadoq are equally dominated by a precedent-based household halakhah:

> Said R. Eleazar b. Tsadoq, "Heads of posts were on the Temple Mount on which craftsmen would sit and polish stones, and the sages did not suspect them in respect to any uncleanness."
>
> And so R. Eleazar b. Tsadoq used to say, "Two blocks were in the house of my father, one unclean, and the other clean. I said to father, 'On what account is this unclean, and the other clean?' He said to me, 'This one which is hollowed out is unclean, and the other which is not hollowed out is clean. And on it sat Haggai the prophet.'"[91]

The Tosefta discusses whether a block of wood, which can serve as a seat but was not originally made to serve as a seat, can contract uncleanness. R. Eleazar b. Tsadoq argues that it cannot. He brings two precedents to support his view. One of them comes from the Temple practice, the other—from the practice of his own household. Both of them agree with each other and prove R. Eleazar's position against that of other sages. The combination of two proofs illustrates a relationship between household practices of R. Tsadoq's household and the Temple halakhah. The reference to Haggai the prophet apparently serves to add more authority to the household halakhah of R. Tsadoq. Yet the centrality of the ancestral practices of R. Eleazar b. Tsadoq for his argument remains unmistakable. The text also helps identify the family of Tsadoq as a priestly family, whose household law is connected with the priestly laws of the Temple.[92]

---

[90] Cf. T Sukkah 2:3.

[91] T Kelim B. Bat. 2:2–3.

[92] T Kip. 1:12 (= T Sheb. 1:4) contains an anecdotal story about a brawl between two priests (brothers, in T Sheb. version), who were running to clean the ashes from the altar (cf. M Yoma 2:1). The brawl ended in the murder of one priest by the other. The story has Tsadoq deliver a sermon after the murder, but this part may be a later interpolation into what appears to be a morality tale criticizing priestly mores. See Lightsone, "Sadoq the Yavnean," 62–64. At any rate, the story may belong to the priestly oral lore transmitted through Tsadoq or his family. Cf.

R. Tsadoq is important because his family establishes an explicit connection between priestly rabbinic families and the family of Rabban Gamaliel. Both groups constitute a distinct category within the early rabbinic movement and provide continuity with the Second Temple period. But only in the case of R. Tsadoq do we find repeated and detailed attestation of close social contacts between them. These contacts manifest themselves, among other things, through shared halakhic traditions and reports about halakhic practices of each other. The embodiment of halakhah through a network of families becomes clearly manifest. This halakhah is not an abstract anonymous law. It is an everyday life of families who share a social space with each other through various forms of interaction, such as visits, banquets, etc. Before it became systematically presented in the Mishnah, the early rabbinic halakhah had evolved within such a close-knit structure of families. As in many other aspects of life in Antiquity, here too, a family and a network of families became the main units of production. The halakhah was embodied not only through individual households and their practices, but also through networks of households sharing common social and ideological space.[93]

Traditions associated with the name of Simeon b. Kahana provide another example of halakhic lore emerging from a social network of households connected to the family of Rabban Gamaliel. R. Simeon b. Gamaliel transmits most of Simeon b. Kahana's traditions either in the form of stories or in the form of testimonies. Thus he illustrates the prohibition on importing heave offering from abroad into the Land of Israel by telling an eyewitness account about Simeon b. Kahana. The latter had to finish drinking the wine from Cilicia, which had the status of heave offering, prior to disembarking from

---

Lieberman, *Tosefta K-ifshutah*, vol. 2 (*Mo'ed*), 735–736, who sees the story as a mixture of different oral traditions.

[93] Such contacts (and not study circles) often serve as formulaic settings for tannaitic stories. See for example a series of anecdotal stories about Rabban Gamaliel and elders traveling on a ship. See M Ma'as. Sh. 5:9 illustrating tithing practices of Rabban Gamaliel and his fellow elders. Cf. T Sukkah 2:11 (= Sifra Emor 16:2), which tells a similar story about Rabban Gamaliel and elders celebrating Sukkot in a particular way while on a ship. Here, again, a network of like-minded men constitutes the prime setting for halakhic practices and innovations. See also M Shabb. 16:8. All these stories belong to the same formulaic literary construct ("rabbis on a ship"), which is used to convey various halakhic messages. See Kanter, *Rabban Gamaliel*, 39. Remarkably, all of them lack the "scholarly" setting of bet midrash. See Hezser, *Social Structure*, 228–31, for further discussion.

the boat in order not to bring it into the Land of Israel.[94] According to another passage, R. Simeon b. Gamaliel stated three rules pertaining to the priests in the name of Simeon b. Kahana. The rules were introduced by the formula "in the time of the priests they used to do X" and dealt with technical aspects of priestly practices, and priestly attitudes toward uncleanness.[95] The transmission of this specific set of rules apparently took place as part of a social interaction between the families of R. Simeon b. Gamaliel and Simeon b. Kahana. The introductory formula may indicate that the rules reflected the priestly family lore of Simon's household made public within a network of families that included the family of Rabban Gamaliel. The household halakhah was disseminated not only through the members of a particular household but also through the members of other socially related families. In this case, R. Simeon b. Gamaliel's testimonies helped disseminate the household halakhic practices of his social circle to a wider audience. A final bit of information we learn about Simeon b. Kahana is not transmitted by R. Simeon b. Gamaliel but also appears in connection with the family law. Upon the testimony of an arrested man, who notifies the wife of Simeon b. Kahana that he has murdered her husband, the sages allow her to remarry.[96] Here the halakhah is embodied in practices of a social network that regulates affairs of individual families included in it.

Overall, legal traditions of rabbis coming from the priesthood provide numerous examples of household halakhah. A number of these traditions are associated with R. Tarfon. They not only repeatedly address issues related to priestly law and practices but also explicitly indicate family traditions as their basis. According to the Tosefta:

> On that day, R. Tarfon observed a lame [priest] standing and blowing the horns. On that basis he observed and said, "A lame [priest] blows the horn in the Temple."[97]

R. Tarfon's observation of a lame priest blowing the horn led him to the conclusion that lame priests are allowed to blow the horn in the Temple. The story derives R. Tarfon's halakhah from a precedent but does not associate it with his family.

---

[94] T Sheb. 5:2.
[95] T Parah 12:6.
[96] T Yebam. 4:5.
[97] T Sotah 7:16.

Sifre Numbers presents a much more elaborate version of the same story, now phrased as a halakhic debate between R. Tarfon and R. Aqiva.[98] R. Aqiva states that priests who blow the horn must be without physical defects just as priests who offer sacrifices in the Temple. R. Tarfon responds by appealing to the practice of his family that he himself witnessed:

> Said to him R. Tarfon, "How long will you put words together and bring them up against us, Aqiva? I cannot endure [this any longer]. May I bury my sons if I did not observe Simeon, my maternal uncle (אחי אימא), who was lame in one foot, standing and blowing the horns."
>
> He said to him, "You are correct, Rabbi, but perhaps you observed this at the festival of Haqhel, for [priests] with defects are fit [to blow the horns] at the festival of Haqhel, and on the Day of Atonement, and at the Jubilee festival."
>
> He said to him, "[I swear] by the Temple service that you did not invent this. How worthy is Abraham, our father, [that he] has Aqiva as his offspring. Tarfon observed [the incident] and forgot. Aqiva explains it by himself in accordance with the law. Behold, anyone who separates himself from you is as if he separates himself from his life."[99]

R. Aqiva responds by interpreting Tarfon's testimony as an exception that proves the rule. R. Tarfon concurs. Aqiva is portrayed as better understanding priestly halakhah than priests themselves do.[100] Despite a clearly pro-Aqivan bias of the final redaction of our story, its presentation of R. Tarfon's opinion is characteristic. He argues halakhah based on the practice of his family, which he himself observed in the Temple. A pro-Aqivan editor responds to this claim to authority that with proper interpretation this precedent-based approach can be essentially explained away and included into an abstract legal construct of later rabbis. The two approaches to the law clash and the Aqivan approach proves victorious. The halakhah of R. Tarfon embodied in the practices of his family proves no match to the abstract reasoning of R. Aqiva. The paradigmatic significance of this passage is such that possibly R. Tarfon stands here for an entire tradition of precedent-based approach to the Jewish law associated here with the priests.[101]

---

[98] See Gereboff, *Rabbi Tarfon*, 102–04, for discussion.
[99] Sifre Num. 75 (Horowitz, 70).
[100] Cf. Hezser, *Social Structure*, 268, for a similar observation.
[101] T Zebah. 1:8 (cf. Sifra Wayikra 4:4–5 [Weiss, 6a]) transmits another debate between R. Aqiva and R. Tarfon constructed along similar lines. There R. Aqiva

R. Tarfon was singled out to personify a precedent-based priestly halakah for a reason. The most explicit example of the relationship between the general halakhah and private practice of R. Tarfon comes from the following story:

> Said R. Judah, "I was spending the Sabbath, and I went to visit R. Tarfon at his home. He said to me, 'Judah, my son, give me my sandal,' and I gave it to him.
>
> He stretched out his hand to the window and he took a staff from there. He said to me, 'My son, with this I have purified three lepers, and I have taught with it seven laws:[102]
>
> That it is made from cypress wood; and its top is smoothed and planed; and its length is a cubit; and its thickness is one-quarter of the thickness of the leg of a bed, one divided into two, and [then] two into four; they sprinkle once, they do it a second time, they do it a third time [with the same piece of cedar wood]; and they purify both while the House [the Temple] is standing and not while the House [the Temple] is standing; and they purify in the provinces [outside of Jerusalem].' "[103]

R. Judah comes to visit R. Tarfon on Sabbath and incidentally learns laws of purification by simply observing the staff with which his master purified "three lepers." When the story talks about Judah giving sandals to R. Tarfon, it clearly reflects the household setting of early rabbinic instruction and the status of a disciple as a subservient member of his master's household. The student acts as R. Tarfon's appren-

---

discusses technical aspects of priestly service solely based on exegesis of Lev 1:5 and Exod 40:15. R. Tarfon objects to him by saying that he has heard a tradition that appears to contradict R. Aqiva's words. In this case, R. Tarfon does not explicitly refer to his own experience, but it is probably implied. The tradition apparently belongs to the professional priestly halakhah, which R. Tarfon knows by virtue of being a priest. R. Aqiva, however, explains this tradition in a way that does not contradict his earlier scriptural exegesis. At the end, R. Tarfon acknowledges that he "heard [the tradition] and could not explain [it]," whereas R. Aqiva "expounds it so that it accords with the law." He thus recognizes the supremacy of R. Aqiva's abstract knowledge and hermeneutic skills over his practical knowledge of the ancestral priestly halakhah. The story addresses the same issue as T Sot. 7:16 and most probably belongs to the same editorial circles. A. Yadin, *Scripture as Logos: Rabbi Ismael and the Origins of Midrash* (Philadelphia: University of Pennsylvania Press, 2004), 151–52, makes a similar observation on this passage in the Sifra: "focusing on the interpretive dynamic between Rabbi Aqiva and Rabbi Tarfon, the derashah contrasts the latter's authority as an eyewitness to the Temple service to the former's interpretive acumen." See further Gereboff, *Rabbi Tarfon*, 135. I do not agree with him, however, that "Tarfon serves merely as a literary device in this pericope."

[102] Or it may be R. Judah himself who speaks: "And I have learned from it seven laws." The Hebrew is ambiguous.

[103] T Neg. 8:2 (= Sifra Metsora 1:13 [Weiss, 70a]).

tice, while his knowledge of halakhah comes from familiarity with R. Tarfon's practices.[104] There is no indication of formal transmission of abstract halakhic knowledge anywhere in this story. On the contrary, R. Judah receives the knowledge he needs by observing and discussing a staff with which his master "purified three lepers." The study of Torah amounts to careful observation and interpretation of R. Tarfon's priestly practices and even tools with which these practices are performed. The instruction deals with the form of the staff, its use during the purification ceremony, and the claim that priests have the exclusive right to purify lepers even after the destruction of the temple (once again based on R. Tarfon's own practice). All this knowledge is transmitted as part of household priestly halakhah, which a student may receive only if he himself has become a member of the priest's household, as R. Judah has.[105]

R. Tarfon's practices are referred to on a number of other occasions. As a priest, he redeems the first-born and his particular way of doing that is taken as halakhically authoritative.[106] He also eats heave offering describing this practice as a sacred act equivalent in its sanctity to the Temple service:

> They said about R. Tarfon that he used to eat heave offering in the morning, and he would say, "I have sacrificed the daily morning sacrifice." And he would eat heave offering at dusk, and he would say, "I have sacrificed the daily afternoon offering."

---

[104] On this mode of discipleship see further Aberbach, "Relations between Master and Disciple in the Talmudic Age," 202–25. Cf. Hezser, *Social Structure*, 332–36, and Sivertsev, *Private Households*, 125–31.

[105] R. Judah transmits several traditions, which he has learned by closely observing R. Tarfon's halakhic routine. In T Yebam. 12:15 (= Sifre Deut. 291) he describes how R. Tarfon told his students to recite the verse from Deut 25:10 during a *halitsah* ceremony. This practice contradicts an anonymous halakhah that exempts students from doing so. On several occasions other rabbis (and R. Yose in particular) question the validity of R. Judah's tradition received in such a way. See M Ned. 6:6, T Sheb. 4:4, and T Bek. 5:6–7. To prove that a minor can read the *Megillah*, R. Judah refers to his own experience of reading the *Megillah* before R. Tarfon while still a minor. Other rabbis put in doubt the halakhic validity of this testimony. See T Meg. 2:8.

[106] T Bek. 6:14. Gereboff, *Rabbi Tarfon*, 388–89, emphasizes the importance of priesthood-related laws in R. Tarfon's legal agenda. In these cases, R. Tarfon consistently rules in favor of priests thus confirming a tannaitic observation that priests tend to interpret the Torah to benefit themselves (M Sheqal. 1:4). In fact, many of his rulings may be just that: remnants of the priestly halakhah. Cf. Schwartz, *Josephus and Judaean Politics*, 104–05.

> And from where do we know that the eating of sanctified food by
> the priests within the boundaries [of the Land of Israel] is equal to
> the Temple service?
> For it says, "I give you the priesthood as the service of gift" (Num.
> 18:7).[107]

In these practices R. Tarfon undoubtedly reflects the halakhic lore of
priestly families that had to adjust in the aftermath of the Destruction.
The latter incident is reported in connection with Rabban Gamaliel,
who asks why R. Tarfon is late to a session in bet midrash:

> R. Tarfon was late in coming to the Bet Midrash.
> Said to him Rabban Gamaliel, "Why did you see [fit] to be late?"
> He said to him, "[I was late] because I was performing Temple
> service."
> He said to him, "Indeed all your words are mysteries. For is there
> now Temple service?"
> He said to him, "Lo, it [Scripture] says, 'I give you priesthood as
> a service of gift' (Num. 18:7). [Scripture says it] so as to make the
> eating of heave-offering within the boundaries [of the Land of Israel]
> equivalent to the service in the Temple.[108]

This story may be another indication of close social interaction
between Rabban Gamaliel and priestly households. More importantly,
R. Tarfon's response implies that eating heave offering has the same
status in respect to Torah study as instruction in the bet midrash.
By eating heave offering, priests perform Torah in the absence of
the Temple. They also teach their version of Jewish law by doing
so, just as R. Tarfon taught seven laws with his staff in the previous story. The setting for this performance is one's household. In
other words, R. Tarfon once again describes halakhah as embodied
in household practices and contrasts it with study of the laws in bet
midrash. According to him the true setting for the law is in practical household halakhah, not in the study session. This approach is
consistent with what we have observed so far regarding R. Tarfon's
approach to Jewish law and the differences between his approach
and the more "impersonal" and distanced approach to the law by
the later editors of the Mishnah.[109]

---

[107] Sifre Zutta 18:7 (Horowitz, 293).
[108] Sifre Num. 116 (Horowitz, 133).
[109] Sifre Deut. 41 (Finkelstein, 85) tells about a discussion among three rabbis
about whether deed or learning is greater. According to R. Tarfon, deed is greater.
According to R. Aqiva, learning is greater. The story, quite predictably, sides with

Priestly Laws and Priestly Families in the Post-70 Period

Before we conclude, it would be worthwhile to compare the scope of tannaitic decisions to those rendered by priestly courts in approximately the same period. The existence of an independent system of priestly legislation at least during the first decades after the destruction of the temple has been convincingly argued by a number of scholars.[110] The paucity of information on these courts prevents us from reaching any definitive conclusions. Still, tannaitic texts occasionally indicate that there was an alternative system of priestly halakhah functioning alongside that of the rabbis. The application of this halakhah seems to have been limited to priestly families and most of the cases associated with it belonged to the realm of family law.[111] According to several tannaitic texts priests as a group followed certain laws and/or legal principles. Thus the Tosefta reports a disagreement between R. Aqiva and R. Ishmael about the time of finishing certain domestic activities on Friday afternoon. It concludes by observing that "the priests customarily do according to the words of R. Ishmael."[112] Priests are also reported to have interpreted the requirement to pay the Temple tax in Lev 6:16 for their own benefit. They did not see it as obligatory for them but required it for

---

R. Aqiva and further elaborates his statement. It is important to notice, however, that R. Tarfon's statement is in full agreement with his understanding of halakhah. It is transmitted and ensouled through one's deeds and practices, not through abstract study in bet midrash. On the two editorial layers of the story see Gereboff, *Rabbi Tarfon*, 251. The original story might have involved only R. Tarfon and R. Aqiva debating this issue "in the upper chamber of the house of Aris in Lydda." Cf. also R. Eleazar b. Azariah's statement in M 'Abot 3:17 that favors deeds over wisdom. As Zahavy, *Traditions of Eleazar Ben Azariah*, 145, observes, it may be reflective of Eleazar's priestly values.

[110] See for example Schwartz, *Josephus and Judaean Politics*, 105–09. Cf. Hezser, *Social Structure*, 480–89, and Cohen, "Rabbi in Second-Century Jewish Society," 942–43.

[111] I believe that our sources do not support a claim that post-70 priests vied for public power and leadership. They might have as well, but all sources reflecting priestly legislation of that period deal with family issues confined to priestly households. In this respect, priestly halakhah is very similar to that of early rabbis. Cf. Schwartz, *Josephus*, 106: "mishnah provides evidence that priests formed a separate body with their own rules, but not that they exerted authority over the population at large." For priests as an organized political power vying for control over Jewish society see R. Kimelman, "The Conflict between the Priestly Oligarchy and the Sages in the Talmudic Period (An Explication of PT *Shabbat* 12:3, 13C = *Horayot* 3:5, 48C)," *Zion* 48 (1983), 135–47 (in Hebrew).

[112] T 'Ed. 1:9.

everyone else.[113] In both cases priests emerge as an anonymous social group sharing certain perspectives on the law. Each case deals with a set of rules regulating particular household practices, such as household work on Sabbath eve or payment of the Temple tax. Similarly to early rabbinic halakhah, priestly traditions appear to have belonged to the realm of household traditions regulating everyday lives of priestly families.

Indeed, our sources contain several case-stories supporting this conclusion. Thus according to M Ketub. 1:5 a priestly court required that a ketubah (marriage contract) of a virgin was worth four hundred *zuz* (against only two hundred in rabbinic halakhah). M Sanhedrin 7:2 describes what appears to be a priestly court of the pre-70 period executing a promiscuous daughter of a priest in a way prohibited by rabbinic law. According to a series of traditions in M 'Ed. 8:2–3, priests take a more stringent view than rabbis and do not follow rabbinic halakhah in the case of genealogical uncertainty about a prospective bride. According to M 'Ed. 8:2:

> Rabbi Yosi the Priest and Rabbi Zechariah ben HaKatsab testified about a young girl who was left as a pledge in Ashkelon, that the members of her family (בני משפחתה) kept her far from them, although she had witnesses who testified that she had not secluded herself [with any man], and thereby been defiled. The sages said to them, "If you believe that she was left as a pledge, believe also that she had not secluded herself and that she had not been defiled. But if you do not believe that she had not secluded herself and that she had not been defiled, do not believe that she was left as a pledge.

In this case, Rabbi Yosi the Priest and Rabbi Zechariah b. HaKatsab (a butcher?) make a legal testimony based on the practice of a particular priestly family. The practice was apparently deemed authoritative, at least among other priests. That is why the two named rabbis (apparently, priests themselves) refer to it as a valid legal precedent. The anonymous sages, however, reject this case as a basis for more general legislation. Interestingly enough, they do it not because they reject the validity of inferring general halakhah from practices of a household but because they view this particular practice as flawed and inconsistent. This debate is preceded by another testimony of a similar kind made by R. Judah b. Baba and R. Judah the Priest. They testified about a minor, the daughter of an Israelite married

to a priest, that she could eat terumah as soon as she entered the
bridal chamber, even though she did not have marital intercourse.
This statement, although apparently derived from the same law of
priestly families as the later one, did not produce the same kind of
a debate and was accepted as authoritative by other sages. In other
words, legal practices of priestly households could be seen as sources
of authoritative halakhah even by the mishnaic authorities, not to
mention other (although not necessarily all) priestly families.

On the other hand, M 'Ed. 8:3 may reflect possible conflicts not
just between sages and legal practices of priestly families, but between
practices of various priestly families themselves:

> Rabbi Joshua and Rabbi Judah ben Bathyra testified that the widow
> of one who belonged to an *'Issah* family (a family of doubtful stock)
> was eligible to marry a priest, since the members of *'Issah* family were
> qualified to testify about which of themselves is clean or unclean, and
> which must be put away, and which may be brought near.
>
> Rabban Simeon b. Gamaliel said, "We accept your testimony, but
> what shall we do? For Rabban Yohanan ben Zakkai decreed that
> courts may not be set up concerning this matter. The priests would
> listen to you in what concerns putting away, but not in what concerns
> bringing near.

It is not immediately clear whether or not R. Joshua's and R. Judah's
testimony reflects the actual practice of some priestly families opposed
by other priests. If indeed it does, the story reflects a split within
the priesthood over different understandings of the purity law, something that was attested during most of the Second Temple period
and in many cases evolved into sectarian antagonism.[114] Alternatively,
it may merely reflect a rabbinic attempt to control priestly family
law. Rabban Gamaliel admits the testimony but cautions that "the
priests" probably will not. Once again, the law appears to be determined within individual families according to their legal practices.
Rabbis had to decide which of those practices they wanted to follow
as their halakhah but could not impose their rulings on priestly families. M 'Ed. 8:7 concludes the entire debate by a colorful eschatological
prediction that Elijah will come to "put away those who have been
brought near by force and to bring near those who have been put
away by force. The family of Beth Zerephah was on the other side

---

of the Jordan and Ben Zion put it away by force, and yet another family was there and Ben Zion brought it near by force." This story reflects, among other things, the arbitrary nature of legal practices as they were shaped in the priestly families. Still, it also tacitly admits their legal validity, at least as far as this age is concerned.[115]

Even when priestly legal activity seems to address issues of public interest, it still may be more reflective of internal halakhah of priestly families. M Rosh Hashanah 1:7 describes practices of a priestly court intercalating the calendar:

> A father and his son who saw the New Moon, they should [both] go [to bear witness], not because they can join with each other [to give testimony as a valid pair of witnesses], but if one of them becomes disqualified, the second may join with another witness.
> R. Shimon says, "A father and his son and all relatives are valid for the testimony of the New Moon."
> R. Yose said, "It once happened that Tobiah the physician saw the New Moon in Jerusalem, he and his son and his freed slave. And the priests accepted him and his son, but disqualified his slave. And when they came before the court, they accepted him and his slave, but disqualified his son."

Although this story may be interpreted as an indication of a post-70 power struggle between rabbis and priests vying for control over the calendar and thus for a dominant position in Jewish society, there are several problems with such an interpretation. First, it is far from clear that the event described in the story took place after the destruction of the Temple and not prior to it. Second, the story illustrates the eligibility of various family members to confirm each other's testimony about the New Moon. Thus it may be just another account of priestly family halakhah detailing religious duties of a household. In this case, priests differed from rabbinic halakhah over who in the household could testify about the New Moon. But the focus of the halakhah was once again on the household and religious responsibilities of its members. As a whole, the bits and pieces of information about priestly halakhah available to us portray it as functioning along the same lines as early rabbinic law. In both cases we have household

---

[115] Satlow, *Jewish Marriage*, 150–51, discusses the development of this tradition in the Amoraic period, when it was used to illustrate rabbis' knowledge of (potentially damaging) facts about priestly genealogies. Rabbis perceived control over priestly family legislation as a source of major social and political clout.

legal traditions (ancestral "traditions of the fathers") shared and followed by particular social groups within Israel. In both cases the family and its everyday concerns represent a prime setting of legal decisions. Both priestly halakhah and early rabbinic law represent a transition from ancestral "traditions of the fathers" to the increasingly more abstract and apodictic legal system of mishnaic Judaism.

Conclusions

Household-based halakhic practices played an important role in the formative stages of post-Destruction Rabbinic Judaism. They were associated with both lay and priestly households. In many cases the origins of these households can be traced back to the Second Temple times. On a number of occasions there is a clear continuity between the familial halakhic traditions of Jewish sectarian movements and those of the nascent rabbinic movement. At the same time, these traditions were becoming increasingly detached from their household carriers as they moved from the realm of family lore into the realm of teachings transmitted within disciple circles. This process would eventually produce the foundational texts and ethos of classical Rabbinic Judaism, which both limited and affirmed the religious role of households. They remained an important part of the rabbinic religious universe, but predominantly as objects of scholastic "holiness discourse," not as full-fledged participants in it. The complexity of relationships between the utopian piety of rabbinic disciple circles and the traditionalist familial piety inherited from the Pharisees and other pre-70 groups would eventually account for the creative richness of mature Rabbinic Judaism.

TANNAITIC CASE STORIES AND THE ROLE OF
FAMILIES IN THE EARLY RABBINIC MOVEMENT

In his detailed discussion of the types of legal issues addressed by
early rabbis, Shaye Cohen has observed that most cases dealt with
either purity issues or family law. The latter included "marriage,
divorce, and levirate marriage, especially the ability of a woman to
marry after her husband's presumed but unverifiable death." Other
types of cases occasionally addressed by the rabbis (but in much
smaller proportion compared to the first two categories) included
oaths and vows, avoidance of idolatry, agricultural tithes, and priestly
offerings. A relatively small number of cases had to do with civil
law, Shabbat laws (especially the laws of *'eruv*), kosher slaughtering,
and festivals.[1] Later, Catherine Hezser has confirmed this distribution of legal cases in tannaitic texts, especially noticing the importance of family law.[2] Both studies have indicated the relatively limited
and selective nature of legal issues addressed by the early rabbis. As
Cohen has summarized, "the rabbis before Judah the Patriarch were
acknowledged experts in the laws of purity and personal status, legal
relics of the sectarian past of the rabbinic movement."[3] This observation is clearly in agreement with Jacob Neusner's theory about the
continuity of legal interests between the Second Temple Pharisees
and the early generations of post-70 rabbis.[4]

I would like to continue this discussion along the lines already
indicated in the previous chapters of this book. Most of the cases

---

[1] Cohen, "Rabbi in Second-Century Jewish Society," 968. I will use Cohen's list
of tannaitic case-stories, appearing on pp. 980–87 as a basis for my discussion.

[2] Hezser, *Social Structure*, 361.

[3] Cohen, "Rabbi in Second-Century Jewish Society," 969.

[4] Neusner, *Judaism: The Evidence of the Mishnah*, 95–97 and 101–110. For a specific
example see his discussion of R. Eliezer in J. Neusner, *Eliezer Ben Hyrcanus: The
Tradition and the Man* (Leiden: Brill, 1973), vol. 2, 298–307. Arguing from his legal
traditions, Neusner sees R. Eliezer as a transitional figure between pre-70 Pharisees
and post-70 rabbis. Cf. B.Z. Bokser, *Pharisaic Judaism in Transition: R. Eliezer the Great
and Jewish Reconstruction after the War with Rome* (New York: Bloch, 1935), 87–116.
He emphasizes R. Eliezer's conservatism and adherence to the patriarchal ideals of
a wealthy landowner.

addressed by tannaitic rabbis belonged to the realm of family law broadly understood.[5] When rabbis were approached by someone else, they almost always were approached as experts in one or another aspect of family law. Most of the cases dealing with either purity or agricultural laws were in fact related to family law since they had to do with the proper functioning of a Jewish household. In other words, we have to understand family law not in the narrow sense of marriage, divorce, and levirate marriage legislation, but in the broader sense of household halakah allowing for the proper religious life of a Jewish family. Most of the tannaitic case stories dealt with exactly this kind of legislation. The legal interests of the early tannaitic movement, reflected in case-stories, were centered around the household halakhah. Most of these stories preserved very vague information about those who approached rabbis seeking their advice. Still, upon close examination we can reach certain conclusions about the social background of these people. Almost always, they can be identified as householders of certain means, concerned about the everyday religious life of their families. They would usually ask very practical and ad hoc questions in the realm of household halakhah. The individual family and its halakhic concerns remained the key social reference within these stories. Questions arrived at in the process of everyday family life formed the core of tannaitic case-stories and rabbinic self-representation.[6]

As both Cohen and Hezser have observed, issues of marriage, divorce, and levirate marriage play a significant role in tannaitic case stories. Rabbis were repeatedly approached about circumstances under

---

[5] Baker, *Rebuilding the House of Israel*, 34–47, 77–94, and 114–22, convincingly demonstrates that our distinction between "private" and "public" space is essentially inapplicable to early rabbinic literature and to Jewish life in second and third century Galilee as a whole. See also C. Hezser, "'Privat' und 'öffentlich' im Talmud Yerushalmi und in der griechisch-römischen Antike," in P. Schäfer, ed., *The Talmud Yerushalmi and Graeco-Roman Culture* (Tübingen: Mohr Siebeck, 1998), vol. 1, 423–579. Cf. M. Peskowitz, "'Family/ies' in Antiquity: Evidence from Tannaitic Literature and Roman Galilean Architecture," in S. Cohen, *Jewish Family in Antiquity*, 24–34 and see n. 56 below.

[6] On case stories in the Mishnah and their literary characteristics see Goldberg, "Form und Funktion des Ma'ase in der Mischna," 1–38. Cf. Hezser, *Form, Function and Historical Significance*, 283–92. It remains unclear whether these stories are historical accounts (as Cohen seems to assume) or represent literary constructs and rhetorical exercises. In either case, however, they reflect a particular reality, either historical or imaginative. We shall study precisely this reality and what it may tell us about the setting of the early rabbinic movement.

which remarriage would be possible. Most of the cases had to do with various types of testimony about the death of one's husband, allowing a woman to remarry.[7] The format of the writ of divorce was another issue addressed by the rabbis: the format of some writs was deemed unacceptable,[8] writs produced abroad required special confirmation,[9] and not all witnesses could be accepted as reliable.[10] A special case concerned a woman and her former husband who continued to have sexual relations after their divorce. The rabbis decided that they did not need another writ of divorce.[11] Finally, cases involving levirate marriage and especially the rite of *halitsah* feature prominently in this type of story. Rabbis would often supervise *halitsah* ceremonies, but how "formal" these ceremonies were remains unclear.[12] In fact, there are indications that at least in some cases the ceremony was fairly informal and private.[13] A rabbi's involvement was indicative of his informal connections with the household in which the ceremony took place rather than his official authority to supervise such procedures. All this evidence indicates that the early rabbinic movement functioned as a network of households following similar halakhic standards in their everyday lives.[14]

In addition, the tannaitic corpus of legal narratives contains a relatively large number of case-stories involving relationships between parents and their children or between masters and slaves. Thus, when a child dedicated a spade to heaven, his father brought him to R. Aqiva to make sure that the boy properly understood his vow.[15] Several stories concern the menstrual impurity of minors.[16] One story

---

[7] See for example M Yebam. 16:4 and 6. Cf. T Yebam. 14:7–8 and 10, 16:7.

[8] T Git. 2:10.

[9] M Git. 1:3.

[10] M Git. 1:5.

[11] T Git. 5:4.

[12] See for example M Yebam. 12:6 and T Yebam. 12:15. In both cases rabbis establish legal precedents by their particular ways of supervising the ceremony. In M Yebam. 12:5, R. Aqiva confirms *halitsah* done in prison without formal supervision.

[13] T Yebam. 12:9 mentions that R. Ishmael supervised a *halitsah* ceremony alone at night.

[14] Satlow, *Jewish Marriage in Antiquity*, 68–89, demonstrates just how much Jewish marriage was a family affair dominated by customary law. In this respect, it corresponded to Greco-Roman perspectives on marriage. According to them, "marriage, and its definition, were largely family affairs, left to the families and their male heads (*paterfamilias*) to arbitrate" (Satlow, 74).

[15] T Nid. 5:16.

[16] T Nid. 5:14 and 6:3. Cf. T Nid. 7:3.

deals with a raped girl's eligibility to marry a priest.[17] Most probably, children's parents initiated these inquiries as well in order to resolve issues emerging within their households. At least two stories deal with the issue of circumcision when it may put a child's life in danger:

> It once happened with four sisters in Sepphoris: the son of the first was circumcised and died, the second—and he died, the third—and he died. The case came before sages, they said: "The fourth should not be circumcised.
>
> Said R. Nathan, "When I was in Caesarea Mazaca in Cappadocia, there was one woman there who gave birth to male children, who were circumcised and died. She circumcised the first and he died, the second—and he died. The third she brought before me. I saw that he was pale. I examined him and did not find in him "blood of the covenant" [enough blood to perform circumcision]. They said to me, 'How shall we circumcise him?' I said to them, 'Wait on him until blood enters into him.' They waited on him and circumcised him and he lived, and they called him, 'Nathan the Babylonian' in my name."[18]

Both stories address the problem of circumcising a child if his cousins or brothers died from circumcision. The first story prohibits such a child from being circumcised. The second story qualifies this decision by quoting an example of R. Nathan, who told parents to wait until their child passes through a certain medical condition and then to circumcise him. The family life and its concerns provide a backdrop for both narratives. Rabbis advise two Jewish households about what to do under extraordinary circumstances. The parents apparently initiated inquiries in both cases to ascertain both the physical and religious wellbeing of their children. In both cases rabbis acted as informal advisors whose knowledge of the Jewish law was relied upon by other Jews. In another story rabbis appear as experts on the question of conversion of the maidservants of one Valeria to Judaism and their subsequent manumission.[19] Valeria's household provides an immediate setting for this relatively rare example of rabbinic involvement with a Jewish conversion ceremony.[20]

Oaths and their annulment represent another significant category of family law occasionally addressed by rabbis. Most of the tannaitic

---

[17] M Ketub. 1:10.
[18] T Shabb. 15:8.
[19] Mek. Pisha 15 (Horowitz-Rabin, 57).
[20] On the somewhat ambiguous attitude of early rabbis toward converts and conversion see Cohen, *Beginnings of Jewishness*, 324–40, and "Rabbi in Second-Century Jewish Society," 944–45.

case-stories involving oaths take place within a household. They usually result from an unwise decision of one of the family's members to make an oath not to derive benefit from other family members. A husband swears not to derive benefit from his wife.[21] A father finds himself under oath not to derive benefit from his son.[22] But there are other cases as well. A man prohibits his wife under oath from going to Jerusalem.[23] An intoxicated woman, apparently during a banquet, makes a vow to become a Nazirite.[24] A woman, troubled by her son, swears to marry the first available man and finds herself in trouble when two unsuitable men ask to marry her.[25] Rabbis seek to annul most of these vows, thus restoring peace to the household. All these cases address concerns of particular households and have an articulated family setting. By addressing them, rabbis tried to help relationships within families by peacefully resolving internal frictions of a religious nature:

> It once happened that a man vowed to have no benefit [i.e. not to marry—A.S.] from his sister's daughter. They brought her to R. Ishmael's house, and he made her beautiful.
>   Said to him R. Ishmael, "My son, did you make an oath concerning this one?"
>   He said to him, "No."
>   And R. Ishmael permitted him [to marry her].[26]

The man who vows not to marry his niece is apparently a friend or maybe even a relative of R. Ishmael. The latter brings up the girl in question in his household and makes her attractive for her prospective husband. Afterwards R. Ishmael releases him from a hastily made oath. This story reflects a household setting of the halakhic problem solved by R. Ishmael. This halakhic problem is a family affair that threatens peace and stability within the household. To resolve the crisis R. Ishmael acts not as a judge but as a family friend (perhaps, relative?) taking the girl under his wing. The entire affair has a markedly family setting. By resolving the prospective husband's oath, R. Ishmael continues to act as an informal family arbitrator, in fact,

---

[21] M Ned. 9:5.
[22] M Ned. 5:6.
[23] T Ned. 5:1.
[24] M Naz. 2:3.
[25] T B. Qam. 8:16.
[26] M Ned. 9:10.

as a *paterfamilias* establishing peace and justice among his friends, relatives, and clients. The legal authority of R. Ishmael comes from
his status within his own household and recognition of this status by
other families. The halakhic practice of R. Ishmael is that of *paterfamilias* acting on an informal but nevertheless very efficient level of
family arbitration.

Many case-stories dealing with purity laws also have an easily
identifiable family setting. In most cases, women who are concerned
about their purity status approach rabbis to get expert advice.[27] Most
of the cases addressed in this context have to do specifically with
menstrual impurity and its implications for family life. Women tend
to approach rabbis to resolve dubious or extraordinary cases. At least
some stories presuppose a certain knowledge on their part about the
basics of the relevant halakhah.[28] A couple of cases that deal with
the impurity resulting from miscarriage also come from the family
setting.[29] Several cases address the susceptibility to impurity of various household utensils.[30] A relatively large group of cases deals with
various aspects of constructing and using ritual baths (*miqvaot*).[31]
Finally, a number of cases reflect the purity concerns of priestly
households and apparently come from them.[32] At any rate, most of
the purity related case-stories reflect a household setting. They are
not directly related to the temple and the purity of its sacred space,
although they may have temple-related considerations in the background. Even the cases that involve priests emerge from a family
setting and not from that of the temple per se.

Very few case-stories involving purity issues provide information
about their social setting. But when they do, the household setting
clearly dominates:

> One woman was weaving a cloth in cleanness, and she came before
> R. Ishmael for inspection. She said to him, "Rabbi, I know that the
> cloth was not made unclean, but it was not in my heart to guard it

---

[27] M Nid. 8:3. Cf. T Nid. 1:9 and 6:17.

[28] Women from rabbinic households were expected to have substantial knowledge of purity laws in general and menstrual impurity laws in particular. See Wegner,
Chattel or Person, 162–65.

[29] T Nid. 4:3–4. The case comes before R. Tsadoq.

[30] T Kelim B. Bat. 2:1–2.

[31] M Miqw. 7:1, T Miqw. 4:6 and 7:10–11 (cf. Sifre Num. 124 [Horowitz, 158]).

[32] T 'Ohal. 16:13 (a priest looks into a cistern, into which the servant-girl of an
olive-farmer [apparently, his neighbor] has thrown her dead baby). T Bek. 5:6–7
(R. Tarfon decides if a birth-deformity of a priest renders him unfit).

[from impurity]." In the course of the questions which R. Ishmael asked her, she said to him, "Rabbi, I know that a menstruating woman came and pulled the rope with me." Said R. Ishmael, "How great are the words of the sages, who used to say, 'If one did not intend to guard it, it is unclean.' "[33]

The woman's inquiry to R. Ishamel comes from her concern about her purity status as a result of participating in a particular type of household work (weaving). Although she herself was ritually pure, she did not have intent to guard herself from coming into contact with impure objects. In the course of questioning, R. Ishmael realizes that the woman indeed was in contact with another woman who helped her with the weaving and who was menstrually unclean. Similar to the story discussed above, this one provides us with a glimpse into the household setting of many (if not most) of the tannaitic case-stories dealing with purity laws. The question to R. Ishmael emerged from a household setting as a result of performance of household work. The question itself comes from a female member of the family (her precise identity is unclear) and presupposes certain knowledge of halakhah on her part. Indeed, R. Ishmael praises the woman's attentiveness to what may seem an excessively strict point of purity law.

Early rabbinic case-stories address various aspects of agricultural halakhah. Rabbis are consulted about the permissibility of mixed plantings under certain circumstances (mixed plantings in a vineyard are especially prominent).[34] The issue of tithing and handling of tithed produce as opposed to non-sanctified produce is another subject of inquiries. A number of Jewish households apparently continued to observe laws of tithing even after the destruction of the temple. Rabbis were often approached as experts in the issue of proper tithing and subsequent handling of agricultural products.[35] The proper handling of priestly heave-offerings constituted a related issue. Once again, householders who wanted to ensure the sanctity of their produce probably initiated inquires.[36] Purity laws related to agricultural produce, especially products of the vine, constituted another area of

---

[33] T Kelim B. Bat. 1:2.
[34] M Kil. 4:9 and 7:5. Cf. T Kil. 2:12, 3:5 and 1:4.
[35] T Demai 4:13 and T Ma'as. Sh. 3:18.
[36] T Ter. 1:15 and 4:13. T Tehar. 8:15 deals with a woman who filtered pure and impure liquids into a jar of priestly offering. The story clearly presupposes a family setting. Cf. T Tehar. 6:1.

concern. Finally, rabbis were sometimes asked about specific application of the law of the Seventh year.[37] Overall, the agricultural laws
addressed by rabbis belong to the realm of household halakhah.
They reflect the interests and concerns of Jewish households trying
to sanctify their agricultural work by following a specific set of laws.
Most of these stories presuppose at least some knowledge on the part
of those who approached rabbis. Inquiries were usually made regarding special cases that did not fit a common pattern. Similar to family law and purity law, tannaitic agricultural law originally took shape
in the context of household practices and halakhic observances. It
was just another area of household practical law deemed to ensure
the righteousness and piety of individual Jewish families. Several stories explicitly identify their household setting, whereas others seem
to presuppose it:

> It once happened that Rabban Simeon b. Gamaliel and R. Judah and
> R. Yose entered the residence of a householder in Kezib (שנכנסו אצל
> בעל הבית לכזיב). They said, "We do not know how this householder
> prepares his produce."
>   When he sensed [their unease], he brought before them a chest full
> of gold dinars.
>   They said to him, "How do you prepare your produce?"
>   He said to them, "Like this: I say, 'The second tithe which is in
> this item is deconsecrated with this issar.'"
>   They said to him, "Go and eat your produce. You have gained the
> coins, but you have lost your life.[38]

Three rabbis visit a householder at Kezib. Before they can partake
of his hospitality they want to make sure that he consecrates his food
correctly by removing the second tithe. In the process of conversation it becomes clear that the householder removes the second tithe
but not in accordance with rabbinic norms. This leads to a sharp
rebuke from the rabbis. The entire story is presented as an informal
encounter and conversation among householders following slightly
different halakhic traditions. What appears to be a private visit to
an apparently affluent head of the family turns into a halakhic debate,
resulting from differences between halakhic practices of individual
households. Household practices and halakhic concerns thus constitute the matrix of early rabbinic legislation. During another similar

---

[37] T Sheb. 4:13. See also M Kil. 7:5.
[38] T Ma'as. Sh. 3:18.

encounter sages told a householder how to purify his field from bones scattered in it.[39] In yet another story sages visited a village of Mahoz and observed the local practice of wiping agricultural products with sand to render them clean. The sages told the people of Mahoz that because of this practice they had never eaten ritually pure food.[40] All these accounts demonstrate that agricultural laws addressed by early rabbis were part of local household halakhic practices designed to preserve the religious purity and piety of Jewish families.[41]

Although these stories divulge very little explicit information about the actual circumstances and identity of people approaching rabbis, almost always those who sought rabbis' help and advice turn out to be local householders making a private inquiry about certain aspects of practical halakhah. There is no indication that they approached rabbis as official religious authorities. Even when a man approaching sages is a local official, he seems to be acting as a private person:

> R. Judah said, "It once happened that Sebion chief of the synagogue of Kezib (ראש הכנסת של כזיב) bought a fourth[-year] vineyard in Syria from a gentile, and paid him for it. He came to ask Rabban Gamaliel, who was travelling from place to place.
>
> He [Gamaliel] said to him, 'Wait until we are [concerned] with halakhah.'
>
> He said to himself, 'There is proof from that.'
>
> But he sent him [a message] by a mute messenger, 'What you have done you have done, but do not teach to do so (לא תשנה לעשות כן).'"[42]

A head of the synagogue from Kezib approaches Rabban Gamaliel during his stay in the area to inquire if his purchase of a vineyard from a gentile in Syria violates the law of *'orlah*. Despite Sebion's official title, his inquiry concerns exclusively his private business. In fact, the title *rosh knesset* may be an honorific title of a local Jewish

---

[39] T 'Ohal. 16:11.

[40] M Maksh. 3:4.

[41] Shaye Cohen observes that prosperous landowners and heads of households constituted the backbone of the early rabbinic movement. Rabbinic legislation often reflects their biases and interests. See Cohen, "Rabbi in Second-Century Jewish Society," 930–36. Neusner, *Judaism*, 250–56, arrives at similar conclusions. Cf. Lapin, *Early Rabbinic Civil Law*, 233–34. Cohen's theory that prior to Judah the Prince the rabbinic movement was predominantly rural has to be revised in the light of the later research by Hezser and Lapin. See Hezser, *Social Structure*, 156–65, and H. Lapin, "Rabbis and Cities in Later Roman Palestine: The Literary Evidence," *JJS* 50 (1999), 187–207.

[42] T Ter. 2:13.

magnate rather than a designation of an official position.[43] The story tells us about a meeting of two respected and influential Jewish house-holders, one of whom tries to clarify a cumbersome halakhic issue.[44] Rabban Gamaliel's response reflects what we have already observed: household halakhic practices can easily become authoritative halakhic prescriptions, especially when they are the practices of a high-placed and socially influential local magnate and his household.[45] Rabban Gamaliel tries to make sure that this does not happen in the case of Sebion. He states that Sebion's purchase is permissible (since it already has happened anyhow) but as an exception and not as a rule. Sebion should not "teach" his one-time practice as an accept-able legal precedent. This story provides more evidence for the legal importance of individual halakhic practices and for the virtual lack of distinction between household law and public law in the early rabbinic tradition. It also illustrates the household setting of agri-cultural halakhah of early rabbis. Agricultural laws were part of fam-ily practices, and these laws entered rabbinic legislation in precisely such a capacity.

A separate category of case-stories deals with business and social interaction between Jews and gentiles. Most of these stories address the problem of using wine that has come into contact with gentiles and may be considered a sub-section of agricultural halakhah.[46] They also seem to have emerged in a household setting and reflect con-cerns of Jewish families about permissible degrees of social and eco-nomic interaction with their non-Jewish neighbors.[47] According to one story wine of a pagan libation accidentally dripped on a ship-ment of figs belonging to Boethus b. Zonen. The sages permitted the use of the figs after rinsing them.[48] Boethus b. Zonen is a well-

---

[43] This, probably, was the case in the Diaspora as well. See T. Rajak and D. Noy, "*Archisynagogoi*: Office, Title and Social Status in the Greco-Jewish Synagogue," *JRS* 83 (1993), 75–93.

[44] On Rabban Gamaliel's status as a civic magnate see Sivertsev, *Private Households*, 19–93. Cf. Jacobs, *Die Institution des jüdischen Patriarchen*, 124–205.

[45] T Naz. 5:1 identifies one R. Judah b. Patera of Ardaskis as a "head (*ha-rosh*), sitting and judging in the *halakhah*." In a dialogue that follows R. Meir commends him as "master of *halakhah*." The exact status of R. Judah remains unclear, although he apparently was a local authority of some sort. Indeed, his status may be close to that of Sebion. See further Hezser, *Social Structure* 286–87.

[46] M ʿAbod. Zar. 4:10 and 12. Cf. T ʿAbod. Zar. 7:4, 6, and 8.

[47] Cf. M ʿAbod. Zar. 1:4, which regulates commercial relations with businesses either decorated or not decorated for a pagan holiday. See also T ʿAbod. Zar. 4:11.

[48] M ʿAbod. Zar. 5:2.

known figure of early rabbinic narratives. He occasionally asked for rabbis' legal advice,[49] and his house served as an informal meeting place for the sages, who apparently frequented Boethus' social receptions and banquets.[50] Boethus b. Zonen thus represents a quintessential tannaitic householder of means, who is sympathetic to rabbis but apparently not a rabbi himself. His practices provide another example of a household halakhah making its way into the formal legislation of the later Mishnaic masters. Socially, Boethus b. Zonen seems to belong to the same group of relatively affluent local magnates as Sebion and Rabban Gamaliel did. All of them belonged to the new Jewish civic elite that had emerged after the destruction of the Temple and transformation of Judaea into a Roman province.[51] If this story is to be believed, in addition to being a landowner Boethus b. Zonen was apparently involved in some form of regional trade. It was in this capacity as a householder conducting his private business that Boethus encountered a halakhic difficulty, which he asked the sages to resolve. This account has a well-articulated household setting and can be compared to a well-known story of Rabban Gamaliel in Aphrodite's bath, analyzed by Seth Schwartz.[52] In both cases halakhic discussion emerges within a context of household practices of influential Jewish families. Both cases reflect a potential conflict between the observance of the Jewish law and cultural interaction with the surrounding non-Jewish society.

In those relatively rare cases when tannaitic case-stories address issues of civil law, they are predominantly concerned with resolving issues among members of the same household or among several households interacting in public space. The Tosefta tells a story about a man who was clearing stones away from his field by tossing them upon public property. A pious man (*hasid*) cursed him and his curse was fulfilled.[53] When a man bared a woman's head in public, thus assaulting her honor and presumably that of her family, R. Aqiva ordered him to pay a fine.[54] Other sages dealt with such issues as

---

[49] In addition to M ʿAbod. Zar. 5:2, see also M B. Metsiʿa 5:3 (which deals with the expropriation of a field from a debtor unable to pay back his debt).

[50] See T Pisha 10:12.

[51] For an attempt to reconstruct the "historical" Boethus based on rabbinic texts see J. Schwartz, "ʿAl Zonen u-Veno Baytos," *Sinai* 103 (1989), 108–22. Cf. further observations in Siversts ev, *Private Households*, 174–78.

[52] M ʿAbod. Zar. 3:4. See Schwartz, *Imperialism and Jewish Society*, 162–76.

[53] T B. Qam. 2:13.

[54] M B. Qam. 8:6.

rent of a bathhouse and loans.[55] All of them involved small business ownership, which was virtually indistinguishable from the family business. In Late Antiquity the family constituted the main unit of production and economic activity. Small businesses were usually family-operated.[56] In other words, the civic cases of tannaitic masters addressed the concerns of households involved in family trade. When R. Tarfon made commerce-related rulings in Lydda, he addressed local merchants and tried to change their practice of doing business. They at first accepted but then rejected his legal opinion.[57] Sometimes our texts explicitly contrast the halakhic opinions of individual sages with household practices in the area of civil law. Thus the Mishnah quotes an opinion of R. Eliezer prohibiting oral deathbed disposition of property, only to counter it with the following account:

> They said to him, "It once happened that the mother of the sons of Rokhel was sick and said, 'Give my veil to my daughter, and it was worth 12 maneh. And she died. And they carried out her words."
> He said to them, "May their mother bury the sons of Rokhel."[58]

The family setting of this story is obvious, although the issue at stake belongs to what we would describe as civil law. The Mishnah determines the validity of a deathbed oral ceremony on the basis of individual family practice contrasted with the opinion of R. Eliezer. The story indicates that rabbis perceived at least some aspects of the civil law as belonging to the realm of households and their practices.

Several tannaitic case-stories deal with Sabbath law. Most of them address the topic of ʿeruv, i.e., the creation of the common domain allowing people to carry items during the Sabbath. The very nature of the ʿeruv puts it into the category of household halkahah emerg-

---

[55] M B. Metsiʿa 8:8 and M B. Bat. 10:8.

[56] See Peskowitz, " 'Family/ies' in Antiquity," 24–34, and Baker, *Rebuilding the House of Israel*, 34–47, 77–94, and 114–22. Both authors correctly observe that the modern distinction between private and public space is inapplicable to social realities of Late Antiquity. They also cite evidence for the economic significance of Jewish households. Cf. Wegner, *Chattel or Person*, 126–27, on woman's eligibility to take an oath as a business partner. M Ketub. 9:4 envisions a household-operated small business (such as stallkeeping), in which all family members play a role. Wegner's cut and dried distinction between public and private space cannot be upheld in light of her own evidence. On the Jewish family in Late Antiquity as the main unit of (re)production see further Satlow, *Jewish Marriage in Antiquity*, 12–21.

[57] M B. Metsiʿa 4:3.

[58] M B. Bat. 9:7.

ing as a result of the cooperation of several families.[59] Most of the cases dealing with *'eruv* seem to focus on the technical details of constructing the Sabbath perimeter. Variations in these details reflect varieties of local customs and demonstrate just how much the rabbinic halakhah was dependent on local customary laws. We learn, for example, about a local practice of constructing the *'eruv* at the synagogue in Tiberias, which was frowned upon by Rabban Gamaliel and the elders visiting the city. Apparently, it was different from their tradition.[60] On the other hand, R. Judah the Prince determined the Sabbath limits of the town of Magdala following the testimony of a local shepherd about the local practice to go as far as the outskirts of a neighboring town (Hammatha) on the Sabbath.[61] In other words, according to the custom of the people of Magdala, the outskirts of Hammatha belonged to the Sabbath travel limit. But the same text states that, according to the Hammatha's custom, Magdala was beyond the Sabbath limit, and so the people from Hammatha would not go to Magdala. The significance of local halakhic practices becomes obvious in this story. Early rabbinic halakhah was a strictly local phenomenon, determined by local practices either on the level of an individual family or on the level of an individual community. The later Mishnaic tradition emerged as a result of the constant interaction and mutual modification of these practices.[62]

In addition to the customary law of local communities, tannaitic texts occasionally refer to the family halakhah of individual households:

> It once happened that R. Eliezer went to Joseph b. Peredah in Ublin. And he saw that he had an alley-entry with only a single sidepost.
> He said to him, "Make a second for it."
> He said to him, "Do you instruct me to close it up?"
> He said to him, "Let it be closed up. On what basis do you spend Sabbath in such wise!"[63]

---

[59] See helpful remarks in Baker, *Rebuilding the House of Israel*, 119–20.

[60] M 'Erub. 10:10.

[61] T 'Erub. 4:16.

[62] In T 'Ohal. 18:18 the sages declare Ashkelon to be a part of the Land of Israel regarding ritual purity based on local halakhic practices. Cf. J Shebi'it 6:1 (36c) and J Yebamot 7:2 (8a), versions of the story where the importance of local practices is even more articulated. On a similar basis, certain areas were exempted from the laws of the Seventh Year. See J Demai 2:1 (22c).

[63] T 'Erub. 1:2.

The story tells about R. Eliezer visiting one Joseph b. Peredah in the town of Abelin and observing his practice of building the *ʿeruv*. R. Eliezer disagrees and suggests a different way of building it. Once again, we observe here an encounter of two slightly different practices of building the Sabbath perimeter. Joseph b. Peredah follows his household halakhah, whereas R. Eliezer follows his. We do not know if R. Eliezer was successful in convincing Joseph to give up his halakhic custom. At any rate, the story reflects the role of household practices in the domain of Sabbath observance. Customary practices played a crucial role not only on the level of town and village communities, but on the level of households as well. Tannaitic case-stories are occasionally constructed around a rabbi encountering a local practice different from his own and dealing with it in one way or another.

A special group of stories comprises cases in which a rabbi introduces changes into local ritual and liturgical practices. Sometimes this happens as a result of a rabbi simply performing a new ritual or saying a new prayer. Thus R. Halapta and R. Hananya would institute a special way of blowing a shofar on the fast day in local communities at Sepphoris and Sikni respectively.[64] R. Tarfon prohibited the men of Lydda from eulogizing a local dignitary (?), Aleksa, because it was a holiday.[65] R. Eliezer and R. Joshua opposed the decision of men at Lydda to decree a fast on Hanukkah.[66] It is not clear if their protests were heard. What we encounter in most of these stories is a conflict between the practices and halakhic opinions of individual rabbis and the local practices of various communities in the Land of Israel. The stories are extremely vague about the identity of the rabbis' opponents. They are usually referred to as "men of such-and-such place" or simply "they." But the anonymous "they" most probably designates a sum total of householders constituting a particular Jewish community. Rabbinic households occasionally dissent from a common decision to decree a fast or to say prayers in a particular way. In the story about R. Eliezer and R. Joshua disagreeing with the people of Lydda, who had decreed a fast on Hanukkah, the two rabbis demonstrate their disagreement by simply continuing with their everyday household practices:

---

[64] T Taʿan. 1:12.
[65] T Hag. 2:13.
[66] T Taʿan. 2:5.

> They decreed a fast on Hanukkah in Lod. They told R. Eliezer about it, and he got a haircut. They told R. Joshua about it, and he took a bath.

Sometimes the rest of the people perceive the dissenting actions of rabbis as authoritative, and sometimes they do not. Local communal halakhah emerges from these stories as a complex fabric of household halakhic practices, which eventually crystallize in ceremonial law.[67]

As we have observed in the previous chapter, early tannaitic texts time and again demonstrate the importance of individual households and their halakhic practices for shaping rabbinic law. The halakhic decisions and actions of individual masters are often seen as testimonies to their ancestral family traditions. Their own practices are important precisely because they either reflect these traditions or represent their legitimate interpretation within the family. We now see that most of the case-stories appearing in tannaitic literature have households and household concerns as their immediate setting. Tannaitic halakhah as it emerges from these stories is first and foremost household-oriented religious law designed to ensure the pure and pious life of individual families. Rabbinic authorities featured in these stories act as informal experts in family halakhah, called upon in especially complicated cases. Thus the halakhic realm of an individual household emerges as the prime setting of early rabbinic law. It is indeed possible that the case-stories in question were produced within rabbinic schools in order to buttress their claims of halakhic control over everyday practices of Jewish households. But even in this case these stories reflect the continuous importance of families in the holiness project of Rabbinic Judaism. In their narratives rabbis present themselves as legitimate heirs to and interpreters of the pre-rabbinic household halakhic lore. The household maintains its function as the locus of sanctity, even though the nature of this sanctity and means to achieve it are now determined by an outside discourse.

---

[67] On local rabbis sometimes credited with particular bodies of halakhic traditions see Hezser, *Social Structure*, 180–84. Cf. further S. Miller, "R. Hanina b. Hama at Sepphoris," in L. Levine, ed., *The Galilee in Late Antiquity* (New York: JTSA, 1992), 175–200, and *"Zippora'ei, Tibera'ei* and *Deroma'ei*: Their Origins, Interests and Relationship," in *Proceedings of the Tenth World Congress of Jewish Studies* (Jerusalem: 1990), Division B, II, 15–22. These groups apparently played a significant role in shaping Judaism in the Land of Israel during the Amoraic period.

CONCLUSIONS

In the early decades of the Second Temple period families and family-based halakhic observances were central elements in Jewish religiosity and piety. Family-based piety became central for the formation of the Jewish religious movements (often called "sects") of the Second Temple period. From the times of the "proto-sectarian" movements of Ezra and Nehemiah until approximately the end of the Hasmonean reign, Jewish sects should be predominantly seen as family alliances bound together by a common interpretation of Torah and common practices of Jewish religious law. The driving force behind such alliances was a notion that patriarchal households and their everyday halakhic practices embody Torah and fulfill its call to be holy. Sociologically, such alliances corresponded very well to the overall structure of Jewish society of the early Second Temple period. As can be seen from numerous sources, individual families constituted the main social, economic, and political units in Second Temple Judah. It was only natural that they constituted the main religious units as well.

As part of the same trend, much of Second Temple Jewish literature portrays Judaism as a body of ancestral traditions preserved and passed on within successive generations of individual patriarchal families. The *Book of Jubilees*, the *Testament of Levi*, and sections of the *Book of Enoch* describe Jewish law as being preserved and transmitted by individual patriarchal clans. The transmission takes place in either oral or written form, but it is always from father to son. Occasionally, specific practices of family ancestors are referred to as valid legal precedents and the basis for future legal rulings. This type of transmission becomes especially obvious in priestly families. Technical skills of temple worship (such as the proper way of slaughtering and offering sacrificial animals, singing, the preparation of incense, etc.) are passed on within the individual families responsible for particular types of tasks. The knowledge of these laws is "owned" by particular families, as many other technical skills were during Late Antiquity. But priests represent only the most well-documented and enduring manifestation of a general trend that dominated Second Temple Judaism: religious traditions were learned, practiced, and transmitted within families. Families "embodied" and sustained Judaism by conducting their everyday lives according to these traditions and passing them on from one generation to the next.

Toward the end of the Second Temple period a new type of religious discourse begins to crystallize in which family-owned traditions are increasingly abandoned and transformed in favor of more universal, eternal, and abstract modes of presentation. The traditions are no longer transmitted as part of ancestral family lore but as anonymous collections of texts organized either by subject or as running commentaries on biblical books. On a social level this development corresponds to the increased prominence of association-type movements uniting like-minded individuals who share common religious ideals. Such groups come to be viewed as depositories of holiness, piety, and sacred knowledge, whereas traditional families and kinship ties are increasingly perceived as religiously neutral at best and spiritually inhibiting at worst. Family life begins to lose its central place in the grand holiness project of late antique Judaism. The inner transformation of the Dead Sea movement serves as an excellent example of this shift in religious thinking.

Study circles, in which traditions are transmitted from teachers to their disciples, not from fathers to their sons, provide another example of association-type movements. In study circles traditions lose their family-based setting and become more universal and abstract. They are no longer "embodied" or "owned" by specific households. This transition from household to disciple study circle as the basic social unit within Judaism is what, I would argue, marks the transition from Second Temple to Rabbinic Judaism (as well as Christianity). The religion of households is transformed into a universal teaching now seen as independent of its original carriers. This process reflects the transformation of the traditional household society of the early Second Temple period into the provincial civic society of the Roman Empire. It comes as a result of the profound absorption and "naturalization" of Hellenistic cultural and educational values among Jews. The "alienation" of ancestral family-based traditions marks the transition to classical Rabbinic Judaism.

On the other hand, Rabbinic Judaism did not simply discard and abandon the social matrix of Second Temple Judaism. Rather, it naturally grew out of this matrix, appropriating its traditions or dismissing them, when necessary. Although disciple circles would eventually play a dominant role in shaping and transmitting rabbinic

Torah, family-based forms of transmission also continued to exist for some time. Unlike other roughly contemporaneous groups (such as the Dead Sea sect and some Christian movements) rabbis continued to see the family and its everyday functions as crucial aspects of their "holiness project." Rabbinic Judaism grew out of an attempt to integrate the "utopian" holiness of disciple circles and familial piety of Second Temple households. Some immediate parallels can be noticed between portions of the Mishnah and the so-called "household codes" prominent in the contemporaneous Greco-Roman literature, such as an idealized description of family life, intended to set philosophical standards for household management. Tannaitic and early Amoraic periods in Roman Palestine witnessed the gradual transition from family-dominated to school-dominated modes of religious consciousness. Throughout this time both modes more or less equally contributed to the development of Rabbinic Judaism. Only by the fourth century (if not later) did classical Rabbinic Judaism come of age when study sessions became the predominant social form embodying rabbinic tradition.

ABBREVIATIONS

AJA	*American Journal of Archaeology*
ANRW	*Aufstieg und Niedergang der römischen Welt: Geschichte und Kultur Roms im Spiegel der neuren Forschung.* Edited by H. Temporini and W. Haase. (Berlin, 1972–)
ATR	*Anglican Theological Review*
BA	*Biblical Archaeologist*
BASOR	*Bulletin of the American Schools of Oriental Research*
CBQ	*Catholic Biblical Quarterly*
CPJ	*Corpus Papyrorum Judaicarum.* Edited by V. Tcherikover, 3 vols. (Cambridge, 1957–1964)
DJD	Discoveries in the Judaean Desert
DSD	*Dead Sea Discoveries*
FJB	*Frankfurter Judaistische Beiträge*
HTR	*Harvard Theological Review*
HUCA	*Hebrew Union College Annual*
IEJ	*Israel Exploration Journal*
INJ	*Israel Numismatic Journal*
JBL	*Journal of Biblical Literature*
JEH	*Journal of Ecclesiastical History*
JJS	*Journal of Jewish Studies*
JR	*Journal of Religion*
JRS	*Journal of Roman Studies*
JSJ	*Journal for the Study of Judaism*
JSQ	*Jewish Studies Quarterly*
JTS	*Journal of Theological Studies*
LCL	Loeb Classical Library
NEAEHL	*The New Encyclopedia of Archaeological Excavations in the Holy Land.* Edited by E. Stern, 4 vols. (Jerusalem, 1993)
NTS	*New Testament Studies*
PAAJR	*Proceedings of the American Academy for Jewish Research*
PW	Pauly, A., *Paulys Realencyclopädie der classischen Altertumswissenschaft.* New edition G. Wissowa, 49 vols. (Stuttgart, 1894–1919)
RB	*Revue biblique*
RevQ	*Revue de Qumrân*
ZAW	*Zeitschrift für die alttestamentliche Wissenschaft*

BIBLIOGRAPHY

Editions of Primary Sources

Aland, B., et al., eds., *The Greek New Testament* (Stuttgart: Deutsche Biblegesellschaft, 1994)
Albeck, H., *Shishah Sidre Mishnah*, 6 vols. (Jerusalem: Bialik, 1959)
Baumgarten, J., and D. Schwartz, eds. and trans., "Damascus Document (CD)," in J. Charlesworth, ed., *The Dead Sea Scrolls: Hebrew, Aramaic, and Greek Texts with English Translations* (Tübingen: J.C.B. Mohr, 1995), vol. 2, 4–57
Baumgarten, J., *Qumran Cave 4.XIII: The Damascus Document (4Q266–273)* (DJD 13; Oxford: Clarendon Press, 1996)
Charlesworth, J., and L. Stuckenbruck, "Rule of the Congregation (1QSa)," in J. Charlesworth, ed., *The Dead Sea Scrolls: Hebrew, Aramaic, and Greek Texts with English Translations* (Tübingen: J.C.B. Mohr, 1995), vol. 1, 108–117
Colson, F., trans., *Philo*, 10 vols. (LCL; Cambridge: Harvard University Press, 1929)
Elliger, K., and W. Rudolph, eds., *Biblia Hebraica Stuttgartensia* (Stuttgart: Deutsche Bible-gesellschaft, 1990)
Finkelstein, L., ed., *Sifra or Torah Kohanim According to Codex Assemani 66* (New York: JTSA, 1956)
Fitzmyer, J., ed. and trans., "Tobit," in M. Broshi, et al., *Qumran Cave 4.XIV: Para-biblical Texts, Part 2* (DJD 19; Oxford: Clarendon Press, 1995)
Hadas, M., ed. and trans., *The Third and Fourth Books of Maccabees* (New York: Harper & Brothers, 1953)
Horovitz, H., ed., *Siphre de-Ve Rav: Siphre ad Numeros adjecto Siphre Zutta, cum Variis Lectio-nibus et Adnotationibus* (Jerusalem: Wahrmann, 1966)
Horovitz, H., and I. Rabin, eds., *Mechilta de-Rabbi Ismael, cum Variis Lectionibus et Adnota-tionibus* (Jerusalem: Wahrmann, 1970)
Knibb, M., *The Ethiopic Book of Enoch: A New Edition in Light of the Aramaic Dead Sea Fragments*, vols. 1–2 (Oxford: Clarendon Press, 1978)
Kugler, R., *From Patriarch to Priest: The Levi Priestly Tradition from "Aramaic Levi" to "Testa-ment of Levi"* (Atlanta: Scholars Press, 1996)
Lauterbach, J., ed., *Mekilta de-Rabbi Ishmael: A Critical Edition on the Basis of the Manu-scripts and Early Editions with an English Translation, Introduction, and Notes*, vols. 1–3 (Philadelphia: JPS, 1976)
Lieberman, S., ed., *The Tosefta According to Codex Vienna, with Variants from Codex Erfurt, Genizah MSS, and Editio Princeps* (Venice 1521), vols. 1–5 (New York: JTSA, 1955–1988)
Milik, J., *The Books of Enoch* (Oxford: Clarendon Press, 1976)
Puech, É., "Le Testament de Qahat en araméen de la Grotte 4 (*4QTQah*)," *RevQ* 15 (1992), 23–54
Qimron, E., and J. Charlesworth, eds. and trans., "Rule of the Community (1QS)," in J. Charlesworth, ed., *The Dead Sea Scrolls: Hebrew, Aramaic, and Greek Texts with English Translations* (Tübingen: J.C.B. Mohr, 1995), vol. 1, 1–51
Qimron, E., and J. Strugnell, eds., *Qumran Cave 4.V: Miqsat Maʿase Ha-Torah* (DJD 10; Oxford: Clarendon Press, 1994)
Rahlfs, A., ed., *Septuaginta, id est Vetus Testamentum graece iuxta LXX interpretes* (Stuttgart: Deutsche Biblegesellschaft, [s.a.])
Strugnell, J., et al., eds., *Qumran Cave 4.XXIV: Sapiential Texts, Part 2. 4QInstruction (Mûsar Le Mevîn): 4Q415 ff.* (DJD 34; Oxford: Clarendon Press, 1999)

Thackeray, H. St. J., et al., trans., *Josephus*, 10 vols. (LCL; Cambridge: Harvard University Press, 1927–1965)

VanderKam, J., ed. and trans., *The Book of Jubilees*, 2 vols. (Leuven: Peeters, 1989)

Weiss, I., *Sifra de-Ve Rav* (New York: Om, 1946)

Zuckermandel, M., ed., *Tosephta, Based on the Erfurt and Vienna Codices, with Parallels and Variants* (Jerusalem: Wahrmann, 1970)

Modern Authors and Translations

Aberbach, M., "The Relations between Master and Disciple in the Talmudic Age," in H. Dimitrovsky, ed., *Exploring the Talmud* (New York, 1976), 202–225

Albeck, H., *Mavo La-Mishnah* (Jerusalem: Byalik, 1966)

Albertz, R., *History of Israelite Religion in the Old Testament Period*, 2 vols. (Louisville: John Knox Press, 1994)

———, *Persönliche Frömmigkeit und offizielle Religion* (Stuttgart: Calwer Verlag, 1978)

Albright, W., *The Archaeology of Palestine and the Bible* (New York: Fleming H. Revell, 1932)

Alexander, P., "*Quid Athenis et Hierosolymis?* Rabbinic Midrash and Hermeneutics in the Graeco-Roman World," in P. Davies and R. White, eds., *A Tribute to Geza Vermes: Essays on Jewish and Christian Literature and History* (Sheffield: JSOT Press, 1990), 101–24

Alon, G., *Jews, Judaism, and the Classical World* (Jerusalem: Magnes Press, 1977)

———, *Toldot ha-Yehudim be-Erets-Yisrael bi-tekufat ha-Mishnah veha-Talmud* (Tel Aviv: Ha-Kibuts Ha-Meuhad, 1967), vol. 1–2

Amoussine, J., "Éphraïm et Manassé dans le Pesher de Nahum," *RevQ* 4 (1963), 389–96

Avery-Peck, A., *Mishnah's Division of Agriculture: A History and Theology of Seder Zeraim* (Chico: Scholars Press, 1985)

Avi-Yonah, M., *Art in Ancient Palestine: Selected Studies* (Jerusalem: Magnes Press, 1981)

Baker, C., *Rebuilding the House of Israel: Architectures of Gender in Jewish Antiquity* (Stanford: Stanford University Press, 2002)

Balch, D., "Household Codes," in D. Aune, ed. *Greco-Roman Literature and the New Testament: Selected Forms and Genres* (Atlanta: Scholars Press, 1988), 25–50

———, *Let Wives Be Submissive: The Domestic Code in I Peter* (Atlanta: Scholars Press, 1981)

Barag, D., "A Silver Coin of Yohanan the High Priest and the Coinage of Judaea in the Fourth Century BCE," *INJ* 9 (1986–1987), 4–21

Barclay, J., "The Family as the Bearer of Religion in Judaism and Early Christianity," in H. Moxnes, ed., *Constructing Early Christian Families: Family as Social Reality and Metaphor* (London: Routledge, 1997), 66–80

———, *Jews in the Mediterranean Diaspora: From Alexander to Trajan (323 BCE–117 CE)* (Edinburgh: T&T Clark, 1996)

Baumgarten, A., *The Flourishing of the Jewish Sects in the Maccabean Era: An Interpretation* (Leiden: Brill, 1997)

———, "Graeco-Roman Voluntary Associations and Ancient Jewish Sects" in M. Goodman, ed., *Jews in a Graeco-Roman World* (Oxford: Clarendon Press, 1998), 93–111

———, "The Name of the Pharisees," *JBL* 102 (1983), 411–28

———, "The Pharisaic *Paradosis*," *HTR* 80 (1987), 63–77

———, "Seekers after Smooth Things," in Schiffman and VanderKam, *Encyclopedia of the Dead Sea Scrolls*, vol. 2, 857–59

Baumgarten, J., "4Q502, Marriage or Golden Age Ritual?" *JJS* 43 (1983), 125–136

———, "Celibacy," in Schiffman and VanderKam, *Encyclopedia of the Dead Sea Scrolls*, vol. 1, 122–24

———, "Form Criticism and the Oral Law," *JSJ* 4 (1974), 34–40

————, "The Pharisaic-Sadducean Controversies about Purity, and the Qumran Texts," *JJS* 31 (1980), 157–170

Baumgarten, J., "The Qumran-Essene Restraints on Marriage" in L. Schiffman, ed., *Archaeology and History in the Dead Sea Scrolls: The New York University Conference in Memory of Yigael Yadin* (Sheffield: JSOT Press, 1990), 13–24

————, "Purification after Childbirth and the Sacred Garden in 4Q265 and Jubilees," in G. Brooke, ed., *New Qumran Texts and Studies* (Leiden: Brill, 1994), 3–10

————, "The Unwritten Law in the Pre-Rabbinic Period," *JSJ* 3 (1972), 7–29

Bernstein, M., "The Employment and Interpretation of Scripture in 4QMMT: Preliminary Observations," in Kampen and Bernstein, *Reading 4QMMT*, 29–51

Berquist, J., *Controlling Corporeality: The Body and the Household in Ancient Israel* (New Brunswick: Rutgers University Press, 2002)

Bickerman, E., "La Chaîne de la Tradition Pharisienne," *Revue Biblique* 59 (1951), 153–65

————, "La charte séleucide de Jérusalem," in idem, *Studies in Jewish and Christian History* (Leiden: Brill, 1980), vol. 2, 44–85

————, "Edict of Cyrus in Ezra 1," in idem, *Studies in Jewish and Christian History*, vol. 1, 72–108

————, *From Ezra to the Last of the Maccabees: Foundations of Post-Biblical Judaism* (New York: Schocken Books, 1962)

————, *The Jews in the Greek Age* (Cambridge: Harvard University Press, 1988)

Blenkinsopp, J., *Ezra-Nehemiah: A Commentary* (Philadelphia: Westminster Press, 1988)

————, "The Family in First Temple Israel," in Perdue, ed., *Families in Ancient Israel*, 78–84

————, "Interpretation and the Tendency to Sectarianism: An Aspect of Second Temple History" in E. Sanders, ed., *Jewish and Christian Self-Definition* (Philadelphia: Fortress Press, 1981), vol. 2, 1–26

————, "A Jewish Sect of the Persian Period," *CBQ* 52 (1990), 5–20

————, "Temple and Society in Achaemenid Judah," in P. Davies, ed., *Second Temple Studies* (Sheffield: JSOT Press, 1991), vol. 1, 22–53

Bloch, H., *Die Quellen des Flavius Josephus in seiner Archäologie* (Leipzig: Teubner, 1879)

Boccaccini, G., *Beyond the Essene Hypothesis: The Parting of the Ways between Qumran and Enochic Judaism* (Grand Rapids: Eerdmans, 1998)

Bokser, B., "Todos and Rabbinic Authority in Rome," in J. Neusner et al., eds., *New Perspectives on Ancient Judaism* (Lanham: University Press of America, 1987), vol. 1, 117–30

Bokser, B.Z., *Pharisaic Judaism in Transition: R. Eliezer the Great and Jewish Reconstruction after the War with Rome* (New York: Bloch, 1935)

Boyarin, D., *Border Lines: The Partition of Judaeo-Christianity* (Philadelphia: University of Pennsylvania Press, 2004)

————, *Carnal Israel: Reading Sex in Talmudic Culture* (Berkeley: University of California Press, 1993)

————, "The *Diadoche* of the Rabbis; or, Judah the Patriarch at Yavneh," in R. Kalmin and S. Schwartz, eds., *Jewish Culture and Society under the Christian Roman Empire* (Leuven: Peeters, 2003), 285–318

————, *A Radical Jew: Paul and the Politics of Identity* (Berkeley: University of California Press, 1994)

Briant, P., "The Seleucid Kingdom, the Achaemenid Empire and the History of the Near East," in P. Bilde et al., eds, *Religion and Religious Practice in the Seleucid Kingdom* (Aarhus: Aarhus University Press, 1990), 40–65

Brooten, B., *Women Leaders in the Ancient Synagogue* (Chico: Scholars Press, 1982)

Bultmann, R., *The History of the Synoptic Tradition* (New York: Harper & Row, 1963)

Camp, C., "The Female Sage in Ancient Israel and in the Biblical Wisdom Literature," in Gammie and Perdue, *Sage in Israel*, 185–203

————, *Wisdom and the Feminine in the Book of Proverbs* (Decatur: Almond Press, 1985)

Campbell, A., *The Elders: Seniority within Earliest Christianity* (Edinburgh: T&T Clark, 1994)

Campbell, J., "Essene-Qumran Origins in Exile: A Scriptural Basis?" *JJS* 46 (1995), 143–156

Charlesworth, J., ed., *Old Testament Pseudepigrapha*, 2 vols. (Garden City: Doubleday, 1985)

Coggins, R., *Samaritans and Jews: The Origins of Samaritanism Reconsidered* (Atlanta: John Knox Press, 1975)

Cohen, N.G., "The Jewish Dimension of Philo's Judaism—An Elucidation of *de Spec. Leg.* IV 132–150," *JJS* 38 (1987), 165–86

Cohen, S.J.D., "Alexander the Great and Jaddus the High Priest according to Josephus," *AJS Review* 7–8 (1982–1983), 41–68

———, *The Beginnings of Jewishness: Boundaries, Varieties, Uncertainties* (Berkeley: University of California Press, 1999)

———, *From the Maccabees to the Mishnah* (Philadelphia: The Westminster Press, 1987)

———, "Hellenism in Unexpected Places," in J. Collins and G. Sterling, eds., *Hellenism in the Land of Israel* (Notre Dame: University of Notre Dame Press, 2001), 218–43

———, ed., *The Jewish Family in Antiquity* (Atlanta: Scholars Press, 1993)

———, *Josephus in Galilee and Rome: His Vita and Development as a Historian* (Leiden: Brill, 1979)

———, "Masada: Literary Tradition, Archaeological Remains, and the Credibility of Josephus," *JJS* 33 (1982), 385–405

———, "Parallel Historical Tradition in Josephus and Rabbinic Literature," *Proceedings of the Ninth World Congress of Jewish Studies* (Jerusalem, 1986), Division B. I, 7–14

———, "Patriarchs and Scholarchs," *PAAJR* 48 (1981), 57–85

———, "The Rabbi in Second-Century Jewish Society," in W. Horbury et al., eds., *The Cambridge History of Judaism* (Cambridge: Cambridge University Press, 1999), vol. 3, 922–90

———, "The Significance of Yavneh: Pharisees, Rabbis, and the End of Jewish Sectarianism," *HUCA* 55 (1984), 27–53

Colledge, M., "Greek and non-Greek Interaction in Art and Architecture of the Hellenistic East," in Bilde, *Religion and Religious Practice*, 134–62

Collins, J.J., *The Apocalyptic Imagination: An Introduction to the Jewish Matrix of Christianity* (New York: Crossroad, 1984)

———, "Apocalypticism and Literary Genre in the Dead Sea Scrolls," in P. Flint and J. VanderKam eds., *The Dead Sea Scrolls After Fifty Years: A Comprehensive Assessment* (Leiden: Brill, 1999), vol. 2, 403–30

———, *Between Athens and Jerusalem: Jewish Identity in the Hellenistic Dispora* (New York: Crossroad, 1983)

———, "Forms of Community in the Dead Sea Scrolls," in S. Paul et al., ed., *Emanuel: Studies in Hebrew Bible, Septuagint and Dead Sea Scrolls in Honor of Emanuel Tov* (Leiden: Brill, 2003), 107–110

———, *Jewish Wisdom in the Hellenistic Age* (Louisville: Westminster John Knox Press, 1997)

———, "Marriage, Divorce, and Family in Second Temple Judaism," in L. Perdue et al., *Families in Ancient Israel* (Louisville: Westminster John Knox Press, 1997), 104–62

Cook, M., *Mark's Treatment of the Jewish Leaders* (Leiden: Brill, 1978)

Crenshaw, J., *Education in Ancient Israel: Across the Deadening Silence* (New York: Doubleday, 1998)

Cross, F., *The Ancient Library of Qumran and Modern Biblical Studies* (Garden City: Doubleday, 1958)

———, "An Aramaic Ostracon of the Third Century BCE from Excavations in Jerusalem," *Eretz Israel* 15 (1981), 67–69

———, "The Development of the Jewish Scripts," in G. Wright, ed., *The Bible and the Ancient Near East: Essays in Honor of William Foxwell Albright* (Garden City: Doubleday, 1961), 133–202

———, "Papyri and their Historical Implications," in P. Lapp and N. Lapp, eds., *Discoveries in the Wadi ed-Dâliyeh* (Cambridge: ASOR, 1974), 18–24

———, "Papyri of the Fourth Century BC from Dâliyeh," in D. Freedman and J. Greenfield, eds., *New Directions in Biblical Archaeology* (Garden City: Doubleday, 1969), 53–61

Cross, F., and E. Eshel, "Ostraca from Khirbet Qumran," *IEJ* 47 (1997), 17–28

Crouch, J., *The Origin and Intention of the Colossian Haustafel* (Göttingen: Vandenhoeck & Ruprecht, 1972)

D'Angelo, M.R., "Εὐσέβεια: Roman Imperial Family Values and the Sexual Politics of 4 Maccabees and the Pastorals," *Biblical Interpretation* 11/2 (2003), 139–64

Danby, H., *The Mishnah* (London: Oxford University Press, 1938)

Daube, D., "Alexandrian Methods of Interpretation and the Rabbis," in H. Fischel, *Essays*, 165–82

———, "Rabbinic Methods of Interpretation and Hellenistic Rhetoric," *HUCA* 22 (1949), 239–64

Davies, G., "The Significance of the Handshake Motif in Classical Funerary Art," *AJA* 89 (1985), 627–40

Davies, P., *Behind the Essenes: History and Ideology in the Dead Sea Scrolls* (Atlanta: Scholars Press, 1987)

———, *The Damascus Covenant* (Sheffield: JSOT Press, 1983)

———, *Scribes and Schools: The Canonization of the Hebrew Scriptures* (Louisville: John Knox Press, 1998)

Delcor, M., "Le temple d'Onias en Egypte," *RB* 75 (1968), 188–205

Destionon, J., *Die Quellen des Flavius Josephus* (Kiel: Lipsius & Tischer, 1882)

Destro, A., and M. Pesco, "Fathers and Householders in the Jesus Movement: The Perspective of the Gospel of Luke," *Biblical Interpretation* 11 (2003), 211–238

Dexinger, F., *Henochs Zehnwochenapokalypse und offene Probleme der Apokalyptikforschung* (Leiden: Brill, 1977)

Dombrowski, B., "היחד in 1QS and τὸ κοινόν: An Instance of Early Greek and Jewish Synthesis," *HTR* 59 (1966), 293–307

Doudna, G., *4Q Pesher Nahum: A Critical Edition* (London: Sheffield Academic Press, 2001)

Eilberg-Schwartz, H., "The Problem of the Body for the People of the Book," in idem, ed., *People of the Body: Jews and Judaism from the Embodied Perspective* (Albany: State University of New York Press, 1992), 17–46

———, *The Savage in Judaism: An Anthropology of Israelite Religion and Ancient Judaism* (Bloomington: Indiana University Press, 1990)

Elgvin, T., "The Reconstruction of Sapiential Work A," *RevQ* 16 (1995), 559–80

Elliott, J., "The Jesus Movement Was Not Egalitarian but Family-Oriented," *Biblical Interpretation* 11 (2003), 173–210

Epstein, J., *Mavo le-Nusah ha-Mishnah* (Jerusalem, 1965)

———, *Mevo'ot le-Sifrut ha-Tanaim: Mishnah, Tosefta, u-Midreshe-Halakhah* (Jerusalem: Magnes, 1957)

Feeley-Harnik, G., "Is Historical Anthropology Possible? The Case of the Runaway Slave," in G. Tucker and D. Knight, eds., *Humanizing America's Iconic Book* (Chico: Scholars Press, 1982), 95–126

Feldman, L., "Masada: A Critique of Recent Scholarship," in J. Neusner, ed., *Christianity, Judaism and Other Graeco-Roman Cults* (Leiden: Brill, 1975), vol. 3, 218–48

Fiensy, D., *The Social History of Palestine in the Herodian Period: The Land is Mine* (Lewiston: Edwin Mellen Press, 1991)

Finkelstein, L., *Pharisees: The Sociological Background of Their Faith* (Philadelphia: Jewish Publication Society, 1962)

Fischel, H., *Rabbinic Literature and Greco-Roman Philosophy: A Study of Epicurea and Rhetorica in Early Midrashic Writings* (Leiden: Brill, 1973)
———, "Story and History: Observations on Greco-Roman Rhetoric and Pharisaism," in idem, ed., *Essays in Greco-Roman and Related Talmudic Literature* (New York: KTAV, 1977), 443–72
———, "Studies in Cynicism and the Ancient Near East: The Transformation of a Chria," in J. Neusner, ed., *Religions in Antiquity: Essays in Memory of Erwin Ramsdell Goodenough* (Leiden: Brill, 1968), 372–411
Fishbane, M., *Biblical Interpretation in Ancient Israel* (Oxford: Clarendon Press. 1985)
Flesher, P., *Oxen, Women, or Citizens? Slaves in the System of the Mishnah* (Atlanta: Scholars Press, 1988)
Flint, P., and J. VanderKam eds., *The Dead Sea Scrolls After Fifty Years: A Comprehensive Assessment*, 2 vols. (Leiden: Brill, 1998–1999)
Flusser, D., "Pharisäer, Sadduzäer und Essener im Pescher Nahum," in Grözinger et al., eds., *Qumran: Wege der Forschung* (Darmstadt, 1981), 121–66
Fonrobert, C., "The Didascalia Apostolorum: A Mishnah for the Disciples of Jesus," *Journal of Early Christian Studies* 9:4 (2001), 483–509
———, *Menstrual Purity: Rabbinic and Christian Reconstructions of Biblical Gender* (Stanford: Stanford University Press, 2000)
———, "When Women Walk in the Ways of Their Fathers: On Gendering the Rabbinic Claim for Authority," *Journal of the History of Sexuality* 10, no. 3/4 (2001), 398–415
Fontaine, C., "The Sage in Family and Tribe," in J. Gammie and L. Perdue, eds., *The Sage in Israel and the Ancient Near East* (Winona Lake: Eisenbrauns, 1990), 155–64
Fraade, S., *From Tradition to Commentary: Torah and Its Interpretation in Midrash Sifre to Deuteronomy* (Albany: State University of New York Press, 1991)
———, "Interpretive Authority in the Studying Community of Qumran," *JJS* 44 (1993), 46–69
Frankel, Z., *Darkhe ha-Mishnah, ha-Tosefta, Mekhilta, Sifra, we-Sifre* (Warsaw: Cailingold, 1923)
Frankfurter, D., *Religion in Roman Egypt: Assimilation and Resistance* (Princeton: Princeton University Press, 1998)
Gammie, J., "From Prudentialism to Apocalypticism: The Houses of the Sages Amid the Varying Forms of Wisdom," in Gammie and Perdue, *Sage in Israel*, 484–85
García Martínez, F., "Qumran Origins and Early History: A Groningen Hypothesis," *Folia Orientalia* 25 (1988), 113–136
———, "The Heavenly Tablets in the Book of Jubilees," in M. Albani et al., eds., *Studies in the Book of Jubilees* (Tübingen: Mohr Siebeck, 1997), 243–60
García Martínez, F., and A. van der Woude, "A 'Groningen' Hypothesis of Qumran Origins and Early History," *RevQ* 14 (1990), 521–541
Gera, D., *Judaea and Mediterranean Politics, 219 to 161 BCE* (Leiden: Brill, 1998)
Geraty, L., "The Khirbet el-Kôm Bilingual Ostracon," *BASOR* 220 (1975), 55–61
Gereboff, J., *Rabbi Tarfon: The Tradition, the Man, and Early Rabbinic Judaism* (Missoula: Scholars Press, 1979)
Gerhardsson, B., *Memory and Manuscript: Oral Tradition and Written Transmission in Rabbinic Judaism and Early Christianity* (Grand Rapids: Eerdmans, 1998)
Goldberg, A., "Form und Funktion des Ma'ase in der Mischna," *FJB* 2 (1974), 1–38
Goldin, J., *Studies in Midrash and Related Literature* (Philadelphia: Jewish Publication Society, 1988)
Golka, F., *The Leopard's Spots: Biblical and African Wisdom in Proverbs* (Edinburg: T&T Clark, 1993)
Goodblatt, D., "The Beruriah Traditions," *JJS* 26 (1975), 68–85
———, *The Monarchic Principle: Studies in Jewish Self-Government in Antiquity* (Tübingen: J.C.B. Mohr, 1994)

————, "Talmudic Sources on the Origins of Organized Jewish Education," in B. Oded, ed., *Studies in the History of the Jewish People and the Land of Israel* (Haifa: University of Haifa, 1980), vol. 5, 83–103 (in Hebrew)

Goodman, M., "A Note on Josephus, the Pharisees and Ancestral Tradition," *JJS* 50 (1999), 17–20

————, *The Ruling Class of Judaea: The Origins of the Jewish Revolt against Rome* (Cambridge: Cambridge University Press, 1987)

————, "Sadducees and Essenes after 70 CE," in S. Porter, et al., eds., *Crossing the Boundaries: Essays in Biblical Interpretation in Honour of Michael D. Goulder* (Leiden: Brill, 1994), 347–56

Grabbe, L., "4QMMT and Second Temple Jewish Society," in M. Bernstein et al., eds., *Legal Texts and Legal Issues: Proceedings of the Second Meeting of the International Organization for Qumran Studies* (Leiden: Brill, 1997), 89–108

————, "Josephus and the Reconstruction of the Judean Restoration," *JBL* 106 (1987), 236–42

————, *Priests, Prophets, Diviners, Sages: A Socio-Historical of Religious Specialists in Ancient Israel* (Valley Forge: Trinity Press, 1995)

————, "Sadducees and Pharisees," in J. Neusner and A. Avery-Peck, eds., *Judaism in Late Antiquity* (Leiden: Brill, 1999), part 3, vol. 1, 35–61

————, "Synagogues in Pre-70 Palestine: A Re-assessment," *JTS* 39 (1988), 401–10

Graetz, H., *History of the Jews* (Philadelphia: Jewish Publication Society, 1891)

Gray, R., *Prophetic Figures in Late Second Temple Jewish Palestine* (New York: Oxford University Press, 1993)

Guttman, A., "The End of the Jewish Sacrificial Cult," *HUCA* 38 (1967), 137–48

Halevy, I., *Dorot Ha-Rishonim: Sefer Divre ha-Yamim Li-Vene Yisrael* (Berlin: Harz, 1923)

Halpern-Amaru, B., "First Woman, Wives, and Mothers in *Jubilees*," *JBL* 113 (1994), 609–26

Harrington, D., "The *Rāz Nihyeh* in a Qumran Wisdom Text (1Q26, 4Q415–418, 423)," *RevQ* 17 (1996), 549–53

Harrington, D., *Wisdom Texts from Qumran* (London: Routledge, 1996)

Hayes, C., *Gentile Impurities and Jewish Identities: Intermarriage and Conversion from the Bible to the Talmud* (Oxford: Oxford University Press, 2002)

Hayward, R., "The Jewish Temple at Leontopolis: A Reconsideration," *JJS* 33 (1982), 432–41

Hempel, C., "Community Structures in the Dead Sea Scrolls," in Flint and VanderKam, *The Dead Sea Scrolls after Fifty Years*, vol. 2, 67–92

————, "The Earthly Essene Nucleus of 1QSa," *DSD* 3 (1996), 253–267

Hengel, M., *The Charismatic Leader and His Followers* (New York: Crossroad, 1981)

————, *The "Hellenization" of Judaea in the First Century after Christ* (London: SCM Press, 1989)

————, *Judaism and Hellenism: Studies in Their Encounter in Palestine During the Early Hellenistic Period*, 2 vols. (Philadelphia: Fortress Press, 1974)

————, *The Zealots* (Edinburgh: T&T Clark, 1989)

Hengel, M., and R. Deines, "E.P. Sanders' 'Common Judaism,' Jesus and the Pharisees: A Review Essay," *JTS* 46 (1995), 1–70

Herr, M., "Continuum in the Chain of Torah Transmission," *Zion* 44 (1980), 43–56

Hezser, C., *Form, Function and Historical Significance of the Rabbinic Story in Yerushalmi Neziqin* (Tübingen: Mohr Siebeck, 1993)

————, "'Privat' und 'öffentlich' im Talmud Yerushalmi und in der griechisch-römischen Antike," in P. Schäfer, ed., *The Talmud Yerushalmi and Graeco-Roman Culture* (Tübingen: Mohr Siebeck, 1998), vol. 1, 423–579

————, *The Social Structure of the Rabbinic Movement in Roman Palestine* (Tübingen: Mohr Siebeck, 1997)

Himmelfarb, M., "'A Kingdom of Priests': The Democratization of the Priesthood in the Literature of Second Temple Judaism," *Journal of Jewish Thought and Philosophy* 6 (1997), 89–104

———, "Levi, Phinehas, and the Problem of Intermarriage at the Time of the Maccabean Revolt," *JSQ* 6 (1999), 1–24

Hoftijzer, J., and K. Jongeling, *Dictionary of the North-West Semitic Inscriptions*, 2 vols. (Leiden: Brill, 1995)

Hoglund, K., *Achaemenid Imperial Administration in Syria-Palestine and the Missions of Ezra and Nehemiah* (Atlanta: Scholars Press, 1992)

Hölscher, G., "Josephus," PW 9:2, 1934–2000

Hölscher, G., *Die Quellen des Josephus für die Zeit vom Exil bis zum jüdischen Kriege* (Leipzig: Teubner, 1904)

Horsley, R., *Archaeology, History, and Society in Galilee: The Social Context of Jesus and the Rabbis* (Valley Forge: Trinity Press, 1996)

———, "The Sicarii: Ancient Jewish Terrorists," *JR* 59 (1979), 435–58

Ilan, T., *Jewish Women in Greco-Roman Palestine* (Peabody: Hendrickson, 1996)

———, *Mine and Yours are Hers: Retrieving Women's History from Rabbinic Literature* (Leiden: Brill, 1997)

Jacobs, M., *Die Institution des jüdischen Patriarchen: Eine quellen- und traditionskritische Studie zur Geschichte der Juden in der Spätantike* (Tübingen: Mohr Siebeck, 1995)

Jaffee, M., *Torah in the Mouth: Writing and Oral Tradition in Palestinian Judaism, 200 BCE–400 CE* (Oxford: Oxford University Press, 2001)

Japhet, S., "Sheshbazzar and Zerubbabel," *ZAW* 94 (1982), 66–98

Jawitz, Z., *Sefer Toldot Yisrael*, 11 vols. (Jerusalem: Ahiever, 1926)

Jones, A.H.M., "Urbanization of Palestine," *JRS* 21 (1931), 78–85

Kampen, J., and M. Bernstein, eds., *Reading 4QMMT: New Perspectives on Qumran Law and History* (Atlanta: Scholars Press, 1996)

Kanter, S., *Rabban Gamaliel II: The Legal Traditions* (Chico: Scholars Press, 1980)

Kasher, A., *The Jews in Hellenistic and Roman Egypt: The Struggle for Equal Rights* (Tübingen: J.C.B. Mohr, 1985)

Kaufmann, Y., *History of the Religion of Israel* (New York: Ktav, 1977)

Kimelman, R., "The Conflict between the Priestly Oligarchy and the Sages in the Talmudic Period (An Explication of PT *Shabbat* 12:3, 13C = *Horayot* 3:5, 48C)," *Zion* 48 (1983), 135–47 (in Hebrew)

Kirschenbaum, A., *Sons, Slaves, and Freedmen in Roman Commerce* (Washington, D.C.: Catholic University of America Press, 1987)

Klinghardt, M., "The Manual of Discipline in the Light of Statutes of Hellenistic Associations," in M. Wise et al., eds., *Methods of Investigation of the Dead Sea Scrolls and the Khirbet Qumran Site: Present Realities and Future Prospects* (New York: The New York Academy of Sciences, 1994), 251–67

Knibb, M., "Rule of the Community," in L. Schiffman and J. VanderKam, *Encyclopedia of the Dead Sea Scrolls* (Oxford: Oxford University Press, 2000), vol. 2, 793–97

Kugel, J., "Levi's Elevation to the Priesthood in Second Temple Writings," *HTR* 86 (1993), 1–64

———, "The Jubilees Apocalypse," *DSD* 1 (1994), 322–37

Kugler, R., "Priesthood at Qumran" in Flint and VanderKam, *The Dead Sea Scrolls after Fifty Years*, vol. 2, 93–116

Kuhnen, H.-P., *Palästina in Griechisch-Römischer Zeit* (Munich: Beck, 1990)

Ladouceur, D., "Masada: A Consideration of the Literary Evidence," *Greek, Roman, and Byzantine Studies* 21 (1980), 245–60

Lapin, H., *Early Rabbinic Civil Law and the Social History of Roman Galilee: A Study of Mishnah Tractate Baba Mesia* (Atlanta: Scholars Press, 1995)

———, "Rabbis and Cities in Later Roman Palestine: The Literary Evidence," *JJS* 50 (1999), 187–207

Lapp, N., ed., *The Excavations at Araq el-Emir* (Winona Lake: Eisenbrauns, 1983)

————, " 'Iraq el-Emir," *NEAEHL*, vol. 2, 646–49

Larson, E., "Greco-Roman Guilds," in Schiffman and VanderKam, *Encyclopedia of the Dead Sea Scrolls*, vol. 1, 321–23

Lassen, E., "The Roman Family: Ideal and Metaphor," in H. Moxnes ed., *Constructing Early Christian Families: Family as Social Reality and Metaphor* (London: Routledge, 1997), 103–20

Lauterbach, J., "A Significant Controversy between the Sadducees and the Pharisees," in idem, *Rabbinic Essays* (Cincinnati: Hebrew Union College Press, 1951), 51–83

Leith, M., *Wadi Daliyeh* (Oxford: Clarendon Press, 1997)

LeMoyne, J., *Les Sadducéens* (Paris: Lecoffre, 1972)

Levine, L., *The Ancient Synagogue: The First Thousand Years* (New Haven: Yale University Press, 2000)

Lieberman, S., "The Discipline in the So-Called Dead Sea Manual of Discipline," *JBL* 71 (1951), 199–206

————, *Hellenism in Jewish Palestine: Studies in the Literary Transmission, Beliefs and Manners of Palestine in the I century BCE–IV century CE* (New York: JTSA, 1950)

————, *Tosefet Rishonim: A Commentary Based Upon Manuscripts of the Tosefta and Works of the Rishonim and Midrashim, and Rare Editions*, 4 vols. (Jerusalem: Bamberger & Wahrmann, 1939)

————, *Tosefta Ki-fshutah: A Comprehensive Commentary on the Tosefta*, 10 vols. (New York: JTSA, 1955)

Lightstone, J., "Sadducees *versus* Pharisees," in J. Neusner, ed., *Christianity, Judaism and Other Greco-Roman Cults* (Leiden: Brill, 1975), vol. 3, 206–17

————, "Sadoq the Yavnean," in W. Green, ed., *Persons and Institutions in Early Rabbinic Judaism* (Missoula: Scholars Press, 1977), 49–147

Liver, J., "The 'Sons of Zadok the Priests' in the Dead Sea Sect," *RevQ* 6 (1967), 3–30

MacDonald, M., *Colossians and Ephesians* (Collegeville: Liturgical Press, 2000)

————, *Pauline Churches: Socio-Historical Study of Institutionalization in the Pauline and Deutero-Pauline Writings* (Cambridge: Cambridge University Press, 1988)

Malbon, E., "The Jewish Leaders in the Gospel of Mark: A Literary Study of Markan Characterization," *JBL* 108 (1989), 259–81

Martens, J., "Unwritten Law in Philo: A Response to Naomi G. Cohen," *JJS* 93 (1992), 38–45

Martin, D., "Slavery and the Ancient Jewish Family," in S. Cohen, ed., *The Jewish Family in Antiquity* (Atlanta: Scholars Press, 1993), 113–29

Mason, S., *Flavius Josephus on the Pharisees: A Composition-Critical Study* (Leiden: Brill, 1991)

Mazar, B., "The Tobiads," *IEJ* 7 (1957), 137–45 and 229–38

McEvenue, S., "Political Structure in Judah from Cyrus to Nehemiah," *CBQ* 43 (1981), 353–64

Meeks, W., *The First Urban Christians: The Social World of the Apostle Paul* (New Haven: Yale University Press, 1983)

Meshorer, Y., *Ancient Jewish Coinage*, 2 vols. (Dix Hills: Amphora, 1982)

Meshorer, Y., and S. Qedar, *The Coinage of Samaria in the Fourth Century BCE* (Jerusalem: Numismatic Fine Arts International, 1991)

Meyers, C., "To Her Mother's House: Considering a Counterpart to the Israelite *Bêt'āb*," in D. Jobling et al., eds., *The Bible and the Politics of Exegesis: Essays in Honor of Norman K. Gottwald on His Sixty-Fifth Birthday* (Cleveland: Pilgrim Press, 1991), 39–51

Mildenberg, L., "Yehud: A Preliminary Study of the Provincial Coinage of Judaea," in O. Mørkholm and N. Waggoner, eds., *Greek Numismatics and Archaeology: Essays in Honor of Margaret Thompson* (Wetteren: Cultura, 1979), 183–96

Milik, J., *Ten Years of Discovery in the Wilderness of Judaea* (London: SCM, 1959)

Millar, F., "The Phoenician Cities: A Case Study in Hellenisation," *Proceedings of the Cambridge Philological Society* 209 (1983), 55–71

Miller, S., "R. Hanina b. Hama at Sepphoris," in L. Levine, ed., *The Galilee in Late Antiquity* (New York: JTSA, 1992), 175–200

———, "*Zippora'ei, Tibera'ei* and *Deroma'ei*: Their Origins, Interests and Relationship," in *Proceedings of the Tenth World Congress of Jewish Studies* (Jerusalem: 1990), Division B, II, 15–22

Müller, "Hebräische Sprache der Halacha als Textur der Schöpfung: Beobachtungen zum Verhältnis von Tora und Halacha im Buch der Jubiläen," in H. Merklein et al., eds., *Bibel in jüdischer und christlicher Tradition: Festschrift für Johann Maier zum 60. Geburtstag* (Frankfurt am Main: Hain, 1993), 157–76

Murphy-O'Connor, J., "The Damascus Document Revisited," *RB* 92 (1985), 223–46

———, "An Essene Missionary Document? CD II,14–VI,1," *RB* 77 (1970), 201–229

———, "The Essenes and Their History," *RB* 81 (1974), 215–244

———, "The Essenes in Palestine," *BA* 40 (1977), 100–124

———, "A Literary Analysis of Damascus Document XIX,33–XX,34," *RB* 79 (1972), 544–564

Najman, H., "Interpretation as Primordial Writing: Jubilees and Its Authority-Conferring Strategies," *JSJ* 30 (1999), 379–410

———, "The Law of Nature and the Authority of Mosaic Law," *The Studia Philonica Annual* 11 (1999), 65–72

Neusner, J., *Development of a Legend: Studies on the Traditions concerning Yohanan ben Zakkai* (Leiden: Brill, 1970)

———, *The Economics of the Mishnah* (Chicago: University of Chicago Press, 1990)

———, *Eliezer Ben Hyrcanus: The Tradition and the Man*, 2 vols. (Leiden: Brill, 1973)

———, "Exegesis and the Written Law," *JSJ* 5 (1974), 176–78

———, "The Fellowship (הבורה) in the Second Jewish Commonwealth," *HTR* 53 (1960), 125–42

———, "The Formation of Rabbinic Judaism: Yavneh (Jamnia) from A.D. 70 to 100," in *ANRW* 19.2 (1979), 3–42

———, *From Politics to Piety: The Emergence of Pharisaic Judaism* (New York: KTAV, 1979)

———, *A History of the Mishnaic Law of Purities*, 22 vols. (Leiden: Brill, 1974)

———, *Judaism, the Evidence of the Mishnah* (Chicago: University of Chicago Press, 1981)

———, *The Mishnah: A New Translation* (New Haven: Yale University Press, 1988)

———, "Oral Torah and Oral Tradition: Defining the Problematic," in idem, ed., *Method and Meaning in Ancient Judaism* (Missoula: Scholars Press, 1979), 59–75

———, *The Rabbinic Traditions about the Pharisees Before 70*, 3 vols. (Leiden: Brill, 1975–1978)

———, *The Tosefta*, 6 vols. (New York: Ktav, 1977–1986)

———, "Two Pictures of the Pharisees: Philosophical Circle or Eating Club," *ATR* 64 (1982), 525–28

———, "The Written Tradition in the Pre-Rabbinic Period," *JSJ* 4 (1973), 56–65

Nickelsburg, G., "The Apocalyptic Message of 1 Enoch 92–105," *CBQ* 39 (1977), 309–28

———, "The Epistle of Enoch and the Qumran Literature," *JJS* 33 (1982), 333–48

———, *Jewish Literature between the Bible and the Mishnah: A Historical and Literary Introduction* (Philadelphia: Fortress Press, 1981)

———, *Resurrection, Immortality, and Eternal Life in Intertestamental Judaism* (Cambridge: Harvard University Press, 1972)

———, "Riches, the Rich and God's Judgement in 1 Enoch 92–105 and the Gospel According to Luke," *NTS* 25 (1979), 324–32

Nitzan, B., "Absalom, House of," in L. Schiffman and J. VanderKam, eds., *Encyclopedia of the Dead Sea Scrolls*, vol. 1, 4–5

Nock, A., *Conversion: The Old and the New in Religion from Alexander the Great to Augustine of Hippo* (Baltimore: Johns Hokins University Press, 1998)

Noy, D., "Jewish Communities of Leontopolis and Venosa," in J.W. van Henten and P.W. van der Horst, eds., *Studies in Early Jewish Epigraphy* (Leiden: Brill, 1994), 162–72

Oppenheimer, A., *The 'Am Ha-Aretz: A Study in the Social History of the Jewish People in the Hellenistic-Roman Period* (Leiden: Brill, 1977)

Osiek, C., and D. Balch, *Families in the New Testament World: Households and House Churches* (Louisville: Westminster John Knox Press, 1997)

Parente, F., "Onias III' Death and the Founding of the Temple of Leontopolis," in F. Parente and J. Sievers, eds., *Josephus and the History of the Greco-Roman Period: Essays in Memory of Morton Smith* (Leiden: Brill, 1994), 69–98

Perdue, L., "The Household, Old Testament Theology, and Contemporary Hermeneutics," in idem, *Families in Ancient Israel*, 223–57

———, "The Israelite and Early Jewish Family: Summary and Conclusions," in L. Perdue et al., *Families in Ancient Israel*, 163–222

Perdue, L., et al., *Families in Ancient Israel* (Louisville: Westminster John Knox Press, 1997)

Peskowitz, M., " 'Family/ies' in Antiquity: Evidence from Tannaitic Literature and Roman Galilean Architecture," in S. Cohen, *Jewish Family in Antiquity*, 24–34

———, *Spinning Fantasies: Rabbis, Gender, and History* (Berkeley: University of California Press, 1997)

Pomeroy, S., *Families in Classical and Hellenistic Greece: Representations and Realities* (Oxford: Clarendon Press, 1997)

Purvis, *The Samaritan Pentateuch and the Origin of the Samaritan Sect* (Cambridge: Harvard University Press, 1968)

Rabin, C., *Qumran Studies* (Oxford: Oxford University Press, 1957)

Rajak, T., and D. Noy, "*Archisynagogoi*: Office, Title and Social Status in the Greco-Jewish Synagogue," *JRS* 83 (1993), 75–93

Rhoads, D., *Israel in Revolution* (Philadelphia: Fortress Press, 1976)

Richardson, P., and V. Heuchan, "Jewish Voluntary Associations in Egypt and the Roles of Women," in J. Kloppenborg and S. Wilson, eds., *Voluntary Associations in the Graeco-Roman World* (London: Routledge, 1996), 226–51

Rivkin, E., "*Beth Din, Boule, Sanhedrin*: A Tragedy of Errors," *HUCA* 46 (1975), 181–99

———, "Defining the Pharisees: The Tannaitic Sources," *HUCA* 43 (1972), 234–38

———, *A Hidden Revolution* (Nashville: Abingdon, 1978)

Rostovtzeff, M., *The Social and Economic History of the Roman Empire*, 2 vols. (Oxford: Clarendon Press, 1966)

Safrai, S., "Home and Family," in idem and M. Stern, eds., The Jewish People in the First Century: Historical Geography. Political History, Social, Cultural & Religious Life & Institutions (Assen: Van Gorcum, 1976), vol. 2, 728–833.

———, *Literature of the Sages* (Assen: Van Gorcum, 1987)

Saldarini, A., "The Adoption of a Dissident: Akabya ben Mahalaleel in Rabbinic Tradition," *JJS* 33 (1982), 547–56

———, *Pharisees, Scribes and Sadducees in Palestinian Society: A Sociological Approach* (Wilmington: Glazier, 1988)

———, *Scholastic Rabbinism: A Literary Study of the Fathers according to Rabbi Nathan* (Chico: Scholars Press, 1982)

Sanders, E.P., *Jewish Law from Jesus to the Mishnah: Five Studies* (London: SCM Press, 1990)

———, *Judaism: Practice and Belief, 63 BCE–66 CE* (London: SCM Press, 1992)

———, *Paul and Palestinian Judaism: A Comparison of Patterns of Religion* (Philadelphia: Fortress Press, 1977)

Satlow, M., *Jewish Marriage in Antiquity* (Princeton: Princeton University Press, 2001)

Schäfer, P., "Das Dogma von der mündlichen Torah," in idem, *Studien zur Geschichte und Theologie des Rabbinischen Judentums* (Leiden: Brill, 1978), 153–97
Schiffman, L., *The Eschatological Community of the Dead Sea Scrolls* (Atlanta: Scholars Press, 1989)
———, *The Halakhah at Qumran* (Leiden: Brill, 1975)
———, "The New Halakhic Letter (4QMMT) and the Origins of the Dead Sea Sect," *BA* 53 (1990), 64–73
———, "Pharisaic and Sadducean Halakhah in Light of the Dead Sea Scrolls," *DSD* 1 (1994), 285–99
———, "Pharisees and Sadducees in *Pesher Nahum*," in M. Brettler and M. Fishbane, eds., *Minhah le-Nahum: Biblical and Other Studies Presented to N.M. Sarna* (Sheffield: JSOT Press, 1993), 272–90
———, "The Place of 4QMMT in the Corpus of Qumran Manuscripts," in J. Kampen and M. Bernstein, eds., *Reading 4QMMT* (Atlanta: Scholars Press, 1996), 81–98
———, *Reclaiming the Dead Sea Scrolls* (Philadelphia: JPS, 1994)
———, *Sectarian Law in the Dead Sea Scrolls: Courts, Testimony and the Penal Code* (Chico: Scholars Press, 1983)
Schiffman, L., and J. VanderKam, *Encyclopedia of the Dead Sea Scrolls*, 2 vols. (Oxford: Oxford University Press, 2000)
Schremer, A., "[T]he[y] did not Read in the Sealed Book": Qumran Halakhic Revolution and the Emergence of Torah Study in Second Temple Judaism," in D. Goodblatt et al., eds., *Historical Perspectives: From the Hasmoneans to Bar Kokhba in Light of the Dead Sea Scrolls. Proceedings of the Fourth International Symposium of the Orion Center for the Study of the Dead Sea Scrolls and Associated Literature, 27–31 January, 1999* (Leiden: Brill, 2001), 105–26
Schuller, E., "Women in the Dead Sea Scrolls," in Flint and VanderKam, *The Dead Sea Scrolls after Fifty Years*, vol. 2, 117–44
Schürer, E., *History of the Jewish People in the Age of Jesus Christ (175 BC–AD 135)*, revised and edited by G. Vermes and F. Millar, 3 vols. (Edinburgh: Clark, 1973–1975)
Schwartz, D., *Agrippa I: The Last King of Judaea* (Tübingen: J.C.B. Mohr, 1990)
———, "Josephus and Nicolaus on the Pharisees," *JSJ* 14 (1983), 157–71
———, "Law and Truth: On Qumran-Sadducean and Rabbinic Views of Law," in D. Dimant and U. Rappaport, eds., *The Dead Sea Scrolls: Forty Years of Research* (Leiden: Brill, 1992), 229–40
———, "On Two Aspects of a Priestly View of Descent at Qumran," in L. Schiffman, ed., *Archaeology and History in the Dead Sea Scrolls: The New York University Conference in Memory of Yigael Yadin* (Sheffield: JSOT Press, 1990), 157–79
———, *Studies in the Jewish Background of Christianity* (Tübingen: J.C.B. Mohr, 1992)
Schwartz, J., "'Al Zonen u-Veno Baytos," *Sinai* 103 (1989), 108–22
Schwartz, J., and J. Spainer, "On Mattathias and the Desert of Samaria," *RB* 98 (1991), 252–71
Schwartz, S., "The Hellenization of Jerusalem and Shechem," in M. Goodman, ed., *Jews in a Graeco-Roman World* (Oxford: Clarendon Press, 1998), 37–45
———, *Imperialism and Jewish Society, 200 BCE to 640 CE* (Princeton: Princeton University Press, 2001)
———, *Josephus and Judaean Politics* (Leiden: Brill, 1990)
———, "A Note on the Social Type and Political Ideology of the Hasmonean Family," *JBL* 112 (1993), 305–09
———, "On the Autonomy of Judaea in the Fourth and Third Centuries BCE," *JJS* 45 (1994), 159–61
Sherwin-White, S., and A. Kuhrt, *From Samarkhand to Sardis: A New Approach to the Seleucid Empire* (Berkeley: University of California Press, 1993)

Sivertsev, A., *Private Households and Public Politics in 3rd–5th Century Jewish Palestine* (Tübingen: Mohr Siebeck, 2002)
———, "Sects and Households: Social Structure of the Proto-Sectarian Movement of Nehemiah 10 and the Dead Sea Sect." *CBQ* 67 (2005), 59–78
Smith, D., "Meals," in Schiffman and VanderKam, *Encyclopedia of the Dead Sea Scrolls*, vol. 1, 530–32
Smith, M., "The Dead Sea Sect in Relation to Ancient Judaism," *NTS* 7 (1960), 347–60
———, *Jesus the Magician* (New York: Harper & Row, 1978)
———, "Palestinian Judaism in the First Century," in M. Davis, ed., *Israel: Its Role in Civilization* (New York: JTSA, 1956), 67–81
———, *Palestinian Parties and Politics that Shaped the Old Testament* (New York: Columbia University Press, 1971)
———, "Zealots and Sicarii, Their Origins and Relations," *HTR* 64 (1971), 1–19
Steckoll, S., "Qumran Sect in Relationship to the Temple of Leontopolis," *RevQ* 6 (1967–69), 55–69
Stegemann, H., "Some Remarks to 1QSa, to 1QSb, and to Qumran Messianism," *RevQ* 17 (1996), 479–505
———, *The Library of Qumran: On the Essenes, Qumran, John the Baptist and Jesus* (Grand Rapids: Eerdmans, 1998)
Stemberger, G., *Jewish Contemporaries of Jesus: Pharisees, Sadducees, Essenes* (Minneapolis: Fortress Press, 1995)
———, "Narrative Baraitot in the Yerushalmi," in P. Schäfer, ed., *The Talmud Yerushalmi and Graeco-Roman Culture* (Tübingen: Mohr Siebeck, 1998), vol. 1, 63–81
———, "The Sadducees—Their History and Doctrines," in W. Horbury et al., *Cambridge History of Judaism*, vol. 3, 428–43
Stern, E., *Material Culture of the Land of the Bible in the Persian Period, 538–332 BC* (Warminster: Aris & Phillips, 1982)
Stern, M., "Aspects of Jewish Society: The Priesthood and Other Classes," in S. Safrai et al., eds., *The Jewish People in the First Century* (Philadelphia: Fortress, 1976), vol. 2, 561–630
Stiegman, E., "Rabbinic Anthropology," in *ANRW* 19 (1977), 508–23
Strack, H., and G. Stemberger, *Introduction to the Talmud and Midrash* (Edinburgh: T&T Clark, 1991)
Talmon, S., "The Emergence of Jewish Sectarianism" in idem, *King, Cult and Calendar in Ancient Israel* (Jerusalem: Magnes Press, 1986) 165–201
Tcherikover, V., *Hellenistic Civilization and the Jews* (Philadelphia: Jewish Publication Society, 1959)
———, "Palestine under the Prolemies," *Mizraim* 4–5 (1937), 9–90
Tropper, A., *Wisdom, Politics, and Historiography: Tractate Avot in the Context of the Graeco-Roman Near East* (Oxford: Oxford University Press, 2004)
Van Henten, W., *The Maccabean Martyrs as Saviours of the Jewish People: A Study of 2 and 4 Maccabees* (Leiden: Brill, 1997)
VanderKam, J., *The Dead Sea Scrolls Today* (Grand Rapids: Eerdmans, 1994)
———, *Enoch and the Growth of an Apocalyptic Tradition* (Washington, D.C.: Catholic Biblical Association of America, 1984)
———, "Enoch Traditions in Jubilees and Other Second-Century Sources," in idem, *From Revelation to Canon: Studies in the Hebrew Bible and Second Temple Literature* (Boston: Brill, 2002), 305–31
———, "Granddaughters and Grandsons of Noah," *RevQ* 16 (1994), 457–61
———, "Identity and History of the Community" in Flint and VanderKam, *The Dead Sea Scrolls after Fifty Years*, vol. 2, 487–531
Vermes, G., *The Complete Dead Sea Scrolls in English* (New York: Penguin Books, 1997)

Von Keinle, W., *Die Berichte über die Sukzessionen der Philosophen* (Berlin, 1961)
Weber, M., *Ancient Judaism* (Glencoe: Free Press, 1952)
Wegner, J., *Chattel or Person? The Status of Women in the Mishnah* (New York: Oxford University Press, 1988)
Weinberg, J., *The Citizen-Temple Community* (Sheffield: JSOT Press, 1992)
Weinfeld, M., *The Organizational Pattern and the Penal Code of the Qumran Sect: A Comparison with Guilds and Religious Associations of the Hellenistic-Roman World* (Fribourg: Editions Universitaires; Göttingen: Vandenhoeck & Ruprecht, 1986)
Werman, C., "*Jubilees* 30: Building a Paradigm for the Ban on Intermarriage," *HTR* 90 (1997), 1–22
White, R., "The House of Peleg in the Dead Sea Scrolls," in P. Davies, ed., *A Tribute to Geza Vermes* (Sheffield: JSOT, 1990), 67–98
Whybray, R., *The Intellectual Tradition in the Old Testament* (Berlin: Walter de Gruyter)
Williamson, H., *Ezra and Nehemiah* (Sheffield: JSOT Press, 1987)
Wilson, S., "Voluntary Associations: An Overview," in J. Kloppenborg and S. Wilson, *Voluntary Associations in the Graeco-Roman World*, 1–15
Wright, B., "Jewish Ritual Baths—Interpreting the Digs and the Texts: Some Issues in the Social History of Second Temple Judaism," in N. Silberman and D. Small, eds., *The Archaeology of Israel: Constructing the Past, Interpreting the Present* (Sheffield: Sheffield Academic, 1997), 190–214
Yadin, A., *Scripture as Logos: Rabbi Ismael and the Origins of Midrash* (Philadelphia: University of Pennsylvania Press, 2004)
Zahavy, T., *The Traditions of Eleazar ben Azariah* (Missoula: Scholars Press, 1977)
Zeitlin, S., *The Rise and Fall of the Judaean State*, 2 vols. (Philadelphia: JPS, 1964)

SUBJECT INDEX

INDEX OF SOURCES

Hebrew Bible

Exod			*Neh*	
12:8	216		1:1–3	33
40:15	248		2:10	42
			2:12	33
Lev			2:16	33
1:5	248		2:19	42
6:16	251		3:4	42
16:12–13	202		3:8	35
19:19	117		3:17–18	35
21:14	81		3:23	35
			3:28–30	35
Deut			3:31–32	35
19:14	161		4:13	35
25:10	249		4:23	33
			5:10	33
Isa			6:17–18	42
19:18–19	60		7:1–2	34
			7:3	34
Zech			7:8–25	35
6:9–14	36		7:10	42
13:7	102		7:26–38	35
			7:39–45	35
Esth			7:44–45	35
6:13	32		7:46–56	36
9:28	32		7:57–60	36
9:31	32		7:61–62	36
10:3	32		7:63–65	36
			8:1–8	116
Ezra			8:1–12	29
1:5	36		8:2	116
2:3–20	35		8:13	29, 30
2:5	42		8:13–18	116
2:21–35	35		8:16	30
2:36–42	35		8:17	29
2:40–42	35		9:16	31
2:43–54	36		9:2	31, 117
2:55–58	36		9:9	31
2:59–60	36		9:23	31
2:61–63	36		9:32	31
2:68–69	36		9:34	31
4:1–3	36		10:21	42
8:1–14	36		10:29–30	116
8:15–20	37		10:29–30	28
8:24–30	37		10:31–32	28
9:2	117		10:32	117
10:8	111			

Deuterocanonical Books

New Testament

Tosefta